Wavell and the Dying Days of the Raj

Britain's Penultimate Viceroy in India

SECOND EDITION

Wavell and the Dying Days of the Raj

Britain's Penultimate Viceroy in India

SECOND EDITION

MUHAMMAD IQBAL CHAWLA

OXFORD
UNIVERSITY PRESS

OXFORD
UNIVERSITY PRESS

Oxford University Press is a department of the University of Oxford.
It furthers the University's objective of excellence in research, scholarship,
and education by publishing worldwide. Oxford is a registered trade mark of
Oxford University Press in the UK and in certain other countries

Published in Pakistan by
Oxford University Press
No. 38, Sector 15, Korangi Industrial Area,
PO Box 8214, Karachi-74900, Pakistan

ISBN 978-0-19-070784-2

Typeset in Minion Pro
Printed on 55gsm Book Paper

Printed by The Times Press (Pvt.) Ltd., Karachi

Disclaimer
There are instances where we have been unable to trace or contact the copyright
holder. If notified, the publisher will be pleased to rectify any errors or omissions at
the earliest opportunity.

This book is respectfully dedicated to
my parents, Mr and Mrs Yousaf Chawla,
my younger brother Khalid Chawla (late),
and my wife, Shabana

Contents

Acknowledgements

This book derives its present form from a dissertation submitted to the Quaid-i-Azam University, Islamabad, in 2007. The dissertation revolves around Lord Wavell's viceroyalty (October 1943–March 1947) which has not received scholarly attention from historians. Therefore, a critical study of the viceroyalty has been attempted here in order to arrive at an understanding of the ever-changing dynamic political relationship amongst the three leading political actors in India of that time, the British, the Hindus, and the Muslims. Although there is ample literature about the viceroyalties of Lords Linlithgow and Mountbatten which informs us adequately about British policies during their tenures at the helm of power in India, the equally important historical period of Lord Wavell's viceroyalty has not received the attention it deserves.

A few articles based on some parts of the dissertation have been published in national and international journals. In this regard, I am grateful to the publishers of *Journal of Punjab Studies* (Berkeley), *Journal of South Asia* (Lahore), *Pakistan Journal of History and Culture* (Islamabad), *Historians* (Lahore), and *Journal of Pakistan Historical Society* (Lahore). But the dissertation as a whole had remained unpublished.

I am greatly indebted to Professor Dr Sikandar Hayat and Professor Dr Sayed Wiqar Ali Shah, my thesis supervisors, for their guidance and valuable suggestions. Their profound knowledge and high standard of scholarship helped me develop a synopsis for the thesis, and avoid many errors in argument and style.

Many teachers, friends and colleagues have helped me in this intellectual quest. I am grateful to my respected teachers at the Quaid-i-Azam University, Dr Rafique Afzal, Dr Naeem Qureshi, Dr Riaz Ahmed, Dr Muhammad Aslam Syed, Mr Masud Akhtar and Mr Aziz Ahmed (late) for their encouragement and valuable suggestions. I am much obliged to my former teacher, Prof. Dr Iftikhar Haider Malik, formerly of the Quaid-i-Azam University, Islamabad, and presently of

Bath Spa University, UK, for his personal interest and support in helping to collect the relevant research material from that country.

In the course of research and writing this work many scholars motivated me to publish my work. I feel honoured in expressing my deepest gratitude to Professor Dr Ian Talbot (Director, Centre for Imperial and Post-Colonial Studies, University of Southampton, UK); Dr David Gilmartin (North Carolina State University); Professor Dr Chad Haines (North Carolina State University); Dr Yasmin Saikia (North Carolina State University); Dr Avril Powell (School of Oriental and African Studies, University of London); Ms Victoria Schofield and Dr David Page; Professor Sharif al Mujahid; Professor Dr Mushirul Hasan; Professor Dr Bipen Chandra, for their valuable suggestions and encouragement. I wish to extend my sincere thanks to Professor Dr Sarah Ansari (Royal Holloway College, University of London) for her suggestion of a suitable title for this book.

To my colleagues at the History Department of the Punjab University, Lahore, I owe debt of gratitude for their great interest in my work, especially Professor Dr S. Qalb-i-Abid, Professor Syed Qamar Abbas, Mr Ghazi Abdullah, Mr Faraz Anjum, and Mr Tauqeer Ahmed Warraich.

My continuing gratitude and appreciation is due to the library staff of the India Office Record at the British Library in London for their wonderful cooperation in helping me to access the relevant material from the library itself as well as the inter-library loan materials. I am also thankful to the staffs of the following libraries: the Bodleian Library at Oxford; the Churchill Archives Centre in Cambridge; the Cambridge University Library; Library of the University of Swansea; Library of the School of Oriental and African Studies in London; and Knowledge House Library in East London for their generous cooperation in helping me with the collection of the relevant material.

I would also like to express my thanks to the staff of the National Documentation Centre in Islamabad, National Archives in Islamabad, Quaid-i-Azam Library in Lahore, Government College University Library in Lahore, the University of Karachi Library and the Sargodha College University Library. I am also grateful to the management and staff of the following libraries in Lahore for their valuable help: Lahore Museum Library, Punjab Public Library, Pakistan Study Library; South Asian Studies Centre Library at the Punjab University, Quaid-i-Azam

University Library and Tulu-i-Islam Trust Library. I am also grateful, especially to the library staff, of my very own History Department at the Punjab University for all their help and cooperation. They generously furnished me with all I ever needed from the library.

Finally, I wish to express my gratitude to my parents Mr and Mrs Yousaf Chawla and all my brothers and sisters for their prayers, encouragement and moral support. Appreciation is due to my children Abdul Wahab Chawla, Noman Chawla, and Ahmad Chawla. My special thanks to my wife Shabana for her persistent support, encouragement and help.

MUHAMMAD IQBAL CHAWLA

Preface to the Second Edition

This is the second edition of the book which has been revised, updated, and enhanced with the addition of one new chapter, titled 'Wavell's Breakdown Plan' in a significantly expanded version of what can easily be characterized as Wavell's most important contribution to a peaceful plan for British departure from India and India's division. Wavell's Breakdown Plan entailed a stepwise plan for the division of Punjab and Bengal in case there was a Partition of India. It would have, most likely, avoided the wide-ranging disturbances and bloodshed, especially in Punjab, which followed the timetable and planning for division as actually put in place by Lord Mountbatten. This resulted in what has been widely criticized as a 'shameful flight' because it caused bloodshed, forced dislocation, and mass migration of millions of people across the new borders unprecedented in world history. Wavell, however, never received any credit for a plan however well-conceived and suited to the actual conditions in India at that time. And the new chapter tries to bring all that out to Wavell's credit. In the end, Mountbatten never followed Wavell's plan and we all know the mayhem that ensued.

Besides that, I have revised the book in the light of newly-published academic literature, especially books and articles, which I could lay my hands on during this time of constrained access due to the global coronavirus pandemic. This new literature mostly deals with the Indian Freedom Movement and its parallel after 1940, the Pakistan Movement, and pertinent new writings on the British Empire. However, I am sticking to my main argument and contents which I offered in the first edition.

The additions and alterations are the results of thorough reading and re-reading of the first edition of my book to bring it up to date, as much as was possible, regarding the main topic. These changes are spread throughout the book and as it is a historically well-researched topic, would be better conspicuous to the judicious bibliophile. Regardless of these changes and/or minor alterations, I am still satisfied with the main theme, presentation, and outline of the book as was the case with the first edition which was published by the OUP in 2011. I have tried to make use of the best possible new material, which is not substantial, on the topic. I have also tried to accommodate what I felt were reasonable points raised by many critics. However, it is a difficult task attempting to accommodate points of view, often well-argued, but which are quite opposed to each other.

However, personally it is very gratifying to me that the OUP has decided to bring out a revised edition although it has taken some time since 2011, the year of the first edition. As this award-winning book's author, however, it is extremely gratifying to me because Wavell never commanded the attention of historians as his successor, Mountbatten, did.

I must thank Ms Ghousia Ghofran Ali for all her help and cooperation. I must also take this opportunity to thank my editor, Ms Sunehra Mehmood.

I am indebted to many friends, colleagues, and scholars, who made helpful suggestions for the revision of the book, both theoretically and empirically. Some of them have been mentioned in the 'Preface' to the First Edition, and I need not recount them, except for Professor Dr Sikandar Hayat who remained quite helpful with this edition also. Here, I would like to express my gratitude to some of those scholars who took the trouble of reviewing the book such as Prof Dr Roger D. Long, Prof Sara F.D. Ansari, and Prof Ian Talbot. I have benefitted from their useful comments and feedback. Some of their concerns, as of other reviewers from abroad, have been duly considered in this revised edition. However, like in the first edition, I alone am responsible for the facts or their interpretation in the book. I am thankful to the staff of the Library of the History Department and the Main Library (PU), Lahore for providing me with much of the material that I needed. I am grateful to all my friends and colleagues for their keen interest and encouragement. I owe a lot to Mr Moazzam Wasti, currently a doctoral candidate, for fruitful discussion and occasional proofreading of the book. Finally, I must thank my wife, Shabana (to whom the first edition of this book was dedicated) for all her urging and support throughout the writing of the book. I must also thank my children, Noman Chawla, Abdul Wahab Chawla, and Ahmad Chawla, for understanding and indeed respecting my passion for time-consuming reading and writing. I dedicate this edition to my father, family, and of course my late mother (Mrs Zohra Yousaf).

Muhammad Iqbal Chawla

Introduction

A critical and historical understanding of Lord Archibald Wavell's viceroyalty (October 1943–March 1947) is important for understanding the rational dynamics amongst the three leading political actors of that time, the British, the Hindus and the Muslims. There is ample literature on the viceroyalties of Lords Linlithgow and Mountbatten which informs us about the British policies during their tenures in India, but the equally important historical period of Lord Wavell's viceroyalty is often overlooked by historians.

This study focuses primarily on Lord Wavell's response to Muslim politics in India in the 1940s. The hypothesis of this study is that Lord Wavell was against the demand for Pakistan, because he believed that India was a natural geographical unit and could be preserved as such. Therefore, during his viceroyalty, he struggled to achieve that aim, and floated and backed schemes that tried to preserve the union of India such as his Wavell Plan, the Cabinet Mission Plan and the Breakdown Plan. However, Pakistan emerged despite Wavell's attempts to sidetrack it. It is important to note that although Pakistan came into being almost six decades ago it still faces the effects of the problems it inherited from the decisions taken by the last two British viceroys. A reappraisal therefore of the circumstances in which Pakistan was born, especially the politics and policies of that time which gave birth to Pakistan, is of immense importance.

This book attempts mainly to investigate the following points:

Firstly, why Wavell was against the demand for Pakistan and the efforts he made to sideline that demand; secondly, the bureaucratic interaction which took place between Wavell and His Majesty's Government in this regard.

In order to find appropriate answers to these important questions it is essential to explore sources and material dealing with Wavell's viceroyalty and Muslim politics of that time.

Wavell's viceroyalty (October 1943–March 1947) was significant and decisive because of the developments that led to a sudden British exit from India under his successor. Wavell struggled from the start of his viceroyalty to keep India united. He suggested that India should be granted independence by March 1948 and in keeping with that timeframe, he suggested appropriate plans for an orderly British retreat from India before they were forcibly thrown out by the ever-increasing strength of the Indian political awakening. However, by the end of Wavell's term, Congress had become convinced by its experiences, especially by its participation in the Interim Government, that the partition of India was the only way out from a very complex situation.

Among the immediate problems that Wavell was faced with, were: firstly, the need to carry the war with Japan to a decisive and speedy victory; secondly, to deal with the Bengal famine; thirdly, to deal with the day-to-day issues of the Indian government; and finally, to break the political deadlock in India, which was his most important concern of all.

The administrative, economic and defence problems of India have been discussed with a view to understanding their impact on the political life of India in general and of the Muslims in particular. Nonetheless, Wavell's policies in dealing with the Muslim problem, especially the Pakistan issue, remain the focus of this study.

Right from the beginning of his term, Wavell saw a variety of complex problems littering the Indian political scene. The main ones were the following: Hindu–Muslim religious friction, which had entered its final phase, in the 1940s. The Muslim League demand for a separate homeland for the Muslims based on the two-nation theory and the multifarious political complexities it had given rise to. This demand (for Pakistan) had divided the Muslims into two groups, its supporters and detractors, which were as sharply opposed to each other as were the Muslim League and Congress. Additionally, the Cripps Proposals had been rejected both by the Congress and the League at a critical juncture of the Second World War and the British government was not ready to break the political impasse.

Muslim politics in India had become quite complicated, for a number of political parties and groups with conflicting ideas and divergent programmes had emerged on the political landscape. Muslim parties like the Unionist Party, the Khudai Khidmatgars, and the Majlis-i-Ahrar, were strongly against the Pakistan demand.

Lastly, it is beyond our scope to discuss Wavell's role as a soldier; however, his Indian experiences first as a soldier and then as the commander-in-chief did help him to understand Muslim politics in India.

As viceroy-designate in 1943, Wavell drafted a plan, which was termed as the Wavell Plan. This plan contained an outline for a peaceful transfer of power in India and incorporated his desire to sideline the demand for Pakistan; both the aims, which he believed, could only be brought about with the formation of coalition governments at the centre as well as in the provinces. Though agreeing with the central idea of the 'Wavell Plan', the India committee did not allow him to decide the timing of its implementation. He was directed to deal with other matters first.

Wavell particularly encouraged those efforts, which could bridge the Hindu–Muslim link. Related political developments like the Rajagopalachari Formula (1944), Gandhi–Jinnah talks (1944), Desai–Liaquat Pact (January 1945), however, are beyond our scope but will be discussed briefly in order to help understand their impact upon Wavell's thinking.

As the result of all these failed political endeavours, the seriousness of the Muslim problem was impressed upon Wavell's mind and he became convinced that the demand for Pakistan could only be sidelined with the formation of coalition governments as a part of a peaceful transfer of power.

Following these failed moves and because the Second World War was approaching its end, Wavell was permitted to go ahead with his Wavell Plan and a conference took place at Simla in 1945, which ended in smoke. The Simla Conference (1945) highlighted the sharp and unbridgeable differences of the Congress and the League. The Congress claimed to speak for all the communities of India, which included the Muslims. But the League rejected Congress's claim to speak for Muslims and instead claimed for itself the role of the sole and authoritative spokesman of Muslims in India.

Only fresh elections could have verified their respective claims and it was already nine years since the last elections. However, for their own individual reasons, neither Wavell nor the Congress wanted early elections. But decisive victory by the Labour Party in England, war promises of the British government and its economic and political problems caused mainly by war and America's consistent pressure to grant independence to India, forced Wavell to hold the elections he clearly wanted to avoid. The election results gave a heavy mandate to Jinnah and made his case for Pakistan stronger.

This study focuses only on the Cabinet Mission Plan (1946) and its impact upon the Muslims in India. Since, as mentioned earlier, Wavell was not at all convinced of the demand for Pakistan, he exerted all his influence to maintain India's geographical unity by trying to provide enough political and constitutional rights to the Muslims of India. Wavell sincerely believed that the Cabinet Mission Plan as outlined in the statement of 16 May could solve the Hindu–Muslim problem in India if the Congress and the League accepted it sincerely.

Congress failed to appreciate the positive aspects of the Plan and made it a controversial document. The Grouping clause became a major cause of its concern because if accepted, the Congress felt, it would enable Jinnah to achieve Pakistan according to the Lahore Resolution after ten years. To push for the Plan's success Wavell wanted London to issue an unambiguous statement regarding the Grouping clause. In fact, British government's own economic and political interests rendered the British policy planners in London indecisive, thereby causing damage to the plan and resulting in its failure.

Wavell was convinced that the Cabinet Mission Plan was the last chance to keep India united, and its failure would end the unity of India, pave the way for Pakistan, and open the floodgates of a blood bath on the road to independence. His fears proved to be true.

Wavell's main goal was the formation of the provisional government. The formation of the provincial governments (1946) took place without much debate but the thorniest problem Wavell had to deal with was the formation of the central government. He chalked out a formula for the composition and strength of the Interim Government (statement of 16 June) at the Centre. Wavell's dream was shattered when the Interim Government failed to bring about the much hoped for harmony.

To provide feedback to his seniors in London and to receive their advice Wavell regularly updated the British government about the

Muslim problem. This study discusses the British policy towards India with special reference to its impact on Muslim politics therein, though its colonial policy is also highlighted.

Wavell showed tremendous interest in resolving the constitutional and political deadlock in India. He was also willing to take bold steps to achieve that goal. However, political leaders and officials in London differed from Wavell in their political outlook. They thought that as a soldier he was incapable of having political insight.

Wavell's liberal ideas about the future of India and his insistence on carrying them out were unacceptable both to Churchill and to Attlee. Wavell's differences with the Labour government especially on the Breakdown Plan created such a serious situation that he became the only governor-general of India to be dismissed before the official end of his tenure (March 1947).

The turbulent and salient features of Indian politics in the 1940s have attracted the attention of a number of historians. This was the time when the raj was withdrawn from India and the role of its Viceroy in the political tangle amongst the political parties assumed critical importance.

As compared to his predecessors Wavell has been little understood and in fact has often been maligned by historians. He has, moreover, not received due attention from them. Even those who have written about him have failed to understand the real motives behind his actions, and there are only a few good biographies of Wavell.

L.G. Pain[1] deals with the genealogical table and history of the origin and development of the Wavell family. He discusses Wavell's life from birth until his viceroyalty. The author, however, fails to dwell on either the general Indian political situation prevailing during his tenure or specifically the Muslim problem of India in his time.

Robert Woollcombe[2] gives us interesting information about Wavell's role during the critical years of the Second World War. He enlightens us about his role as the Viceroy of India. The author maintains that Wavell was called to deal with a heavier task than was faced by Allenby in Egypt, and he thinks that the political climate under which he was asked to break the communal deadlock in India might even have baffled the diplomatic skills of a Marlborough. The author seems intent on portraying Wavell as the greatest hero in British history, which is only partially true, but shows no interest in analyzing the Muslim problem in India.

Michael Carver[3] concentrates on Wavell's activities in Africa, particularly his Italian campaign. The most interesting point he raises is that Churchill at a distance was more impressed by Wavell. Wavell had resisted orders to send troops to Britain at the height of the disaster in France. However, the author shows no interest in Wavell's role as the Viceroy of India.

Donald Cowie[4] discusses in detail the campaigns of Wavell as a general. He remarks that Wavell was the first British general in several generations to achieve what he had set out to do, namely, the conquest of Cyrenaica, Eritrea, Italian Somaliland, Abyssinia, and the re-conquest of British Somaliland. But, although the book shows an interesting aspect of Wavell's life as a soldier, it does not deal with his life as a viceroy.

Rowan Robinson[5] deals exclusively with Wavell's role as a soldier and general and throws no light upon his viceroyalty.

William F. Burbridge sheds light only on the brief tenure of his viceroyalty.[6] Bernard Ferguson gives a critical appreciation of Wavell's role as a soldier. Having been closely associated with Wavell, he describes his personal relationship with him and dwells on military duty with him.

R.H. Keirman[7] covers the story of only one-and-a-half years of Wavell's viceroyalty. He tells us how Wavell accepted the viceroyalty and he sheds light on Wavell's actions in dealing with the Bengal famine and war against Japan. However, this author also fails to deal with the Muslim problem in India as faced by Wavell.

Sir George Arthur[8] briefly describes Wavell's services as a soldier but is not interested in his viceroyalty.

Bernard Fergusson[9] gives a critical appreciation of Wavell's role as a soldier. Because of his close association with Wavell as a soldier, he describes his personal as well as military experiences with Wavell. He critically evaluates Wavell's relationship with Churchill. He criticizes Churchill for not attending Lord Wavell's funeral; but this author also is least interested in Wavell's role as viceroy.

John Collins, R.J.[10] deals with Wavell's life before becoming the Viceroy of India. In his second book, edited by Michael Roberts,[11]

Collins gives interesting aspects of Wavell's life as a soldier-writer but also fails to deal properly with his viceroyalty.

Ronald Lewin[12] has written a scholarly work about Wavell's life. He also analyzes mostly his military career and deals only casually with the Muslim problem in India.

H.M. Close has penned a valuable work,[13] on the last days of Wavell's viceroyalty. The author has compared three British politicians, Wavell, Attlee, and Mountbatten, who were responsible for shaping British policies in India during the closing period of the raj. He attempts a defence of Wavell's role during the last days of his viceroyalty but, unfortunately, this author is also not interested in the Muslim politics in India of that period and as a result fails to appreciate Wavell's dilemma during his political actions. While discussing Wavell's Breakdown Plan he has wrongly concluded that he had come to support the demand for Pakistan at the close of his tenure as viceroy.

Victoria Schofield's work[14] is probably better than the rest as it also throws light on the viceroyalty of Wavell. She has rediscovered Wavell through unpublished letters and diaries, and by means of interviews with those who knew Wavell. She analyzes Wavell's military life and his role in Indian politics and dwells upon the differences in the thinking of Wavell, Churchill and those at Whitehall, regarding policy towards Indian political problems. Unlike some other Western scholars, she gives a balanced picture of the Hindu–Muslim problem in India. Since she has not focused solely on the Muslim problem in India she concludes wrongly that in the Breakdown Plan Wavell had endorsed the creation of Pakistan.

In a recent study on the period under discussion, Rabia Umar Ali has focused on the crucial last days of British rule in India when the situation was completely out of their hands and the incompetent decision-making of Mountbatten et al. complicated the already confusing situation. In this, she seems to be following the broader lines of Stanley Wolpert's *Shameful Flight*. She has built up the argument that the premature replacement of Wavell by Mountbatten was based on the realization by the British government that a plan to divide the subcontinent had become inevitable.[15] The hasty transfer of power, viceroy's friendship with Nehru, the leading Hindu leader, and his not so cordial relations with Jinnah, besides other factors, helped push the situation towards widespread massacres, carnage and colossal damage to property. The hasty division of subcontinent resembled more of a hasty retreat rather than any planned operation and the British authorities, especially the viceroy Lord Mountbatten, completely failed to play their respective roles as wise and just arbiters. Wavell was abruptly replaced as the viceroy by Mountbatten who proved to be a much less competent successor whose less than satisfactory grasp of the situation resulted in a highly traumatic situation for millions of people.

Besides these biographies, there are a number of personal accounts, interviews, travelogues and personal diaries which reveal other aspects of Wavell's life as well. However, there is hardly any book which deals prominently with the viceroyalty of Wavell or his response to the Muslim problem in India.

H.V. Hodson[16] claims that Wavell promoted dissension between Hindus and Muslims, which hardened their approach. He blames Wavell for making Mountbatten's job difficult; he could not keep India united. He failed to access Wavell's papers; therefore, he evaluates his viceroyalty on the basis of Lord Mountbatten's paper. Perforce he ended up exalting his hero, Mountbatten's, role and thereby condemning Wavell's.

Similarly, Leonard Mosley's book,[17] which is based upon interviews and personal contacts, exaggerates the efforts of Mountbatten, ignoring the real contributions of other viceroys like Wavell.

Penderel Moon,[18] a civil servant, experienced the extremely fast moving but complicated process of the partition of India. He reveals an interesting story about the last days of British rule in India. He thinks that the Congress ministries of the 1930s paved the way for Pakistan, but he strongly believes that the 1940 Pakistan Resolution was 'a technical move and bargaining counter.' He believes that Pakistan could have been sidelined if the Congress leaders had made positive steps to conciliate Jinnah. Besides the Congress, he also holds the Muslim League responsible for the partition of India. He, however, has also failed to analyze Wavell's measures to sidestep the demand for Pakistan.

Mushirul Hasan[19] analyzes the support of the Muslim nationalists to the All-India National Congress. His main argument is that an important section of Muslim society remained pro-Congress and was opposed to the demand for Pakistan. However, he admits that a large section of the society was dissatisfied and disappointed with the

Congress Ministries 1937–1939, and the Congress leadership did not try to address their complaints and thus paved the way for the rise of communal feeling among the Muslims.

Ayesha Jalal[20] concentrates on the leadership role of Jinnah in the creation of Pakistan. She argues that the Lahore Resolution was a 'bargaining chip' and Jinnah was not serious in achieving Pakistan but was forced into it by the British and the Congress. In the end, he had to compromise on a smaller Pakistan. She advocates that Jinnah acted unilaterally and became the sole spokesman, which is a partial truth. Her position has already been challenged by Pakistani historians like Professor Sikandar Hayat[21] who has argued that the Lahore Resolution was not a bargaining counter. Muhammad Reza Kazimi[22] has also rejected Ayesha Jalal's thesis that Jinnah's lieutenants such as Liaquat Ali Khan were not serious in getting Pakistan.

In the 1980s some new research on partition focused on regions. Indeed amongst the manifold themes addressed are the roots of separatism and working of power sharing in the provinces particularly in the Muslim-majority provinces. They discuss how various interest groups especially industrialist, labour, and peasant movements coalesced with the mobilization for Pakistan. Ian Talbot[23] did the pioneer work on the Muslim majority provinces. Since then, he has focused on Punjab. Besides David Gilmartin,[24] Sarah Ansari,[25] Joya Chatterjea,[26] S. Qalb-i-Abid,[27] and Sayed Wiqar Ali Shah[28] have done work on the regional history perspective.

A variety of memoirs, autobiographies, biographies have been penned by contemporaries, participant observers, and historians on the partition of India in 1947. Many of them are solid works, which provide valuable insight and information about Wavell and Muslim politics, yet there is a need to throw fresh light on the subject, based on recent material made available for study and research. Wavell and Mountbatten papers available since 2000 in the British Library, London, and various personal diaries of the then provincial governors, bureaucrats, weekly reports of the governors and volumes of *Transfer of Power*, the Quaid-i-Azam papers edited by Zawar H. Zaidi and *Leo Amery's Diaries* published in 1988, have all become available for public access.

Numerous volumes of Wavell collections, various personal diaries of the then governors of provinces, bureaucrats, and weekly reports of the governors and volumes of *Transfer of Power* reveal the fact that the British government created all sorts of hurdles on the road to Pakistan. Wavell, the British government, and the Congress formed a united front against the League and were fierce enemies of the demand for Pakistan.

Literature available on this topic reveals a considerable gap in information. No single work available on this topic has dealt at length with Lord Wavell and Muslim politics in India.

As pointed out earlier, this study centres on an area of the topic not covered by earlier research. It refutes the allegation that the 'demand for Pakistan' was a bargaining counter. It also attempts to study the freedom struggle of the Muslims of South Asia in the 1940s. This research is significant because it analyzes the role of different political parties like the League, the Congress, the Unionists of Punjab and other important political parties of India. It also deals with the British policy towards the Muslim problem. It also discusses the role of Jinnah in the achievement of Pakistan. Finally, Wavell's role as Viceroy of India in dealing with the Muslim problem, with special reference to the demand for Pakistan is analyzed.

This study employs the historical-descriptive approach, based on primary and secondary sources. The book contains five chapters along with an introduction and a conclusion. Chapter 1 deals with the political scenario in India on the eve of Wavell's appointment as Viceroy of India. It traces the origin of the political parties and their aims and objectives. Chapter 2 concentrates on the Wavell Plan, which aimed at establishing an executive council comprising the main political parties. Chapter 3 is primarily concerned with the Cabinet Mission Plan and its repercussions upon Muslim politics in India. Chapter 4 explains Wavell's efforts in finalizing the strength and composition of the Interim Government of 1946–47, and the response of the main political parties to Wavell's move. Chapter 5 analyzes Delhi–London relations during Wavell's viceroyalty.

NOTES

1. L.G. Pain, *The House of Wavell* (London: typed, 1948).
2. Robert Woollcombe *The Campaigns of Wavell: 1939–43* (London: Cassell & Company Ltd., 1959).
3. Michael Carver, *Wavell and the Middle East: 1940–1* (Austin: Harry Ransom Humanities Research Centre, 1993).

4. Donald Cowie, *Campaigns of Wavell: The Inner Story of the Empire in Action*, second part: *September 1940 to September 1941* (London: Chapman & Hall Ltd., 1942).
5. Rowan Robinson, *Wavell in the Middle East* (London: Hutchinson and Co. Ltd., nd.).
6. William F. Burbridge, *Wavell: The Military Viceroy* (London: Sydenham and Co. Ltd., 1944).
7. R.H. Keirman, *Wavell* (London: George Harper & Co., 1945).
8. Sir George Arthur, *From Wellington to Wavell* (London: Hutchinson & Co. Ltd., 1947).
9. Bernard Fergusson, *Wavell: Portrait of a Soldier* (London: Collins Clear-Type Press, 1961).
10. John Collins, R.J., *Lord Wavell: A Military Biography* (London: Hodder & Stoughton, 1964).
11. John Collins, R.J., *Wavell: Supreme Commander* (London: Hodder & Stoughton, 1968).
12. Ronald Lewin, *The Chief, Field Marshal Lord Wavell, Commander-in-Chief and Viceroy 1939–1947* (London: Hutchinson & Co., 1980).
13. H.M. Close, *Wavell, Mountbatten and the Transfer of Power* (Islamabad: National Book Foundation, 1997).
14. Victoria Schofield, *Wavell, Soldier and Statesman* (London: John Murray, 2006).
15. Rabia Umar Ali, *Empire in Retreat: The Story of India's Partition* (Karachi: OUP 2012), p. 185.
16. H.V. Hodson, *Great Divide, Britain-India-Pakistan* (London: Oxford University Press, 1969).
17. Leonard Mosley, *The Last Days of British Raj* (London: 1961).
18. Penderel Moon, *Divide and Quit* (London: Chatto & Windus Ltd, 1961).
19. Mushirul Hasan, *Muslim Politics in Modern India, 1857–1947* (Meerut: Meenakshi Prakashan, 1970).
20. Ayesha Jalal, *The Sole Spokesman: Jinnah, the Muslim League and the Demand for Pakistan* (Cambridge: University Press, 1985).
21. Sikandar Hayat et al., *Aspects of Pakistan Movement* (Lahore Progressive Publishers, 1991).
22. Muhammad Reza Kazimi, *Liaquat Ali Khan: His Life and Work* (Karachi: Oxford University Press, 2003).
23. Ian Talbot, *Provincial Politics and the Pakistan Movement* (Karachi: Oxford University Press, 1988).
24. David Gilmartin, *Empire and Islam: Punjab and the Making of Pakistan* (London: I.B. Taurus & Co Ltd., 1988).
25. Sarah Ansari, *The Sufis, Saints and State Power: The Pirs of Sindh* (Cambridge, 1992).
26. Joya Chatterjea, *Bengali Divided Hindu Communalism and Ethnicity in Partition, 1932–1947* (Cambridge, 1994).
27. S. Qalb-i-Abid, *The Muslim Politics in Punjab 1923–1947* (Lahore: Vanguard, 1992).
28. Sayed Wiqar Ali Shah, *Ethnicity, Islam and Nationalism: Muslim Politics in the North-West Frontier Province, 1937–47* (Karachi: Oxford University Press, 1999).

1

Political Picture of India at the Time of Wavell's Viceroyalty

The Hindu–Muslim conflict in India had entered its final phase in the 1940s. The Muslim League, on the basis of the Two-Nation Theory, had been demanding a separate homeland for the Muslims of India. The movement for Pakistan was getting into full steam at the time of Wavell's arrival in India in October 1943, although it was opposed by an influential section of the Muslims.

This chapter investigates Muslim politics in India and also highlights the background of their demand for a separate homeland. It analyzes the nature, programme, and leadership of the leading Muslim political parties in India. It also highlights their aims and objectives, with the purpose of gaining an understanding of their future behaviour. Additionally, it discusses the origin and evolution of the British policy in India, with special reference to the Muslim problem. Moreover, it tries to understand whether Wavell's experiences in India, first as a soldier and then as the Commander-in-Chief, proved helpful to him in understanding the mood of the Muslim political scene in India.

British Policy in India

Wavell was appointed Viceroy of India upon the retirement of Lord Linlithgow in October 1943. He was no stranger to India, having served there on two previous occasions. His first-ever posting in India was in Ambala, in 1903, and his unit moved to the North-West Frontier Province (NWFP) in 1904 as fears mounted of a war with Russia.[1] His stay in the NWFP left deep and lasting impressions on him. He had passed his Lower and Higher Urdu examinations while at Ambala so he was able to communicate with the local people.[2] He found the Pathans (also known as 'Pashtoon' or 'Pakhtun'), the dominant ethnic community of the province, attractive, with a good sense of humour. Another effect of Wavell's stay in the NWFP was that he realized the strategic importance of the area because of its location. He never forgot these experiences during his later assignments.

Wavell served in India again as Commander-in-Chief, and member of the Governor General's Council for Defence and Military[3] from July 1941 to April 1943. This assignment, with its manifold responsibilities, was not an easy job to handle, as expected by Churchill.[4] Constitutionally, he took second place to the Viceroy.[5] His duty on several occasions was to sit and speak in the Legislative Assembly. As head of the armed forces in India he undertook three main tasks: Firstly, he was responsible for efforts to bring about the military defeat of Japan. Secondly, he built the foundations of a new relationship with Asia in the midst of the swirling tide of war and revolution. Lastly, he initiated steps to reach some understanding with the Indian nationalist aspirations in 1942 to help in partially allaying American concerns which had come to regard India as part of their overall strategic picture of Asia centred on China.[6]

Besides the obvious fact that the defence of India against a Japanese conquest, because of its vast military and manpower resources, was the prime concern of the British authorities, there were other strategic factors as well which helped enhance its importance. One very important goal was to put a stop to the idea of Japanese invincibility amongst Indians and thereby prevent the rise of the idea of 'Asians as a superior group' from taking a strong hold in the minds of the Indian people. Another was to prevent the Japanese domination of the Indian Ocean which could have jeopardised the Allies's oil supply from Iran and the Middle East. Wavell, as Commander-in-Chief in India, was also responsible for the direction of military operations in Burma and at the same time for a continuous expansion and professional training of the Indian Army.[7]

By the end of 1943, the Japanese were still at the gates of India, but the overall situation had changed substantially. They had lost air and sea supremacy to the American forces while on the Burmese front, Britain was not only hitting back aggressively but was ready to take the offensive into Burma. Because of India's pivotal importance, it could not any more be taken for granted psychologically or politically. In the midst of all these concerns of His Majesty's Government, Wavell was also plunged into a major political crisis.

CRIPPS PROPOSALS

On 11 March 1942 Churchill announced that he was sending Sir Stafford Cripps to Delhi with a draft declaration of British plans regarding 'self-government' for India. The main issue was the grant of the Dominion status to India after the war, with the right to secede, but with the provision that the self-governing States would have the right to opt out of the union and retain their existing constitutional position *vis-à-vis* the British government. Cripps, who arrived on 22 March, was full of optimism but soon found that neither Jawaharlal Nehru nor Gandhi, the Congress leaders, shared this feeling. During the early stages of the talks, the greatest stumbling block was the proposed right of non-accession of the self-governing States. Britain felt that it had a moral obligation to the Princely States, which in the past had been whole-heartedly loyal to the Crown, to ensure that they should have some say in their future.

Right from the start it appeared as if Cripps wanted to ensure the participation of the Congress at all cost. To remove the latter's reservations regarding the creation of Pakistan, Sir Sikandar Hayat, Punjab Premier, came to Delhi on the directive of the Viceroy and Cripps to give assurances to the Congress leadership that if the matter was put to vote in the Punjab Assembly, its decision would be on national and not on communal lines. After this assurance, Congress suggested that discussions should be confined to the immediate defence problem.[8]

Victoria Schofield has recorded, 'Wavell was not directly involved in discussions regarding the future of India, but his role as Commander-in-Chief was relevant to the question of how much responsibility Indians should bear for the defence of their country.'[9] In fact, his strong stand on the defence issue brought about the failure of the Cripps Proposals. Cripps had suggested that the Defence Ministry should also be transferred to the Indian political elements. But Lord Linlithgow and Wavell had different points of view.[10] Wavell sought a middle way and suggested creating the position of Deputy Commander-in-Chief or Defence Coordination Member to relieve some of the main burden of administrative work and internal security.[11] It was proposed that the Commander-in-Chief should remain on the Viceroy's Council as War Member and that there should be an Indian member for Defence. Discussion on the demarcation of duties between the Commander-in-Chief and the Defence Member soon ran into difficulties.

Cripps personally took Nehru and Maulana Azad to Wavell to clarify and give assurances regarding the offer.[12] They discussed the responsibility of the Indian member of the Council. When Wavell was asked whether the role of the Indian member of the Council would be that of a responsible cabinet minister, he gave no direct reply. Maulana Azad writes that Wavell spoke more like a politician than a soldier and insisted that during the war, strategic considerations must take precedence over all other issues.[13]

In fact, the British government could not afford to separate the British and the Indian armies at this critical juncture. On the same matter, Lord Linlithgow expressed his views in a telegram to the Prime Minister:

> Commander-in-Chief and I feel that no very serious risks are involved in setting up and handing over to an Indian Member of Council a portfolio Defence Co-ordination including duties of present Defence Co-ordination section along with such other non-essential functions of present Defence department as Wavell thinks he can safely include in the new portfolio. But we are both satisfied that in existing circumstances it is not (repeat not) possible to take away from Commander-in-Chief the substance of the defence portfolio as now held by him in order to entrust it to a representative Indian.[14]

Likewise, Wavell wrote to Churchill, '...I am convinced after careful consideration that it would not be possible to separate my dual functions as civil (Commander-in-Chief?) and defence member without causing a complete dislocation of machine....'[15] Deep differences arose and no agreement was reached between the British government and the Congress. No clarification or assurance could change the mindset of Congress leaders like Gandhi who believed that the presence of the British in India was an invitation to Japan to invade their country and, therefore, their withdrawal would remove the threat. He thought that a free India would be better able to cope with the invasion. Therefore, he decided to launch a 'Quit India' movement which he thought would wrap up the British rule in India.[16]

Jinnah and the Muslim League had no doubt that Japanese aggression had to be resisted, and consequently they created no trouble during the war.[17] The Muslim League also rejected the Cripps Proposals because they did not ensure the creation of Pakistan.

Though Wavell might have been 'on the tarmac to see the delegation off'[18] and his stand might have provided an excuse to Congress to reject the Cripps offer but his ideas about transfer of power to Indians as early as possible to get the best results in the war began to mature. His experience in the political affairs of the country opened new realities to him. Firstly, he noticed that Cripps did not care to take into confidence either the Governor General of India or the Commander-in-Chief of the army while dealing with the future political structure of India and the transfer of the British power to the Indians. It was unethical and authoritative rather than democratic to bypass the crown's representatives. It also made his task more difficult, for a single person could not bring a solution to the Indian problem. Cripps's authoritative manner in dealing with the Indians and his unflinching support and leaning towards the Congress, too, brought home to Wavell that Cripps's credibility as an honest peacemaker was doubtful.

Wavell had a different mindset. He realized that the two leading political parties of India had to be brought into government as soon as possible to help them in overcoming their differences and helping the British government to utilize all the resources of India with their kind cooperation in the war.[19]

WAVELL AS SUPREME COMMANDER OF ABDA

Wavell was appointed the Allied Supreme Commander of ABDA (American, British, Dutch, and Australian forces in the West Pacific). Laboriously, Wavell tried to build up a capacity, first, to resist the Japanese attack, and then, to strike back, but, being short of trained troops and modern equipment and plagued by the need to maintain security in India itself, he made little headway.[20]

He underrated the Japanese fighting capabilities and tried to block their military progress but he had insufficient air cover[21] to prevent the Japanese from overrunning Malaya. In December 1942, his troops attacked in the Arakan[22] without making a breakthrough because Wavell insisted on frontal assaults. When a limited offensive was begun in the Arakan Peninsula on the Burmese coast, Wavell seemed to make the same mistakes as he did in the previous campaign.

Churchill was very critical and even unpleasant about the Arakan operations, and regarded them as failures worthy of disgrace. Wavell resigned his command of ABDA.[23] He returned to India where he marshalled his resources to prepare an offensive on Burma. In January 1943, he was made Field Marshal.[24] Immediately taking charge, Wavell on his own responsibility[25] supported the first Wingate expedition to recapture Burma from the Japanese.[26] The idea was to send Wingate's 3000 men, supported by air cover, into Burma as a kind of extended cavalry raid, accomplished by an invasion by a much larger force which later on brought victories for the Allies.[27] But he was called back to London in April 1943 and returned as the Viceroy of India.[28]

Paying tribute to Wavell's services, the editor of *The Statesman* wrote: '…there have been, throughout history men to whom Governments tend to turn when a difficult task or situation arises and Wavell was such a person.' It would not be wrong to suggest that 'Wavell had often been sent to do the near-impossible, owing to his potentials and achievements.'[29]

Linlithgow was due to relinquish his viceroyalty in 1941, and almost as soon as Amery, the Secretary of State for India, took office, he began to inquire about a new Viceroy.[30] He discussed the matter with Churchill[31] and they failed to find a suitable substitute for Linlithgow for three years, till Wavell's appointment to that post.[32]

APPOINTMENT AS VICEROY

Amery told Linlithgow, 'He is excellent company and most interesting once he starts to talk. But it is not always easy to get him started.'[33] Churchill informed Attlee from North Africa that in the opinion of Brooke and Lord Ismay, Wavell had aged considerably. Churchill thought that Wavell would not be the best man to command in East

Asia. In his view, Auchinleck was a better person to deal with the enlarged Indian army.[34] He concluded that he would be sorry to leave Wavell unemployed, as he had just acquired a high reputation, due to his war services.[35] He had to be accommodated[36] and it was advised that an officer who had been Commander-in-Chief in India should not be employed in a subordinate position.[37] Hence, a suggestion that he should be made Inspector General of the Indian army was rejected. Churchill was apprehensive about how to fit in this outstanding soldier and also find a place for Wavell, and this produced a difficult problem. The solution they decided upon was to appoint Mountbatten as the Supreme Allied Commander South East Asia, with operational responsibility for the war against Japan; Auchinleck was restored to the post of Commander-in-Chief, India, which had been his from 1940–41.

Following a shuffling of various positions, Wavell was assigned the viceroyalty of India in 1943. Wavell himself has written about the rather curious circumstances under which Churchill made the decision to appoint him Viceroy of India; Wavell adds, he accepted it as a military officer would in time of war.[38] He was dissatisfied as Churchill had not written to him anything about the tenure of his appointment but only had suggested that the government might, at the end of three years, possibly wish to replace him by a politician, but he hoped that that would not, in fact, be the case.[39] Wavell suggested to Churchill the name of Evan Jenkins as his private secretary and that was accepted.[40]

Churchill was happy that Wavell's appointment had been so well received by the people.[41] Wavell had certainly got a broader outlook and wider reading than most soldiers of his time. He had dealt with many political figures in the Middle East and had the advantage of having been on the Executive Council in India and of knowing the political and constitutional problems and personalities.

Lord Wavell, the Viceroy-designate, along with his wife reached Delhi on 17 October 1943. He was sworn in as the new Viceroy on 20 October 1943.[42] Wavell was briefed by Linlithgow about the political situation in India.[43]

British Administration in India

Wavell's initiation as Viceroy coincided with the British administration beginning to lose its previously tight grip in India due to political pressures and the aftermath of war. When Wavell became Viceroy, the Governor General's Council consisted of fourteen members, of whom ten were non-official Indians and four British.[44] The Government of India Act 1935 had granted the provinces of India parliamentary self-government.[45] The need to introduce Section 93 arose shortly after the outbreak of the Second World War when the Congress ministries holding office in seven of the eleven provinces resigned and no provincial government with a satisfactory majority could be formed other than in Assam and the NWFP where a non-Congress coalition government and a government led by Sardar Aurangzeb, held offices, respectively.[46]

In Orissa, due to a change of allegiance by seven Congress members in 1941, a coalition government had been formed.[47] In May 1943, in the absence of a Congress member of the legislative assembly, the Muslim League under Sardar Aurangzeb was able to form a coalition government in the NWFP.[48]

Since 1858 the British government had been governing India directly from London.[49] In spite of promising India dominion status by the end of the Second World War, the British had not designed any special plans for quitting India. The Secretary of State for India, who was also a member of the Cabinet along with his Council, was responsible for Indian affairs.[50] The Second World War had turned India into a strategically sensitive country. Therefore, India Committee,[51] War Cabinet Committee[52] and the Secretary of State took keen interest in the internal and external affairs of India. They would not let any Governor General of India act independently. Churchill presided over most of the meetings and took decisions regarding India. As they ignored the Indian government while making decisions, Linlithgow had protested against these decisions many times.[53]

At the outbreak of the Second World War, the British government promised to grant 'Dominion Status' to India after the end of the war, due to internal and external political pressures. The August Offer of 1940, the enlargement of the Executive Council of the Viceroy in 1941 and the Cripps Proposals of 1942 were a few of the steps taken in this direction. Nonetheless, they had no clear-cut plan of leaving India in the near future, nor were they clear as to how and to which party they would transfer power in case of a breakdown.[54]

All the leading politicians as well as a majority of the British public opinion were opposed to the demand for Pakistan. However, at the same time, they believed this could best be served in a united India. Hence, the majority of the British policy makers including Churchill, Amery, Attlee, and Cripps strongly supported the unity of India and were absolutely opposed to the idea of Pakistan.[55] Likewise, the British public and press were also opposed to the demand for Partition.[56]

Though Wavell was no stranger to India, the political problem he had to encounter was complex and deeply complicated by historical forces.[57] The Muslim League was not only the strongest Muslim party in India but also an outspoken proponent of the demand for Pakistan, although a few lesser Muslim groups were opposed to it. These parties and groups had conflicting ideas and divergent programmes. Therefore, it is essential to discuss the nature, programmes and the personalities of the main Muslim political parties in order to understand Muslim politics in India better.

MUSLIM POLITICS IN INDIA: A HISTORICAL BACKGROUND

The Muslims ruled India from 712 to 1857.[58] Their decline brought them face to face with many new problems and ushered in a new era in the history of the Muslims of India.[59] Following the British conquest of India, but especially after the failed attempt to oust them in 1857, the three-way relations between the Muslims, Hindus, and the British passed through several stages. In this whole game Muslims were the biggest losers financially, politically, educationally and socially, while, carefully nurtured by the British, the Hindus and Sikhs were the biggest beneficiaries. This completely reversed the political situation.

Muslims suffered heavily wherever the British took control. Deprived of property, government jobs, discrimination in language and thereby in education, their position went down from being the leaders and elite in India to an existence at the lowest social level, just a notch above the 'untouchables'. On the other hand, the Hindus, and later the Sikhs as well, rose to the top. The Muslims' loss was the Hindus' gain and thereby the political situation of the two communities was totally reversed. This point is critical in understanding the dynamics of politics between the communities right up to 1947 and even afterwards.

The general policy of the East India Company towards the Muslims was of severe discrimination and involved replacing Muslims with Hindus wherever possible. The Hindus, on the whole, remained loyal to the foreign power and benefited immensely from the situation over a long period of time. No wonder, this generated in them the expectation of succeeding the British and becoming the overlords of South Asia after the departure of the British. Thus, when the Muslims were struggling for their very survival, the Hindus were dreaming of political power through the vehicle of democracy.

Following the events of 1857, the British tried to introduce in India the institution of democracy based on the 'Westminster' model, aimed at enlisting the support of the loyalists amongst the Indians. As a result the Indian National Congress came into being in 1885.[60] Its aim was to promote the social, economic, political interests of the Indian people regardless of their background. The dreams of its founders, however, began to shatter when it fell prey to Hindu extremist elements that began to turn it into a purely Hindu body.[61]

During the critical years of the second half of the nineteenth century, Sir Syed Ahmed Khan (1817–1898) emerged as a champion for the cause of Muslims.[62] He found his community broken by the trials and tribulations of the War of Independence, and the stormy decades that succeeded it. He undertook the responsibility of bringing about a renaissance in Muslim India. Only a full-spectrum political loyalty to the British raj, he thought, could ensure Muslim survival. The British also appreciated his efforts and realised that the Indian Muslims could not be ignored any more, so they encouraged them to get a modern education and helped Syed Ahmad Khan in establishing a number of institutions in this connection.[63]

Syed Ahmad Khan was also the first of the Muslim leaders to consistently dwell on the 'Two-Nation Theory' and held that besides other communities the two leading ones, Muslims and Hindus, formed two distinct nations.[64] He predicted, after a detailed examination of the drift of the Congress, that it would eventually turn out to be a predominantly Hindu party. He called upon Muslims to abstain from politics and refrain from joining Congress. The Muslims, heeding his advice, began to pay more attention to their educational needs. As a result of his efforts, the Congress failed to attract a large number of Muslims to its fold.

Select opposition to British rule in India had begun to mount in India in the late 1870s and early 1880s. However, till the partitioning of Bengal in 1905, there was no national political movement worth the name. Congress agitation against the partition of Bengal had two immediate effects: it turned Congress into a national organization; secondly, it created the deep chasm between the Muslims and the Hindus which kept on widening till it led to the creation of Pakistan. Two other political moves of immense historical importance resulted from the anti-government Congress agitation, seen by a majority of Muslims as strongly affecting the Muslim interests as well: Muslims decided to form their first political party and called it Muslim League, in 1906; and, following the repeal of the Bengal partition in 1911 due to Hindu/Congress agitation, Muslims realised for the first time the raw power of concerted, aggressive and sustained political agitation which could even bend the might of the powerful British Empire in India.

Not only the overwhelmingly Hindu agitation against the partition of Bengal but nearly all Hindu and Congress protests seemed to pose a direct threat to Muslim interests. Congress's opposition to the Land Alienation Act of 1901 in Punjab and to the Muslim demand for separate electorates are good examples of such a political approach. Concerning the partition of Bengal and its effects on Muslim interests, Sikandar Hayat wrote that:

> even if one were to grant the argument that the partition of Bengal was a deliberate move on the part of the British government to sow the seeds of conflict between the Hindus and the Muslims, the question still remains, why did not the Hindus put forward "an alternative scheme" to satisfy legitimate grievances of the Muslims in Bengal. After all, they were fully aware that the partition meant great relief to many Muslims in East Bengal.[65]

The Hindu political groups, press and professionals banded together to openly condemn, abuse and politically attack those Muslims who supported the partition of Bengal.

All of the above political activity created amongst the Muslims a sense of deprivation and loss, for the Congress could not endorse those reforms which would further Muslim development. The Muslims felt that as a community they were totally separate from the Hindus. The one-dimensional understanding of the Congress leadership towards the Muslim problems led them to denounce and reject all other political view points. They became prone to the 'conspiracy theory'. They themselves had been created, nurtured and promoted by the British, and believed that whatever had occurred and was going to occur in India, happened with the backing or prior approval of the British government. As a result Hindus branded Sir Syed as a British loyalist, anti-nationalist and a communalist. Similarly they declared Simla Deputation of 1906 and the creation of the Muslim League in 1906 as a 'command performance'.[66] This kind of approach had serious implications and needed readjustment and rectification in the light of the Muslim intellectual experience and the emerging problems of the Muslims in the first half of the twentieth century.

However, the new century required openness, large heartedness and political insight from the Indian leadership in order to end British Raj in India. Unity of purpose among the different communities of India could have facilitated it, but unity was a factor that was sorely lacking among them.

The Hindus, however, had become the most politically conscious community since 1857. They had not only been aspiring for total political ascendancy in India upon the departure of the British but had also declared India 'a land only for the Aryans', a declaration that denied a homeland to Muslims and Christians in the Hindu, holy motherland.[67] Sikhs also had been forming, for a long time, their separate associations for promotion and protection of their religious and political rights. On 30 October 1902, they formed the Chief Khalsa Diwan by merging 29 of the Singh Sabhas.[68]

At this critical juncture, the Muslims at large could not afford to remain aloof from the complexities of Indian national politics. They expected, from the Muslim political elite, some bold political steps to safeguard their future destiny. Unlike the creation of the Sanskrit College, Hindu Benares University and the Indian National Congress, the Simla Deputation of October 1906 and the establishment of the Muslim League (December 1906) by the Muslim leaders was neither engineered nor sponsored or commanded by the British authorities.[69] This change in the Muslim political thought was the outcome of the origins of Hindu–Muslim tussles, the introduction of the democratic institutions in India and independent growth of separate nationalistic aspirations, of the Muslims of South Asia.[70] Although, Sir Syed Ahmad Khan, Waqar-ul-Mulk, and Syed Ameer Ali[71] had founded some political associations at the national level, these failed to achieve popularity among the rank and file of the Muslims mainly because their founders had neither the intention nor the capacity to extend them on a large scale. However, their main thrust remained the securing of safeguards for the Muslims in the fields of culture, education, economics and politics. The Muslim League right from its commencement demanded safeguards for Muslims in every field, and claimed for itself the status of the only representative of the Muslims. Whether its establishment was justified or not, the response of the Congress leaders to its establishment was unfortunate. They took ten years to recognize the significance of its role in the liberation of India.

The Lucknow Pact of 1916 provided a basis for an eventual rapprochement between the Congress and the Muslim League; however it was to be of short duration. The outcome of this agreement was that it enabled them to work collectively and vigorously to achieve home rule through the efforts of the Home Rule League (1916–1920), opposing the Rowlatt Act of 1919, protesting against the tragedy of Jallianwalla Bagh 1919, and boycotting the elections in 1920 under the Montagu–Chelmsford Reforms of 1919. Moreover, they started the Non-Cooperation Movement (1920–22) as part of the Khilafat Movement. But this honeymoon period soon came to an end and the 'accord' between the two communities struggled in the stormy politics of the 1920s.[72] The new constitutional reforms and the inception of new Hindu religious extremist movements and organizations like Shuddhi, Sangathan, and Hindu Mahasabha polluted the recently created atmosphere of Hindu–Muslim unity and exposed the mutual trust, respect and the reliance of the two political parties on each other to mutual hostilities.

Jinnah was praised for his efforts for Hindu–Muslim unity. He however, left the Congress in 1920, as his rational approach towards politics[73] did not permit him to accept the emotionalism of Gandhian philosophy, which he thought would lead nowhere. Therefore, he did not endorse the philosophy and the methods adopted by the Congress under the instructions and influence of Gandhi for the Non-Cooperation Movement in the Khilafat Movement. He felt that Gandhi was taking India to a destination where everything would end in disaster.[74] His prediction proved correct and not only did the Khilafat Movement end in failure but it also led to communal riots which became routine afterward.

Jinnah always thought in terms of a unified approach by the two leading communities to the political problems then faced by India.[75] It was with this spirit that he endorsed the Congress decision to boycott the Simon Commission in 1927 and presented the Delhi Muslim Proposals in 1927.

With a view to carrying on League–Congress concurrence and Hindu–Muslim unity, Muslim League under Jinnah's direction even showed its willingness to surrender the two principles of separate electorates and weightage in the provinces. These two constitutional provisions formed the bedrock of what they thought was essential for the preservation of their identity and interests.[76]

This stance soon divided not only the Muslim League but also the whole Muslim community between proponents and opponents of separate electorates. No doubt, according to David Page, the Unionists in the Punjab who were against the Delhi Muslim Proposals were more interested in preservation of their class interests than any communal interests.[77] But there were genuine reactions of the Muslims who considered it a political mistake to rely so heavily on the Congress leaders without prior assurances.[78] Though it could have put his political career at stake, Jinnah was ready to make an extremely courageous and risky move for the sake of Hindu–Muslim unity. In fact, the proposals were not a political mistake on the part of Jinnah, rather a calculated move masking Jinnah's political expediency.

While the Muslims were divided on this point, the Hindus had become united against the demand for separate electorates. In 1928, the All-Parties Convention approved the Nehru Report drafted by the Nehru Committee.[79] It not only rejected the Muslim demand for separate electorates but also refused to accept the Muslim claim to one-third of seats in the Central Legislature.[80] Thus the Nehru Report killed the spirit and substance of the Lucknow Pact of 1916. Shoaib Qureshi, a member of the Nehru Committee, disagreeing with its proposals did not sign it while the other Muslim member Sir Ali Imam was ill and did not take part in its proceedings. The report was considered by the Muslim League as a charter of slavery for the Muslims, for it aimed at establishing the Hindu Raj in India by Congress and the Hindu Mahasabha. According to Uma Kaura, 'The failure of the Convention can only be attributed to the inability of the Congress leaders to stand up firmly against the pressures of the Hindu Mahasabha.'[81]

To Jinnah, it was a 'parting of the ways' but according to Abdul Hamid, Jinnah's brief and pointed comment at this stage was more apparent than real, as he did not lose heart and continued to seek Hindu–Muslim unity even during the Round Table Conferences.[82] In response to the Nehru Report Jinnah presented his 'Fourteen Points' but Allama Iqbal had a unique remedy to solve the Hindu–Muslim problem.[83]

ALLAMA IQBAL'S ALLAHABAD ADDRESS (1930)

Allama Iqbal had a clear vision and profound outlook regarding the future of Indian Muslims. Like Jinnah, he had also passed through stages of political evolutionary growth to arrive at the conclusion that the best alternative for Muslims was to have a separate homeland of their own. He conceptualized the idea of a separate homeland for the Muslims in his presidential address of 1930 at Allahabad during the annual session of the Muslim League.

Based on the Two-Nation Theory, his address shed light on the incongruity and divergent philosophies of the Muslims and Hindus that had persisted for centuries. He maintained that both Muslims and Hindus had failed to merge into one nation. All efforts to forge them into a single nationhood in the past through such means as the Bhagti

Movement and Akbar's Deen-i-Ilahi ended in failure. He did not deem it fit for the Muslims and the Hindus to live together in an atmosphere where the practice of the basic principles of co-existence had become impossible due to mutual jealousies, rioting and economic and political clashes. Therefore, he proposed the division of India on communal grounds, i.e., Hindu and Muslim zones.

Despite the forceful arguments and logic of the Allahabad address, Allama Iqbal failed to attract a large following within the Muslim League to his concept of the division of India but ended up laying the intellectual foundation of Muslim nationalism in India, which led in March 1940 to the demand for Pakistan.[84]

In 1933, Chaudhry Rahmat Ali, a student at Cambridge University along with his two friends, coined the name 'Pakistan',[85] keeping in view those areas and provinces which were designated by Allama Iqbal as forming part of a separate Muslim 'homeland'. They also started the 'Pakistan Movement' to achieve this separate homeland as described by him. However, the movement for Pakistan could not become a popular movement till the passage of the Lahore Resolution in 1940.

THE CONGRESS MINISTRIES (1937–1939)

The main feature of the Muslim politics in India in the 1930s was its shift from the provinces to the Centre. The upshot of the three Round Table Conferences held in 1930–1932 was the enactment of the Government of India Act 1935.[86] Although it could neither satisfy the Muslim League nor the Congress, both decided to make the best of it by agreeing to follow it.[87] The general elections of 1936–37 failed to prove that the Congress was the single representative body of all the communities in India. It contested only on 58 seats out of 482 seats reserved for the Muslims in the provinces and won only 24 of them. Although the Muslim League proved to be the largest single party of the Muslims it acquired only 104 seats. Congress secured 711 out of 1585 seats in the provincial elections.[88] Though it did not win a majority of seats in the general constituencies, it had enough strength, however, to give the party an absolute majority in five provinces and control in three others.

According to its critics, these unexpected results deceptively intoxicated the Congress leaders with a mistaken sense of power. Overriding and ignoring the growing intensity of the Muslim League's opposition to their anti-Muslim policies, they started believing that it was the only party with the sole right to rule India once the British departed. After occupying power at the provincial level they started thinking of capturing it at the centre as well, but the onset of the Second World War shattered their dreams.

In fact, the Congress ministries (1937–39) had further widened the gulf between the Muslims and the Hindus, mainly due to their irresponsible and blatant anti-Muslim policies. The 'Gentleman's Agreement', between the Governor General and Gandhi, had put the Congress on the driving seat, for the Governor was forbidden to use his special powers. Thus, the Congress secured for itself a position in which it could disregard altogether the safeguards that the Act had provided as a brake upon the powers of the majority.[89] At the outset of the formation of its ministries, the Congress refused to form a coalition government with the League in the United Provinces.

Refusal of the Congress to form a coalition government with the League was their legitimate right but they exercised this right in an awkward and indecent manner. They put humiliating terms to include one minister of the League in the United Provinces (UP) government. The Muslim League leaders felt that Gandhi and his followers wished to absorb the League into the Congress.[90]

On failing in their aim in the UP, the Congress launched the 'Mass Contact' movement[91] with great zeal and commitment to enlist Muslim voters, which also proved counter-productive.[92] But not only did it annoy the Muslim masses and the provincial governments of Bengal, Punjab and Assam but also forced the League to counter the propaganda unleashed by the Congress.[93] The Muslims complained that Congress ministries had adopted policies that aimed at making Hindu extremists happy at the cost of Muslim peace of mind.

The League's offices all over India overflowed with letters and applications from Muslims regarding their sufferings in the Muslim-minority provinces.[94] Neither the Congress nor the British government took notice of these sufferings which emboldened the Hindu extremists, and they unleashed a reign of terror by converting Muslims into Hindus through the agency of Rashtriya Swayamsevak Sangh, Hindu Sabha, Shuddhi and Sangathan.[95] The climate became ripe for the Hindu–Muslim riots which claimed the lives and properties of thousands of innocent persons.[96] The Muslims thought that a Hindu raj had come into full play where they had no part to play in the society.

Leading Congress leaders like Gandhi and Jawaharlal Nehru also did not display political wisdom and sagacity regarding the complaints of the Muslims. Nehru's statements such as 'there were only two parties, Congress and the British in India' was enough proof for the majority of Muslims and the League to believe that as far as the Congress was concerned Muslims had no place in Indian politics.

Gandhi's policies of educational and cultural innovations, aimed at diluting the national identity of Muslims, were probably the most serious political mistake at an inopportune time. The most unfortunate aspect of Congress's attitude was that it highly overestimated its popularity and standing among the Muslims, vis-à-vis that of the League, in the mature political culture of the 1930s. Congress continued to show a general lack of wisdom and statesmanship in the coming years as well. Mistakes committed by the Congress during this period, along with the missed opportunities, rendered all the later efforts to keep the country united, worthless.

The Second World War provided an opportunity for the Indians to forge unity amongst themselves to pressure the British Indian government for independence, but this did not happen. Penderel Moon points out,

> The outbreak of war afforded a splendid opportunity of repairing the damage that had been done during their ministries. On the plea of national emergency Congress could have retraced their steps and sought to join with the League in coalition both in the provinces and at the centre. It was politically unwise to display dissent and division between them, for they could not force the British to evacuate South Asia at the crucial time of the Second World War. The Congress chose to follow the barren path of non-co-operation with both the British and the League.[97]

Gandhi, like Nehru, also asserted that there were only two parties in India, namely those who supported the Congress and those who did not, and then added that between the two there was no meeting ground without the one or the other surrendering its purpose.[98] Consequently when the Congress Ministries resigned from the provinces, Jinnah called upon Muslims to celebrate the 'Day of Deliverance'.[99] Thus Jinnah, at the Patna session of the League held in 1938, declared that the Congress was a Hindu body and aimed at Hindu Raj because the Vidya Mandir Scheme,[100] the Rajkot Affairs, Hyderabad Satyagraha and the singing of Bande Matram[101] were enough reason for the Muslims to quit the Congress and despise it.[102]

At the end of the Congress ministries, putting the blame for the fragile and tense communal situation existing in India squarely on Congress Jinnah claimed, 'The Musalmans cannot expect any justice or fairplay at their hands.'[103] He now felt that a federal form of government for united India, a separate electorate for the Muslims, reservation of one third seats in the centre and provincial autonomy were not enough safeguards for the Muslims of India. A feeling of despondency and helplessness prevailed amongst the Indian Muslims,[104] therefore, there was only one path left for them and that was the division of India into Hindu and Muslim zones. It could save the Muslims of the Muslim-majority areas from complete annihilation at the hands of the Hindus.

Ian Stephens has recorded, 'whereas in the 1920s, Muslims were worried mainly about how diarchy would work under the Montagu-Chelmsford system, in the 1930s their chief concern was to prevent a future Central or Federal Government from getting too strong, from obtaining powers wide enough to put Muslims permanently at a Hindu majority mercy.'[105]

THE LAHORE RESOLUTION (1940)

The Lahore Resolution of March 1940 was the result of an independent evolution of the Muslim political thought.[106] It was neither dictated by the British nor encouraged by Lord Linlithgow as some Congress party historians have alleged[107] but was a natural result of the Muslims' aspirations, interests and ideals shaped by the evolving political situation in India.[108] Jinnah, like Allama Iqbal, after exploring all other avenues of Muslim survival and security in India, had reached the conclusion that the only way the Muslim could save themselves from the stranglehold of a Hindu majority government and secure their future life in line with their ideals, 'religious,[109] spiritual, economic,[110] social[111] and political,' was to have their own homeland, territory and state. His rationale of the two-nation theory was almost on the same lines, tone and style as had been expounded by Allama Iqbal.[112] But he elaborated it in a manner clearer to the Muslims at large to explain the contradictions which had existed between the Hindus and the Muslims for a long time. He tried to prove that the Muslims of India had survived with a separate identity and deserved to be considered as a separate nation, for their separate identity fulfilled every sense of the meaning of the word 'nation' prevalent in the political dictionary of the time.

It is rightly pointed out that the Muslims of India had been wandering in a political wilderness but the Lahore Resolution of March 1940 gave them a sense of identity and purpose. Some historians tend to declare the Lahore Resolution 'ambiguous' and a 'bargaining counter'. Although Viceroys Linlithgow, Wavell, and Mountbatten frequently had used the word 'bargaining counter' for the Lahore Resolution of 1940, historians like Ayesha Jalal have also reinterpreted it sensationally.

Sikandar Hayat has pointed out, 'So-called ambiguities in the Lahore Resolution were tactical in nature and put deliberately to save it from attacks from Muslim League's powerful adversaries, the British and the Congress.'[113] The fact was that the Muslims of India responded quickly and positively to Jinnah's call and began to join the League and supported the demand for Pakistan. He deliberately left vague the whole plan although he called for establishing independent states in the North-West and North-Eastern zones for the Muslims of India. This placed Jinnah at the top in his ability to negotiate with the opponents of the demand for Pakistan during the British transfer of power to India.

As both the British and the Congress stood for the unity of India, the resolution failed to make either of them happy, due to a variety of reasons. As in earlier instances Hindus admonished the Muslims for passing such a resolution and declared that it was dicta.

Instead of trying for a truer understanding of the Muslims' problems and complaints, the Congress, as a result of the Pakistan Resolution, became even more hostile towards them and adopted a strategy aimed at dividing their ranks.[114] They encouraged all those groups, leaders and associations whom they thought would oppose the League, Jinnah and the Lahore Resolution, by providing them economic, political and other assistance. Increased Congress opposition to the League, Jinnah and the Lahore Resolution had the reverse of the intended effect, for it increased their popularity amongst the Muslim masses. Like the Hindus, the British government was also opposed to the Lahore Resolution, but being the governing power it could not afford to ignore the growing influence of Jinnah and the League among the Muslims of India, whose valuable military and other services were badly needed for the Second World War.

Lord Linlithgow, Viceroy of India (1936–1943), was concerned about the Lahore Resolution and termed it a 'silly Muslim scheme for partition' but could not ignore the Muslims as a unique community in India.[115] In August 1940, Linlithgow issued a declaration in which he pledged that the government would accept, at the earliest possible moment after the war, the right of India's free and equal partnership in the British Commonwealth under a constitution of her own making. He also announced:

> His Majesty's Government could not contemplate transfer of their present responsibilities...to any system of government whose authority is directly denied by large and powerful elements in India's national life. Nor could they be parties to the coercion of such elements into submission to such government.[116]

At the same time, he invited party leaders to cooperate in the war effort by joining the Viceroy's Executive Council. Congress refused even to discuss the offer and started 'Satyagraha movement' against India's participation in the War. The Satyagraha campaign proved a complete fiasco and died out in 1941.

Muslims, in the late 1920s and early 1940s were divided into a number of groups. However, the All-India Muslim League was the largest, most important and influential amongst them. Even some Muslim parties and leaders and almost all the non-Muslims of India opposed the demand for Pakistan. Despite the bitter opposition of the British, Hindus, Sikhs and even some Muslim circles, the Pakistan movement was fast gaining popularity among the Muslim masses in India.[117]

V.P. Menon's conclusion that the League maximized its gains from estrangement between Congress and the British[118] while the Congress leaders were in jail does not accord with facts.[119] In the by-elections from 1 January 1938 to 12 September 1942 the League won 46 Muslim seats out of a total of 56 whereas the Congress could win only three.[120] The voting pattern remained nearly the same in the succeeding by-elections as well and all this had nothing to do with the Congress being absent from the political scene, for the Congress had yet to start the Quit India Movement.[121] However, between 1943 and 1945 only 11 by-elections took place of which the League won eight, the Independent Muslims three while the Congress failed to win any seat.[122] Therefore, by the time Wavell became viceroy, the Muslim League had emerged as the most powerful Muslim organization in all of India. It had grabbed power in Bengal,[123] Assam,[124] Sindh[125] and the NWFP.[126] The head of the Punjab government was not a member of the League but referred to himself as 'a Leaguer'.[127] The League now controlled, directly or indirectly, the provincial governments of all the provinces that it wanted included in its proposed Pakistan. This new situation made Jinnah's claim for the establishment of Pakistan much more forceful.[128]

By this time, Jinnah, the driving force and moving spirit behind the Pakistan demand, had assumed the undisputed leadership of the League. He also enjoyed the full support and respect of the Muslim masses throughout India which[129] were solidly arrayed behind his leadership.[130] Subsidiary organizations of the Muslim League such as the Muslim Students Federation[131] and the All-India Women's Organization[132] were playing a strong role in spreading the message of the Pakistan movement throughout India.[133] The Muslim League National Guard[134] was also a great source of strength and security for the League and its leadership. Above all, the League's allied leaders and organizations including Jamiatul Ulama-i Islam, under the leadership of Maulana Shabbir Ahmad Usmani,[135] Jamiat Ahle Hadith led by Maulana Ibrahim Sialkoti[136] and Maulana Sanaullah Amritsari also provided great strength and solidarity to the Pakistan demand.

Besides all the above activists for the Pakistan movement, the Sufis also played an important role in various parts of India, particularly in Punjab and Sindh, in popularizing the Pakistan cause.[137] Likewise, some prominent Ulema and Mashaikhs under the leadership of Pir Jamat Ali Shah of Alipore Suadan in the Punjab[138] and Pir Sahib Amin-ul-Hasnat of Manki Sharif[139] in the NWFP were also playing an inspired role in advancing the cause of Pakistan.[140] A section of Muslim press was also playing a commendable role in propagating the Pakistan plan.[141] A number of Muslim-owned newspapers like the *Dawn* (Delhi),[142] *Morning News* (Calcutta),[143] *The Eastern Times* (Lahore)[144] and *Nawa-i-Waqt* (Lahore)[145] were in the forefront of popularizing the demand for Pakistan.

In short, the Pakistan movement, which promised a homeland for Muslims in distinct zones of India in the North-West and North-East, had captured the imagination of the Muslim masses.[146] The demand for Pakistan had assumed serious dimensions worthy of a serious consideration by everybody, although Jinnah had yet to explicitly define the precise boundaries of the proposed homeland for the Muslims, which remained a source of anxiety and debate among all the parties.[147] He used every opportunity to exploit the then existing Congress–British estrangement. It was expected that he would not compromise on the 'Pakistan Plan' until both the Hindus and the British had accepted it on principle. The Cripps Proposals and some Hindu leaders like Rajagopalachari had indirectly accepted the Muslims as a separate nation with the right of self-determination in the Muslim majority provinces. By the time Wavell reached India, it was claimed by the Muslim League circles that the 'Pakistan Plan' had achieved a solid footing amongst the Muslim masses. Most of the Muslim middle- and lower-middle classes supported it. By 1942, 'Jinnah actually assumed a position like Gandhiji so far as Muslims were concerned and thence Pakistan dominated the political discourse.'[148]

Jinnah claimed to be the unchallenged and undisputed leader of the Indian Muslims, but neither the British government, nor the Congress or the Sikhs agreed with these claims. Certainly India had entered a political era which it had never experienced before. Any mishandling on the part of the British government regarding the Muslim problem might bring a civil war in India.

NATIONALIST MUSLIM PARTIES

Those Muslims who opposed the Muslim League programme and its Pakistan plan can be termed as 'Nationalist Muslims'.[149] Maulana Abul Kalam Azad, President of the Congress (1940–46), was the leader of these Congressite and 'Nationalist' Muslims. 'Nationalists' were divided into groups such as the Unionists, the Ahrar, Khudai Khidmatgars, the Khaksars, etc., and were in the forefront of opposition to the Pakistan scheme. Azad, along with his Muslim supporters, was dead set against the idea of Pakistan and left no stone unturned to denounce Jinnah, the League and the demand for Pakistan.[150] They believed in the 'composite' Indian nationalism[151] and were determined to maintain the unity of India.[152]

THE UNIONIST PARTY

Sir Fazl-i-Husain founded The Unionist Party in 1923; its membership mostly consisted of Muslims, Hindus, and Sikhs besides some others from Punjab.[153] It was a multi-communal party with a secular outlook which was committed to protecting the interests of all the communities inhabiting the Punjab. However, Fazl-i-Husain was also a member of the Muslim League and his conflicting loyalties were tested to the hilt during the provincial elections of 1936–37.

Before the provincial elections of 1936 Jinnah demanded of Sir Fazl-i-Husain that his members should contest the elections on the Muslim League platform, but Sir Fazl-i-Husain, citing the reduced numerical strength of the Muslim League following the Communal Award, refused. He contended that since cooperation with other parties would definitely be required, he could not go along with Jinnah's request. Therefore, it was more appropriate to let the Muslim members of the Unionist Party fight elections on its platform. Jinnah failed to change the provincial leadership of the Punjab and Bengal.

After the death of Sir Fazl-i-Husain, Sir Sikandar Hayat became the Unionist leader in Punjab. The Muslim League could not fare well in the elections as its leaders chose to fight them from other platforms. The Unionists won a landslide victory in the 1936–37 provincial elections.[154] The provincial-oriented Muslim leaders, however, soon suffered setbacks which forced them to review their political position.

Sikandar Hayat (the Unionist Premier of the Punjab, 1937–42) was forced to abandon the path treaded by Sir Fazl-i-Husain and sought help from the Muslim League to ensure his power as it was threatened by the Congress.[155] It resulted in the conclusion of the Sikandar–Jinnah

Pact of 1937 which made the Muslim members of the Unionist Party members of the Muslim League as well.[156]

Sikandar took part in the proceedings of the Lahore Resolution but was opposed to the division of India.[157] According to Qalb-i-Abid, 'Sir Sikandar did everything possible to prevent the Pakistan Scheme from establishing its roots in the Punjab, but failed owing to the rapid growth of the Muslim League during the war.'[158] His divided loyalties led him nowhere as he needed the backing of all three leading communities, Muslims, Hindus and Sikhs, in the Punjab. He also had to resign[159] from the Viceroy's Defence Council[160] as per Jinnah's instructions because his 1937 pact with Jinnah had considerably reduced his manoeuvring space.[161] He was succeeded by Khizar Hayat Khan Tiwana,[162] who was unwilling to work smoothly under the League's directions. When Wavell assumed viceroyalty, the Unionist Party had been losing its support amongst the Muslim masses of the Punjab due to the rising popularity of the Pakistan demand.

Jamiat Ulema-i-Hind

Jamiat Ulema-i-Hind (JUH),[163] founded in 1919, was another important party of the Muslims. It mostly consisted of religious scholars[164] who believed in composite nationalism and, therefore, condemned the Pakistan demand.[165] From the League's point of view the Jamiat was a subordinate organization of the Congress party.[166] Under the leadership of Maulana Hussein Ahmad Madni (1879–1957)[167] and Kifayatullah (1852–1952), the group worked hard at promoting the aims of the Congress, thereby hurting the League's cause. Ajmal[168] and Al-Jamayat (Delhi),[169] the two important periodicals of Jamiat, strongly condemned the Pakistan demand. JUH had divided into pro-Pakistan and anti-Pakistan groups, and Maulanas Ashraf-Ali Thanvi[170] and Shabbir Ahmad Usmani[171] et al. of the former joined the Muslim League and supported the Pakistan plan.[172]

As per the Jamiat Ulema-i-Hind it was the British government[173] which was chiefly responsible for creating a fear-complex in the minds of the Muslims.[174] They thought that Imperial England, in order to keep its hold on a rich country like India, had to have its domination over the Muslim countries in the Middle East.[175] The enslavement of India was the cause of the British supremacy over all lands and seas through which the strategic line of imperial communications passed. Therefore, the independence of India would mean the liberation of a vast Muslim area.[176]

Division amongst various Muslim leaders and parties confused the Muslim masses.[177] The non-League Muslim organizations responded to the Lahore Resolution by convening an Azad Muslim Conference at Delhi in April 1940 and passed resolutions or presented programmes for the religious and cultural safeguards of the Muslim community. In 1942 the Jamiat came out with its own recommendations as well, in a programme known as the Jamiat Formula[178] which was almost identical to Jinnah's Fourteen Points.

Majlis-i-Ahrar-i-Islam

As observed by Janbaz Mirza, persuaded by Maulana Abul Kalam Azad,[179] some prominent Indian Ulema, mostly from the Punjab, decided to establish a separate political party known as the Majlis-i-Ahrar-i-Islam.[180] Maulana Syed Ataullah Shah Bokhari, Chaudhry Afzal Haq,[181] Maulana Zafar Ali Khan,[182] and Maulana Mazhar Ali Azhar[183] were its founding leaders. These leaders had also been active in the Khilafat Movement.

The Khilafat Movement's leaders were divided about the Nehru Report of 1928. The Central Khilafat Committee under the presidentship of Maulana Muhammad Ali Jauhar[184] condemned the Nehru Report while some members of the Punjab Khilafat Committee were in favour of accepting the Nehru Report.[185] Since they believed that the principle of joint electorates was not harmful to the Muslims of the Punjab they decided to set up their own political party.

Most of the Indian Ulema believed that the British rule in India was a curse and they supposed the Congress to be anti-raj as opposed to the All-India Muslim League which they considered pro-British,[186] therefore, they leaned towards the Congress. In 1929–30, after Congress had declared the achievement of complete independence as its ultimate goal it went looking for the support of the Muslim Ulema,[187] and Maulana Abul Kalam Azad was able to persuade some important ones to form their own parties.[188]

In the first two years of its existence, Majlis-i-Ahrar worked in close contact with the Congress taking an active part in Gandhi's Civil Disobedient Movement of 1930.[189] Ram Gopal stated, 'Working steadily, fervently and inspiringly, the Ahrars played their noble part in the struggle.'[190] Its active part in the pro-Muslim movements in Kashmir[191] and in Kapurthala State in 1931[192] brought it into the limelight. It was popular among the middle and the lower classes of Muslims.[193] Their indecisive stand on the Shahid Ganj Mosque tragedy[194] and, following that, a tussle with the Unionist Government lost them supporters.[195]

The Ahrar was pro-Congress and anti-Pakistan and via its politico-religious philosophy claimed to establish a 'Godly State' or 'States' in the world.[196] It lacked a clear vision of its path in politics except for its opposition to the proposed Pakistan scheme.[197] Although on the decline in Punjab, the Ahrar seriously challenged the British government in 1930, 1940, and 1941 and also during the Congress rebellion of 1942.

Although, Peter Hardy's argument that the 'Ahrar movement co-operated politically with Congress, it stood for an India of federated, religiously-inspired radicalism, rather than for a national secular state,'[198] seems fair, the Congress was able to use it against the Muslim League.

The bitter reality for all Muslim groups like the Jamiat-ul-Ulema, the Ahrar Party and the Nationalist Muslims Conference, which had been created as counters to the Muslim League, was that they were not able to convert many Muslims to the creed which gave nationalism a place subordinate to religion.[199]

THE KHUDAI KHIDMATGARS OF NWFP

It was founded on 1 April 1921, as a social movement, by Khan Abdul Ghaffar Khan (1890–1988), popularly known as Bacha Khan (Badshah Khan), who named it Anjuman-i-Islahul-Afghania (the association for the reformation of the Afghan). Although the organization aimed primarily at countering social evils and forging unity in the Pukhtoon ranks, with the passage of time it assumed a definitive political character. In May 1928, Bacha Khan started the *Pukhtoon*, a monthly journal and in November 1929 organized the movement of Khudai Khidmatgars (the Servants of God).[200] The organization had numerous aims and objectives, however, the real objective of this movement was to organize the Pukhtoon, and awaken them for the services of their country in the name of God. Its chief aim was to work for the betterment of mankind regardless of religion, sect or ethnicity.[201]

This organization created awareness in the poor people of the province, who were mostly disorganized and exploited by the vested interests including feudal Khans and Maliks. They aimed at the social uplift of the Pakhtoons and opposition to British colonialism. After the firing incident in Peshawar, the movement became extremely popular, with its membership growing to more than 40,000 people. It remained popular amongst the Pakhtoons of the Pashto-dominated districts of NWFP.[202] The British and local elites were threatened by the popularity of the movement because of its demands for the end of colonialism, the redistribution of land, etc.

Deeply influenced by Gandhi's philosophy, Bacha Khan attended the Lahore Session of the Congress[203] and endorsed the Congress's programme of complete independence.[204] He took an active part in the Civil Disobedient Movement of 1930–34 launched by Congress and later on merged the Khudai Khidmatgar organization with Congress, though retaining its separate identity. It increased the popularity of his organization to an all-India level.[205] Thereafter, the Khudai Khidmatgars and the Congress worked together till the partition.

Elections for the provincial legislative assembly of NWFP were held in the first week of February 1937.[206] Dr Khan Sahib, younger brother of Ghaffar Khan, took over the Congress leadership in the province because Bacha Khan was in prison but he guided his brother from his cell.[207]

For an assembly of 50 members Congress fielded 36 candidates.[208] Following the election results Congress emerged as the single largest group while the United Muslim Nationalist Party had 16 members, Hindu–Sikh Nationalist Party had 8; Hazara Democratic Party had 4, Khuda Bakhsh and Pir Bakhsh were the two independents while Sardar Abdur Rab Nishtar had no political affiliation. During these 1937 elections Muslim League had practically no support in the NWFP and not even a single candidate contested on a Muslim League ticket. The provincial Congress chose not to form the ministry, so on 1 April 1937 Sir Sahibzada Abdul Qayyum Khan in alliance with Hindu–Sikh

Nationalist party, the Hazara Democrats, and individual Khans formed a ministry.[209] The assembly held only two sessions during this period.

By autumn 1937, however, the Congress high command instructed its NWFP organization to form a new ministry. Dr Khan Sahib was able to remove the Sir Abdul Qayyum Khan ministry following a no-confidence motion on 7 September 1937 and after securing the support of some members from other groups[210] formed a Congress-led ministry. Sir Abdul Qayyum Khan retired from public life and passed away three months later on 4 December 1937.[211] His death marked the end of any credible personality to pose a constructive opposition to the government as he was the man whom everybody looked to for advice in serious political matters.

The ministry had to cope with a number of internal and external problems including communal riots.[212] However, it performed well and introduced various reforms in the province. It introduced the Teri Dues Regulation Act, X of 1938,[213] the Prohibition Act, XI of 1938,[214] the Agricultural Produce Markets Act, XIV of 1939,[215] the Punjab Tenancy (NWFP) Amendment Act, XX of 1939, etc.[216]

When Lord Linlithgow unilaterally declared war against Germany in 1939 the Congress decided to resign its ministries in the provinces (eight) held by them and the governors took over control of the administration.[217] The Congress-led ministry in the NWFP also followed and resigned on 7 November 1939. This meant that Congress abandoned the 'constitutional' politics and once again plunged into politics of protest.[218] During the war years, Bacha Khan had endorsed the Individual Satyagraha (1940) and the 'Quit India' (1942) Movements of the Congress. However, as compared to other parts of British India, NWFP remained relatively peaceful. According to Wiqar Ali Shah: 'The Khudai Khidmatgars were induced by those leaders who were still outside prison not to pay their revenues; government servants were asked to leave their jobs; and army men were requested to desert the army. But, contrary to the expectations of the Congressites, the general public had lost interest in civil disobedience.'[219]

After a small time gap, on 25 May 1943, the provincial Muslim League leader, Sardar Aurangzeb Khan,[220] was able to form a coalition ministry with the help of the Sikhs.[221] When Wavell assumed office in India the popularity of the demand for Pakistan had spread deeply amongst the Muslims of the NWFP.[222] However, because of their longstanding political roots in certain areas of the province, the Khudai Khidmatgars, were deemed a potential threat to Mr Jinnah's demand for Pakistan especially when he needed the Pathan support later on in his campaign in the province.[223]

THE KHAKSAR MOVEMENT

Inspired by Hitler and with the aim of reviving the Islamic military tradition, the Khaksar Movement was founded by Allama Inayatullah Mashriqi at Lahore in April 1931.[224] He organised the rank and file of his party on para-military lines, with workers dressed in 'khaki' military style uniforms and parading in streets, carrying spades.[225]

Khaksar's first showdown took place with the UP government at a place called Bulandshaher in 1939 resulting in several deaths.[226] Although the UP government had banned their entry into the province they still somehow managed to defy the orders.

It was followed by an even bigger confrontation with the Unionist regime of Sir Sikandar Hayat in Lahore.[227] The Khaksars had asked the Punjab government for permission to open a radio station at Lahore which was declined by the government.

The Punjab government had issued an order in 1940 banning all military-style drills or processions. On 19 March 1940, despite this ban on the parade and drill, the Khaksars paraded the streets and police opened fire killing a number of Khaksar volunteers.[228] The government banned the Khaksar party and arrested all its leaders and locked its offices.[229] Jinnah's gesture of visiting the injured Khaksar workers in the hospital during his visit to Lahore for the Muslim League meeting helped ease Muslim League –Khaksar relations from 1940–43 but an assassination attempt by a Khaksar worker on Jinnah in 1943 strained them irreparably.[230]

Mashraqi's political attitude proved puzzling because he was not a supporter of the Congress[231] but his animosity to the Muslim League and Jinnah did end up helping the Congress.[232] Their leading voice in press, *Al-Islah*[233] of Lahore, played a major role in widening the gulf between the Khaksars and the League.

JAMAAT-I-ISLAMI

It was established by Maulana Abul Ala Maududi (1901–1979)[234] at Lahore in 1941.[235] Its main objective was to establish an Islamic state in India but like other Muslim Ulema, Maududi lacked a practical political methodology to achieve his goals.[236] He believed in the Two-Nation Theory, though his interpretation differed greatly from that of the Muslim League. This difference in understanding the political situation made him critical of Jinnah and the Muslim League.[237] Though he had a very small following, yet he had the potential to influence the public opinion against the Muslim League and its demand for Pakistan, therefore indirectly serving the cause of the Congress.[238]

THE INDIAN NATIONAL CONGRESS

The Indian National Congress claimed to be the sole representative party of Indians of all shades of public opinion and from all religious backgrounds including the Muslims.[239] For this purpose they elected Maulana Abul Kalam Azad their president (1939–1946) at the crucial time when the League had begun to demand a separate homeland on the basis of the 'two nation' theory.

Although Congress had a few Muslim and Sikh members in its fold, an overwhelming majority of the Muslim population had refrained from joining it ever since its establishment.[240] At that time Sir Syed Ahmad Khan had declared that Congress was against the Muslim interests and it would remain a Hindu party so he advised the Muslims to stay clear of it.[241]

The Congress agitation against the partition of Bengal, which began in 1905, fully exposed its Hindu character. Without a doubt, it could be termed as an authoritative representative body of Hindu community.[242] Not only was it opposed to the idea of Pakistan it also challenged the League's claim as the sole representative of the Indian Muslims.[243] Congress incited a rebellion in 1942 to uproot the British rule in India with the aim of taking over full control of the government at the centre. At the time Wavell assumed charge of the highest post in the land, Congress was in deep political waters. Its leaders were in prison, and its vast organisation had been rendered ineffective following its unsuccessful rebellion of 1942. As it was in no mood to compromise with the British its leaders were being kept in jail without any contact with their followers, thus leaving the field open to the Muslim League. This was a big tactical mistake which Jinnah exploited to the maximum for his party's benefit.

Amongst all the top-ranked leaders of the Congress, Rajagopalachari was the only one who led a revolt from within the ranks of the Congress high command against its rigid policies. Contrary to his counterparts he opposed the 'Quit India' movement, supported the Cripps Proposals and was in favour of granting the Muslims their demand for a separate homeland.[244] However, all this failed to have appreciable impact on any of his noteworthy colleagues.

Gandhi, who was the initiator of the 1942 rebellion, still commanded great influence in the party.[245] He was considered a pacifist to the core, and a master of evasive tactics.[246] For whatever motives, he wanted to avoid a negotiated settlement with the British and the League.[247] In this situation, for Wavell to try to build a 'constructive partnership' between the leaders of two leading political parties, the Congress and the Muslim League, would have been very difficult indeed.[248]

THE HINDU MAHASABHA

This extremist Hindu party stood for a united India. It believed India to be a sacred land reserved for the Hindus only where it wanted to establish *Akhand Bharat* (Sacred and Great India).[249] The Hindu Mahasabha, as is obvious from its name, was entirely a Hindu organization.[250]

It was founded in 1915 in Punjab.[251] It became active especially after the Moplah uprising[252] of 1921 against the Hindu landlords.[253] Since its leader Dr Moonje felt that the Hindus were weaker in comparison to the Muslims he wanted to organise them into purely Hindu forums.[254] The Mahasabha had been successful in the provincial elections in 1920–37 and had prevented the Congress from making inroads into urban centres, especially, of Punjab.[255] It experienced internal rifts during the 1940s and thereby was weakened as a political force.

The Depressed Classes[256] were in a weak position and could hardly assert themselves so they looked towards the British and the Congress to get a fair deal.[257]

THE SIKHS

The Sikhs, though numbering only about six million and concentrated mostly in the Punjab, constituted another important factor on the Indian political scene of the early 1940s. This was especially due to their valuable services for the British Indian army during the Second World War and their generally proven loyalty to the British rule. The other two main religious groups of the Punjab were the Muslims and the Hindus which constituted respectively 57 and 25 per cent of the population.

Founded by Guru Nanak during the sixteenth century they started off as a reformist sect of the Hindus[258] but soon branched off and assumed a separate identity.[259] Professionally they were concentrated in commerce, agriculture and trade. Although constituting only 14 per cent[260] of the total population of the Punjab they, however, wanted to politically dominate the province.[261]

As soldiers and peasants, the community's loyalist tradition was grounded in material advantages derived from government wages and pensions, colonists' incomes and land preferential policies of the British Indian government which had cemented a special Anglo–Sikh political union.[262] Though their relationship had undergone some change due to a number of reasons including the Jallianwala massacre of 1919, the two had continued to retain a strong affinity[263] for each other in the 1940s as well. Realising their important contribution as soldiers in the Second World War, the Sikhs, in light of the rising chorus of the demand for Pakistan by the Muslims in the 1940s had countered with their own demand for a partition of the Punjab based mainly on what they described as their 'unique position' in various districts of the province, which included some districts in which they were in a distinct minority like Lahore and some others.[264]

By the beginning of the 1940s however, the Sikhs had become divided into various political factions, most of them lacking any clear-cut political agenda. Some of them had begun to demand a separate Sikh homeland, which they referred to, variously, as 'Azad' Punjab, Sikhistan or Khalistan.[265] Lahore's important daily newspaper, *The Tribune*,[266] was their main supporter. Though they were deeply anti-Pakistan in their general political stance, as stated above, they kept pace with the popularity of the demand for Pakistan amongst the Muslims and came up with their own formulas for the partition of the Punjab in case things went as far as the creation of Pakistan. The Sikhs' anti-Pakistan stance is clearly evident in the position taken by their most prominent political parties and leaders including the National Khalsa Party[267] and the Shiromani Akali Dal[268] and their prominent leaders like Master Tara Singh (1885–1967),[269] Giani Kartar Singh,[270] Yadavender Singh (1913–1973),[271] Maharaja of Patiala[272]and Baldev Singh.[273] All these well-known leaders were stridently against the demand for Pakistan and Master Tara Singh and Giani Kartar Singh especially were making fiery speeches against the Muslim demand for Pakistan.[274]

Khushwant Singh has also written on the lines that in the 1940s the Sikhs had begun to react actively to the increasing popularity of the demand for Pakistan.[275] All the leading Sikh political parties and their leadership, especially those referred to above, had begun to arouse virulent hatred in the majority of Sikhs against the Muslims, and this was the main cause of the civil war in India at the time of the British departure. These Sikh fears were fully exploited by the Hindu leaders and press as well.

As stated earlier, Wavell became the Viceroy at a time of great political division in India. All the leading religious communities of India had come up with deeply conflicting demands which were put forth by their respective political leaders. The most important political development was the demand by the All India Muslim League for a separate Muslim homeland. This demand was opposed by the British, Hindus, Sikhs and a small though vocal group of Muslims as well. In such an acrimonious and fractured political atmosphere Wavell had to tread carefully lest any misstep lead to a break up of India. He, therefore, came up with a plan known as the 'Wavell Plan'.

NOTES

1. K.K. Aziz, *Britain and Muslim India* (London: Heinemann), p. 188.
2. John Connell, *Wavell Scholar and Soldier* (London: Collins Clear-Type Press, 1964), p. 48.
3. John Connell, *Wavell: Supreme Commander* (London: Hodder & Stoughton, 1968), pp. 18–20.
4. John Connell, *Wavell Scholar and Soldier*, p. 125.
5. Wavell as the Commander-in-Chief was also called His Excellency.
6. Halifax to Eden, 20 March 1942, L/PES/12/2315: f 237.

7. In 1939 the army in India numbered some 50,000 British and 180,000 Indian soldiers. All these were professionals, whose main duties were defence of the North-West Frontier Province and police service. By the end of 1943 half a million Indian troops had served in France, Libya, Abyssinia, Italian East Africa, Palestine, Syria, Iraq, Hong Kong, and other places.

8. John Connell, *Wavell: Supreme Commander*, pp. 18–20.

9. Victoria Schofield, *Wavell Soldier & Statesman* (London: John Murray 2006), p. 258.

10. Lord Linlithgow once wrote to Amery how he was sure his present Council would break up at once if they were told them that they had nothing to do with the general conduct of a campaign for the defence of India. Linlithgow to Amery, 24 March 1942, *Transfer of Power*, Vol. V, p. 466.

11. Linlithgow to Amery, 20 March 1942, ibid., p. 447.

12. Wavell had just returned from Burma and discussed this matter with Nehru and Azad. Victoria Schofield, *Wavell Soldier & Statesman*, p. 259.

13. Maulana Abul Kalam Azad, *India Wins Freedom: An Autobiographical Narrative* (Calcutta: Orient Longmans, 1959), pp. 57–64.

14. Linlithgow to Messrs. Amery and Churchill, 6 April 1942, MSS Eur F 125/22, Oriental and India Office Library, London (hereafter referred to as OIOL).

15. General Wavell to Prime Minister Churchill, 6 April 1942, L/PO/6/106c: f 46.

16. Gandhi, *Harijan*, 22 March 1943, p. 88; *The Indian Annual Register 1943*, Vol. II, pp. 207–241.

17. Matlubul Hasan Saiyid, *Mohammad Ali Jinnah: A Political Study* (Lahore: Shaikh Muhammad Ashraf, 1953), pp. 260–61.

18. Victoria Schofield, *Wavell Soldier & Statesman*, p. 259.

19. Ibid., pp. 260–61.

20. The British troops were untrained for jungle warfare. For details see: Jeremy Black, *World War Two: A Military History* (London: Routledge, Taylor & Francis Group, 2003), p. 97.

21. Louis Allen, *Burma: The Longest War 1941–45* (London: Butler & Tanner Ltd., 1984), p. 106.

22. Lawrence James, *Raj: The Making of British India* (London: Little, Brown and Company, 2001), p. 548.

23. Wavell Papers, L/PO/4/25(i); L/PO/5/36(i); John Connell, *Wavell: Supreme Commander*, pp. 27, 229, 244–52, 252–256.

24. Ibid.

25. Orde Wingate, Brigadier, later Major General, was an expert in guerrilla warfare and inflicted great damage on the Japanese during his expeditions in Burma. Victoria Schofiled, *Wavell Soldier & Statesman*, pp. 117–8.

26. Wavell Papers, L/PO/4/25(i); L/PO/5/36(i); John Connell, *Wavell: Supreme Commander*, pp. 27, 229.

27. After the Casablanca Conference in January 1943, Churchill had decided to remove Wavell. Their relations became strained and Wavell returned to England.

28. Wavell wanted to end his career with another active military command such as becoming the Supreme Commander of the Joint Command for South East Asia, instead of the viceroyalty.

29. 'Tribute to Lord Wavell', *The Statesman*, 20 March 1947.

30. Wavell, *Viceroy's Journal*, p. 2.

31. Hugh Tinker, *Viceroy: Curzon to Mountbatten* (Karachi: Oxford University Press, 1997), pp. 179–223.

32. Churchill had many names in his mind. For details see, ibid., Wavell, *Viceroy's Journal*, p. 5.

33. Ibid.

34. Wavell, in all likelihood, prepared to get this assignment.

35. Hugh Tinker, *Viceroy: Curzon to Mountbatten*, pp. 179–223.

36. Ibid.

37. Ibid.

38. Wavell, *Viceroy's Journal*, pp. 8–9; there was a mixed reaction to the appointment of Wavell as viceroy in India. Generally it was not that bad. Leo Amery, *The Empire At Bay: The Leo Amery Diaries, 1929–45*, ed., John Barnes and David Nicholson (London: Hutchinson and Co. Ltd., 1988) (hereafter referred to as Barnes, *Amery's Diaries*).

39. Accordingly, on Amery's suggestion Churchill accepted an amendment to the Cabinet Minutes, which made it quite clear that there was no suggestion of a three-year period but only an intimation, which would prevent a sense of disappointment if after three years the suggestion of a change was made. Ibid.

40. Barnes, *Amery's Diaries*, p. 895.

41. Churchill to Amery, 20 June 1943, Churchill Papers, Chur 2/43, Churchill Centre, Cambridge, England.

42. At Durbar Hall of Viceroy's House, Delhi, his swearing-in-ceremony passed off without a hitch. Linlithgow was in remarkably good mood and greeted Wavell at the top of the great flight of steps in front of the Viceroy's House.

43. Linlithgow told him that before the Cripps' proposals were made, the British government should become the Constitution-making body and should also assist in running the war. Wavell, *Viceroy's Journal*, pp. 32–4.

44. Members of the Executive Council were as follows: Sir Auchinleck (C-in-C), Sir Reginald Maxwell (ICS, Home Member), Sir Jeremy Raisman (ICS, Finance Member), Sir Ramaswami Mudaliar (Member for Industry and Civil Supplies), Sir Sultan Ahmed (Member for Information and Broadcasting), Sir Firoz Khan Noon (Defence Member), Sir Edward Benthal (Member for Posts and Air), Sir Mohammad Usman (Member for War Transpor), Dr B.R. Ambedkar (Member for Labour), Sir J.P. Srivastva (Member for Food), Sir Jogendra Singh (Member for Education, Health, and Lands), Sir Aziz-ul-Haque (Member for Commerce), Dr N.B. Khare (Congress Premier of Central Provinces at the time, Member for Commonwealth Relations), and Sir Asoka Roy (Law Member).

45. Ministers responsible to the provincial legislatures formed the governments of these provinces.

46. R.G. Coupland, *India Restatement* (London: Oxford University Press, 1968), p. 45.

47. In these Section 93 provinces, the governors carried on the government with the aid of official ICS advisers and constitutional government remained in abeyance. Peter Hardy, *The Muslims of British India*, p. 234.

48. When Wavell assumed office as Viceroy, ministries responsible to the legislatures were in office in six provinces of Bengal, Assam, Orissa, NWFP, Sindh, and the Punjab. The other five provinces of UP, CP, Bihar, Bombay and Madras were in full control of governors under Section 93. Ibid.; S.M. Ikram, *Modern Muslim India and the Birth of Pakistan* (Lahore: Research Society of Pakistan, 1970), p. 323; Anwar Khan, *The Role of NWFP in the Creation of Pakistan*, pp. 173–74.

49. By 1919, the British were mainly dependent on the Indian co-operation for the governance of the country. There had been strains among the European element since the beginning of the Second World War because they could not find time to see their families. Another reason for this strain was that the government had not recruited fresh European staff to share the burden of administration.

50. When the Government of India Act came into force in 1935, an Indian High Commissioner assumed some of the functions of the Indian Council in England.

51. Hugh Tinker, *Experiment with Freedom* (Karachi: Oxford University Press, 1967), p. 24.

52. R.J. Moore, *Churchill, Cripps, and India, 1939–45* (London: Oxford University Press, 1979), p. 74; Hugh Tinker, *Viceroys of India: Curzon to Mountbatten*, pp. 142–178.

53. *Indian Annual Register 1943*, Vol. I, p. 128.

54. H.V. Hodson, *Great Divide, Britain-India-Pakistan* (Karachi: Oxford University Press, 1997), p. 119.

55. R.J. Moore, *Escape From Empire: Attlee Government and the Indian Problem* (Oxford: Clarendon Press, 1963), pp. 69–108.

56. One thing, however, was quite obvious, that they wanted to maintain the unity of India at all costs as they considered it to be their proud legacy. They also did not hesitate to express their desire to preserve and promote their political, economic and geo-strategic interests in India. K.K. Aziz, *Britain and Muslim India*, (London: Heinemann, 1963), pp. 143–208.

57. In 1943 India's population totalled over 400 million with Muslim comprising about 100 million of that total. The Princely States scattered all over India numbered 560 of whom only few were large.

58. A number of writings deal with the Muslim rule in India such as S.M. Ikram's *Muslim Civilization of Indo–Pakistan* (Lahore: Research Society of Pakistan, 1966); I.H. Qureshi, *The Muslim Community of Indo–Pakistan* (Hague: 1962).

59. The conflict amongst the British, Hindus and the Muslims originated mainly after the War of Independence of 1857 and subsequent direct rule of the British crown. Razi Wasti has recorded the Pakistani point of view in his book *Political Triangle in India* (Lahore: People's Publishing Company, 1976); the Indian point of view is well projected by Ashoka, Mehta and Patwardhan, *Communal Triangle in India* (Allahabad: Kitabistan, 1942); Rajendra Prasad, *India Divided* (Lahore: Book Traders, 1978).

60. A.O. Hume, founded the Indian National Congress in 1885 with the prior approval of the Liberal Prime Minster Gladstone. For details see: P. Sitaramayya, *The History of the Indian National Congress*, Vol. II, (Bombay, 1947).

61. There are some historians in India who believe that the important role of Hindu extremists like Bal Gangadhar Tilak, Lala Lajpat Rai and Madan Mohan Malviya in the making and unmaking of the Congress party's policy had confused the

Muslims because they could not tell whether it was a Hindu or a secular party. For details see: Bipen Chandra, *Nationalism and Colonialism in Modern India* (Hyderabad: Orient Longman, reprinted 2004).

62. F.G. Graham's book entitled *Sir Syed: Life and Times*; and Altaf Hussain Hali's book entitled *Hayat-i-Javaid* (Agra, 1901) are still considered the best writings on Sir Syed Ahmed Khan.

63. For details on the Muslim Educational Conference and its activities see: Abdul Rashid Khan, *The All India Muslim Educational Conference, Its Contribution to the Cultural Development of Indian Muslims 1886–1947* (Karachi: Oxford University Press, 2001).

64. Sir Syed's political views can be found in Francis Robinson, *Separatism Among Indian Muslims, The Politics of the United Provinces Muslims: 1860–1923* (London: 1974); Altaf Hussain Hali, *Hayat-i-Javaid*, (Urdu) (Lahore: National Book Foundation, reprinted, 1986).

65. Sikandar Hayat has recorded that there were other factors besides the religious which had generated the Hindu–Muslim conflict and which became formed the genesis of the Pakistan demand. He argues that it was mainly the failure of the leaders from the two communities to compromise on their interests that led inevitably to the demand for Pakistan. Sikandar Hayat, 'Hindu–Muslim Communalism and its impact on Muslim Politics in British India: The Making of the Pakistan Demand', in *Proceedings of the Tenth International Symposium on South Asian Studies* (Hong Kong: Asian Research Service, 1989), pp. 969–86.

66. Razi Wasti refutes the allegation that the 'Simla Deputation' in 1906 was a 'command performance' in his book *The Political Triangle in India*.

67. Sharif al Mujahid, 'The Hindu Revivalist Movements', in *a History of the Freedom Movement*, Vol. III, Part II (Karachi: Pakistan Historical Society, 1970).

68. Chiefly based in the Punjab, they demanded political, economic and religious rights for the Sikhs. In this connection they demanded a separate electorate for the Sikhs which the British Government conceded in the Montagu–Chelmsford Reforms of 1919.

69. For details see: Razi Wasti, *Lord Minto and the Indian Nationalist Movement, 1905–1910* (London: Oxford University Press, 1963).

70. Ibid.

71. Ameer Ali founded Central Mohammadan Association in Calcutta in 1877. It aimed at looking after the concerns of the Indian Muslims but remained active chiefly in the province of Bengal. K.K. Aziz, *Ameer Ali: His Life and Work* (Lahore: Publishers United Ltd., 1968), pp. 44–56.

72. For details about the Muslim response to the new system of the British Government in 1920s in India, see: David Page, *Prelude to Partition: The Indian Muslims and the Imperial System of Control, 1920–1932* (Delhi: Oxford University Press, 1982).

73. Sachinananda Sinha blames Jinnah's conversion from nationalism to communalism on the 'Pathology of the Super-Ego'. This book is typical of the Hindu mindset *vis-à-vis* the Muslim leadership. For details see: Sachchidananda Sinha, *Jinnah as I Knew Him* (Patna: Khuda Bakhsh Oriental Public Library, second impression, 1993), pp. 1–16.

74. S.K. Majumdar, *Jinnah* (Patna: Khuda Bukhsh Oriental Public Library, 1996), pp. 1–15.

75. Sharif al Mujahid, 'Jinnah's Rise to Muslim Leadership (1906–1940)', in Ahmad Hasan Dani, ed., *World Scholars on Quaid-i-Azam Mohammad Ali Jinnah* (Islamabad: Quaid-i-Azam University, 1979), pp. 379–395.

76. Saeed R. Khairi, *Jinnah Reinterpreted* (Karachi: Oxford University Press, 1995), p. 201.

77. David Page, *Prelude to Partition: The Indian Muslims and the Imperial System of Control, 1920–1932*, p. 61.

78. S. Qalb-i-Abid, *The Muslim Politics in Punjab 1923–1947* (Lahore: Vanguard, 1992), pp. 104–110.

79. The Committee consisting of Motilal Nehru, M.R. Jayakar, Tej Bahadur Sapru, M.N. Joshi, M.S. Aney, G.R. Pradhan, Mangal Singh, Ali Imam, and Shoaib Qureshi.

80. Richard Symonds, *The Making of Pakistan* (London: Faber and Faber, 1950), p. 51.

81. Uma Kaura, *Muslims and Indian Nationalism the Emergence of the Demand for India's Partition 1928–40* (New Delhi: Manohar, 1977), p. 46.

82. Abdul Hamid, *On Understanding the Quaid-i-Azam* (Karachi: National Book Foundation, 1977), p. 22.

83. The Nehru Report united the Muslim League. All-India Muslim Conference met at Delhi in 1929 under the chairmanship of Sir Aga Khan.

84. Sikandar Hayat, *Aspects of the Pakistan Movement* (Lahore: Progressive Publishers, 1991), p. 16.

85. In a pamphlet entitled 'Now or Never' Chaudhry Rahmat Ali explained the term 'Pakistan'.

86. For details see: A.B. Keith, *A Constitutional History of India 1600–1935* (Lahore: Lawyer's Home, Reprinted, 1961).

87. Farzana Sheikh, *Community and Consensus in Islam: Muslim Representation in Colonial India, 1860–1947* (Cambridge University Press, 1989).

88. K.K. Aziz, *Historical Handbook of Muslim India, 1700–1947*, Vol. II, p. 419.

89. Zafrullah Khan, *The Forgotten Years: Memories of Sir Muhammad Zafarullah Khan*, ed., A.H. Batalvi, (Lahore: Vanguard Book Ltd., 1991), pp. 97–98.

90. The Congress's president put forth five conditions which aimed at annihilating the Muslim League and establishing one party system in India. Chaudhry Khaliquzzaman, *Pathway to Pakistan* (Lahore: Brothers Publishers, 1961) p. 16.

91. With its vast organizational strength, financial backing, the press and the newly found power and authority, the Congress started the Muslim Mass Contact campaign. A special department for Muslim Mass Contact was set up in the office of the All-India Congress Committee.

92. The Muslim Mass Contact failed to produce any positive results, because of its negative approach. It caused severe anxiety among the ministries of Bengal, Assam and the Punjab. The chief ministers of these provinces felt insecure and sought help from Jinnah. Sikandar–Jinnah Pact was concluded between Sikandar, the premier of Punjab, and Jinnah, president of the Muslim League. Fazlul Haq wrote a pamphlet titled, '*Muslim Suffering under the Congress Rule*' in December 1939.

93. The League had to counter propaganda and so became actively involved in mass politics which increased its popularity. As a result, the All-India Muslim League Council also passed a resolution at New Delhi on 4 December 1938. It was decided that in order to counter the Muslim Mass Contact Movement launched by the Congress, the following measures would be adopted: Brief 'Fatwas' and manifestos should be issued on behalf of the Ulema in which the Muslims should be warned against joining the Congress. Qualified Muslims should be appointed to address Friday congregations and other Muslims gatherings as well as meetings held in rural areas on the subject of religious and secular harm which is likely to result for the Muslims by their joining the Congress. The Council of the All-India Muslim League was asked to direct influential and leading members of the League to move Government Officers responsible for the maintenance of law and order to check such unlawful abuse of powers. For details see: K.K. Aziz, *Muslims Under the Congress Rule*, Vol. I, pp. 165–166.

94. A number of reports, articles and books were written explaining these atrocities. For example, the Muslims constituted a special committee under the presidentship of Raja Syed Muhammad Mehdi of Pirpur, which submitted its report known as *The Pirpur Report*. This gives an account of events in all the Congress provinces save the NWFP. Another important book the *Shareef Report* mainly consisted of a full description of the injustices to the Muslims done by Hindus at various places in Bihar. Another book entitled *C.P. Main Congress Raj* was written by Hakeem Israr Ahmed Kuravi, reveals the history of Congress ministries in CP and Berar. These reports show that Congress failed to inspire confidence in the minorities and continued to be a Hindu organization. It followed a 'closed-door' policy by refusing to form coalitions with any other party in the legislature. The aim of Muslim League during and after the elections was not to wage war against other communities but to organize the Muslims and to find a solution for the political and economic problems facing India as a whole. For details see: Jamil-ud-din Ahmed, *Historic Documents of Muslim Freedom Movement*, (Lahore: Sh. M. Ashraf Press, 1970); G. Allana, ed., *Pakistan Movement: Historic Document* (Lahore: Islamic Book Service, 1977), p. 153.

95. Ishtiaq Ahmad, 'Competing Religious Nationalism and the Partition of British India,' *Pakistan Journal of History & Culture*. Vol. XXVI, No. 2 (Islamabad: Quaid-i-Azam University, July–December 2005), pp. 1–11.

96. R.G. Coupland writes, 'The worst and most dangerous cause of disorder was, as it had always been, communal strife. The barometer of rioting and fighting, which had stood so steady for some years past began to fall again, when the Congress ministers resigned in the autumn of 1939, there had been 57 communal outbreaks in their provinces and more than 1700 casualties of which over 130 had been fatal. By the end of 1939, it was widely believed that, if the Congress Governments had lasted much longer, communal fighting would have broken out on an unprecedented scale.' R.G. Coupland, *India: A Restatement* (London: Oxford University Press, 1945), p. 158.

97. Penderel Moon, *Divide and Quit* (London: Chatto & Windus Ltd, 1961), p. 273.

98. *Harijan*, 15 June 1944.

99. Reminiscences of the Day of Deliverance (Islamabad, National Committee For the birth celebration of Quaid-i-Azam Mohammad Ali Jinnah, 1976).

100. The Congress ministry in Central Provinces started a scheme for the education of children called Vidya Mandir Scheme (Primary School for boys and girls). Any institution which fulfilled certain conditions could start education in Marathi, Hindi or Urdu. Muslim children were forced to join Hindi or Marathi Vidya Mandir if they wanted to be educated. The most painful complaint for the Muslims was that the Muslim students were also ordered to worship the portrait of Gandhi, for the chairman of the *chandwara* issued orders officially asking for worshiping the portrait of Gandhi.

101. This controversial song was introduced in a Bengali novel, *Anandamath*, written by the Bengali novelist, Bankim Chandra Chatterji and published in 1882.

102. Khurshid Ahmed Enver, *Life Story of Quaid-i-Azam* (Lahore: Young People Publishing Bureau, 1950), pp. 108–9.

103. Jamil-ud-din Ahmed, ed., *Speeches and Writings of Mr Jinnah*, Vol. I (Lahore, Shaikh Muhammad Ashraf, 1968), p. 29.

104. Syed Shamsul Hassan, *Plain Mr Jinnah* (Karachi: 1976), p. 54.

105. Ian Stephens, *Pakistan: Old Country, New Nation* (London: Ernest Benn, 1967), p. 75.

106. Hundreds of proposals had been presented by various individuals which included Hindus, British and Muslims for the division of India into various parts. An authoritative research has been conducted by K.K. Aziz in his book, *The History of the Idea of Pakistan*, 4 volumes(Lahore, 1987).

107. Lord Linlithgow considered India as a natural geographical unit; therefore was against the creation of Pakistan. For details see Riaz Ahmed, 'Quaid-i-Azam's Pakistan Scheme and the British Government (1940–1941),' in Riaz Ahmad, *World Scholars on Quaid-i-Azam*, pp. 13–30.

108. Sikandar Hayat, 'Quaid-i-Azam and the Demand for a Separate Muslim State: Lahore Resolution Reappraised,' *Journal of Research Society of Pakistan* (Lahore: Punjab University Press), Vol. XXIV, No. 4 (October 1987).

109. I.H. Qureshi emphasises the Two-Nation Theory based on religion as the main factor in the establishment of Pakistan. For details see Ishtiaq Hussain Qureshi, *The Struggle for Pakistan*, (Karachi: University Press, 1965); *The Muslim Community of Indo-Pakistan*, (Karachi: 1967).

110. For details see: Naureen Talha, *Economic Factors in the Making of Pakistan: 1921–1947* (Karachi: Oxford University Press, 2000).

111. An interesting discussion on the intellectual and social foundations of the Pakistan demand could be found in Waheed Quraishi, *Ideological Foundation of Pakistan* (Lahore: Islamic Book Foundation, 1987).

112. Shafique Ali Khan, *Two Nation Theory* (Hyderabad: 1973); Hafiz Malik, *Moslem Nationalism in. India and Pakistan* (Washington D.C.: Public Affairs Press, 1963).

113. Sikandar Hayat, 'Quaid-i-Azam Jinnah and the Demand for a separate Muslim State: Lahore resolution Reappraised,' in *Journal of the Research Society of Pakistan* (Lahore), Vol. XXIV, No. 4 (Oct. 1987), pp. 1–44.

114. The Congress encouraged those Muslims parties and leaders who could oppose the demand for Pakistan.

115. A rejoinder to the allegation that Lord Linlithgow played an important role in persuading Jinnah to come up with a 'constructive policy' is well defended by many historians like Sikandar Hayat, Riaz Ahmed, and Qalb-i-Abid and Mussarat Abid, 'The British Response to the Lahore resolution and the British Reaction,' *Journal of Research Humanities* (Multan), vol. 19, (2002), pp. 75–108.

116. Attlee Collection MSS Eur 212.

117. For details see: Ian Talbot, *Freedom's Cry: The Popular Dimension in the Pakistan Movement and the Partition Experience in North-West India*, (Karachi: Oxford University Press, 1996), pp. 81–104.

118. V.P. Menon, *The Transfer of Power*, (Princeton University Press, 1957), pp. 336–40.

119. Ibid.

120. K.K. Aziz, (ed.) *Historical Handbook of Muslim India, 1707–1947*, Vol. II, Vanguard Books Ltd., 1995), pp. 433–37.

121. For detailed results of this by-election see: R.G. Coupland, *India: A Re-Statement* (London: Oxford University Press, 1945), pp. 184, 242.

122. K.K. Aziz, (ed.) *Historical Handbook of Muslim India*, Vol. II, pp. 433–37.

123. Khawaja Nazim-ud-Din, who had been the leader of Opposition from1941 to 1943, formed a ministry on 24 April 1943, after Fazulul Haq's resignation as Premier of Bengal.

124. S.M. Ikram, *Modern Muslim India and the Birth of Pakistan*, (Lahore: Sh. Muhammad Ashraf Press, 1965), p. 294.

125. In Sindh after the dismissal of Allah Bukhsh in September 1942, Sir Ghulam Hussain Hidayatullah joined the Muslim League and managed to hold office with League support. Peter Hardy, *The Muslims of British India* (Karachi: Cambridge University Press, 1972), p. 236.

126. Sardar Aurangzeb Khan formed the ministry on 25 May 1943 in the NWFP which could be called a League–Akali coalition. Dr Muhammad Anwar Khan, *The Role of N.W.F.P. in the Freedom Struggle* (Lahore: Research Society of Pakistan, 2000), pp. 173–74.

127. Ian Talbot, *Punjab Under the Raj, 1848–1947*, New Delhi: Manohar Publication, 1988), pp. 170–74.

128. Jamil-ud-Din Ahmad (ed.), *Speeches and Writings of Mr Jinnah*, Vol. VII (Lahore: Sh. Muhammad Ashraf, 1960), p. 529.

129. Matlubul Hasan Saiyid, *Mohammad Ali Jinnah: A Political Biography* (Lahore: Shaikh Mohammad Ashraf, 2nd ed., 1953), p. 196.

130. A number of Muslim leaders like Nawabzada Liaquat Ali Khan, Chaudhri Khaliquzzaman, Chaudhry Mohammad Ali, Sardar Shaukat Hayat Khan, Khawaja Nazimuddin and Huseyn Shaheed Suhrawardy, not only accepted Jinnah as undisputed leader but supported the Pakistan demand. For details see: Z.A. Suleri, *My Leader*, (Lahore: S.A. Latif, 1945), pp. 137–174; Sarfaraz Hussain Mirza, *Muslim Students and Pakistan Movement: Selected Documents (1937–1947)*, (Lahore: Pakistan Study Centre, 1988).

131. For details see: Shaista Ikramullah, *From Purdah to Parliament* (Karachi: Oxford University Press, 1998), p. 128; Sarfaraz Hussain Mirza, *The Role of Women in the Freedom Movement* (Lahore: Research Society of Pakistan, 1981).

132. Salahuddin Khan (ed.), *Speeches, Addresses and Statements of Madr-i-Millat Mohtarma Fatima Jinnah: 1948–1967* (Lahore: Research Society of Pakistan, 1976), pp. 18–19.

133. Riaz Ahmad (ed.), *Madr-i-Millat Miss Fatima Jinnah: A Chronology* (Islamabad: History Commission, 2003), p. 14.

134. Sikandar Hayat, *Some Aspects of Pakistan Movement* (Lahore: Progressive Publishers, 1991), pp. 165–192.

135. Khalid bin Sayeed, *Pakistan: The Formative Phase, 1857–1948* (Karachi: Oxford University Press, 1968), p. 203; I.H. Quershi, *Ulema in Politics*, 2nd ed. (Karachi: The Inter Services Press, 1974), p. 221.

136. H.B. Khan, *Bar-i-Sagheer Pak-o-Hind Ki Siyasat Main Ulema Ka Kirdar* (Urdu) (Islamabad: National Institute of History and Culture, 1985), pp. 371–81.

137. Sarah Ansari, *The Sufis, Saints and State Power: The Pirs of Sindh* (Cambridge, 1992); A. Sattar Khan, 'The Role of Sindh in the Pakistan Movement,' *Journal of the Research Society of Pakistan*, Vol. XXX, No. 1 (Lahore: Punjab University, April 1993).

138. Muhammad Khurshid, 'The Role of Landlords and Pirs in the Punjab Politics and its After-effects,' *Journal of the Research Society of Pakistan*, Vol. XXXI, No. 2 (Lahore: University of the Punjab, April 1994).

139. Syed Mohammad Rooh-ul-Amin, 'Quaid-i-Azam Aur Sooba-i-Sarhad Ke Musha'ikh' in Riaz Ahmad (ed.), *Pakistani Scholars on Quaid-i-Azam*, pp. 439–55.

140. Ibid.

141. Ian Talbot, *Inventing the Nation: India and Pakistan*, (London: Oxford University Press, 2000), pp. 60–85.

142. *Dawn* was the English daily published from Delhi. Its proprietor was All-India Muslim League and its first editor was Pothan Joseph; later Altaf Husain became its editor. K.K. Aziz, *Historical Handbook of Muslim India*, Vol. VII, pp. 634–689.

143. *Morning News* English daily published from Calcutta. Its proprietors were Khawaja Nuruddin and Abdur Rahman Siddiqui.

144. *The Eastern Times* a daily English news paper published from Lahore was considered a spokesman of the Muslim League.

145. *Nawa-i-Waqt* an Urdu daily, published from Lahore. First appeared in March 1940, its editor/proprietor was Hamid Nizami.

146. M.R.T., *Nationalism in Conflict* (Bombay: Home Study Circle, 1943).

147. 'Memorandum by the Secretary of State for India,' 15 September 1943, L/PO/108a: ff 83–6.

148. V. Pala Prasad Rao, K. Nirupa Rani, and Dhuskara Rao, *India-Pakistan, Partition Perspective in Indo-English Novels* (New Delhi: Discovery Publishing House, 2004), p. 15.

149. The term 'Nationalist Muslim' was used for the first time in 1929 when some pro-Congress Muslim leaders disagreeing with League's opposition to the Nehru Report called a separate meeting of their own.

150. *Indian Annual Register, 1942*, Vol. I.

151. Abul Kalam Azad, *India wins Freedom*, p. 29.

152. The Diarchy was introduced in the Montagu–Chelmsford Reforms of 1919. It further exposed the communal tangle because ministers from different religious

groups favoured their respective communities. Azim Husain, *Sir Fazl-i-Husain: A Political Biography* (Bombay, 1946); S. Qalb-i-Abid, *The Muslim Politics in the Punjab*, 1921–47 (Lahore: Vanguard Books Ltd, 1992), pp. 30–70.

153. Ibid., *The Muslim Politics in the Punjab*, pp. 30–70.

154. In the elections of 1936, the Unionist party won 96 out of 175 seats. Ikram Ali Malik, *A Book of Reading On The History Of The Punjab, 1799–1947* (Lahore: Research Society of Pakistan, 1970), p. 483.

155. The Unionists soon faced the undue interference of the Congress in the provincial administrative matters which created insecurity in the Muslim majority provinces such as Punjab, Assam, and Bengal. The Congress unleashed a programme of Mass-Contact Movement which had been denouncing the policies of the Unionist Party and the Muslim League in a bid to win the Muslim voters.

156. Ibid., pp. 490–93.

157. Sikandar Hayat Khan was against the division of India and, therefore, with the official backing, presented his scheme for the Indian federation, before the Lahore Resolution, so that the idea of Pakistan should not become popular among the Muslims of India and particularly of Punjab. Lahore was chosen as the venue for the occasion but Sikandar tried his level best to postpone the meeting of the All-India Muslim League which was being held to pass the historic resolution in March 1940. On failing, he took part in it.

158. S. Qalb-i-Abid, *Muslim Politics in Punjab*, p. 235.

159. Aslam Ganaira, 'National Defence Council, 1941: Britain, India and the War', *Pakistan Vision*, Vol. 1, No. 2 (Lahore: Pakistan Study Centre, University of the Punjab, 2000).

160. In 1941, Government of India established the National Defence Council in order to get more active cooperation of the Indians in the Second World War. The four Muslim prime ministers of Punjab, Bengal, Assam and the NWFP were nominated for the Council. These ministers accepted the invitation without consulting the president of the League and Jinnah as the president of the Muslim League directed them to resign which they did. This sent a strong message to the British that in no way could they bypass Jinnah.

161. The Pakistan demand had sharply divided the pro-Pakistan and anti-Pakistan groups in the Unionist Party which continuously threatened the position of Sir Sikandar Hayat. Iftikhar Haider Malik, *Sir Sikandar Hayat: A Political Biography* (Islamabad: National Institute of Historical And Cultural Research, 1985).

162. Ian Talbot, *Khizar Tiwana, the Punjab Unionist Party and the Partition of India* (London: Oxford University Press, 1996), p. 34.

163. Ziya-ul-Hasan Faruqi, *The Deoband School and the Demand for Pakistan* (Bombay: Asia Publishing House, 1963), p. 2.

164. The establishment of a separate political party of the ulema had synchronized with the Khilafat Movement 1919–22. The majority of Jamiat's members consisted of the Ulema of Deoband. Darul Aloom Deoband was founded in 1866 in UP, India. It became the most important religious institution in the Muslim World after the al-Alzhar of Egypt. S.M. Ikram, *Mauj-i-Kausar* (Urdu) (Lahore: Ferozsons, 1966), pp. 219–239.

165. Mushirul Haq, 'The Ulema and the Indian Politics,' in *Islam in South Asia*, Rashid Jallandhri and Muhammad Afzal Qarshi (eds.) Lahore: Institute if Islamic Culture, 1986), pp. 75–96.

166. I.H. Qureshi, *The Struggle For Pakistan* (Karachi: University of Karachi, 1987), pp. 184–94.

167. Maulana Hussain Ahmad Madni propounded his theory of 'composite nationalism' in a treatise, 'Muttahidah Qaumiyyat aur Islam', at a time when the Muslims were fast becoming conscious of their separate identity. This brought an instant reaction from Allama Iqbal and became the subject of a lengthy controversy. Rafique Afzal, *Political Parties in Pakistan 1947–58* (Islamabad: National Commission on Historical and Cultural Research, 1976), p. 33.

168. *Ajmal*, an Urdu daily published from Bombay, was a pro-Congress newspaper.

169. *Al-Jamiat*, published from Delhi, was an organ of the Jamiat Ulema-i-Hind. See, Ahmad Saeed, 'Muslim Sah'aft Aur Jado Jehd-i-Azadi,' *Journal of the Research Society of Pakistan* (Lahore: University of the Punjab) Vol. XVIII, No. 1, January 1981, pp. 85–127.

170. Ibid.

171. Shabbir Usmani, *Hamara Pakistan* (Urdu), (Lahore, n.d.), pp. 65–66.

172. The party was organized with the exclusive purpose of safeguarding the Shariah and giving the Muslim community religious and political guidance according to Islamic principles and commandments. This rigid and orthodox stand of theirs was bound to create a rift, as it actually did, in the communal life of the Muslims, who, in course of time, were led to depend more upon the leadership of their western-educated intelligentsia. The Ulema were in favour of unconditional co-operation with the Congress so far as the cause of freedom was concerned. They claimed that once the British regime was dissolved, the Hindus would come to terms with the Muslims who formed a strong minority and could not be deprived of their legitimate rights.

173. Rashid Jallandhari, *Dar-ul-Uloom Deoband* (Urdu), (Islamabad: National Book Foundation, 1989), pp. 193–208.

174. Azad, *India Wins Freedom*, p. 59.

175. Ibid.

176. Ibid.

177. The Jamiat and the Muslim League showed an occasional unity as in the Khilafat Movement and its opposition to the Nehru Report. They always disagreed with each other after 1940 and there was a complete parting of ways. Jamil-ud-Din Ahmed, *Middle Phase of Muslim Political Movement* (Lahore: Publisher United Ltd., 1969), pp. 42–57.

178. Janbaz Mirza, *Caravan-i-Ahrar* (Urdu), Vol. I (Lahore: Maktaba Tabsara, 1975), pp. 81–84.

179. The Majlis-i- Ahrar-i- Islam was founded in December 1929 in Lahore during the Congress session of 1929–30 in which the Congress adopted the resolution for complete independence of India.

180. Azad, *India Wins Freedom*, p. 64.

POLITICAL PICTURE OF INDIA 57

181. Afzal Haq (1895–1942) was the founder of the Majlis-i-Ahrar. Ahmad Saeed, *Muslim India (1858–1947) A Political Biography* (Lahore: Institute of Pakistan Historical Research, 1997), p. 54.
182. Maulana Zafar Ali Khan (1873–1956), was a journalist, poet, writer and politician.
183. Afzal Iqbal, *Life and Times of Muhammad Ali Jauhar and Analysis of the Hopes, Fears and Aspirations of Muslim India from 1878 to 1931* (Lahore: Islamic Research Institute, 1974), p. 3.
184. For details see: K.K. Aziz, *All India Khilafat Conference, 1928–1933: A Documentary Record* (Karachi: National Publishing, 1972).
185. Afzal Haque, *Tarikh-i-Ahrar* (Lahore, 1968), p. 10.
186. K.K. Aziz, *The Making of Pakistan: A Study in Nationalism*, (Islamabad, 1977), pp. 41–43; Syed Noor Ahmed, *Marshal Law Say Marshal Law Tak* (Lahore: Malik Deen & Sons, 1967), pp. 79–88.
187. Janbaz Mirza, *Caravan-i-Ahrar*, pp. 81–84.
188. Chaudhry Afzal Haq, *Tehreek-i- Ahrar*, p. 19.
189. Partha Sarathi Gupta, *Power, Politics and the People: Studies in British Imperialism and Indian Nationalism* (London: Anthem press, 2002), pp. 96–97.
190. Ram Gopal, *The Indian Muslims: A Political History (1858–1947)* (Lahore: Book Traders, 1976), p. 224.
191. Mohammad Iqbal Chawla, 'The Role of Majlis-i-Ahrar in Kashmir Movement of 1931,' *Sanger Maal* (Lahore: University of the Punjab, 2001), pp. 7–38.
192. Janbaz Mirza, *Caravan-i-Ahrar: Tareekh-i-Azadi-i-Bar-i-sigher*, Vol. VII (Lahore: Maktaba-i-Tabsara, 1975).
193. Samina Awan, 'Subaltern Studies or Regional History: Explorations in Nationalist Movement with Special Reference to the Majlis-i-Ahrar-i-Islam,' in *Pakistan Journal Of History & Culture* (Islamabad), Vol. XXVI, No. 2, July–December 2005, pp. 41–54.
194. Ian Talbot, *Punjab under the Raj*, p. 94.
195. Ikram Ali Malik, *A Book of Reading, 1799–1947*, pp. 489–90.
196. *The Indian Annual Register 1943*, Vol. I.
197. Afzal Haque, *Tarikh-i-Ahrar*, p. 18.
198. Peter Hardy, *Muslims of British India*, p. 216.
199. Ram Gopal, *The Indian Muslims: A Political History* (Lahore: Book Traders, 1976), p. 227.
200. In September of 1929 Bacha Khan decided to set up an army of Pukhtoon, fierce soldiers, but with no weapons. They would be soldiers for non-violence, drilled and disciplined, with uniforms, a flag and officers. They would fight not with guns but resist oppression with their lives. He named it Khudai Khidmatgars (Servants of God). When the Congress started Satyagraha movement, the Khudai Khidmatgar also took part in it.
201. Sayed Wiqar Ali Shah, *Ethnicity, Islam and Nationalism: Muslim Politics in the North-West Frontier Province, 1937–47* (Karachi: Oxford University Press, 1999), pp. 29–30.
202. Ibid.
203. Ibid.

204. Ibid.
205. On 23 April 1930, the British killed at least 200 unarmed volunteers of Congress, Khilafat Committee and Khidmatgars members in Qissa Khani Bazar, Peshawar.
206. Sayed Wiqar Ali Shah, *Ethnicity, Islam and Nationalism*, p. 53.
207. Ibid., p. 54.
208. Ibid., p. 57.
209. Ibid., p. 92.
210. Ibid., p. 95.
211. S.M. Ikram, *Modern Muslim India and the Birth of Pakistan*, p. 13.
212. Communal riots erupted in Dera Ismail Khan in January 1939 in which eight persons were killed; twenty-one injured and 150 shops were gutted resulting in loss of over rupees two lacs to the public.
213. The Nawab of Teri used to collect house tax, grazing tax, feudal royalty (*haqi taluqdari*) etc, which were abolished with the passage of this bill.
214. The possession and sale of liquor and drugs was prohibited in Dera Ismail Khan and certain restrictions were imposed on possession in other districts. This had a negative effect on its possession in other districts.
215. The agricultural produce markets Act, XIV of 1939. This bill opened the way for the agriculturists to take their produce directly to the market instead of depending up the middleman.
216. The Punjab tenancy (NWFP) Amendment Act, XX of 1939 enforced Shariat in inheritance of occupancy tenants.
217. For details see: Wiqar Ali Shah, *Ethnicity, Islam and Nationalism*.
218. Ibid., p. 83.
219. Ibid., p.136.
220. Ian Talbot, *Pakistan A Modern History* (Lahore: Vanguard Book, 1999), p. 83.
221. Tara Chand, *History of the Freedom Movement in India*, Vol. IV (Lahore: Book Trader, 1972), p. 262.
222. The results of the by-elections which took place from 1937–43 witnessed that the Muslim League was becoming popular particularly after the Lahore Resolution in 1940. For details see: Wiqar Ali Shah, *Ethnicity, Islam and Nationalism*, pp. 95–114.
223. Ibid.
224. A.D. Muztar, *Khaksar Tehreek Aur Azadi-i-Hind*, Vol. VII (Islamabad: National Institute of History and Culture, 1995), p. 1; *Jang* (Urdu), Lahore, 13 May 1983.
225. Mr Aslam Malik has discussed the life and work of Allama Mashriqi in very interesting manner. His chapter 'Mashriqi and the All-India Muslim League' gives a good insight about Khaksar's relations with the League. He has shed a new light on the personality of Jinnah and maintains that the British created a hurdle for Jinnah by their efforts to bring Khaksar and Ahrar close to the Muslim League's demand for Pakistan. For details see: Muhammad Aslam Malik, *Allama Inayatullah Khan Mashriqi: A Political Biography* (Karachi: Oxford University Press, 2000).
226. Iftikhar Haider Malik, *Sir Sikandar Hayat*, pp. 64–74.
227. *India Annual Register 1939*, Vol. II, p. 80.
228. Abid, *Muslim Politics in Punjab*, pp. 232–4.
229. *Civil and Military Gazette*, Lahore, 20 March 1940.

230. Statement of Quaid-i-Azam and his secretary on the deadly attack made on the life of the Quaid. See Jamil-ud-Din Ahmad, *Speeches and Writings of Mr Jinnah*, Vol. I, pp. 523–24.

231. Safdar Salimi, *Khaksar-i-Azam aur Khaksar Tehreek* (Lahore, 1957), p. 32.

232. Agha Bashir, *The Khaksar Movement, Past and Present: An Appraisal* (Lahore, n.d.), p. 6.

233. *Al-Islah*, a newspaper which was a mouthpiece of Khaksar movement. It published from Lahore and was popular among the lower-middle class of the Punjab and the NWFP; Safdar Salimi, *Khaksar Tehreek Ki Sola Sala Jadojehad*, p. 45.

234. Seyyed Vali Reza Nasr, *Mawdudi and the Making of Islamic Revivalism* (New York: Oxford University Press, 1996), pp. 39–41.

235. Seyyed Vali Reza Nasr, *The Vanguard of the Islamic Revolution: The Jama'at-i-Islami of Pakistan* (Berkeley: University of California Press, 1994), pp. 141–46.

236. Leonard Binder, *Religion and Politics in Pakistan* (Berkeley: University of California Press, 1961), pp. 22–40.

237. Mohammad Iqbal Chawla, *Islamic Writings in Pakistan: A Case Study of Allama Ghulam Ahmad Parwez* (Lahore: Al-Noor Printing Press, 1991).

238. Rafiuddin Ahmed, 'Redefining Muslim Identity in South Asia: The Transformation of the Jama'at-i-Islami,' in Martin E. Marty and R. Scott Appleby (eds.), *Accounting for Fundamentalism: the Dynamic Character of Movement* (Chicago: University of Chicago Press, 1994), pp. 669–705.

239. Jawaharlal Nehru, *The Discovery of India* (New York: The John Day Company, 1946), pp. 237–38.

240. Maulana Abul Kalam Azad remained President of the All India National Congress 1940–46. Quaid-i-Azam called him the 'showman' of the Congress.

241. Sir Syed's predictions became reality in his lifetime when Congress made a number of demands, which were viewed against the interests of Muslims. For instance Congress's opposition to Punjab Land Alienation Act 1900 and movement against the 1905 Partition of Bengal were viewed as anti-Muslim stands. The Nehru Report of 1928 and the Congress Ministries 1937–39 were proof of their being a Hindu party.

242. See results of the 1936–37 elections. They could hardly secure 20 odd Muslim seats.

243. The Congress–League accord in 1916 was the first and last effort on the part of the Congress to accept ground realities. The bitter reality was this that the League represented the Muslim aspirations. Instead of accepting it Congress encouraged other small and unimportant groups to counter balance the League.

244. Mohammad Iqbal Chawla, 'Quaid-i-Azam and Rajagopalachari Formula', (Lahore) *South Asian Studies*, Vol. 17, No. 1, 9 (January 2002), pp. 1–16.

245. 'Memorandum by The Viceroy-Designate, 15 September 1943, *Transfer of Power*, Vol. IV, p. 261.

246. *Wavell, Viceroy's Journal*, p. 17.

247. The Marques of Linlithgow to Mr Amery, 6 September 1943, *Transfer of Power*, Vol. V, p. 212.

248. Memorandum by The Viceroy-Designate, 15 September 1943, *Transfer of Power*, Vol. V, p. 261.

249. Ian Talbot, *Inventing the Nation: India & Pakistan*, pp. 49–52.
250. Peter Robb, *A History of India*, (London: Palgrave, 2002), p. 201. For detail see *The Indian Annual Register*, 1940–1947.
251. Jamil-ud-Din Ahmed, *Middle Phase of Muslim Political Movement*, pp. 42–57.
252. Ian Talbot, *Inventing the Nation: India & Pakistan*, p. 122.
253. Romila Thapar, 'Religion as History in the making of South Asian Identities', in S.M. Naseem and Khalid Nadvi (eds.), *The Post-Colonial State and Social Transformation in India and Pakistan* (Karachi: Oxford University Press, 2002), pp. 283–312.
254. Azim Husain, *Fazl-i-Husain: A Political Biography*, (Bombay: Longman & Green company, 1946), pp. 243–65.
255. It claimed to represent the Hindus and denied the Congress claim of representing the whole of India.
256. For detail see: B.R. Ambedkar, *Pakistan or the Partition of India* (Bombay: Thacker & Co., 1946).
257. Peter Robb, *A History of India*, pp. 228–29.
258. A. Sattar Khan, 'Punjab's Role in the Pakistan Movement,' *Journal of the Research Society of Pakistan* (Lahore: University of the Punjab), Vol. XXXII, No. 1, January 1995, pp. 29–50.
259. Muhammad Munawwar, *Dimensions of Pakistan Movement* (Lahore: Pap-Board Ltd., 1987), pp. 159–71.
260. Darshan Singh Tatla, *The Sikh Diaspora: The Search For Statehood* (London: UCL, 1990), p. 18.
261. Ian Talbot, *Inventing the Nation: India & Pakistan*, pp. 69–71.
262. Darshan Singh Tatla, *Sikh Diaspora*, p. 18.
263. Ibid.
264. Peter Robb, *A History of India*, p. 236.
265. Ibid.
266. Ian Talbot, *Inventing the Nation: India & Pakistan*, 69–71; See Punjab Native Newspapers Reports 1937–47; Punjab Police Secret Reports for the years 1940–43.
267. Darshan Singh Tatla, *Sikh Diaspora*, pp. 18–19.
268. Ibid.
269. Tara Singh (1885–1967) was a Khatri Sikh who got prominence in the Akali Dal, due to its role in the Gurdwara Reform movement.
270. He was a Jat Sikh leader from the Lyallpur (now Faisalabad) district.
271. Kirpal Singh, *The Partition of Punjab* (Patiala: Punjab University, 1972), p. 16.
272. Ibid.
273. Qalb-i-Abid, *Muslim Politics in the Punjab*, pp. 250–55.
274. Michael Edwards, *The Last Years of British India* (London: Cassel, 1963), p. 176.
275. Khushwant Singh, *Train to Pakistan* (London, 1965), p. 19.

2

The Wavell Plan

Just prior to taking over as the Viceroy of India but immediately following the announcement of his appointment in 1943, Wavell had devised a scheme, thenceforth known as the 'Wavell Plan'. The scheme envisaged the establishment of a Federal Executive Council composed of leaders from the main Indian political parties to ensure smooth running of the government during the war and peaceful transfer of power later on to the Indians.

He announced that except for the posts of the Viceroy and the Commander-in-Chief, the Executive Council would consist entirely of Indian members. It would have full control of all portfolios including exercising sway over Finance, Home, and External Affairs. All these steps were part of Wavell's attempt to solve the then prevailing administrative, political and constitutional problems of India. To achieve this goal he convened a conference at Simla in 1945 and invited important Indian leaders including Jinnah and Gandhi. He assured them that if they promised to support the war effort of the British Government, he would proceed with his plan. This chapter deals with that Wavell Plan and the response to it of the main political parties in India.

There are three interpretations commonly put forward in historical literature regarding failure of the Simla Conference and the Wavell Plan. The first one puts the blame on Jinnah's intransigence. The second blames mostly the politicians involved and their failure to affect a compromise concerning a suitable allocation of seats. The third current of historical thought mostly blames Wavell's lack of political training and farsightedness for his failure to secure an agreement between the two leading parties. All these three lines of thinking will be analyzed in the following pages.

The present author thinks that contrary to the three lines of historical thinking referred to above, the real reason for the failure of the Wavell Plan was the failure of the parties involved to deal adequately with the burning issue of the time, the demand for Pakistan. This issue brought Wavell face to face with a situation where he could not ignore the demands of the Congress, the Muslim League or the Unionist Party, (the last named being the leading political party of Punjab in the 1940s). This chapter, therefore, tries to deal in depth with the forcefulness of the demand for Pakistan.

Churchill's appointment of Wavell, a professional soldier, as the Viceroy of India in 1943, was aimed at blocking any unexpected major political change during the war because he wanted everybody involved to devote all energies towards contributing to a victory in the war. However, his judgement was off the mark because Wavell, besides being a good soldier was a politically astute person as well.[1] He had clearly demonstrated this in his earlier dealings with the Egyptians and now he wished to display his political acumen in India as well.[2] He was also concerned about the tense relations then existing between the Indians and the British government and wanted to normalize them because his plan aimed at building a better understanding between the people of India and the ruling British government.

Soon after his announcement as the new viceroy, but before taking over of his new assignment, Wavell began to prepare a plan to bring Congress and the Muslim League together in a national government within the existing constitution of the Government of India Act 1935.[3] He thought that he should attempt to secure a provisional government at the Centre on the lines of the Cripps proposals, composed mainly of party leaders. Such an act, he believed, would lead to a decrease in political and communal tensions besides lessening the sense of political deprivation of the Indian people.

He believed that the main reason for the failure of the Cripps offer had been the strong conviction in India at that time that there was no reason to compromise with the British, as they would eventually lose the war. Later when the tide turned in the Allies's favour by mid-1943, Wavell expected that Indian thinking would have undergone a corresponding change as well, and, therefore, they would welcome the offer. He discussed his plan with Amery,[4] who saw an opening in it for a constitutional disquisition.[5]

At this juncture, the India Committee that had been formed in February 1942 under the chairmanship of Attlee was reconstituted for an evaluation of the existing political situation in India and for making appropriate recommendations.[6] Wavell, as the Viceroy-designate attended a few meetings of the committee where he submitted his plan in a long memorandum.[7] He sought permission to hold a secret conference of the ten top leaders[8] of Indian political parties to implement his plan. He visualized almost the same kind of Executive Council as proposed in the Cripps offer. He thought that besides the viceroy who was named by the sovereign, His Majesty's Government should only nominate the Commander-in-Chief of the British Indian army. However, the Governor General was to maintain his power to overrule his council on any measure whereby 'the safety, tranquillity or interests of the British India or any part thereof are or may be in his judgment essentially affected.'[9]

He proposed the establishment, both at the Centre and in the provinces, of coalition governments committed to an acceptable support for the war. However, the main part of the change at the Centre would be the establishment of a coalition government of party leaders. The new Executive Council would consist of various political leaders selected 'for their representative character and for their influence with the Indian people'[10] and not for their individual qualities.[11] In the provinces, it would be necessary to reconstruct some of the governments then functioning, depending upon the nature of agreement between the parties. But the main task would be to revive provincial autonomy where it had lapsed, and to ensure that the resultant governments were genuine coalition governments. He asked that the timing of the initiative and composition of the Executive Council be left to his good judgment.[12]

India Committee

Wavell's Plan underwent many revisions in the light of discussions in the various meetings of the India Committee.[13] Sir James Grigg, the Secretary of State for War,[14] thought that it was almost impossible to reach any agreement in Gandhi's presence. He maintained that any Congress member appointed to the Viceroy's Council would be under Gandhi's control; he opined that the situation would be: 'there would be two Kings in Brentford.'[15]

Attlee pointed out that Cripps had proposed that a Constitution-making body should be set up after the war and that, only if this were agreed to, the politicians should be invited to participate in the councils. He held that the present proposal reversed these two stages and the reversal was a fundamental and most serious change. He asked whether the radical changes would not greatly weaken the responsibilities of the Viceroy and of the Secretary of State. He doubted the success of such a council in case it failed to receive a sincere and serious response from the Indian leaders.[16] Pointing to the many shortcomings in the plan, he said that no reference had been made to the British responsibility to the minority communities. He agreed that Wavell should be able to make a fresh approach to the Indian political leaders, provided an assurance of the goodwill and cooperation of the Indian leaders was taken first. Following that, they might be willing to consider some interim arrangement whereby the recognized leaders of the Indian political parties would be trusted with a greater degree of responsibility.[17]

The India Committee[18] approved the Wavell plan but decided that the Viceroy-designate could only invite the Indian leaders for participation in such discussions with the prior and specific approval of the War Cabinet,[19] regarding both the timing of the approach as well as concerning the terms of the invitation.[20] Churchill, however, cancelled the meetings and privately detailed to Wavell his priorities for India which included making efforts for improving the Indians' economic lot, attempting restoration of peace between Hindus and Muslims, but did not rule out completely making some political progress during the war; Wavell thought of Churchill's ideas as meaningless.[21] Churchill was opposed to making any approach to Gandhi.[22] Wavell resented this comment and inferred from Churchill's cautious approach that he either feared a split in the Conservative Party or some kind of trouble in parliament if they took any fresh step regarding political reforms in India; certainly, Churchill was against taking such a risk during his tenure.[23]

Rejecting the plan put forth by Wavell, the War Cabinet, decided that he could, at an opportune time, submit recommendations for taking some steps that could assist in a solution of the constitutional problem. Actually, they tried to direct his attention away from emphasizing the constitutional and political problems of India and towards preparation for offensive operations against Japan, regulation of food supplies to counter the famine conditions and preparation of a sound legislative policy to help improve the social conditions.[24] Thus not only did the Wavell plan go into cold storage, but the course proposed and endorsed by a majority of the India Committee was also ruled out.[25]

By the time Wavell took over the top job in 1943, Jinnah had established himself as the most important leader of the Muslims in India. Wavell, therefore, would be compelled to invite him as the recognised representative of the Indian Muslim community if in the future he ever decided to invite Gandhi, Rajagopalachari and Nehru as representatives of the Congress, Savarkar as a leader of the Mahasabha and Dr Ambedkar, as leader of the Untouchables; Jam Sahib and Zafarullah, the other Muslim claimants, acted as representative of the States and law expert, respectively.

Wavell considered India's geographical and political unity as a 'natural' one and was, therefore, dead-set against any division.[26] Although he had no definite plans to totally bypass the Muslim demand for the separate state of Pakistan he certainly harboured vague ideas in that regard through the adoption of various schemes. Most importantly, however, he thought of giving appropriate representation to various communities in the legislature, the new central executive and the services. He wished to see the same kind of treatment being given to the Royal States.[27]

The India Committee's rejection of Wavell's proposals for progress on the Indian political scene forced Wavell into a corner and now he felt that minus the plans for any definite policy, all he could do was to give promises to the Indians without any sincere intention of fulfilling them.[28] It became very clear from their rejection that the British policy-makers had no interest whatsoever in helping Indians move towards achievement of a self-governing status.[29] They were still too busy making all efforts to preserve their own political and economic interests in India. Indeed, very few in Whitehall had displayed any eagerness to go along with Wavell's latest proposals concerning India.

THE BENGAL FAMINE

Primarily, Wavell had to cope with the economic problems of India. The most urgent problem in India was the food crisis, particularly in Bengal, where a famine had broken out.[30] Many factors had combined in contributing to the severe famine in Bengal which reached its peak of death and desolation in 1942 and continued unabated in the year 1943.[31] The famine was a serious disaster and claimed the lives of millions of men, women and children.[32] Linlithgow himself had feared that the death toll might rise to one and a half million in July 1943.[33]

Addressing the legislative assembly of Bengal, Maulvi Fazlul Haq, the Bengal premier, alleged that John Arthur Herbert, the Governor of Bengal, and his official advisers had ignored the council of ministers, therefore, he held the governor responsible for the whole catastrophe.[34] Then and afterwards, the Hindu dominated press of India, and the Western press as well, blamed the Muslim League government particularly that of Khawaja Nazimuddin, who had replaced Fazlul Haq as the new Bengal Premier, for a tragedy which was not of its making.[35]

When Nazimuddin came into office in 1943, the province was already heading towards a breakdown.[36] Although, Wavell thought that the Bengal government was weak and had failed in delivering the goods, he rejected the Hindu allegations that the Bengal government was doing nothing.[37] Writing to the King-Emperor, he said, 'we are hampered everywhere by the weakness of the administrative machine in Bengal and the lack of real public spirit.'[38]

Wavell would have been able to do a better job of alleviating the sufferings in Bengal if better coordination had existed between London, Delhi, and Calcutta but the response from the British government, the main player, was weak.[39] In spite of the administrative handicaps, Wavell worked hard to eradicate the famine[40] and worked round the clock to restore confidence, to get more crops grown,[41] and imported food from abroad.[42]

Despite Wavell's untiring efforts, the Bengal famine could not be controlled[43] and he felt frustrated.[44] While expressing his views before the Bengal ministers, he alleged that they lacked the ability to run the government.[45] No minister, including Chief Minister Khawaja Nazimuddin, disagreed with him.[46] He also held Rutherford responsible for the plight of the people but he appreciated the role of the army in controlling the food crisis in Bengal.[47]

The famine had revealed the weaknesses in food administration. The government appointed an Enquiry Commission in 1944, presided over by Sir John Acroyd Woodhead, who had spent almost his entire career as an ICS officer in Bengal.[48] Wavell wanted the enquiry limited to Bengal[49] but Amery thought it should be at an all-India level.[50]

The Viceroy's Executive Council met on 29 December 1943 to discuss the food crisis in India. Dissolution of the Bengal Ministry and imposition of Section 93 was suggested by many Hindu members. Mohammad Usman was the only Muslim who supported them. He did not bother if the Muslim League Ministry would fall. Wavell suggested to the Secretary of State for India the removal of the Nazimuddin government but his suggestion was turned down at that point, though later, in March 1945, it was admitted.[51] The fact of the matter was that it could have been handy for the Muslims of Bengal, particularly, and the Muslims of India, in general, had the Muslim League government been in power in the critical years of 1945 and onward. But Wavell had no sympathy with the Muslim League and its political interests in Bengal.

WAR EFFORTS

Wavell greatly admired the role the Indian army played during the war and he was convinced of its soundness and professionalism.[52] Churchill, however, was sceptical, and blamed Wavell for increasing the size of the Indian army and putting modern weapons in their hands fearing a rebellion at any time. Wavell, however, did not doubt the loyalty of the Indian army and assured Churchill of this.[53]

Wavell did not like Churchill's proposal recommending the creation of a new command to control all operations in South East Asia,[54] but not under the control of the Commander-in Chief of India.[55] He also sent an indignant telegram to the Secretary of State on 19 October 1944 when he came to know that His Majesty's Government had decided to increase the pay and allowances of British forces serving in the East. He objected to it for two reasons: Firstly, it would increase the cost of defence expenditure for India as the burden would be borne by the Indian treasury already in a critical stage. Secondly, the Viceroy wanted to increase the pay and allowances of the Indian army as well. But His Majesty's Government increased the soldiers' pay, which added some fifty million pounds of extra expenditure to the Indian treasury. Wavell strongly resented it and considered it unjustified, for it would add to their financial miseries.[56]

POLITICAL DEVELOPMENTS IN INDIA 1943–45

Wavell's most difficult task in the political realm was to find an acceptable compromise between the Hindus and Muslims. The British policy hitherto had been inclined towards the maintenance of India 'as a single administrative and political entity'. Conservatives like Lord Linlithgow had emphasized this as much as the soldier-statesman Wavell. Naturally, the latter was against the demand for Pakistan and, perhaps unwillingly, adopted a course of action that in the end facilitated rather than hindered the partition of India.

He chalked out a programme to deal with the issue of Pakistan with manifold strategies. In the first place, he encouraged all those forces, which could bring about unity and compromise between the League and the Congress. Secondly, after the failure of these efforts, he got involved fully in efforts to sidetrack the Pakistan demand.

Wavell, in his new post, desired cooperation from the major political leaders of India, particularly from Gandhi and Jinnah. He hoped that they would move beyond slogans like the 'Quit India Movement' and 'Demand for Pakistan'. Nonetheless, he promised the Indian leaders that London was ready for transfer of power and that he would consider the Pakistan issue at a time when the country was out of danger.

Politics in India was at a standstill towards the end of 1943; while the Congress leaders were in jail, the British were fully engaged in pursuing the war[57] so, for them, the Indian problem had dwindled in importance.[58]

THE RAJAGOPALACHARI FORMULA

Rajagopalachari, also known as Rajaji (1879–1972) was probably the first important Hindu leader to realize the genuineness of the Muslim League's demand for a separate Muslim state[59] and tried to convince his fellow Congress leaders to accept the division of India on the basis of the Lahore Resolution.[60] Gandhi gave importance to his views but had not considered them worthy of attention till the failure of the 'Quit India Movement'. Wavell allowed Rajagopalachari to see Gandhi in prison. Following its approval from Gandhi he presented his formula to Jinnah for his consent in April 1944.[61] Jinnah was ready to refer it to the Muslim League Working Committee for approval,[62] but Rajaji demanded that Jinnah should accept it first and approve it forthwith before taking it to the Working Committee. However, Jinnah turned down this demand.[63] As a result, Rajagopalachari announced[64] the failure of his secret negotiations with Jinnah and held him responsible for its failure.[65] But the overall formula itself was extremely vague.[66] Therefore, Jinnah turned down Rajagopalachari formula as 'it was offering a shadow and husk, a maimed, mutilated and moth-eaten Pakistan'.[67]

Wavell was hopeful of a settlement between Gandhi and Jinnah on the basis of Rajaji's formula. Although he felt that any agreement would be a valuable preliminary step towards constitutional progress, he found any reference to Pakistan impossible to deal with.[68] Even Rajagopalachari himself accepted the weakness in his formula, and said, 'If the Muslims are told they have it, they will in time cease to want it.'[69]

Following the failure of Rajaji's proposals, Wavell criticized them as vague and without clear definition. But he also surmised that Gandhi just might have been wishing to assess the strength of Hindu feeling against Pakistan and, at the same time, attempting to decrease Jinnah's prestige by sponsoring an, outwardly speaking, generous scheme but which was sure to be rejected by him. He was of the view, 'We shall never have any chance of a solution till the three intransigent, obstinate, uncompromising principals are out of the way: Gandhi (75), Jinnah (68) Winston (nearing 70).'[70] The failure of talks, he predicted, would lead to further trouble. Incidentally, Wavell later on incorporated almost the entire Rajagopalachari Formula to force Jinnah to accept the unity of India and give up the demand for Pakistan.

Rajagopalachari was not an accredited nominee of the Congress for settling matters with the Muslim League. Although he accepted the division of India in principle, he was not ready to implement it before the departure of the British. Jinnah, on the other hand, wanted a guarantee of complete sovereignty and independence before the British withdrawal. The Rajagopalachari formula was viewed as a try-out by the Congress leadership with the expectation that Gandhi would adapt future policy to the reactions it aroused. Gandhi, who had control and command over the Working Committee of the Congress, might settle the Hindu–Muslim problem.[71]

GANDHI–JINNAH TALKS 1944

In 1944, Gandhi had approached Wavell with the proposal that he should hold talks with him and the Working Committee of Congress as well[72] but Wavell had refused the request by stating, 'In consideration of the radical difference in our point of view, a meeting between us at present could have no value and only could raise hopes which would be disappointed.'[73]

Rejected by Wavell, Gandhi turned his attention towards Jinnah and put forward the argument that unless Congress and Muslim League agreed to take joint political action, the British would not grant independence to India.[74] He wrote to Jinnah on 17 July 1944, suggesting talks which the latter accepted without any reservations.[75] Jinnah had already asked Gandhi for such talks in April 1943 and had suggested a man-to-man and heart-to-heart meeting with Gandhi saying that such an event would be the greatest day for the Congress and the League.[76]

Gandhi–Jinnah talks commenced on 9 September 1944 and continued till 27 September.[77] The talks began first on the basis of the Rajagopalachari formula, which, Jinnah found not good enough on numerous counts and referred instead to the Lahore Resolution of 1940 instead as the basis for talks.[78] Gandhi did not accept Jinnah's thesis that Muslims were a separate nation and that they had the right to a separate homeland. He said, 'You do not claim to be a separate nation by right of conquest but by reason of acceptance of Islam. Will the two nations become one if the whole of India accepted Islam?'[79] He considered the Lahore Resolution worthless, and likely to bring nothing but ruin to the

whole of India. He held that attainment of India's independence must
be the primary aim[80] and further expressed his desire that the British
should first transfer power to Congress who would then allow Muslim
majority areas to vote for separation. He proposed that Balochistan,
Sindh, and the North-West Frontier Province where Muslims constituted
a majority and those parts of Bengal, Assam, and the Punjab where
Muslims were a majority, should vote on whether to secede from the
Indian union or not. If the vote was in favour of separation it should be
agreed upon that these areas would form a separate state as soon as
possible after India was free.[81] He suggested that the two states would
then set up one, unified administration of foreign affairs, defence,
internal communication, customs, commerce and the like.[82]

Jinnah regarded Gandhi's views as a negation of Pakistan. He told
him that the Muslims and Hindus were separate nations by any
definition. He stated:

> We are a nation of a hundred million, and, what is more, we are a nation
> with our own distinctive culture and civilization, language and literature,
> art, and architecture, names and nomenclature, sense of value and
> proportion, legal laws and moral codes, customs and calendar, history and
> traditions, aptitudes and ambitions—in short, we have our own distinctive
> outlook on life and way of life. By all canons of international law we are a
> nation.[83]

Jinnah felt convinced that the true welfare not only of the Muslims but
also of the rest of India lay in the division as proposed in the Lahore
Resolution.[84] He said that he wanted the partition of India before the
British departed, not after that.[85] He demanded a complete separation,
with no unified administration.[86] He wanted only Muslims to vote in a
plebiscite and if the majority of them voted for separation then the
entire province would go to Pakistan.[87]

Jinnah–Gandhi talks broke down due to a number of factors. Gandhi
had himself stated that he represented no recognized political body;
therefore, there could have been no real use of an agreement between
him and Jinnah who claimed that he was the leader of the Muslim
nation and the president of the League.[88] Jinnah did not trust Gandhi
who was giving just lip service to the Muslim cause and not responding
from his heart to the proposed division of India.[89] Despite his wishful

thoughts, Gandhi failed to prove to Jinnah that the Pakistan proposition was wrong on any account.

Amery, the Secretary of State for India, seemed happy over the failure of the Jinnah–Gandhi talks and said that 'The Gandhi–Jinnah conversations only confirm my growing conviction that the two main organized parties are incapable of finding a solution and that further efforts on our part to bring them together at present will not only fail but that their failure will be blamed on us and incidentally weaken and discredit such instrument of government as we possess today.'[90] He, therefore, recommended that Wavell should not include either Congress or the League in the Executive Council.[91]

Contrary to Amery, Wavell, during the talks, had his hopes raised high but with the passage of time, he also became depressed. Although he did not anticipate any feats of statesmanship or a practical solution to result from the talks, still, he thought, the talks could create an atmosphere which might help him to convince His Majesty's Government to accept his plan. In disappointment, he remarked that the correspondence between Gandhi and Jinnah was a deplorable exposure of Indian leadership.[92] Further he said, 'The two great mountains have met and even a ridiculous mouse has not emerged.'[93] He accused both Gandhi and Jinnah for the failure. He commented, 'Jinnah was arguing for something which he has not worked out fully and Gandhi was putting forward counter-proposals in which he did not really believe at all.'[94] Actually, Wavell always wanted to know the definition of Pakistan that could satisfy him, and he was unhappy that Jinnah had not disclosed the exact definition and boundary of Pakistan during these talks either.

Wavell was extremely unhappy with Gandhi's statesmanship, which he considered as unbalanced.[95] His views were shared by one section of the Hindu society in the Punjab who also believed that Gandhi was 'suffering from insanity in his old age.'[96] Gandhi wanted the independence of India first and did not show interest in the formation of an Interim Government under the existing constitution, which was Wavell's main concern.[97] Wavell thought, 'The talks would blast Gandhi's reputation as a leader.' In his view, Jinnah had an easy task as 'he merely had to keep on telling Gandhi he was talking nonsense, which was true.'[98] He believed the main aim of Jinnah was 'to use Gandhi's mood to secure the acceptance of the Pakistan claim as much as possible.'[99] He frankly admitted to Jinnah's outstanding statesmanship exposing Gandhi's weak arguments without disclosing any of his own weaknesses.[100] He deplored the fact that it would help increase Jinnah's prestige amongst his followers. He also held that it would not be appreciated by reasonable men who wished to see the settlement of the Muslim problem.

While Whitehall was concerned about the Hindu–Muslim unity, suspecting that it might result in their combined efforts to achieve independence as it would have been difficult for the Government of India to resist such a combined effort in the forties.[101] Wavell, on the other hand was equally upset over the failure of the talks for two reasons: Firstly, the failure was likely to widen the gulf between the Hindus and Muslims, making the solution of the communal problem impossible and resulting in a continued political stalemate.[102] Secondly, he feared that this would further add to the dislike of His Majesty's Government for a fresh political move in India as was his desire; in fact he had already sent a fresh letter to the Secretary of State on 20 September 1944, containing his proposals for initiating a new political move in India.[103]

Regardless of Gandhi's earnest desire for a united India, according to Louis Fisher, the tragedy of partition hung over Gandhi's head from 1944 to the day of his death in 1948. Gandhi wanted to use the cement of nationalism to keep India united while Jinnah wanted to use the political force of Islam, to break it into two. [104] Although Gandhi had begun to realize that harmony in India lay in the better understanding and solid agreement between the League and the Congress, he failed to perceive the reality of the existence of two nations. He remained mentally strapped with the Muslim ideals of the 1920s when the League had been demanding only political, social, religious and economic safeguards under one Indian union. Still, quite surprisingly, Gandhi, who had described the division of India as a sin, now became ready to discuss the machinery for the exercise of the right of self-determination on the basis of the Rajagopalachari formula, which 'apparently accepted the demand for Pakistan'.[105] According to B.R. Nanda, 'these conversations were no more than a kind of reduction for Gandhi; to

Jinnah they brought an accession of political strength. The fact that Gandhi had knocked at his door raised Jinnah's prestige.[106]

Viewed in the long-term strategy of the demand for Pakistan, the Jinnah–Gandhi talks were another milestone, marking further progress on the August 1940 Offer, the Cripps Proposals, 1942, and the Rajagopalachari formula, 1944.[107] They added to the popularity of the demand for Pakistan and were another feather in Jinnah's political cap.[108] The Jinnah and Gandhi encounter was not merely a personal clash as viewed by Louise Fisher but it was a clash of two different religions and ideologies.[109]

NON-PARTY CONFERENCE 1944

On the failure of his negotiations with Jinnah, Gandhi began to encourage all those elements which were against the League's demand for Pakistan.[110] Although he also pretended to withdraw into the background, he still persuaded[111] Tej Bahadur Sapru, who in August 1944, called the session of the standing committee of the Non-Party Conference, to study the communal and minorities' problem from a constitutional and political point of view and to suggest a solution. According to A.A. Ravoof, Tej Bahadur Sapru was 'a political orphan, who played the part of the saviour whenever Congress was in a tight corner.'[112] The Non-Party Conference set up a Conciliation Committee, known as the Sapru Committee, to recommend proposals after meeting the top leaders of the major political parties. Both Jinnah[113] and Dr Ambedkar refused to cooperate with the Sapru Committee.

Sapru proposals were embodied in no less than fifteen resolutions.[114] The Sapru Committee rejected the idea of the division of India and the principle of separate electorates. However, it recommended that a constitution making body, a central legislature and a central executive be constituted on the basis of parity between Hindus, other than the scheduled castes, and Muslims.[115] To the Muslims it seemed that 'the proposals aimed at a gradual political annihilation of Muslims.'[116] V.P. Menon writes, 'its rejection of the Pakistan idea and the recommendation of joint electorates made the Muslim League's attitude all the more hostile.'[117] Jinnah rejected the proposals and referred to the members of the Reconciliation Committee as 'nothing but hand-maids of the

Congress who have played and are playing to the tune of Mr Gandhi.' Probably, the committee consciously or unconsciously accepted the question of Muslims being a separate entity and the principle of parity between the Muslims and the Caste Hindus that loomed large on the political horizon for a long time to come. Besides Hindus, the Sikh leaders were equally opposed to the parity principle.[118]

Wavell, though he appreciated the indigenous efforts to bring about a rapprochement between the Hindus and the Muslims, showed great anxiety over its timing.[119] The Sapru Committee was formed when Wavell was working hard to impress upon His Majesty's Government to accept his proposals. He feared that the Sapru Committee would give another excuse to the British government to postpone consideration of his proposals. Therefore, he insisted that His Majesty's Government consider his proposals first, even if Sapru's Committee had reported to the British government.[120] Tej Bahadur Sapru also met Wavell and requested him to press the British government to accept his proposals.[121] Wavell had a poor opinion of Sapru and considered him a bitter and intolerant person. These weaknesses in his character, Wavell thought, would fail Sapru in getting the desired results.[122]

DESAI–LIAQUAT PACT, 1945

In the meantime, Bhulabhai Desai, the leader of the Congress party in the Central Assembly, brought to the Viceroy a plan on 20 January 1945, which, he claimed, had been discussed with Liaquat Ali Khan, leader of the League assembly party.[123] He also claimed that Gandhi was in agreement with it, and that Liaquat Ali Khan also had the support of Jinnah on this proposal.[124] The Desai–Liaquat pact recommended an Interim Government under the existing constitution. It also recommended Congress–League parity. No new election in the centre or in the provinces should be held during the war and coalition governments would be formed in the provinces, etc.[125]

Desai told the Viceroy that he wanted a national government under the present constitution with the members drawn from the existing legislature.[126] Wavell found his proposals reasonable and thought they could ease the political situation, for Desai's views were almost identical to his own proposed plan which he had sent to His Majesty's

Government.[127] Although, Wavell found the proposals reasonable, he was not sure of the support they would receive from other leaders and parties. Still, he decided to refer the proposals to His Majesty's Government for their opinion and also sent along his personal observations in which he maintained that the British government had the best chance in a long time.

On the other hand, Wavell also wanted to get confirmation of the pact from Jinnah. Wavell directed John Colville, the Governor of Bombay, to see Jinnah, who happened to be in Bombay, and seek his views on the Desai–Liaquat Pact.[128] The governor asked Jinnah his views on the pact, but the latter denied any knowledge of the Desai–Liaquat Pact.[129] The same was the case with other League leaders such as Chaudhry Khaliquzzaman.[130] Except for Gandhi, all Hindu leaders also repudiated it. Moreover, Liaquat Ali Khan himself disclaimed the pact, which was a serious blow to Desai's reputation as a leader.[131] According to a press report, Liaquat Ali Khan stated on 1 September 1945 that he would not deny the talks with Desai. His personal opinion was that the proposals could be made the basis for further discussion but he had made it clear to Desai that Jinnah, the President of the Muslim League, was the only proper authority to entertain proposals on behalf of the League and that he, i.e. Liaquat Ali Khan, was merely expressing his personal opinion.[132]

Desai had to pay a heavy price for his endeavour, which led to his political extinction, as the Congress denied him a ticket for the general elections in 1945–46. Desai could not bear this insult. It deeply affected his health and he died soon after of a heart attack.[133]

Wavell was not ready to believe that Jinnah had no knowledge of Liaquat's talks with Desai. To him, Jinnah wanted to divert the attention of the Muslim League supporters from the difficulties the party had been facing at the time. In Wavell's eyes, 'The Sind Government seems to be revolting from the League control, the N.W.F.P Government likely to fall, and the Unionist Ministry in the Punjab consolidating itself.'[134] He feared that the His Majesty's Government, due to the Desai–Liaquat Pact, would once again apply delaying tactics and consequently no political progress would be made. He wanted to go to England immediately to plead his case but the British government was inclined to delay his departure as long as possible. Wavell was also frustrated by the mounting pressure from the Indian politicians in the aftermath of the Desai–Liaquat Pact.[135] He thought that Desai and Liaquat were obviously out to show him how to get rid of his Executive Council.[136] He also learnt about Desai's claim that 'Wavell was in his pocket,'[137] and that Desai was so optimistic of his success that he had gone to the extent of offering portfolios to his friends. Wavell became so angry with Desai's tactics and propaganda that he decided not to see him again until he had received approval of his own plan from the British government. He redoubled his efforts to go to England to explain his own plan after the announcement of the Desai–Liaquat Pact, probably suspecting that a united front of the League and Congress could pose a serious challenge to the British authority. On failure of the Indian leaders to settle their dispute among themselves, Wavell now decided to take the initiative in his own hands after the failure of Desai–Liaquat Pact in 1945.

THE WAVELL PLAN (1945)

At the start of 1945, it was expected that the Allies would defeat Germany within that year and Japan approximately six months after that. Wavell had for the time being, accepted the advice of His Majesty's Government to put off going public with his plan. But he continued trying to remind the British government about the urgency for the formation of the coalition government in India. Gandhi had been released in 1944 but he had not budged from his original stand that Congress alone should form the national government. Still, it seemed that he was actively seeking some kind of agreement with Jinnah. It was expected that talks would fail, as any partition formula would not be acceptable to Gandhi. Similarly, Jinnah would also not like to see power handed over to the Congress before the British departed. Wavell had realized that His Majesty's Government had no interest in the Indian problem during the war because they were preoccupied with their vast undertakings elsewhere, and had little time for any political development in India.

Wavell called an informal Governors' Conference on 31 August 1944 to assess the political situation in India.[138] He sought their opinion regarding the political future of India. The obvious question was: should we sit back and await developments or attempt a positive move; if so, when and of what kind? He wanted to know whether governors of the Section 93 provinces visualized any advantage in summoning their legislatures; if not, whether they could control the situation in India till the end of the war.[139]

Wavell had planned to meet with the political leaders as early as possible in 1945 to discuss both short and long-term plans. For the short-term he wished to form a transitional government in which leaders of the political parties would take office, to restore provincial autonomy where it was then in abeyance, and to set up some kind of Constitutional Assembly to begin discussion of the Constitutional Settlement.[140] Concerning the long-term plan, all the governors were unanimously of the view that the British government could not afford to let things drift until the war with Japan had ended, and that if the main political parties failed to reach an agreement in the meantime, a proactive move must be made by His Majesty's government, preferably at the end of the war with Germany.[141] Some governors thought that a conference between political leaders and the Viceroy would do no good, and that the political leaders must settle the main communal issue without any British intervention. Some of them favoured general elections to the provincial assembly on the Cripps model.[142] All the governors except Casey (Bengal) and Rutherford (Bihar) agreed that political disturbances during the war were unlikely. Rutherford said that it would be 'comparatively easy for Congress to make trouble in Bihar where there was still a good deal of political crime.'[143] Casey was apprehensive about the communal situation in eastern Bengal and thought that it might flare up again at any time.[144]

Thus, Wavell took the initiative in addressing his superior in London in the second half of 1944 and requested that certain measures for pacifying the Congress be taken without, at the same time, alienating the League. Wavell addressed Churchill directly on 24 October 1944, pleading for a change of spirit which would convince the Indians of Britain's goodwill.[145] He also told Amery that he was prepared to visit London to urge their acceptance. Wavell was asked on 20 December 1944 to visit London in the second half of March 1945 to explain the main features of his plan to the British Cabinet,[146] and he eventually arrived there on 23 March 1945.[147]

Wavell apprised the India Committee on 26 March 1945 that the problem of India was most important and urgent because the economic future, the security and the reputation and prestige of the British Empire in the East depended on finding some solution of the Indian problem. In his judgment, there was a danger of its (his plan's) failure but his considered opinion was that there was more risk in sitting still and letting things get worse.[148] He suggested that he should be given authority to try to form an Executive Council comprising some of the political leaders to work under the present Constitution. Wavell found it very difficult to convince Churchill and his cabinet as his plan was deemed undemocratic. However, after Wavell's three-month's efforts in London the British Cabinet approved his plan on 31 May 1945.[149] The hard reality was that whereas in 1942 the British government had been desperately anxious to secure Indian cooperation in the war, they were now not ready to grant India any kind of self-rule or interim government as envisaged in Wavell's Plan.

The war with Germany ended on 9 May 1945 and in the same month on 23 May 1945 the coalition government was replaced by a caretaker one.[150] Thus Wavell was allowed to carry out his plan by His Majesty's Government.[151] Upon his return to India, Wavell met his council on 6 June and discussed his proposals with the members of the council. Except Archibald Rowlands,[152] no one supported his proposals. All the Indian members of the council[153] got together and produced a written indictment of the proposals, recommending instead, the grant of dominion status, holding of general elections and an immediate release of political prisoners. It was also demanded that the conference should be confined to those leaders who had supported the war.[154]

The Hindu members of the council like Dr Ambedkar; Dr Narayan Bhaskar Khare (Chief Minister [Central Provinces and Berar 1937–39] and Member, Viceroy's Executive Council for Indian Overseas [May 1943–1946]); and Sir Jawala Prasad Srivastva (Member, Civil Defence, Viceroy's Executive Council 1942–3; Food Member from August 1943–46) sent a written protest against Wavell's proposal to introduce parity between Hindus and Muslims on the council.[155] Ambedkar also sent a passionate protest about the representation of the Depressed Classes and he demanded two seats in the new council for the Scheduled

Castes. He threatened to boycott the whole scheme and even hinted vaguely at a revolution.

SIMLA CONFERENCE, 25 JUNE–14 JULY 1945

On 14 June 1945, Mr Amery officially announced the Wavell Plan in the House of Commons. On the same day, Wavell in his broadcast speech announced his decision to convene a conference at Simla and said that he proposed to invite Indian political leaders to it with a view to the formation of a new Executive Council, comprising representatives of organized political opinion, including an equal number of Caste Hindus and Muslims.[156] Except for the Viceroy and the Commander-in-Chief, it would be a Council composed entirely of Indians, and for the first time the Home, Finance and Foreign Affairs portfolios would also be in Indian hands.[157] It was proposed that the Council would work within the framework of the existing Constitution.[158]

The tasks for the new Executive Council would be as follows: firstly, to execute the war against Japan with the utmost energy till its final defeat; secondly, to carry on the government of British India, with all the manifold tasks of post-war development, until a new, permanent constitution could be agreed upon and came into force; and finally to consider when the members of the government thought it possible, the means by which an agreement regarding constitution could be achieved.[159]

Wavell added that the government had not lost sight of the need for such an agreement and the above-mentioned proposals were intended to make it easier to arrive at one. It would make possible the formation of responsible governments in the provinces with a coalition of the main political parties.[160] He invited Indian political leaders to take counsel with him at Simla. The same day he released Maulana Abul Kalam Azad, Jawaharlal Nehru and other Congress leaders who had been in prison since 9 August 1942.[161]

More or less all political circles of India hailed the Viceroy's speech.[162] Invitations were extended to the various leaders and were accepted by all but Gandhi.[163] He proposed the name of Maulana Abul Kalam Azad, then president of the Congress[164] who was then duly called.[165]

Gandhi registered two objections to the plan and demanded their acceptance. He objected to the term 'Caste Hindus' and suggested the term 'Non-Scheduled Hindus' instead. He said that while parity between the Congress and the League could be understandable parity between Caste Hindus and the Muslims was unreasonable.[166] He threatened that if those two changes were not made, it would lead to the failure of the conference.[167]

Jinnah also had some reservations about the Wavell Plan and wanted clarifications of the points before the start of the conference. The Viceroy turned down the requests of Jinnah[168] and Gandhi[169] to postpone the conference at least for a fortnight. Jinnah wanted to discuss the Wavell Plan with the Muslim League Working Committee before the conference[170] whereas Gandhi wanted the terms of parity between Muslims and Caste Hindus determined first. As Wavell refused to postpone the conference, political leaders arrived in Simla on 24 June.

The Viceroy invited Jinnah, Maulana Abul Kalam Azad and Gandhi, for a personal meeting on 24 June. Maulana Abul Kalam Azad, then president of the Congress, came first. He was accompanied by Govind Ballabh Pant (UP's ex-Premier 1937–9, and Member, Congress Working Committee) as an interpreter; for though Azad could understand English he was shy of conversing in it. He accepted the main principles underlying the proposals but he deprecated the haste with which the Working Committee had been compelled to act, and the government's failure to release all Congress prisoners. He said that Congress would accept equality of Caste Hindus and Muslims. He demanded that the Congress have a voice in the selection of non-Hindus and Muslims in particular.[171]

Gandhi's role at Simla aroused much suspicion. He claimed to represent 'nobody' but obviously, he was a part of the Hindu group and stayed around to 'advice the Viceroy'. Why was that the case even when Gandhi had himself said that he was a party-less worker? B.R. Nanda frankly admits, 'Gandhi was not a delegate to the Conference, though he was consulted by the Viceroy and the Working Committee.'[172] Actually, Gandhi had left the Congress in 1943 and insisted on the 'fiction that he is not the member of Congress and cannot represent them.'[173] But he remained active and keenly promoted the interests of the Congress, as Fisher writes, 'Gandhi made Congress policy behind the Simla scene.'[174]

Wavell tried to benefit from the services of Gandhi who had the habit of using religion to achieve his political ends. Wavell also used him to get better results in the conference. Wavell conceded that 'a democracy will only survive where the people are led by aristocrats, that is, their best men, irrespective of class, birth or wealth; and this combination of Aristocrats and People must control their Priests and not be controlled by them, while recognizing and using their value to guide and stimulate thought.'[175]

Gandhi came to see Wavell alone on 24 June which was their first meeting. He refused to acknowledge himself as the leader of the Congress party and frankly told Wavell that he had been offended just like all 'politically minded Hindus'[176] might have been because of the use of the word Caste Hindus by Wavell. He raised objection to it and said that he would prefer to use 'Non-Scheduled Hindus' instead. He said that in spite of severe pressure he would be prepared to accept parity between Caste Hindus and Muslims as a temporary settlement. He made it clear that it should be open to the Congress to put forth the names of Muslims or the Scheduled Castes. Wavell agreed in principle to this demand but subject to his own approval of the names.[177] Wavell's general impression of the interview with Gandhi was that it was 'mainly a discursive monologue by Mr Gandhi, interspersed by numerous digressions, such as most graphic descriptions.'[178] Wavell's general impression of Gandhi was almost identical to the assessment by Jinnah. Therefore, even in his first meeting with Gandhi, Wavell thought of him 'friendly for the time being, but perfectly prepared to go back at any time on anything he had said.'[179]

Wavell's meeting with Jinnah on 24 June went well as many issues were discussed in a friendly manner. Jinnah presented his case and said that parity between Muslim and Caste Hindu would adversely affect the Muslims, who would be in a minority in the new Council, as the Sikhs and the Scheduled Castes (who belonged to the Hindu community) would always vote against the Muslims and that the Viceroy would be reluctant to exercise his veto. On this, Wavell assured him that the Viceroy would exercise his veto if there was any injustice to the Muslims. Jinnah further demanded that if a majority of Muslims was opposed to any decision, it should not go by vote, but Wavell refused to accept this demand as he thought that the proposal was contrary to all principles of government. Jinnah asked the Viceroy to give a fair share of the key portfolios[180] to the League a request with which Wavell agreed. Jinnah, additionally, claimed that the Muslim League had the right to nominate all members of the Executive Council. He was also strongly opposed to Wavell's proposal for the inclusion of a Muslim member from the Unionist Party in the council. He said that the by-election results were sufficient evidence to prove that the League was the sole representative of the Muslims. He claimed that the Unionist Party had been running a coalition government only because of support of the League members. Anyhow, Wavell refused to accept the proposition that the Muslim League reserved the right to nominate all the Muslims on the Executive Council.

During the inaugural session of the Simla Conference on 25 June 1945, Wavell explained the goals and scope of the proposals embodied in his plan. Azad expressed his party's point of view. He thrashed out seven points and maintained that the proposals were acceptable only for an interim arrangement. The Congress could not be a party to anything, however temporary, that prejudiced its national character, or reduced it directly or indirectly, to the level of a communal body. Azad writes, 'I placed before the Conference the point of view of the Congress Working Committee. The Viceroy's reply on all the points raised was favourable.'[181] Desai, Rajagopalachari and Khare supported Azad. Rajagopalachari explained privately to Jenkins that he was supporting Azad in order to present his own views later.[182]

Dr Pramatha Banerjea, leader of the Nationalist Party (Hindu Mahasabha) suggested the enlargement of Conference to include the Mahasabha, the Muslims outside of the Congress and the League, and the Indian Christians. He advocated parity between Hindus and Muslims and also urged the release of political prisoners. Sir Muhammad Saadullah, the Premier of Assam and Sir Ghulam Hussain Hidayatullah (1942–46), the Sindh Premier, ridiculed Banerjea's speech and said that the Conference was fully representative. Siva Raj, a leader of the Scheduled Castes hoped that the Scheduled Castes would not be accused of obstruction if they claimed essential safeguards. Tara Singh supported the proposals and stated that though the Sikhs had much in common with the Congress, he must claim separate representation for the Sikhs.[183]

Khizar Hayat Khan Tiwana, Premier of the Punjab (1943–47)[184] and leader of the Unionist Party in that province, expressed some concern about the future of the army with finance entrusted to an Indian member and about the law and order situation in the States. He said he could not criticize the proposals until he knew more about the composition of the Executive Council. [185]

Jinnah advocated the case for the Muslim League.[186] He pleaded that the conference must face realities, and recognize where the true right to Muslim representation lay. He pleaded that just as Tara Singh represented the majority of the Sikhs and Siva Raj the majority of the Scheduled Castes, so the Congress represented the vast majority of the Hindus and the League the vast majority of the Muslims.[187] He believed that he looked on the proposals as a stopgap measure but in no way affecting the Congress demand for independence or the Muslim League stand for Pakistan. He said that the League could not agree to a constitution other than the one which guaranteed the creation of Pakistan.[188] However, he did not demand Pakistan immediately. He gave the impression that the Wavell Plan was acceptable to him, provided, he had his way on communal parity.[189]

The Viceroy felt satisfied with the first day's proceedings though he thought that Jinnah was a bit difficult. Wavell remarked, 'Jinnah has a good legal brain, so I think has Rajagopalachari. Of the rest, perhaps Kher for the Congress and Saadullah for the League are the best, but they are second class. The remainder are poor stuff, I think. If we can build a self-governing India on this sort of material, we shall have emulated the legendary rope-trick.'[190] Wavell was not optimistic about the final outcome of the Conference or ability of the leaders present to cooperate with one another.

Next day, on the advice of Evan Jenkins, his private secretary, Wavell offered to the conference a definite agenda for decision in two parts. Part A was for settlement primarily between the individual parties and himself as the representative of His Majesty's Government. The two points in Part B were for the settlement primarily between the parties themselves. Wavell thought that the council would understand that even if agreement were reached on both parts of the statement the final responsibility for advising His Majesty's Government rested with him alone.[191]

Wavell had created such a friendly atmosphere that the plan was approved by the conference without great opposition and without much debate. The delegates reached a consensus with regard to Part A. However, the conference had a difference of opinion on Part B. Wavell asked the conference delegates whether they wished to handle it by private discussion (even if necessary, discussions between leaders and him), or by the appointment of a committee, or by the combination of both these methods. Moreover, Wavell suggested that Part B would have to be considered by the full conference at a later stage.[192] Jinnah and Rajagopalachari, with whom the other delegates also agreed, suggested that private discussions were essential at this stage and that the strength of the council could not be considered independently of its composition. They asked for adjournment to enable delegates to consult one another, to which Wavell agreed.[193] Thus the conference was adjourned till the following day so that the two major parities could reach an agreement on Part B. In fact, the crux of the whole matter was to settle the strength and composition of the council and the method by which panels of names were to be submitted to the Viceroy for his selection. Congress wanted to see the door through which the members would enter. It had already accepted parity and now demanded that the council be appointed on a political and not on a communal basis.[194]

Wavell wanted to make his effort a success but as time passed it was becoming more and more obvious that it would end in smoke. The conference re-opened on the morning of 26 June but dispersed before lunch so that the delegates could discuss the issues amongst themselves. The next session took place on 27 June. Jinnah informed the conference that he and Pant had exchanged the points of view of the Congress and the League at a discussion the previous day but had failed to reach an agreement. Upon this Wavell suggested that further private meetings or discussions between the leaders be held, including those not belonging to the major parties, and him. He also proposed that the conference should appoint a committee of leaders, including those not belonging to the major parties, to bring about a rapprochement between the Congress and the League. He promised to extend all possible help for this noble cause and promised that he would be at the disposal of the delegates at all times.[195]

According to Azad, 'Mr Jinnah had expressed a wish to have an informal discussion with the Congress. I nominated for the purpose Pandit Govind Ballabh Pant, who, I thought, would be the right person to negotiate with Mr Jinnah.'[196] According to Wavell's version Maulana Azad, who was evidently sore at Jinnah's refusal to see him, raised the question of Pant's status and asked whether Jinnah would prefer to deal with a properly authorized representative of the Congress. Jinnah had informed his party leaders and supporters about the failure of the talks but Pant had apparently not informed the Congress Working Committee or Maulana Azad, then president of the Congress, who seemed to be angry. The conference got over this difficulty by agreeing that Pant should report to Azad before committing from the Congress side. After discussions, the conference agreed that there should be a further meeting between Jinnah and Pant and the result of this meeting would be reported to the Viceroy.[197] After about three-quarters of an hour, the League and Congress representatives having exploded into an open conflict twice, the Viceroy adjourned the session till 29 June to give the parties an opportunity for private negotiations.

The talks between Jinnah and Pant failed due to lack of flexibility on both sides. So eager was the Congress for a settlement that it accepted the formula, which suggested equal proportion of Muslims and Caste Hindus.[198] The Congress now claimed that since it was the largest national and secular party of India it had the right to nominate two Muslims out of the quota of five.[199] They feared that if they accepted Jinnah's claim that the League had the right to nominate all Muslim members, the Congress would become identified as representative of a particular religious community only.[200]

When the conference re-opened on 29 June, it was known to everybody that the Congress and the League had failed to reach an agreement. Therefore, Wavell proposed his own alternative line of approach with regard to the composition and procedure of the Executive Council. He said whatever the composition of the Executive Council would be he had three obligations to fulfil. Firstly, he would maintain the parity between Muslims and Caste Hindus. Secondly, he would make the selection of names and would not accept names only on the basis of party affiliation. Thirdly, he had to satisfy himself that the persons selected would function as a team.[201] After some discussion all agreed to do so except, Jinnah and Siva Raj. They maintained that they could not submit their lists of the names without consulting their respective Working Committees. It was agreed that those who agreed to submit their list, including the Congress, would do so within a week. Then the conference was adjourned for a fortnight.[202]

On sensing failure of the conference, Wavell began to hold Jinnah responsible for it. He observed that they had reached the critical point of the conference and that the 'main stumbling bloc is the attitude of Jinnah, i.e. his claim to nominate all Muslim members.'[203] He recorded in his diary,

> Jinnah was very difficult and argumentative, trying to corner me on some lawyer's point and refusing to give a straight answer; at last I had to say to him: "I am no dialectician and do not propose to argue, I have put a simple proposal which everyone else seems to understand, are you or are you not prepared to submit to me a list of names?"[204]

Wavell thought Jinnah might bring about the break up of the conference due to his intransigence and, therefore, he thought of making a shadow government and tried to get approval of this shadow council from His Majesty's Government and the provincial governors.[205]

Wavell sent a written statement to Jinnah outlining the procedure he had suggested.[206] On Jinnah's request, the Working Committee of the Muslim League held its session on 6–14 July at Simla.[207] After giving careful deliberations on the Viceroy's proposals, it authorized Jinnah to send the reply.[208]

Jinnah met Wavell on 8 July and discussed the procedure laid down by Wavell for the selection of the Executive members for almost one and a half hour. He tried to persuade him to accept the principle that all Muslims in the new council must be his nominees but Wavell refused to do so. Anyhow, Wavell, who had been working indefatigably at Simla, again invited Jinnah for talks on 11 July to settle disagreements between him and Jinnah about the procedure of selection. Wavell explained to Jinnah the proposed composition of the council. In fact, in the meantime, he had prepared his own list for the membership of the proposed council. This consisted of sixteen people. Besides the Viceroy and Commander-in-Chief were five Caste Hindus (two of whom were not from the Congress), five Muslims (four of who were members of the Muslim League and the fifth a nominee of the Punjab Premier), one Sikh, two Scheduled Castes and one Indian Christian.[209] Wavell did not disclose the names of the four Muslim League Members but did mention Muhammad Nawaz Khan, a Muslim of the Punjab from the Unionist Party. Jinnah stuck to his previous stand and refused even to submit or discuss names unless he was given the absolute right to select all Muslims and unless the Governor General's veto power was reinforced by special safeguards so that no decision objected to by Muslims should be taken in the council except by a clear two-third majority of the Muslims.[210]

Wavell truly believed that the League did not represent all Muslims in India and considered that one section of the Muslims not only in the Punjab but elsewhere would be outraged if he were to accept the demand of the Muslim League. He thought that he would alienate the Congress if he conceded the point in Muslim League's favour by excluding Nationalist Muslims who were disliked by Jinnah. Wavell refused to accept Jinnah's second condition as well, as the existing constitution did not allow it.[211]

The final session of the Simla Conference took place on 14 July during which Maulana Azad and Rajagopalachari exhorted the Viceroy to form a government without the League, which he declined to do.[212] Wavell announced the failure of the conference and took full responsibility for its breakdown; Maulana Azad, however, blamed Jinnah's intransigent attitude for its failure. On the contrary, according to careful reading of the conference proceedings it is beyond any doubt a proven fact that the Viceroy Lord Wavell brought about its failure.

CAUSES FOR THE FAILURE OF THE SIMLA CONFERENCE

A number of factors led to the failure of the Simla Conference. The Congress first rejected and then accepted the principle of parity with the hope that even then they would command a majority in the cabinet, for the members of the Sikh and the Scheduled Castes communities would always vote in their favour.[213] But they were not ready to allow Jinnah to nominate all Muslim members, which became a stumbling block. The Congress believed that the League's claim to represent all the Muslims of India was belied by the fact that it had problems in the Muslim-majority provinces.[214] However, the fact of the matter was that the demand for Pakistan had become very popular in all the Muslim-majority provinces. Wavell could not afford to ignore this reality.

After the failure of their 1942 anti-British movement, the Congress leaders had reviewed their policy towards the British government. According to Penderel Moon, 'After the folly of the "Quit India" rebellion, Congress was in a chastened mood and ready to co-operate.'[215] Under the Wavell Plan, they had a chance to establish a national government of their liking for the achievement of Indian independence. They, however, refused to accept the two-nation theory or the League's claim that it was the representative of all the Muslims of India. On the other hand, they were trying to create divisions amongst the Muslims by encouraging the nationalist Muslims to challenge this very claim of the League.[216] Wavell wrote to Amery on 9 July that

> I have seen an Intelligence report of attempts by Azad to consolidate the minor parties with the Congress against the Muslim League. He is said to have offered Tara Singh full Congress support for the Sikhs in the Executive Council if an agreed Sikh name were sent in through the Congress. This report is confirmed by statement of two Sikhs to my Private Secretary to whom they came for advice. Report goes on to say that Azad's line with the Sikhs was that if the League stood out, the other parties must prevail upon the Viceroy to go ahead and that the Congress intention was to secure the greatest possible control over affairs of Council. He believed that on this basis Jinnah and the League could be broken.[217]

A number of the statements, policies and actions of the Congress during the conference created distrust in the minds of the Muslim delegates.[218] Jinnah neither trusted Azad, with whom he even refused to negotiate during the conference concerning the Hindu–Muslim problem, nor the Congress. Wavell confirmed it and wrote to Amery, 'Their fear that the Congress by parading its national character and using Muslim dummies will permeate the entire administration of any united India is real, and cannot be dismissed as an obsession of Jinnah and his immediate entourage.'[219]

The Congress had claimed two Muslims and the Unionist Party one, a formula, which if accepted, would have left the League with two Muslim seats only. Wavell himself revealed to Jinnah that he had not discussed his selection of members of the Executive Council with the Congress, which may or may not accept them. Jinnah feared that though it was a temporary settlement, the Congress would make use of it to consolidate its position and gradually to strangle the demand for Pakistan.[220] Smith has recorded, 'Many Congressmen have unrealistically thought of crushing the League or of bypassing it. Many have been content to hold up the freedom of India until the Muslims should "come to their senses" and League die of stalemate.'[221] Thus the Conference proved a failure on the rocks of the unresolved Hindu–Muslim problem the crux of which was represented by the question of the communal representation.[222]

Despite his earnest desire and untiring efforts, Wavell failed to bring about a rapprochement between the Hindus and Muslims. It happened not because he lacked the political will, training and the art of dealing with the Indian politicians but primarily[223] like his predecessor, Linlithgow, he considered and declared India a natural geographical unit and, therefore, indivisible.[224] He called upon the two major nations namely Hindus and Muslims to make arrangements to live together, in spite of different cultures and religions.[225] He had visualized that by appointing a Punjabi Unionist Muslim, he would sidetrack the demand for Pakistan. His ideas about the demand for Pakistan and his efforts to maintain the unity of India were not unknown to Jinnah. Even though he had promised to use his veto power in the assembly in case of any discrimination against the Muslims he failed to convince Jinnah regarding his sincerity for the Muslim cause. Jinnah had demanded some effective safeguards other than the Viceroy's veto to protect Muslim interests from majority decisions of the Executive Council. Jinnah stated:

> On final examination and analysis of the Wavell Plan, we found it was a snare. There was the combination consisting of Gandhi's Hindu Congress, who stand for India's Hindus' national independence as one India, and the latest exponent of geographical unity, Lord Wavell, and Glancy–Khizar, who are bent upon creating disruption among the Muslimans in the Punjab. We

are sought to be pushed into this arrangement, which if we had agreed to, as proposed by Lord Wavell, we should have signed our death warrant.[226]

Some critics believed that Wavell should have formed the Interim Government without the League. It is argued that the Congress might have accepted a Unionist Muslim in lieu of their own nomination of two Muslims, for they came to Simla in a mood to conform; Jinnah was not strong enough to bargain further; the Unionist Party was still very strong, and Liaquat Ali Khan favoured a settlement. It was also perceived that there were many uncommitted Muslims in the country who might change their loyalty from the Muslim League. Hodson argues,

> It is arguable that if the Viceroy had been as adamant as Mr Jinnah, the latter would have been obliged himself to give in; that the destruction of the Unionist Party, which paved the way for partition of the Punjab, would have been averted; and that an effective all-community political Government of India would have operated for the rest of the war and perhaps for some time afterwards.[227]

In fact, if Wavell had gone ahead without the League, the communal problem would, in all likelihood, have become worse.[228] It might have resulted in bloodshed, chaos and civil war, as happened later when Wavell handed over the interim government to the Congress Party in September 1946.

According to Menon,

> Lord Wavell was blamed for not following up his initiative by imposing an award of his own. But it must be said in his justification that the war with Japan was still to be won; that His Majesty's Government would not have supported the formation of an Executive Council which did not include the Muslim League—those 90 million Muslims who, according to Churchill, had eschewed any such non-cooperative tactics as had been adopted by the Congress and had consistently refrained from doing anything that would tend to thwart the war effort.[229]

On the contrary it was equally true that war was expected to last one or two more years. Azad had expected the independence of India at the end of the war which had alarmed Wavell who desired 'to disabuse him of this idea.'[230] In the prosecution of war, a Congress-dominated council was likely to cause a grave embarrassment as its leaders had recently been released from imprisonment[231]and it was still viewed with considerable suspicion in the British governing circles.[232]

Though Jinnah claimed that there must be no Muslim stooges of Congress, like Maulana Abul Kalam Azad, nor possible Muslim 'Quislings' like Khizar or any other Punjabi Muslim belonging to the Unionist Party element between the League and the Unionist Party. Wavell said, 'Jinnah is apparently nervous: he has approached Unionists through various agents to effect compromise but these advances have been nebulous and unsatisfactory.'[233] But, Wavell deplored, 'Khizar has so far submitted no list and is waiting definite move by Muslim League. He has made no effort to reach agreement with the League and is said to have refused to advise Sikhs on their list. He has I think lost a considerable opportunity of influencing final decisions.'[234]

Wavell had suggested a panel system primarily to ensure the representation of the Unionist Party; however, that system was totally unacceptable to the League because it was in principle opposed to the nomination of any non-League Muslim to the Executive Council, not selected by the League president himself. According to Jinnah, the conference failed because the Viceroy had reserved the right to select the members himself and to include non-League men among the Muslims. He believed that this panel system affected the character and status of the League.

However, the best solution to break this impasse was suggested by Khawaja Nazimuddin. He told Casey[235] that according to him, 'Jinnah would accept a Punjabi Muslim who is neither a member of Congress nor of League, provided the individual were to be jointly agreed upon by himself and Punjab Premier and provided he were called a "Punjabi Muslim" and not a "Punjabi Union member".'[236] He made it clear that Jinnah would not accept a Muslim nominated by the Congress; he suggested the name of Firoz Khan Noon as a suitable choice.[237]

However, Khizar was thinking on totally different lines. He was expelled from the League, for he showed no willingness to compromise or to act upon the discipline imposed by Jinnah.[238] The Unionist Party had begun to disintegrate, as has been recorded by Penderel Moon, that there had been since the time of Sikander 'a clique of communal extremist, out of sympathy with Sikander's moderate policies and wholehearted supporters of the demand for Pakistan.'[239] Firoz Khan Noon has recorded, 'the Unionist Party of the Punjab was convinced by some very high up British officials that the British were not quitting and that they would be able to form a Government with Hindu and Sikh support though the Muslims would be only a few.'[240] Khizar thought that Jinnah would always try to undermine his position and tighten his grip over Punjab to achieve his goal of Pakistan.[241] He never thought of rapprochement with Jinnah and, therefore, during the conference remained close to the inner circle of the Congress party and its allies. He was suspected of negotiating with the Viceroy through the Congress President, Maulana Azad, for securing a seat from the Muslim quota representing Punjab.[242]

Khizar knew, 'The Punjab has played a leading part in the war, its soldiers and its people should not be allowed to go uninvolved. Moreover, the Punjab is the only Province which has maintained a popular Government continuously since the beginning of the autonomy and that too a Government representative of all the main communities of the province.'[243] He was also aware of the historical fact that it was an exclusive privilege of Punjab that it had been represented continuously by a Punjabi Muslim representative in the Executive Council since 1910. He was confident that since the province of Punjab had been playing a key role in the affairs of the central government it would not ignore his services.[244]

Khizar held, 'Mr Jinnah's totalitarian claim to monopolize Muslim seats, so that Muslims who do not belong to the League go unrepresented. I can safely assert that a Punjabi Muslim would be not a whit behind a Muslim drawn from any other source in maintaining the rights and claims of Indian Muslims.'[245] He insisted that Wavell should fill up the Muslim quota at once from elsewhere if Jinnah remained intransigent. He believed that in this way the League and Pakistan would begin to lose their power forthwith.[246] Besides, Gandhi impressed upon Wavell, 'His Majesty's Government would have to decide sooner or later whether to come down on the side of Hindu or Muslim, of Congress or League, since they could never reconcile them.'[247]

These suggestions impressed Wavell. Fearing the failure of the conference, Wavell thought of forming the Executive Council without the League, but was not sure of its success.[248] According to Choudhry Khaliquzzaman, 'As the terms were not acceptable either to the Government or the Congress the inclination of the Viceroy was to bypass the League and form his National Government by choosing Muslim representatives either from other parties or independents.'[249] However, on 30 June, Wavell sought the advice of His Majesty's Government and all the governors[250] through secret telegrams on whether or not to go ahead without the League.[251] The British government turned down the proposal and it was 'one of the last memorable acts of Mr Amery before he handed over the charge of his office to Lord Pethick-Lawrence ten days later.'[252]

Glancy, who had been advocating the Unionist stand said that Jinnah's claim to nominate all Muslims in light of the League's meagre hold on Muslim-majority provinces was outrageously unreasonable. He said:

> I agree with you that it would be inadvisable if Jinnah maintains his present attitude, to attempt forming Council without League representation. This would place Congress in an unduly dominating position. Muslim members apart from Unionist and Congress nominees would probably be of dubious value: every individual Muslim representative would be subjected to continual vilification from League-controlled Press and would be likely to feel insecure. Jinnah would pose as Islamic hero and though after some interval the falseness and untenability of his position might be appreciated and his power for mischief broken, it seems not unlikely that meanwhile the central machine would collapse.[253]

Further he said, 'Personally I doubt whether such substitutes except perhaps one or two would be strong enough to stand up to a storm of criticism and abuse without leaning heavily on Congress support. I still think on the whole it would be better to suspend Conference....'[254] Therefore, he did not agree with Khizar's suggestion that an Executive Council should be formed without the League.[255]

Glancy was fully conscious that Khizar's stand might bring about the failure of the Simla Conference but he was also worried about the latter's reputation and the future of Punjab. He said,

I am not entirely clear whether the present proposal means that there is to be no Muslim nominee from Congress and if so whether there is reason to believe that Congress will be prepared to accept this arrangement. But I trust that the impression will not be allowed to arise that the sole organization responsible for Jinnah failing to get his way is the Unionist Party. If this were to happen, the position of Khizar would become more difficult than ever.[256]

Glancy could not hide his grudge against Jinnah. Not only did he suggest to Wavell that the real cause (Khizar's intransigence) of failure of the conference should not be mentioned, but proposed, 'For purpose of discussion on the 14th and subsequent broadcast perhaps the point could be met by stressing that Jinnah, in spite of being assured of majority of Leaguers among Muslims representatives, still remained intransigent.'[257]

In the light of the aforesaid views of the governors of India, especially of the Punjab, Wavell dropped the idea of forming a council without the League. But Khizar Hayat Tiwana blamed it upon the differences between the Muslims and the Hindus which brought about the failure of the conference. He said,

There is nothing to show that the Congress has abandoned its claim to represent a section of Indian Muslims or its demand that some of the Muslim representation must go to its nominees. Lord Wavell has made it clear that he never showed his complete tentative list of nominations to any one of the leaders. Thus the Conference never reached the state at which I had to press my demand for the inclusion of a Punjab Muslim, nor did it break down on that account. Mr Jinnah seems to desire to divert attention from his differences with Congress and to concentrate it upon me. I do not propose here to discuss the merits of the League and the Congress cases. But I must repeat that differences between them were the cause of the failure of the Conference—not the allotment of a seat to a Punjabi Muslim. The present negotiations failed on account of certain fundamental differences between Mr Jinnah and the Congress—differences which have been evident during the Cripps negotiations and again during the Gandhi–Jinnah talks—and therefore the failure can in no way be attributed to the claim for the inclusion of a Punjabi Muslim in the Executive Council.[258]

Lord Wavell showed remarkable political insight and will to break the political deadlock in India. He managed to convince the British government about the wisdom of carrying his plan through. He attempted to help the Indians by trying to bridge their differences at the Simla Conference. Initially it appeared that the conference would be successful because it got to a hopeful start. Congress had not only agreed to the principle of parity but also had agreed to nominate only the non-Muslim members[259] but the real damage was caused by the Unionist Party's stand. It showed inflexibility in its demand that at least one Muslim member from the Unionist Party should be included in the Muslim quota and it was over this issue that the conference broke down. Wavell's dilemma was that he could neither ignore the advice of the governor of the Punjab nor could he bypass the Unionist Party. He was now left with no alternative but to announce the failure of the conference. He had failed to detour the demand for Pakistan but began to consider it a serious issue which needed to be dealt with sooner or later. The elections to the Constituent Legislative Assembly could corroborate Jinnah's claim for the 'Pakistan scheme.'

Notes

1. R.J. Moore, *Churchill, Cripps, and India 1939–4* (Oxford: Clarendon Press, 1979), p. 138.
2. Wavell said, 'I have a great love for the country and I hope in my new post to do something to repay the debt I owe'. He was called to a heavier responsibility as statesman than Allenby in Egypt. Robert Woollcombe, *The Campaign of Wavell: 1939–43*, London: Cassell & Company Ltd., 1959), p. 210.
3. Wavell took up his office in the India Office London on 21 June 1943 and began his study of the problems as seen from this end, as well as of those sides of it which he had not been mindful of hitherto. Amery to Linlithgow, 21 June 1943, *Transfer of Power*, Vol. IV, p. 25.
4. Wavell, *Viceroy's Journal*, pp. 1–15.
5. Amery to Wavell, 1 September 1943, L/PO/6/108a:ff 100–5.
6. War Cabinet Paper W.P. (43) 436, 4 October 1943, *Transfer of Power*, Vol. IV, p. 160.
7. Attlee, Amery, Lord Halifax, Sir John Anderson, Lord Simon, Sir James Grigg, and Wavell attended its first meeting held on 17 September 1943. War Cabinet Committee on India, 1 (43) First Meeting L/PO/6/108a: ff 78–82.

8. He proposed the names of Jinnah, Gandhi, Nehru, Dr Ambedkar, Rajagopalachari, Savarkar, Jam Sahib, Mudaliar and Zafarullah Khan and one representative from the business class, probably the head of Birla or Tata group.

9. War Cabinet Committee on India 1 (43) First Meeting 17 September 1943, L/PO/6/108a: ff 257–8.

10. War Cabinet Committee on India 1 (43) First Meeting L/PO/6/108a: ff 78–82.

11. Wavell did not wish to have the alternative, as he saw 'no halfway house between an official Government and a Government of Political leadership.' To his mind, official government might be efficient but could not in any circumstances plan and exercise political and constitutional reforms, for the simple reason that its members did not have political backing. But in the proposed plan the Executive Council would not only be efficient but also capable of taking initiative in the political and constitutional fields. Ibid., p. 258.

12. Victoria Schofield, *Wavell Soldier & Statesman*, pp. 298–99.

13. Halifax (1881–1959), who attended only the first meeting, gave wholehearted support so that the existing political deadlock could be resolved. However, he thought that it was undesirable to use such a phrase as 'men nominated by the political Parties.' *Transfer of Power*, Vol. IV, pp. 276–7.

14. Lord Simon and Sir James Grigg were real diehards.

15. A phrase taken from the Duke of Buckingham' *The Rehearsal* (1672). He said this of persons who were once rivals but had become reconciled. Ibid., p. 275.

16. Ibid., pp. 275–77.

17. Wavell held that the Constitution making body proposed in the Cripps offer was too big, and unwieldy ever to be effective. He thought it preferable and even necessary to reverse the order of its two parts, and did not consider that any radical departure from the precedent of the Cripps offer was involved. Ibid., p. 332.

18. India Committee met again on 29 September 1943 to discuss the modified draft.

19. The case was referred to the War Cabinet which proposed that the Conference leaders disavow their present attitude. Eden misconstrued the plan as an attempt to enthrone Gandhi. Churchill worked himself up into producing a tirade against Congress and its policies and then digressed into the dangers of an Indian army becoming political minded and anti-British. It was decided that Churchill would prepare a revised draft of the statement in which he would emphasize the defence of India and not much more. Attlee said that he would ask the Indian people to have patience.

20. Cripps who was not present in the earlier meeting supported the Wavell Plan.

21. Directive to the Viceroy Designate, 8 October1943, L/PO/108a: f 27.

22. Ibid.

23. Ibid.

24. War Cabinet Meeting, (43) 136th Conclusions, L/PO/6/108a: ff 43–5.

25. Mr Turnbull to Sir E. Bridges, 8 October 1943, L/PO/6108a: f 36.

26. Qazi Saeed-ud-Din, 'Is India Geographically One', in Rafique Afzal, ed., *The Case for Pakistan* (Islamabad, 1988), pp. 67–76.

27. *Transfer of Power*, Vol. IV, pp. 331–38.

28. According to Lewin, though there was no guarantee that such an effort would be a success, still it would have been an initiative, and a positive, undeniable gesture of British intent. Ronald Lewin, *The Chief*, p. 228.

29. Wavell observed that it had become obvious that the Cabinet showed no interest in laying down, at this stage, a precise and unambiguous course of action.

30. Though the war was apparently bringing prosperity to the peasantry, large profits to traders and businessmen, and better employments to all classes, there was a famine in Bengal. For some years before the Second World War, India had started importing food grains, particularly rice, from Burma. Japan occupied Burma in 1942, which stopped the import of rice from there. Linlithgow address in the Central Legislative Assembly of India, *Indian Annual Register 1943*, Vol. II, p. 328.

31. Ibid.

32. Wavell, *Viceroy's Journal*, p. 96.

33. Ibid., p. 226.

34. Sir T. Rutherford to Linlithgow, 2 October 1943, *Transfer of Power*, Vol. IV, p. 357.

35. Begum Shaista Suhrawardy Ikramullah, *Huseyn Shaheed Suhrawardy: A Biography* (Karachi: Oxford University Press, 1991), p. 44.

36. Bengal presented a separate and most intractable problem. In August 1942 Indian crops were poor, and in October there was a catastrophic cyclone, followed in the spring of 1943 by devastating floods. In addition, the war denied India crops from Burma, and all Indian communications were overtaxed by war-transport. Such were some of the reasons for the famine. Wavell, *Viceroy's Journal*, p. 35.

37. Keirman, *Wavell* (London: George Harper & Co., 1945), pp. 116–7.

38. Wavell to the King-Emperor, 4 January 1944, Wavell Collections, OIOL, MSS Eur D 977/1, pp. 1–12.

39. Wavell to Amery, 29 October 1943, *Transfer of Power*, Vol. IV, pp. 413–6.

40. Wavell visited the provinces of the Punjab and NWFP on 23–30 November 1943, to enlist the support of these governments to help supply food to Bengal, at cheaper rates. Wavell to Amery, 23 November 1943, *Transfer of Power*, Vol. IV, pp. 489–500.

41. Wavell went to Bengal many times in October 1943. He went around the streets of Calcutta by night to witness the state of the destitute. Wavell to Amery, 1 November 1943, ibid., pp. 430–42; Wavell to Amery, 2 November, ibid., pp. 474–8.

42. Wavell to Amery, 2 November 1943, ibid., pp. 474–8.

43. Wavell passed the judgment that the chief political problem in Assam was the desire of Muslim ministers to provide the Muslims the opportunity to get uncultivated government lands under the slogan of 'Grow more food.' Wavell, *Viceroy's Journal*, p. 41.

44. Even then he did not rest and he toured Orissa, Assam, and Bengal a number of times. He urged the people of Orissa and Assam to grow more food. Wavell, *Viceroy's Journal*, p. 41.

45. Huseyn Shaheed Suhrawardy was appointed Minister for Finance and Civil Supplies. He worked day and night organizing food distribution centres, and gruel kitchens all over the city. He mobilized the students for this work. By threatening

dire punishment, he did get rice holders and black-marketers (mostly Hindus) to disgorge their ill-gotten stocks and the rice did appear in the shops of Calcutta sooner than it would have, otherwise. Begum Shaista Suhrawardy Ikramullah, *Huseyn Shaheed Suhrawardy: A Biography*, pp. 44–5.

46. Wavell, *Viceroy's Journal*, p. 42.

47. Wavell to Amery, 2 November 1943, *Transfer of Power*, Vol. IV, pp. 443–4.

48. Amery to Wavell, 22 January 1944, ibid., pp. 663–4.

49. The Famine Enquiry Commission tried to find out the causes and gave recommendations to battle the famine. The British government took little interest in knowing the real causes behind the famine and remained busy with the war against Japan. However, Lord Linlithgow had removed Lt.-Col. Sir John Arthur Herbert from the governorship of Bengal on 18 October 1943. Wavell was equally critical of Rutherford, the new governor of Bengal, who he thought had neither the will nor the courage to drive the ministry to deal with the food crisis. Wavell to Rutherford, 8 November 1943, ibid., pp. 428–9.

50. Wavell disliked the idea to constitute an Enquiry Commission but could not ignore public opinion. It had been the British policy in India to blame Indians for their problems in order to conceal their own weaknesses. Amery to Wavell, 9 November 1943, ibid., pp. 463–4.

51. H.V. Hodson, *The Great Divide: Britain-India-Pakistan* (Karachi: Oxford University Press, 1997), p. 126.

52. Wavell on becoming the Viceroy of India utilized all resources of India to reinforce the Allied army. Directive to the Viceroy-designate, 8 October 1943, *Transfer of Power*, Vol. IV, p. 387.

53. Wavell, *Viceroy's Journal*, p. 3.

54. General Auchinleck had succeeded Wavell, resuming his former duties as Commander-in-Chief in India, and in November 1943 South East Asia Command took over the direction of the war from India. Wavell's son Major A.J. Wavell, was severely wounded in the fighting, and lost his left hand. Keirman, *Wavell* (London: George G. Harper & Co., 1945), pp. 217–9.

55. In November 1944, Chinese troops were fighting in co-operation with the British Imperial army, but this time in an offensive. Wavell to Amery, 19 October 1944, Wavell Paper, L/PO/10/21.

56. Ibid.

57. Contrary to the First World War, the Second World War had involved India in a different way. Not only had India supplied arms, ammunition and men but also defended its integrity and border from the Axis powers. Therefore, Wavell's efforts to implement his political plan (Wavell Plan) were turned down by His Majesty's Government. The Viceroy with the military background was expected to maintain a status quo and not to initiate risky political moves.

58. Jamil-ud-din Ahmad, ed., *Speeches and Writings of Mr Jinnah*, Vol. II, Lahore, 1946, pp. 78–83.

59. Rajagopalachari was one of the prominent Hindu leaders of the Congress Working Committee who was ready to compromise with the Muslims even on the basis of the Lahore Resolution. He was against the 'Quit India Movement' and was in favour of the Cripps Proposals. In 1942, he presided over a meeting of forty-six Madras

Congress legislators and got passed two resolutions in which he urged the Congress to concede the Muslim demand for Pakistan. He thought that the Congress and the Muslim League had to come to terms not only to break the political impasse in India but also for getting independence from the British Raj. K.K. Aziz, *The Making of Pakistan* (Islamabad, 1977), p. 64.

60. Rajagopalachari, born in Madras (now Chennai), began his career as a lawyer. He joined the Congress and came under the influence of Gandhi. Taking an active part in the Non-cooperation Movement in 1920–22, he became general secretary of Congress in 1921–22. He acted as the premier of Madras 1937–1939 and so occupied a prominent position in the Congress hierarchy.

61. Rajagopalachari to Jinnah, 8 April 1944, *Jinnah–Gandhi Talks* (Lahore: Book Talk, 1991), p. 16.

62. Jamil-ud-din Ahmad, *Speeches and Writings of Mr Jinnah*, Vol. II, pp. 57–64.

63. In his foreword to the publication of a book, namely *Jinnah Gandhi Talks*, Nawabzada Liaquat Ali Khan writes that Jinnah had a meeting of the Council of the Muslim League at Lahore where he publicly examined the proposal of Rajaji's formula pointing out how the proposal was a disfigured caricature of the Pakistan idea.

64. Rajagopalachari to Jinnah, 4 July 1944, *Indian Annual Register*, 1944, Vol. II, p. 130.

65. It was unacceptable to the Muslim League as it was offered with a view to bamboozling the world into the belief that the essence of the demand for Pakistan had been met. Jamil-ud-din Ahmad, *The Final Phase of Pakistan* (Lahore: Publisher United Ltd., 1964), p. 3.

66. It did not include the communal composition of the provisional governments which was a matter of great importance to the Muslim League. Moreover, if the word 'district' was used in the sense generally understood in India, the demarcation would apparently relegate 11 Punjab districts (including Amritsar), and 12 Bengal districts (including Calcutta) to Hindustan. Wavell to Amery, 19 October 1944, Wavell Paper, L/PO/10/21.

67. *Jinnah–Gandhi Talks*, p. 7.

68. Wavell to Amery, 11 July 1944, *Transfer of Power*, Vol. V, pp. 1083–5.

69. Wavell to Amery, 12 July 1944, L/P&J/8/519: ff 310.

70. Wavell, *Viceroy's Journal*, p. 79.

71. Louis Fisher, *The Life of Mahatma Gandhi* (London: HarperCollins Publishers, 1951), p. 499.

72. B.R. Nanda, *Mahatma Gandhi: A Political Biography* (London: Unwin Books, 1958), p. 237.

73. Details of correspondence could be found in *Gandhiji's Correspondence with the Government: 1942–44* (Ahmedabd: Navajivan Publishing House, 1945), pp. 1–360; Wavell to Gandhi, 22 July 1944, L/P&J/8/623: f 49.

74. Gandhi wrote a letter to Jinnah.

75. Sharifuddin Pizada, ed., *Quaid-i-Azam Jinnah's Correspondence* (Karachi: East and West, 1977), pp. 99–129.

76. S. Qalb-i-Abid, *Jinnah and Second World War II and the Pakistan Movement* (Multan: Beacon Books, 1999), p. 207.

77. G. Allan, ed., *Pakistan Movement Documents* (Lahore: Islamic Book Service, 1977), pp. 341–75.
78. Jinnah to Gandhi, 10 September 1944, *Jinnah–Gandhi Talks*, pp. 32–4.
79. Gandhi to Jinnah, 15 September 1944, *India Annual Register*, 1944, Vol. II, p. 140.
80. Gandhi to Jinnah, 14 September 1944, ibid.
81. Mr Gandhi's interview to *News Chronicle*, 29 September 1944; *Jinnah–Gandhi Talks*, p. 85.
82. Pyarelal, *Mahatma Gandhi: The Last Phase*, Vol. I (Ahmadabad: Navajivan Publishing House, 1956), p. 91.
83. Jinnah to Gandhi, 17 September 1944, G. Allana (ed.), *Pakistan Movement Documents*, p. 354.
84. Ibid., p. 356.
85. Jinnah to Gandhi, 23 September 1944, ibid.
86. Jinnah's interview to the Representative of the *Daily Worker*, 5 October 1944.
87. Jinnah to Gandhi, 17 September 1944, *Jinnah–Gandhi Talks*, p. 80.
88. 'Joint statement of Jinnah and Gandhi' released to the Press along with the text of correspondence on 27 September 1944; Jinnah's interview to the representative of the *News Chronicle*, London, 4 October 1944; Jinnah to Gandhi, 10 September 1944.
89. Jinnah's statement at the Press Conference on 14 October 1944.
90. Amery to Wavell, 10 October 1944, Wavell Collections, *Political Series April 1944- June 945*, Vol. I, pt. I, p. 85.
91. Ibid.
92. Wavell, *Viceroy's Journal*, p. 91.
93. Ibid.
94. Wavell to Amery, 3 October 1944, *Transfer of Power*, Vol. V, pp. 62–63.
95. Wavell came to know from the Secretary of State that Gandhi had written a letter to the Prime Minister. Wavell writing to Amery on 20 September 1944 wrote 'I cannot imagine anyone with Gandhi's reputation writing so stupid a letter and I think it shows that Gandhi's mental powers are failing. I can well imagine the PM's reactions and I hope that this stupidity will not make him refuse to consider my proposals for a move'. Wavell to Amery, 20 September 1944, L/PEJ/8/623: ff 16–29.
96. Glancy to Wavell, 25 October 1944, Wavell Paper, L/PE/5/247: ff 27–8.
97. Note by Mudie, Wavell Papers, Political Series, April 1944–July 1945, Pt.1, pp. 91–4.
98. Wavell, *Viceroy's Journal*, p. 79.
99. Wavell to Amery, 20 September 1944, *Transfer of Power*, Vol. V, pp. 44–6.
100. Wavell to Amery, 3 October 1944, Wavell Papers, L/P&J/8/520: f 237.
101. Aziz Beg, *Jinnah and His Times* (Islamabad: Babur & Amer Publications, 1986), p. 647.
102. Wavell said, 'I believe that most educated people are tired of the deadlock and ashamed of the futility of the Gandhi–Jinnah discussion...Gandhi seems to be thinking of a fast, but has received no instructions from his 'inner voice' to begin it', Wavell to Amery, 12 October 1944, Wavell Collections, Political Series, April

1944–June 1945, Vol. I, Pt. 1, p. 107; Wavell to Amery, 12 October 1944, L/P&J/8/519: f 46.

103. Wavell to Amery, 20 September 1944, Wavell Papers, L/P&J/8/520: ff 238–44.

104. Louis Fisher, *The Life of Mahatma Gandhi*, p. 499.

105. Ayesha Jalal, *The Sole Spokesman: Jinnah, the Muslim League and the Demand for Pakistan* (Lahore: Sang-e-Meel Publications, 1999), p. 121.

106. B.R. Nanda, *Mahatma Gandhi: A Political Biography* (London: Unwin Books, 1958), p. 237.

107. A meeting with Gandhi was an acknowledgement of Jinnah's equality of status. Michael Edwards, *Nehru: A Political Biography* (London: Cox & Wyman Ltd., 1971), p. 155.

108. Ziauddin Ahmad Suleri, *My Leader* (Lahore: The Lion Press, 1945), p. 146.

109. Louis Fisher, *The Life of Mahatma Gandhi*, p. 497.

110. The day after the breakdown, Gandhi's own paper, came out saying that the Muslim League should repudiate Mr Jinnah's leadership and find someone else to speak for Muslim India. *Jinnah–Gandhi Talks*, p. 7.

111. I.H. Qureshi, *The Struggle for Pakistan* (Karachi: University of the Karachi, 1987), pp. 218–23.

112. A.A. Ravoof, *Meet Mr Jinnah* (Lahore: Sh. Muhammad Ashraf, 1955), p. 156.

113. Jinnah to Tej Bahadur, 14 December 1944, in Jamil-ud-din Ahmad, *Speeches and Writings of Mr Jinnah*, Vol. II, pp. 240–1.

114. Matlubul Hasan Saiyid, *Mohammad Ali Jinnah: A Political Study* (Lahore, 1953), p. 277.

115. Full texts of the proposals see: *Indian Annual Register*, 1944, Vol. II, p. 239.

116. Matlubul Hasan Saiyid, *Mohammad Ali Jinnah: A Political Study*, p. 277.

117. V.P. Menon, *The Transfer of Power in India* (Calcutta, 1957), p. 179.

118. Hindu Mahasabha leaders and other Bengali leaders opposed the proposals on the ground that the recommendation provided for Hindu–Muslim parity. For detail see: K.P. Bhagat, *A Decade of Indo-British Relations* (Bombay, 1959), pp. 300–2.

119. Wavell, *Viceroy's Journal*, p. 101.

120. Wavell to Amery, 21 November 1944, L/P&J/8/520: f 113.

121. Sapru along with Menon came to see Wavell and protested that Wavell was against his proposals. Menon told Wavell that he had satisfied Sapru to the effect that Wavell was not against his proposals. Thus, Sapru said that a move by His Majesty's Government would be welcome even if his Committee had not reported. Wavell, *Viceroy's Journal*, p. 109.

122. Wavell to Amery, 21 November 1944, L/P&J/8/520: f 113.

123. Wavell to Amery, 21 January 1945, L/P&J/8/521: f 97.

124. Wavell to all provincial governors, Wavell Papers: Political Series, April 1944–July 1945, Pt. 1.

125. Wavell to Amery, 19 November 1944, L/P&J/8/520: f 113.

126. Wavell to Amery, 20 January 1945, *Transfer of Power*, Vol. V, pp. 423–5.

127. Having met Liaquat Ali, Desai once again met the Viceroy and gave details of his proposals. He argued that the best solution was to get the main parties working together in the administration, and if this could be achieved he felt that a communal and constitutional settlement might be easier. Ibid.

128. Wavell, *Viceroy's Journal*, p. 114; V.P. Menon, *The Transfer of Power*, pp. 177–8.
129. Colville writes that Jinnah was emphatic that any impression that there had been an authorized discussion between Desai and Liaquat is entirely false' However, Colville had the impression that 'Jinnah is not (repeat not) altogether averse to suggestions put forward though he did not commit himself and described them as not new'. Sir John Colville to Wavell, Wavell Papers: Political Series, April 1944 to July 1945, Pt.1, pp. 192–3.
130. Chaudhry Khaliquzzaman, *Pathway to Pakistan* (Lahore: Brothers Publishers, 1961), p. 327.
131. I.H. Qureshi, *The Struggle for Pakistan*, p. 226.
132. India and Burma news summary, compiled from official and Press sources. Vol. V, week ending July to September 1945, Lumby Collection, MSS Eur D 1033/3, pp. 3–4.
133. S. Qalb-i-Abid, *Jinnah and Second World War and the Pakistan Movement*, p. 207.
134. Wavell, *Viceroy's Journal*, p. 114.
135. Wavell to Amery, 20 January 1945, Telegram, L/PO/6/108 b: f 38.
136. Wavell was told that Desai had been putting about that he had him in his pocket'. Wavell, *Viceroy's Journal*, p. 138.
137. Ibid., p. 116.
138. Note by Evan Jenkins, Wavell Papers: Political Series, April 1944–July 1945, Pt. 1, pp. 43–7.
139. Ibid.
140. Note by Wavell, ibid., pp. 47–9.
141. Note by Evan Jenkins, ibid., pp. 43–7.
142. Ibid.
143. Wavell to Amery, 5 September 1945, L/PO/10/21.
144. Ibid.
145. Wavell to Churchill, 24 October 1944, L/P&J/8/520: f 237.
146. Amery to Wavell, 22 December 1944, L/P&J/8/520: f 50.
147. S.M. Burke and Salim Al-Din Quraishi, *The British Raj in India: An Historical Review* (Karachi: Oxford University Press, 1999), p. 411.
148. War Cabinet, India Committee 1(45) 13th Meeting, L/PO/6/108c: ff 286–96.
149. Cabinet C.M. (45) 3rd Conclusions, Minute 1, R/30/1/5/: ff 23–6.
150. Chris Cook & John Stevenson, *Modern British History, 1714–1987* (Essex: Longman Group UK Ltd., 1992), p. 31.
151. Wavell came back to India on 14 June 1945 and disclosed the proposals. Michael Edwards, *Nehru: A Political Biography* (London: Penguin Books Ltd, 1971), pp. 156–9.
152. Sir Archibald Rowlands was adviser to the Viceroy on War Administration 1943–5 and became Finance Minister, Viceroy's Executive Council from 1945. Wavell to Amery, 7 June 1945, L/PO/10/18: f 183.
153. However, Sir Mohammad Usman, Member for Post and Air, Viceroy's Executive Council, from July 1942 to 1946, did not like the proposal but assured Wavell of support, and Asoka Roy (Law Member Executive Council 1943–46) wanted an election at once.
154. Wavell to Amery, 7 June 1945, Telegram, L/P&J/8/522: f 214.

155. Ibid.

156. Wavell to Amery, 8 June 1945, ibid.

157. Amery to Churchill, 14 June 1945, *Transfer of Power*, Vol. V, pp. 1118–21.

158. Broadcast Speech by Field Marshal Viscount Wavell at New Delhi, L/P&J/8/524: ff 7–8; *Transfer of Power*, Vol. V, pp. 1122–4.

159. Ibid., p. 1123.

160. Ibid.

161. The following political leaders of India were invited in their respective capacities to participate in the conference. The leader of the Congress party and the deputy leader of the Muslim League in Central Assembly; the leader of the Muslim League and the Congress party in the Council of State; the leader of the Nationalist party and the European group in the Assembly. Mr Gandhi and Jinnah were recognized as leaders of the two main political parties; Rao Bahadur N. Siva Raj to represent the Scheduled Caste; Master Tara Singh to represent the Sikhs; Those holding offices as premiers in provincial governments; All those who lost offices of premiership due to imposition of Section 93. Broadcast Speech by Field Marshal Viscount Wavell at New Delhi, L/P&J/8/524: ff 7–8.

162. Wavell, *Viceroy's Journal*, p. 142.

163. Gandhi telephoned the Viceroy on 14 June and said that he could not attend the conference as representative of Congress and the correct representative of Congress would be the president or the president's nominee. In Wavell to Amery, 15 June 1945, Gandhi to Wavell, *Indian Annual Register*, 1945, Vol. II, pp. 128–144.

164. Gandhi to Wavell, 14 June 1945, ibid.; Wavell to Amery, 17 June 1945, Telegram, L/P&J/8/522: f 115.

165. Michael Edwards, *Nehru: A Political Biography* (London: Penguin Books Ltd, 1971), p. 158.

166. Gandhi's Press statement, 15 June 1945, Press Report, Wavell Papers, Political Series, April 1944–July 1945, Pt. I, pp. 244–5.

167. Gandhi was able to get a declaration from Wavell that 'Non-Scheduled Hindus' meant Hindus other than the scheduled castes. Gandhi to Wavell, 17 June 1945, *Indian Annual Register*, Vol. I, 1945, p. 245.

168. Quaid-i-Azam Mohammad Ali Jinnah Papers (Henceforth QAP), File No. 132 (Islamabad: National Archives), pp. 40–42; Sher Mohammad Garewal, *Jinnah–Wavell Correspondence*, Lahore: Research Society of the Punjab); Wavell to Jinnah, 16 June 1945, Wavell Papers, Political Series, April 1944–July 1945, Pt. I, p. 248.

169. Wavell to Amery, 18 June 1945, L/P&J/8/522: f 109.

170. Stanley Wolpert, *Jinnah of Pakistan* (Karachi: Oxford University Press, 1999), p. 243.

171. Wavell to Amery, 25 June 1945, Telegram, L/P&J/8/524: ff 25–6.

172. B.R. Nanda, *Mahatma Gandhi: A Political Biography*, p. 239.

173. Ibid.

174. Fisher, *The Life of Mahatma Gandhi*, p. 510.

175. Archibald Wavell, 'The Triangle of Forces in Civil Leadership', a lecture delivered in the University of St. Andrews, 22 October 1947, *Walker Trust Lectures on Leadership No. IX* (London: Oxford University Press, 1948), pp. 1–24.

176. Gandhi's Press Statement, 14 June 1945, Wavell Papers, Political Series, April 1944–July 1945, Pt. I, pp. 244–5.
177. Ibid., p. 1153.
178. Wavell, *Viceroy's Journal*, p. 146; Stanley Wolpert, *Jinnah of Pakistan*, p. 243.
179. Wavell, *Viceroy's Journal*, p. 146.
180. In Jinnah's eyes, key portfolios in the new Executive Council were Home, Finance, War and Transport, and External Affairs etc. *Transfer of Power*, Vol. V, p. 1154.
181. Maulana Abul Kalam Azad, *India Wins Freedom: An Autobiographical Narrative* (Calcutta: Orient Longman, 1959), p. 109.
182. Wavell to Amery, 25 June 1945, L/P&J/8/524: ff 25–6.
183. Ibid.
184. Very few historians have paid attention to the role of Sir Khizar Hayat Tiwana. However, Ian Talbot wrote an interesting biography. Ian Talbot, *Khizar Tiwana, the Punjab Unionist Party and the Partition of India* (Surrey: Curzon Press, 1996), pp. 137–40.
185. Wavell to Amery, 25 June 1945, L/PO/10/22.
186. Azad stressed seven points which were mostly irrelevant.
187. Wavell to Amery, 25 June 1945, Telegram, L/P&J/8/524: ff 26–7.
188. Ibid.
189. H.V. Hodson, *The Great Divide: Britain-India-Pakistan* (Karachi: Oxford University Press, 1997), p. 122.
190. Wavell, *Viceroy's Journal*, p. 147.
191. Wavell to Amery, 26 June 1945, L/P&J/8/524: ff 27–8.
192. Ibid.
193. Wavell to Amery, 27 June 1945, *Transfer of Power*, Vol. V, p. 1166.
194. Maulana Abul Kalam Azad, p. 109.
195. Ibid.
196. Ibid., p. 110.
197. Wavell to Amery, 27 June 1945, L/P&J/8/524: ff 28–9.
198. Fisher, *The Life of Mahatma Gandhi*, p. 510.
199. Wavell to Amery, 28 June 1945, *Transfer of Power*, Vol. IV, pp. 1170–1.
200. Maulana Abul Kalam Azad, p. 110.
201. Jamil-ud-din Ahmad, *The Final Phase of the Struggle for Pakistan* (Lahore: Publishers United Ltd., 1964), p. 8.
202. Wavell to Amery, 29 June 1945, L/P&J/8/524: f 30.
203. Ibid.
204. Wavell, *Viceroy's Journal*, pp. 150–1.
205. Wavell to all Provincial Governors, 11 July 1945, Wavell Papers, Political Series, April 1944–July 1945, Pt. I, pp. 97–8.
206. Sir E. Jenkins to Jinnah, 29 June 1945, Wavell Papers, Political Series, April 1944–July 1945, Pt. I, p. 63.
207. Sharifuddin Pirzada, ed., *Foundation of Pakistan: All-India Muslim League Documents, 1906–1947*, Vol. II (Karachi, 1970), pp. 500–5.
208. The League did not approve the plan for submitting a panel of names but preferred the procedure which had been agreed to by the former Viceroy Linlithgow, in connection with his offer of August 1940, namely that the selection of

representatives, while resting with the Governor General, should be based on confidential discussion between the leaders of the party concerned and the Viceroy. Secondly, the Muslim members should be chosen only from the Muslim League. Thirdly, while the League appreciated the Secretary of State's remarks that the Viceroy's power of veto would be exercised to protect the minority interests, however, the League felt that some other effective safeguards against unfair decisions of the majority would be necessary.

209. Wavell had five Muslims in his mind. They were Liaquat Ali Khan, Khaliq-uz-Zaman, Sir Nazimuddin, Essak Sait (Leaguer) Nawaz Khan (Unionist) in Wavell to Amery, 9 July 1945, L/P&J/8/524: ff 33–4.

210. Wavell to Amery, 11 July 1945, L/P&J/8/524: ff 34–5.

211. Wavell to Amery, 11 July 1945, *Transfer of Power*, Vol. V, pp. 1224–26.

212. Minutes off final meeting of Simla Conference on 14 July 145, L/P&J/8/524: ff 50–2.

213. Rajagopalachari, Bhulabhai Desai, and Tej Bahadur Sapru had acknowledged this principle of parity before the start of the Conference and even Gandhi accepted it in the Simla Conference. If they had been sincere about accommodating Muslim League or reaching an acceptable and reasonable agreement with it, they could have gone one step forward and could have accepted the exclusive right of the Muslim League to represent the Muslims of India.

214. Maulana Azad pleaded that in the provinces where Muslims were in majority, there was no League ministry. In the NWFP there was a Congress Ministry; in the Punjab it was a Unionist Ministry; in Sindh, Ghulam Hussain depended on Congress's support and the same was the position in Assam. Thus there was a large bloc of Muslims who had nothing to do with the League. But it is also true that this situation did not reflect the growing popularity of League in the Muslim-majority provinces. It was an outcome of internal dissension and personal jealousies of some members of the Muslim League which had brought about these changes. The hard facts were different from the aforesaid assumptions. Ram Gopal in his book, *Indian Muslims*, correctly remarked that 'this seemingly sombre picture was no index of the tremendous popularity the League had gained among the Muslims, who were flocking to it as Hindus flocked to the Congress'. In the Punjab, the Unionist Party was losing its ground. Several well known Punjab Muslims of Unionist and Congress parties had announced their support for the League. In Bengal Fazlul Haq, the Premier since 1937 had dared to defy the authority of the Muslim League High Command. As a result, he was overthrown in 1943 by Khawaja Nazimuddin, a whole-hearted Leaguer. Though Governor Raj had been introduced in Bengal, popularity of the League and of the Pakistan demand had been increasing day-by-day. Congress and its allies, despite the support of Fazlul Haq were never in a position to form a Government, In Sindh and Assam; the Muslim League had formed governments. Even in the NWFP, the solitary Muslim province attached to the Congress, a League's Ministry had been working during the absence of the Congress allies, the Red Shirts, who remained in jail during (1943–45). In the by-elections for 61 Muslim seats in the various provincial assemblies that took place from 1937 to 1943 the League won 47; independent Muslim 4 and the Congress captured only 2. By 1943, in the by-elections to Muslim seats, the League had won

8; independent Muslims 3 and Congress none. Moreover, Muslim League won all the four by-elections to the Muslim seats in the Central Legislature. Thus, the League was able to prove that it had gained a heavy mandate from the Muslim masses for its goal—the achievement of Pakistan. The League was the most popular party of the Muslims, and Rajagopalachari, Gandhi and others had recognized Jinnah as the one and only undisputed leader of the Muslims of India. Jinnah was not wrong in claiming that the League was the sole representative and authoritative organization of over 90 per cent of the Muslims of India.

215. Penderel Moon, *Divide and Quit* (London: Chatto & Widus Ltd, 1961), pp. 40–1.

216. Choudhry Khaliquzzaman and Sir Nazimuddin met Sir Mudie on 16 July and expressed their views on the Simla Conference. They said that the Muslim League Working Committee fully supported Jinnah in his stand on the right of the League to nominate all Muslim members of Council. They resented Azad's attempt to bring pressure to bear on the Congress Working Committee by sending for Husain Ahmad Madni and other Nationalist Muslims to Simla. Sir F. Mudie to Jenkins, 16–17 July 1945, *Transfer of Power*, Vol. V, pp. 1269–70.

217. Wavell to Amery, 9 July 1945, *Transfer of Power*, Vol. V, pp. 1210–11.

218. Wavell noted that 'Azad summoned to Simla the leaders of various nationalist Muslim organizations who are much disliked by the Muslim League, and it was, I think, generally known that he was attempting to consolidate all the minor parties with the Congress against the League. He certainly initiated discussions with the Sikhs and probably with the Scheduled Castes also.' Wavell to Amery, 15 July 1945, L/PEJ/524: ff 22–4.

219. Ibid.

220. Wavell observed that 'The failure of any political move narrows the field for future negotiations and now that Jinnah has rejected a move with the present Constitution based on parity between the Caste Hindus and Muslim it is not clear what he would be prepared to accept short of Pakistan.' Wavell to Amery, 15 July 1945, *Transfer of Power*, Vol. V, p. 1263.

221. W.C. Smith, *Modern Islam in India: A Social Analysis* (Lahore: Ripon Printing Press, 2 ed., 1947), p. 350.

222. Maulana Azad issued a statement from Simla on 17 July 1945. He said that 'So far the Congress is concerned, it has repeatedly declared its readiness to take up the responsibility of administration. If the British government were really anxious to settle the issue they should have foreseen and realized the communal and other difficulties and should have not given the right of veto to any particular group to hold up the progress of the country.' *India Annual Register, 1945*, Vol. II, pp. 131–3.

223. Wavell suggested holding meetings and tried to form a committee to find out some solution but all his efforts went in vain as he found no change of spirit among the leaders. Wavell as a third party could facilitate the dialogue. He could not interfere in their communal dispute. Qazi Saeed-ud-Din, 'Is India Geographically one', Rafique Afzal, ed., *The Case for Pakistan* (Islamabad, 1988), pp. 67–76.

224. Qazi Saeed-ud-Din, 'Is India Geographically one', Rafique Afzal, ed., *The Case for Pakistan* (Islamabad, 1988), pp. 67–76.

225. Wavell, *Viceroy's Journal*, p. 157.

226. Statement at a press conference, Simla, 14 July 1945, in Khurshid Ahmad Khan Yusufi, ed., *Speeches, Statements & Messages of the Quaid-e-Azam*, Vol. III (Lahore: Bazm-i-Iqbal, 1996), pp. 2025–28.

227. H.V. Hodson, *The Great Divide: Britain-India-Pakistan* (Karachi: Oxford University Press, 2001), p. 125.

228. Chaudhri Muhammad Ali, *The Emergence of Pakistan* (Lahore: Research Society of Pakistan, 1989), pp. 75–76.

229. V.P. Menon, *The Transfer of Power*, p. 215.

230. Azad said that the qualification we have sought in each case has been the greatest ability available, the common factor being the independence as the immediate objective after the war. Azad to Wavell, 7 July 1945, Wavell Papers, Political Series, April 1944–July 1945, Pt. II, pp. 77–80.

231. Wavell announced the release of the members of the Congress Party before the opening of the Simla Conference.

232. Therefore, it was highly undesirable to take the risk of allowing the Congress to form a new Executive Council, as the confidence of the British government in the Congress had not been restored completely. Congress was still planning to repeat the 1942 rebellion, the goodwill created by Azad's attitude, seemed dissipated.

233. Sir B. Glancy to Wavell, 3 July 1945, Wavell Papers, Political series, April 1944–July 1945, Pt. II, pp. 74–5.

234. Wavell to Amery, 9 July 1945, *The Transfer of Power*, Vol. V, pp. 1210–11.

235. Governor of Bengal.

236. Casey to Wavell, 3 July 1945, Wavell Papers, Political Series, April 1944–July 1945, Pt. II, p. 75.

237. Ibid.

238. Jinnah placed three demands before Khizar in April 1944: (1) every member of the Muslim League in the Punjab Assembly should declare that he owed allegiance solely to the Muslim League in the assembly and not to the Unionist Party or any other party; (2) the present label of the coalition, namely the Unionist Party should be dropped; and (3) the name of the proposed coalition should be the Muslim Coalition Party. On refusal to accept these demands, Khizar was expelled by Jinnah from the Muslim League on 27 April 1944. See, K.C. Yadav, 'The Partition of India: A Study of the Muslim Politics in Punjab, 1849–1947', *The Punjab Past and Present*, Vol. XVII-I, Serial No. 331 (Patiala: Department of Punjab Historical Studies, Patiala University, April 1983), pp. 36–37; and Ian Talbot, *Khizar Tiwana*, pp. 111–124.

239. Penderel Moon, *Divide and Quit* (London: Chatto & Windus, 1961), p. 39.

240. Firoz Khan Noon, *From Memory* (Lahore: Ferozsons Ltd., 1966), p. 188.

241. David Gilmartin has recorded that the League's influence rapidly increased in 1944–45, due to a number of factors. The Unionist Party was loosing its basis and ideology and suffered from factions. David, Gilmartin, *Empire and Islam*, pp. 199–223.

242. Choudhry Khaliquzzaman, *Pathway to Pakistan*, p. 328.

243. Press statement of Malik Khizar Hayat Khan at Simla on 15 July 1945, *India Annual Register1945*, Vol. II, ed., H.N. Mitra and N.N. Mitra (New Delhi: Gian Publishing House, 1990), pp. 136–7.

244. Wavell said: 'I certainly wish to avoid any political upheaval in the Punjab, where the Unionist Ministry is still doing well, thanks mainly to Khizar himself.' Wavell to Amery, 25 June 1945, *Transfer of Power*, Vol. V, p. 1157.

245. Press statement of Malik Khizar Hayat Khan at Simla on 15 July 1945, *India Annual Register 1945*, Vol. II, pp. 136–7.

246. Sir B. Glancy (Punjab Governor) to Wavell, 7 July 1945, Wavell Papers, Political series, April 1944–July 1945, Pt. II, pp. 74–5.

247. Wavell to Amery, 15 July 1945, *Transfer of Power*, Vol. V, p. 1263.

248. The governors of the important Muslim provinces of Bengal and the Punjab stated that it would be extremely unwise to form the government without the League, for a concession to the Congress was likely to drive the Muslims to rally solidly behind Jinnah. Moreover, Casey, the Governor of Bengal, pointed out that to form an Executive Council comprising members of the Congress and non-League Muslims was not workable. He informed the Viceroy that the Bengal Muslims would support Jinnah, whatever the result of his stand. He suggested announcing general elections to determine the credibility of each party. He further pointed out that elections could decide whether Congress could secure a sufficient percentage of Muslim seats to justify a claim to nominate a Congress Muslim out of the Muslim quota of seats on the Executive Council. It could also clarify the League's claim to be the sole body representative of the Muslims to the exclusion of both the Congress and other political parties.

249. Choudhry Khaliquzzaman, *Pathway to Pakistan* (Lahore: Brothers Publishers, 1993), p. 328.

250. Wavell to all Governors, 30 June 1945, Wavell Papers, Political series, April 1944–July 1945, Pt. II, pp. 63–64.

251. Casey to Wavell, 3 July 1945, Wavell Papers, Political Series, April 1944–July 1945, pt. II, p. 75.

252. Choudhry Khaliquzzaman, *Pathway to Pakistan*, p. 328.

253. Sir B. Glancy to Wavell, 3 July 1945, Wavell Papers, Political series, April 1944–July 1945, Pt. II, p. 76.

254. Sir B. Glancy to Wavell, 6 July 1945, ibid.

255. Sir B. Glancy to Wavell, 3 July 1945, ibid., pp. 74–5.

256. Sir B. Glancy to Wavell, 11 July 1945, ibid., p. 97.

257. Ibid.

258. Punjab Premier's Reply to Jinnah, 14 July 1945, *Indian Annual Register*, 1945, Vol. II, pp. 136–7.

259. H.M. Seervai, *Partition of India: Legend and Reality* (Rawalpindi: Service Book Club, 1989), p. 27.

3

The Cabinet Mission Plan (1946)

This chapter discusses Wavell's role in the initiation of the Cabinet Mission Plan. It also highlights the nature, character and significance of the Cabinet Mission Plan, reaction and response of various political parties and leaders to it, and reasons for its failure.

Wavell believed that the Cabinet Mission Plan was the last effort to preserve the geographical unity of India, his cherished dream, so he pressed hard for its acceptance by the Muslim League and the Congress, besides regularly impressing upon the His Majesty's Government and Whitehall to honour and respect their own undertaking sincerely; but ultimately his efforts ended in failure. The Muslim League, believing the Cabinet Mission Plan contained the intent and substance of Pakistan, accepted the plan in full whereas Congress accepted it with reservations. His Majesty's Government and Whitehall were also found wanting in implementing their own plan faithfully. Its failure meant the end of Indian unity leading to the mass killings of 1947.

Writings on the Cabinet Mission Plan generally adhere to one of the two following viewpoints: One point of view holds that Jinnah's insistence on the demand for Pakistan was responsible for its failure. The second view blames irresponsible speeches and statements of the Congress leaders, especially of Nehru, for the failure. This group also includes the so-called 'revisionist' school of historians which holds the Congress mainly responsible for the Cabinet Mission Plan's failure but Jinnah does not escape its censure either. However, in the following pages the present author takes the position that all approaches are only partial explanations and therefore reveal an incomplete picture. This chapter only analyzes the working of the Cabinet Mission Plan during Wavell's tenure.

GENERAL ELECTIONS (1945–1946)

The Simla Conference had ended in failure. However, it made one point clear: that only a general election could verify the respective parties' claims that largely, they were indeed the true representatives of their constituencies. The Muslim League had been confidently pressing the government to hold elections.[1] The Second World War (1939–1945)[2] had held up the political process in India for six years. The new Labour government in England,[3] under mounting political pressure from Indian politicians,[4] was obliged to hold elections in the winter of 1945–46, so Wavell announced on 21 August 1945 that election to Central and Provincial assemblies would be held in winter.[5]

There was a mixed reaction in India to these announcements. Almost every political leader and newspaper made appreciative comments except the Congress.[6] For various reasons it did not like the British announcement for holding the general elections.[7] Unlike the 1937 elections when there was an informal understanding between the two parties, neither the Congress nor the Muslim League showed the least inclination for any compromise at this critical juncture.[8] To Nehru, it was 'in the best interests of the country to keep away from the Muslim League leaders hereafter.'[9] He thought that the League had 'put up obstacles in the way of the country's freedom and made us gulp many a bitter cup, with them we can have no truck.'[10]

Jinnah, welcoming the election announcement, made it clear that 'no attempt will succeed except on the basis of Pakistan and that is the major issue to be decided by all those who are well-wishers of India and who are really in earnest to achieve real freedom and independence of India and the sooner it is fully realized, the better.'[11] He argued that the division of India was the only solution of this most complex problem of India[12] and this was the road to happiness, prosperity, welfare and freedom for the 400 million inhabiting this subcontinent.[13]

When the British government decided to prosecute the soldiers of Subhas Chandra Bose's anti-British, Indian National Army (INA), the anti-British feeling rose to a much higher level in India.[14] But Wavell proceeded with the elections as scheduled.[15]

For the Muslim League the elections were a matter of life and death as the case for Pakistan could be proved only by a convincing electoral victory so Jinnah tried to mobilize the Muslim masses throughout India for winning this electoral battle.[16] Sikandar Hayat while elaborating the charismatic personality of Jinnah, has recorded, 'However, like any charismatic leader, Jinnah had the support of some enthusiastic followers who saw the demand for Pakistan as primarily their own call to duty, and thus were prepared to contribute crucially to its realization.'[17] He enlisted the support of the civil society, Muslim women,[18] students,[19] labourers, workers, businessmen, industrialists,[20] *pirs*,[21] and *ulema*, etc., promising them a country where they would find a panacea for all the ills facing them in a united India. Muslims mostly believed in his promises.

During the election campaign, Muslim League's popular appeal was mostly based on the demand for Pakistan but its election manifesto covered many other aspects of concern for Muslim India in the political, economic, cultural and educational spheres.[22] The strongest appeal to the voters was of the promise for enforcement of Islamic principles[23] in the proposed Muslim state of 'Pakistan'.[24] The enthusiasm and fervour of the Muslims for the Muslim League and demand for Pakistan was evidently visible in all the provinces including the ones with Hindu majorities.[25] The two-and-half years of Congress rule (1937–1939) had left painful memories of injustices and repression for the Muslims. The propaganda against the Muslim League and its leaders during the election campaign of 1945–1946, further annoyed them. The vision of an independent Muslim state of Pakistan, in which they would have a larger share in the administration and economic resources vis-à-vis a Hindu-dominated, united India, made the Muslim population rally for the cause of Pakistan as espoused by the Muslim League.[26]

ELECTION RESULTS

Vijai Shankar Rai observes, 'The elections to the Central and Provincial legislatures were fought not over independence but on the issue of a united or divided India.'[27] In polls for the Central Assembly held on 4 December 1945, the Muslim League bagged all the 30 seats reserved for Muslims whereas Congress won 57 out of the 62 general seats. These election results sent the League's political stock soaring in India and abroad. Both the League and its supporters became more confident of

the League's victory in the following provincial elections.[28] Consequently,
a number of Muslim nationalists began to join the Muslim League.[29]

In February 1946, countrywide provincial elections for the Muslim
seats were held.[30] In Punjab, the Muslim League won 79 out of 86 seats;
in Bengal 113 out of 119; in Sindh 28 out of 35;[31] in the NWFP 17 out
of 38; in Bihar 34 out of 40; in Assam 31 out of 34; and in UP 54 out of
66. It won a good number of Muslim seats in other provinces as well,
such as Bombay, Madras and CP. On the whole, on an all-India basis,
the Muslim League had captured 440 out of a total of 495 Muslim seats,
giving it a victory in approximately 87 per cent of Muslim constituencies.[32]
The turnout of Muslim voters was fairly large; elections were fair and
impartial. The League alleged that its adversaries used resources such
as vote-buying or impersonation and failed to maintain a high standard
in the election.[33]

The Muslim League had to face a formidable task in the Central and
Provincial elections.[34] It had to contend with several hostile parties and
elements—the Congress with its mighty organization, propaganda
machinery and finance; the 'quisling' Muslim groups encouraged by the
Congress,[35] last but not the least, the Unionist Party in the Punjab, a
group of landlords and moneyed classes enjoying the blessing and
support of the British authorities.[36]

The most decisive election battle, in Wavell's eyes, was fought in the
Punjab, on 1 February 1946, considered the cornerstone of the whole
plan for 'Pakistan'.[37] Here a mighty combination of feudal landlords,
militant Akali Sikhs, and Hindu *banias* (money-lenders) backed by the
British authorities resorted to every conceivable method of corruption,
graft, intimidation and coercion to force Muslim voters to vote for
Unionists against their will. Ian Talbot has recorded that 'They
(Unionist) relied heavily on their control of patronage and the
machinery of government in fruitless effort to stem the Muslim League
tide.'[38] All such attempts failed in the face of the awakened national
consciousness of the Muslims and the slogan that '*Pakistan ka Matlab
kya: La ilaha illa Allah*', had become part and parcel of the election
campaign. David Gilmartin[39] and Sarah Ansari have recorded the role
of *pirs* of Punjab and Sindh respectively but overall appeal for the
protection and promotion of Islam during election campaign was the

most effective propaganda and became the real reason for the Muslim League's victory in the elections.[40]

Nazimuddin[41] and his followers worked zealously for the success of the Muslim League's candidates with the result that the Muslim League captured 95 per cent of seats in Bengal.[42]

According to Norman Brown the nationalist Muslims made a poor show and, 'the nationalists won only 11 against the Muslim League's total of 42 in the 1946 provincial elections; the Jamiat-e-Ulema-e-Islam won only 5; the Momins 5, the Ahrar 1'.[43]

Much has been written on the results of the elections of 1945–46 but there has been little scrutiny of the factors which led to decisive victories for the League and the Congress. Quite interestingly, both the parties ultimately proved to be representing either the one community or the other, as almost the whole of the Hindu community chose Congress as its true representative[44] and the Muslims chose the League.[45] The Sikhs, Caste Hindus, and Scheduled Caste Hindus[46] vehemently supported Congress and did not show confidence in smaller parties whether extremist Hindu Mahasabha[47] or Marxists or communists.[48]

It has been a general tendency among the historians in their writings on the Pakistan Movement to oversimplify the factors other than religious that brought about a glaring victory for the Muslim League in these elections.[49] In the recent past, however, some work has thrown light on other aspects of the Pakistan movement[50] and the manifold dynamics which resulted in the success of the Muslim League.[51]

The Muslim League's victory in the 1946 elections particularly in the provinces of Bengal and Punjab ensured that its political base for the demand for Pakistan was secure.[52] Jinnah who had begun to emerge as the sole accredited representative of the Muslim community during the period of the Second World War, especially during the Simla Conference, further strengthened his position; the electoral victory in the Muslim majority provinces (except NWFP) made his conviction for Pakistan stronger. Wavell, however, was unhappy at the massive victories scored by the Congress and the League.[53]

Parliamentary Delegation (January 1946)

His Majesty's Government did not accord proper respect to the League's victory at the recent polls.[54] So to get a truer idea of the political situation on the ground in India, the British government sent a fact finding mission under the chairmanship of Professor R. Richards[55] which is known as the Parliamentary Delegation.[56]

The delegation made the finding that both the Congress and the League disagreed about everything. It frankly admitted that since the creation of Pakistan could hardly be prevented, therefore, necessary action should be taken to circumvent it.[57]

Their findings led to the idea of sending a high-powered delegation later which became known as the Cabinet Mission Plan.

The Cabinet Delegation (March–June 1946)

The Labour government had close ties with the Congress with whom they shared common ideas of socialism. By virtue of his good understanding with Nehru and the Congress, Cripps expressed to Nehru his desire to understand the Indian situation through the Congress point of view.[58] Nehru in his reply gave a critical appreciation of the political situation in India[59] and blamed the Muslims for the communal problems confronting India.[60] He said that the British could not force Pakistan on India, in the form demanded by Jinnah,[61] for it would certainly lead to a civil war.[62]

He demanded that the British government 'declare in clear terms possible that they accepted the independence of India and constitution of free India will be determined by India's elected representatives without any interference from the British government or any other external authority.'[63] In addition he urged the British government to declare that it considered any division of India harmful to India's interest.[64] He warned that if this important aspect of the Indian problem was ignored, there would be severe conflict between the British and the Indians.[65]

Following the election results Wavell regularly communicated his views about the rapidly evolving political situation in India through telegrams and letters to the Secretary of State for India. The Labour government gave his proposals careful consideration, and decided to send a Cabinet Mission to India in an attempt to resolve the constitutional deadlock of India through negotiations.[66] The proposed delegation would consist of three British cabinet ministers, Pethick-Lawrence, Lord Cripps, and A.V. Alexander.

Nehru's response to Cripps had worked, for Attlee spoke almost in the same vein and language. In a debate in the House of Commons on 15 March 1946, concerning the Mission's visit to India,[67] Attlee remarked,

> I am well aware that when I speak of India I speak of a country containing congeries of races, religions and languages, and I know well the difficulties thereby created but these difficulties can only be overcome by Indians.... We are mindful of rights of the minorities and the minorities should be able to live free from fear. On the other hand we cannot allow a minority to place veto on the advance of majority.[68]

While the Congress welcomed the British prime minister's announcement, Muslim League on the other hand thought it was controversial.[69] Jinnah noted that Attlee 'had fallen into a trap of false propaganda that has been carried on for some time....there was no question of holding up the advance of constitutional progress or of obstructing the independence of India. I want to reiterate that the Muslims of India are not a minority, but a nation, and self-determination is their birthright.'[70]

Wavell called the Cabinet Mission, the 'three Magi';[71] they reached India on 24 March 1946 and stayed there till the end of June.[72] During this time, alongside Wavell, they discussed with the Indian leaders and elected representatives, ways of speeding up the transfer of power to the Indians.[73]

It was contemplated that in pursuit of the Cabinet Mission's task of seeking accord with Indian leaders on the principles and procedures to be followed in framing a new constitution for an independent India, Wavell in consultation with the Mission would open negotiations with the two main political parties, the Congress and the League, for the formation of a new 'Interim Government.'[74] The Mission promised to work with a positive frame of mind, for 'we have not come with any set views. We are here to investigate and inquire.'[75]

The elections had proved the ascendancy of the two parties in their respective constituencies. According to K.M. Munshi 'these results of the elections should have been an eye opener to some of the Hindu leaders who would not believe that Jinnah had acquired complete hold over the Muslim masses.'[76]

Azad, as president of the Congress, had gradually begun to realize the gravity of the communal problem; he met with the Mission and presented to them a formula for resolving the communal problem.[77] His formula was for a federation with limited control over various subjects other than defence, foreign affairs and communications and a limited number of others necessary for effective running of government. Probably the most important gesture on Azad's part was that he admitted the right of a province or area to stand out altogether under certain conditions.

Gandhi, who was interviewed in his personal capacity, denounced the Two-Nation Theory propounded by Jinnah. He alleged that it was a British creation. Wavell's meeting with Gandhi proved a deplorable affair, for Gandhi refrained from doing any productive work for a Hindu–Muslim agreement. No wonder, unafraid of any risk of a civil war in case the League was bypassed, Gandhi like Nehru suggested to the delegation:

> The difficulty would not be solved if the Muslim League refused to join the Constitution-making body. After having exhausted all friendly resources, if you feel a stage must arrive when you feel you must say that there shall only be one Constitution-making body, you must take the risks of that. There must be a considerable interim period. What is to happen in that period and what is to happen to your promise?[78]

The discussion between Jinnah and the Mission focused on the demand for Pakistan.[79] Jinnah explained that the unity of India was a British creation and an artificial one[80] and it would vanish the day that foreign power would depart from India.[81] He cited the example of Europe, where, in spite of one religion and common culture, a number of states, much smaller than Pakistan, had emerged. To Jinnah even the Irish example did not provide for a true understanding of the Indian phenomenon,[82] therefore, he shed light on the history of the growth of the Two-Nation Theory.[83] To his mind, the only solution was to divide

India into Pakistan and Hindustan. On Wavell's enquiry,[84] Jinnah contemplated treaties and agreements between the two countries, once the fundamentals of Pakistan were agreed upon.[85]

The Mission's parleys with Jinnah were crucial and in the course of those parleys the Mission gave him a tough time.[86] Pethick–Lawrence was unmoved by Jinnah's rationalization of the two-nation theory. He and Cripps usually remained hostile towards Jinnah.[87] But according to Stanley Wolpert, 'Jinnah remained firm and cogently advocated the case for Pakistan.'[88]

Attlee in his letter of 13 April 1946 to the Mission and the Viceroy directed them to adopt a method which included a loose all-India federation. He warned that the creation of Pakistan would prove disadvantageous both for India and for England. He said that the Indian army would be divided and the future of the Princely States would be in jeopardy. He advised them that a united India was the best scheme.[89] Therefore, before the interview with Jinnah, the Cabinet Mission and Wavell made a strategy to counter Jinnah's claim for Pakistan.[90] They informed Jinnah that agreement might be reached on a separate sovereign state of Pakistan consisting of Sindh, Balochistan, and NWFP, the Muslim majority districts of the Punjab, except perhaps Gurdaspur, the Muslim majority areas of Bengal, and the Sylhet district of Assam. But they argued that the most promising alternate could be a three-tier solution. Jinnah showed no interest in this alternate, and was not ready to budge an inch from his demand for Pakistan.[91] He said that any form of Union or unity was impossible in India, and reiterated his claim to all six Muslim majority provinces and complete sovereignty for Pakistan. Nonetheless, he agreed that if Congress admitted the principle of Pakistan he was prepared to discuss its boundaries. Wavell thought at the end of the first round of talks with Jinnah that 'Congress has not, on paper and in public at all events, retreated one inch from their demands; nor has Jinnah given up one acre of his Pakistan.'[92]

Meanwhile, other communities like the Sikhs and the low-caste Hindus[93] also became active in claiming their rights. The Sikhs showed concern about the Muslim demand for the division of India into Pakistan and Hindustan. They demanded 'Sikhistan/Khalistan' or a separate Sikh state.[94] According to Baldev Singh, 'Khalistan' could be formulated in the Punjab excluding the Multan and Rawalpindi divisions, with an approximate boundary along the Chenab River. But he strongly favoured a united India and considered the division of India unwise.[95]

The Mission seemed to value their grievances and thought that the Sikhs could not be ignored[96] but it was also suggested that the Sikh demand for an autonomous 'Sikhistan' could not be fulfilled as Sikhs were not in a majority in any compact area of the Punjab.[97]

Jinnah never liked the proposal about the division of the Punjab and Bengal. He issued statements about Sikhs, telling them of their greater significance in a smaller Pakistan than they would have in a larger India. He could have done more for Muslim–Sikhs rapprochement but on the one side, he was preoccupied with much graver issues and on the other, the history of Muslim–Sikh antagonism played a major role in such efforts at rapprochement between the two communities.

Later, Cripps met Azad, Gandhi, and Nehru[98] to persuade them to accept some form of a compromise formula but they remained unyielding in their opposition to any form of government which furthered in any way the cause of Pakistan.[99] In their letter to [100]Attlee, dated 18 April, the delegation wrote that interviews with Indian leaders had failed to bring about a compromise on Pakistan. They held that there was 'no prospect of settlement of the Pakistan issue on the basis of agreement, and failing some unexpected development we shall have to propound the basis for settlement ourselves.'[101]

SIMLA CONFERENCE (5–12 APRIL 1946)

Having failed in their first attempt to bring the parties closer, the Cabinet Mission,[102] after a short break, drafted a three-tier plan, which envisaged autonomous provinces combined into separate groups in an overall federal structure. Since the Mission's negotiations failed to produce an agreement, on 27 April, the Secretary of State wrote letters[103] to the presidents of the Congress and the League inviting them to try to reach an accord on two fundamental principles, i.e. (a) a union government dealing only with foreign affairs, defence and communications; (b) two groups of provinces, one predominantly Hindu the other Muslim, dealing with the remaining subjects.[104] Both the parties accepted the invitation to meet at Simla.[105] The Simla

Conference took place on 5–12 April 1946 but failed mainly due to the failure of the Congress and the League to come to an agreement on the Mission's three-tier proposal.[106]

In fact this meeting was 'to make a final attempt to reach agreement between the parties.'[107] Rejecting both the League demand for Pakistan and the Congress demand for one Federal Centre the Mission specified a form of Central Union for India to deal with certain compulsory subjects and a grouping of provinces which provided the best hope of dealing with the communal problem.

If Jinnah was opposed to the strong Centre, the Congress also had reservations about the Indian Union and the Grouping.[108] Nehru thought that a union without a sovereign legislature would be futile and entirely unacceptable. He said that the Congress was against the Grouping but believed in the provincial autonomy.[109] He thought that some provinces might wish to group themselves while others might not and the rest might be divided almost equally on the subject. But Sikhs and Hindus in the Punjab who were a potential minority might be averse to Punjab being grouped with the North-Western Province. He said if any province declined to come into the Constitution-making body it would function without it. He declared categorically that if Congress's terms and conditions were unacceptable, it was ready to pay a high price for freedom.[110]

Sensing that Nehru's point of view might lead to the division of India, Wavell argued that if the provinces stayed out of the Indian Union, there would be dismemberment of India, which he hated the most. He said that the Cabinet Mission was trying to avoid the division of India and he advised the path of compromise in advance of the Constitution-making body to avoid the risk of a disastrous conflict.[111]

Disagreeing with Wavell, Jinnah maintained that the only way to prevent complete division was that provinces should group themselves together by choice. These group constitution-making bodies would deal with all matters, including the provincial constitutions and only three subjects would be given to the Union.[112] On the question of the right of secession, Jinnah made it clear that the union should not be for more than a period of five years in the first instance.[113]

The conference ended in failure because of a lack of compromise between the Muslim League and the Congress.[114] Regardless of the negative feelings dominating at the end of the conference there was a general impression that there were some positive developments which could help to preserve a union of India. But Wavell was not satisfied with the outcome of the conference.[115] He said:

> The close contact and discussion between Congress and Muslim League has merely enhanced their dislike of one another...I am afraid that further negotiations are more likely to be more difficult. The depressing thing that one should have to hand over the control of India to such small men; the mentality of most of them is that of small *bania*. I feel sometime inclined to cry.[116]

Wavell thought it was quite unfair and morally wrong on the part of delegates like Cripps to make daily contacts with Congress which jeopardized the Delegation's reputation for fair dealing and honesty.[117]

THE CABINET MISSION PLAN (16 MAY–16 JUNE 1946)

After the failure of the conference Wavell and the Cabinet Mission put forth a plan which is called the Cabinet Mission Plan. Their experiences and observations about the Indian situation, before and after the talks,[118] enabled them to formulate this plan.[119] The plan had two parts: long-term and short term. The long-term plan was announced 16 May 1946. This plan envisaged a three-tier plan, visualizing autonomous provinces and groupings of such provinces that wanted to take certain subjects in common and a Federal Centre or Union. However, the essence of the scheme was its three-tier grouping-scheme, placing predominantly Muslim-majority provinces in the North-West and North-East in Groups B and C, respectively, whereas the predominantly Hindu-majority provinces, i.e. Bombay, United Provinces, Madras, Central Provinces, Orissa, and Bihar were placed in Group A. The Province or the Group of Provinces was given the right to opt out from the proposed Indian union. And under the short-term scheme, it was laid down that an interim government would be constituted immediately.[120]

Elaborating on the Mission's intentions and views as outlined in his inaugural broadcast, Lawrence said that they had prepared a method to make a new constitution of India which would provide a smooth and rapid transition. He said that the statement offered an honourable and peaceful method to all parties and if they would accept it, the British government would exercise all its powers to help speed up the constitution-making process, so as to arrive at the speediest possible settlement. He reiterated that the British government under the Labour Party wanted to transfer power as early as possible and they wanted it done in a peaceful and friendly manner.[121]

THE LEAGUE'S RESPONSE

The Cabinet Mission Plan provided an opportunity in which a single Indian union could have emerged after ten years.[122] The crux of the whole plan, from the Muslim point of view, was that it also had the seed and substance of Pakistan.[123]

Jinnah's first impression was that he was palpably despondent with the plan and thought that the plan was simply a move to appease and placate the Congress.[124] But the Congress and Hindu euphoria proved short-lived,[125] as Jinnah in his speech at the meeting of the Muslim League Council held in June 1946 pointed out,

> The Congress Press and Hindus, when they heard these phrases and had this sugar coated pill that Pakistan was rejected, there was jubilation and, naturally, among the Muslims there was the strongest condemnation and resentment. But it was a sugar coated pill and there was so little sugar that within a short time the Congress Press felt that it was a pill minus sugar.[126]

Similarly, the plan unleashed a strong debate between the Congress and the League on the status of the proposed Federal Constituent Assembly,[127] nature of the Grouping System[128] and party representation in the Interim Government.[129] In the face of these controversies, Wavell and the Cabinet Mission had to make an explanatory statement on 25 May 1946 in which they maintained, among other things, that those parties who would accept the plan would be asked to form the government.[130]

As a matter of fact, the League had the following reservations about the Statement of 16 May:

1. The Muslim group of provinces was not given equal representation with the others at the centre.

2. There was no real protection for the Muslims in the Constituent Assembly, because from the very beginning the chairman would be a Hindu, unless the Muslims were to say that the election of the chairman was a communal issue, in which case the constituent assembly would break down straight away.
3. The position of the states was left far too vague.
4. Provinces had not been given the right to secede after ten years although Congress had always been willing to give the right to secede and had raised no real objection at Simla during the second Simla conference.
5. The Union had been given the power to raise money. This was not a communal issue and would inevitably lead to taxation from the centre with other subjects being added later to the short list of the subjects to be handled by the Union Government.[131]

The League Council meeting was held on 6 June 1946 and Jinnah placed the Cabinet Mission Plan before it.[132]After careful deliberations and rebuttal of the Mission's arguments against a sovereign Pakistan, and pointing out the inconsistencies in their statement, the council in the end accepted it. The Muslim League accepted it, prompted by its desire for a peaceful solution, and because the foundation and nitty-gritty of Pakistan were inherent in the Mission's scheme by virtue of the compulsory grouping of the six provinces in Sections B and C, and in the hope that it would, eventually, result in the establishment of a completely sovereign Pakistan. Jinnah was the moving spirit behind this acceptance.[133] M.A. Ispahani has recorded that Jinnah remained apprehensive about the question of the plan's acceptance for days. He repeatedly weighed the pros and cons of the problem, and finally reached the conclusion that the plan should be accepted.[134] The Muslim League press and politicians hailed Jinnah and the Muslim League Council's decision to accept the plan and they congratulated Jinnah for his farsightedness and statesmanship.[135] But the irony was that neither the Congress nor the Cabinet Delegation showed the courtesy to appreciate and congratulate Jinnah for such a move.

The following is a careful study of those clauses of the Cabinet Mission Plan which the League felt substantiated its stand:

1. It had been demanding undivided Punjab and Bengal and those were embodied in the plan.
2. It had demanded a Pakistan consisting of six provinces, i.e. Punjab, Sindh, NWFP, Assam, Balochistan and Bengal and these were included in the Groups B and C of the Plan.
3. These groups could, by simple majority, frame both provincial and group constitutions with regard to all but three subjects, and the framing of these constitutions was to precede that of the Union Constitution.[136]
4. The provision relating to major communal issues could be used to safeguard Muslim interests in the Union Assembly and prevent the Centre from encroaching on the autonomy of the provinces and groups.[137]
5. Muslim majorities in Groups B and C were in a position to negotiate with the Hindu Majority in Group A to ensure safeguards for minorities on a reciprocal basis.
6. The whole constitution would be open to revision at the end of ten years which meant, by implication, that the provinces and groups would have the freedom to opt out of the Union, if they so desired.[138]

A superficial reading led many to conclude that the demand for Pakistan was buried for good, but as Jinnah, clarifying the rationale for the Pakistan demand, stated, 'The Lahore Resolution, which embodied the Pakistan demand, did not mean that when Muslim put forward their demand, it must be accepted at once. It is a struggle and a continued struggle...Acceptance of Mission's proposals was not the end of their struggle for Pakistan. They should continue their struggle till Pakistan was achieved.'[139] But according to Hector Bolitho, Jinnah insisted that the Mission plan was no more than a 'half-way house to Pakistan,' however, 'he warned the British Government and the Congress's that the 'quickest way' to the independence of India was 'to agree to Pakistan'.[140]

However, the delegation failed to act like an honest broker. This is evident from the talks that followed the statement of 16 May, during which the Cabinet Delegation in its earnest desire to make their plan a success was ready to appease Congress at all costs.[141] Jinnah got discouraged but remained cool in the hope that a peaceful settlement between Hindus and Muslims at this critical juncture was essential. But he thought it was immoral for the Cabinet delegation to ally itself with one party at the cost of the other's interests. He criticized the partiality and integrity of the members of the Mission who had been secretly trying to convince Congress leaders like Gandhi and Nehru to accept the Cabinet Mission Plan.[142] The Muslim League had taken a calculated risk in accepting the Cabinet Mission Plan.

CONGRESS'S REACTION

Congress was conscious of the implications inherent in the Cabinet Mission Plan as it contained the seeds of Pakistan. They were in a state of confusion; they were neither ready to accept it nor to reject it in its entirety and they did not want the League to take the lead in the decision-making process in the final years of the British Raj. They also could not afford to annoy the Labour government which had been their friend for decades and had now put forth a plan which could have helped the Congress to preserve its dream of maintaining Indian unity.

In order to thwart the League and to keep attention focused on itself, Congress soon began to twist and distort the provisions of the plan, particularly the grouping scheme. The Congress Working Committee held, 'in the first instance the respective provinces shall make their choice whether or not to belong to the sections in which they are placed.'[143] Gandhi, who always cherished the desire to lead from the front, suggested in his article published in *Harijan*:

> The Cabinet Mission's statement is not an award. The Mission and Viceroy had tried to bring the parties together but they could not bring about an agreement. So they had recommended to the country what in their opinion was worthy of acceptance by the Constituent Assembly. It was open to that body to vary the proposals, reject them or improve upon them. There was no 'take it or leave it' business about their recommendations. If there were restrictions, the Constituent Assembly would not be a sovereign body. Thus the Mission had suggested certain subjects for the Centre. It was open to the Assembly, the majority vote of Muslims and non-Muslim separately, to add to them or even reduce them. It was good that they were not described as

Hindus, Muslims and Sikhs and other religious communities. That was an advance. What they aimed at was absence of all religious divisions for the whole of India as a political entity. And it was open to the Constituent Assembly to abolish the distinction of Muslim and non-Muslims which the Mission had felt forced to recognize. Similarly, about grouping, the provinces were free to reject the very idea of grouping. No province could be forced against its will to belong to a group even if the idea of grouping was recognized.[144]

To the Muslim League and the Cabinet Mission, interpretations by Gandhi and the Congress Working Committee were clearly inconsistent with the letter and spirit of the Cabinet Mission Plan. H.V. Hodson writes, 'Sir Stafford Cripps' fixation on the importance of Mr Gandhi, whom he considered as the only man who could persuade the Congress to acquiesce in the Mission's Statement, was proven wrong. The defect of relying on Mr Gandhi was exposed, as with whom nothing was certain, nothing decisive.'[145] To clear up the confusion thus caused by Congress the Cabinet Mission was forced to issue a clarification on 25 May 1946, stating that:

> the interpretation put forward by the Congress resolution on paragraph 15 of the Statement to the effect that the provinces can, in the first instance, make the choice whether or not to belong to the section in which they are placed does not accord with the delegation's intentions. The reasons for the grouping of the provinces are well known, and this is an essential feature of the scheme and can only be modified by agreement between the parties. The right to opt out of the groups after the constitution-making has been completed will be exercised by the people themselves, since at the first election under the new provincial constitution this question of opting out will obviously be a major issue, and all those entitled to vote under the new franchise will be able to take their share in a truly democratic decision.[146]

Even Congress's sincerest friend in the delegation, Sir Stafford Cripps, could not fail to criticize its interpretation of the Cabinet Mission Plan. He made it clear that firstly, the provision for the provinces' right to opt out of the group after the inauguration of the new constitution followed the suggestion put forward by the Congress as regards the provinces and a single federation, e.g., all provinces, should come in at the beginning but could not opt out if they did not like the constitution when they had seen it; secondly, the existing legislatures were not truly representative of the whole population because of the effect of the provisions of weightage contained in the Communal Award. The existing legislatures should, therefore, be discarded and the right of option should be exercised after the first new elections had taken place when there would be no doubt and would be a much fuller franchise and the precise issue could be raised at the election. According to Cripps, the Congress had been wishing to get everything without losing anything. The Congress would not allow the provinces to decide, in the first instance, to keep out of single federation but must insist on the provinces enjoying this right in relation to groups simply because it could not countenance the idea of Muslim provinces getting together even for a limited purpose.[147]

Congress remained unmoved in spite of such categorical clarifications by the Cabinet Delegation and Wavell, and Gandhi stated that the British were playing old tactics and further alleging that the Delegation said one thing and meant another.[148] In Pethick–Lawrence's eyes, 'Gandhi is provokingly enigmatic and blows hot and cold'.[149] But he believed, 'Azad and Nehru and Congress generally were willing to waive any formal or legal change in the interim constitution, and they wanted absolute power in reality'.[150] Wavell had the identical opinion when he interviewed Gandhi and Nehru, on 11 June 1946. When Gandhi went off into long legalistic arguments about the interpretation of the Mission's Statement, Wavell became impatient and said, 'I was a plain man and not a lawyer, and that I knew perfectly well what the Mission meant and that the compulsory Grouping was the whole crux of the plan.'[151]

Wavell viewed Nehru as a revolutionary with a sentimental approach towards the problems of India which lacked realism. He preferred law and order and peaceful means to achieve his goal whereas Nehru was a revolutionary. He also concluded that Congress was thinking much more of party politics and party advantage than the good of India as a whole.[152]

The Congress Working Committee, by its resolution of 25 June, reiterated its objections to the limitation of the central authority and the system of grouping of provinces. In communicating the resolution to the Viceroy, the Congress president stated that he and his party accepted the proposals and were prepared to work with them with a view towards achievement of their objectives, but they adhered to their own interpretation of some of the provisions of the statement such as that relating to the grouping of provinces.[153] On acceptance of the Cabinet Mission Plan by the Congress, the pro-Congress newspaper wrote that the three ministers achieved a task which the past British politicians had made almost impossible. If the Labour government and the Viceroy maintained the spirit shown by Lord Pethick-Lawrence and his colleagues, India would before long enjoy independence and peace, and Britain would find in independent India its most valued friend and ally in the East.[154]

The pro-League newspaper *Dawn* bitterly criticized this declaration and suspected that it was a first step towards a double-cross of the Muslim League and the Muslim nation. It still refused to believe that categorical promises made by the Viceroy to Jinnah would be broken. It held that the British pledges were at stake, so was the peace of India.[155] The fears of the Muslim League leaders and press were not groundless.[156]

If there was any doubt about Congress's real intention and attitude with regard to the Cabinet Mission's statement of 16 May it was effectively set at rest by the speeches and statements of Nehru after he had taken over as the president of the Congress in July 1946.

It needs to be understood that even before the advent of the Cabinet Mission Plan and certainly after it, Nehru remained the most dominant figure amongst the leaders of the Congress; in the eyes of the Congress, Maulana Azad, a Muslim, had become a spent force and it needed a Brahmin Hindu leader who would not only be more acceptable for the Hindus who formed the backbone of the Congress membership but their allies as well. One section of the Party wanted Sardar Patel to be the president of the Congress, for they wanted a strong and inflexible policy to be carried out in the final phase of the freedom struggle. However, at the instigation of Gandhi who had been acting as the 'super-president' of the Congress, Nehru was elected as the new president of the Congress. Besides, Nehru was acceptable to all shades of opinion, particularly the left wing of the Congress party and Gandhi seemed to be convinced that Nehru would be more acceptable to the Labour party in London.[157]

Nehru, quite frankly, revealed, 'as far as he could see it was not a question of the Congress accepting any plan, long or short; it was merely a question of their agreeing to enter the Constituent Assembly and nothing more than that.' He further added, 'We are not bound by a single thing except that we had decided for the moment to go to the Constituent Assembly.'[158] Speaking later at a press conference, he asserted that in agreeing to go into the Constituent Assembly, the Congress had inevitably agreed to a certain process of entering it, i.e. the election of the candidates, but 'what we do there we are absolutely and entirely free to determine.'[159] He ridiculed particularly the scheme for grouping and said that it would never come to fruition. Even with regard to the limited powers of the Centre of which so much was made by the Cabinet Mission, Nehru argued that it would have to be considerably enlarged both as regards its functions and powers.[160]

Such statements of Nehru had profound and historical implications on the politics of India. According to Azad, Nehru's statements as president of Congress altered the course of history.[161] No doubt, Nehru could not ignore the leaders of Assam and NWFP and, therefore, he had to disapprove the grouping clause of the Cabinet Mission Plan. He was also under attack from the left wing of the Congress, which seemed to think that nothing had changed since 1942 and the real enemy was still Britain. But more importantly it was Nehru's mindset which was chiefly responsible for his provocative utterances.

In 1937, after the decisive Congress election victory, he had declared that there were only two parties in India, the British and the Congress. Similarly, even after the elections of 1945–46, he had criticized the League as a 'British creation'. Additionally, his close association and friendship with important British policy makers like Cripps might have made him confident of the British support for his stand. More ironical were the ground realities which indicate that not a single important leader in the Congress except Azad would advise him to honour the Cabinet Mission Plan because Gandhi and Patel were also against the plan. Nonetheless, the timing of these remarks has been a ground for inquiry. One finds it difficult to get satisfactory answers to these questions. However, Michael Breecher has recorded that 'Nehru's utterances were among the most fiery and provocative statements in his forty years of public life.'[162] Maulana Azad also judged Nehru's statements as 'one of those most unfortunate events which changed the course of history.'[163] He also regarded Nehru's statements as an outright repudiation of those basic terms and conditions upon which the compromise plan of the Cabinet Mission rested and was supposed to have worked.[164]

Whether on purpose or unconsciously, Nehru's statements and speeches, along with Gandhi's press statements about the Cabinet Mission Plan, convinced Jinnah and the Muslim League all the more that the Congress with its majority intended to establish a one party rule, in the Constituent Assembly. The League obviously concluded from these statements that Congress had every intention of changing the true intent and spirit of the Cabinet Mission Plan through a majority vote in the Constituent Assembly, thus placing the minorities at their mercy. Though the Cabinet Mission, in their distress and disappointment, were prepared to clutch at any convenient straw, the pusillanimous attitude of the British Government only encouraged the Congress to persevere in its unjustified and misplaced claims, leading to India's eventual break up.

Yogesh Chadha has stated that Nehru's press conference in Bombay virtually repudiated the basis laid down by the Cabinet Mission for accommodation of the minorities; this forced Jinnah to repudiate and say good bye to the Cabinet Mission Plan.[165] The League already had been alienated by Wavell's refusal to allow it to form the Interim Government earlier, and now the Congress's real intentions regarding the long and short-term parts of the plan had became reasonably clear to everybody. According to A.A. Ravoof, 'Sandwiched, as it was between the Congress and the British, the League had no other alternative but to face facts and take decisions, however drastic they might be. Deceived by the Congress and let down by the British, there was no alternative but to trust in its own power.'[166] It was in these circumstances that the League Council met at Bombay on 27–29 July 1946 where Jinnah stated that the Congress never intended to accept either of the two parts of the Cabinet Mission Plan.[167] Under these circumstances the Muslim League Council resolved to withdraw its earlier acceptance of the Cabinet Mission Plan, 'due to the intransigence of the Congress, on the one hand, and the breach of faith with the Muslims by the British on the other.'[168] It was also resolved to resort to Direct Action to achieve

Pakistan and to immediately renounce the titles conferred upon the Muslims by the British.[169]

There was only one person in the Congress, Azad, who was stunned at these developments. According to Syeda Saiyidain Hameed, 'In a last ditch effort, he persuaded the All-India Congress Committee to pass a resolution reaffirming its acceptance of the Cabinet Mission Plan in its entirety. But Jinnah, Azad writes, had lost faith in the integrity of the Congress.'[170]

Cripps, addressing the House of Lords on 18 July 1946, explained the Mission's difficulties in bringing about an agreement in India. He also stated the diametrically opposite positions of the two leading parties concerning the formation of the Interim Government and the Constituent Assembly. Cripps said that they had not gone out to India with any cut and dried plan but with open minds, since their object was not to impose a plan on India, but to help the Indians to agree to a plan amongst them.[171] Cripps and company thought that they were successful in bringing the two parties into an acceptable agreement but they were incorrect in their assessment.

However, Hopkins wrote in his letter to his wife that the Cabinet Delegation had failed to bring about any change of heart in either of the two parties.[172]

The Congress Working Committee in its session of 25 June, while rejecting the short-term plan, accepted the long-term part of the Plan.[173] But the Muslim League on 25 June[174] accepted the short-term statement of the Viceroy as well. The British Cabinet directed Wavell to announce that the agreed proposals would not be pursued, but further negotiations would be opened after a few months' reflection. Meanwhile a Council of civil servants would be set up. Not only had the Muslims, but the minorities, particularly the British community felt this move to be a dreadful breach of faith, and a big blunder.[175] The Muslims were so disgusted that they said, 'they were driven into wilderness.' They thought that they could trust neither the Hindus nor the British. Stung by the perfidious blow, Jinnah wrote to the Viceroy, 'You have chosen to go back on your pledged word', therefore, he thought they would go for 'Pakistan or nothing'.[176]

Ultimately, Wavell considered it better to form an interim government of officials rather than to form one without the Congress.[177] Wavell informed Jinnah that because of Congress rejection of the 16 June offer the whole scheme had broken down, but he would be willing to reopen negotiations after a short interval.[178] In the meanwhile, new elections would take place for the constituent assembly and it would probably be better to get over them first.[179]

By the end of July 1946, the elections to the proposed Constituent Assembly were almost complete for the 296 seats assigned to the representatives of the British Indian provinces. The Congress secured 205 out of 209 seats for the general constituencies. The Muslim League won all but one of the 79 seats reserved for the Muslims. Ironically, the results delighted both parties but neither was prepared to inject life into the assembly.[180] The Sikhs, at first, declared their boycott of the elections owing to the dissatisfaction with the Mission's Plan but on receiving encouragement from the Congress, they retracted their earlier stand and sent four representatives. They frankly attributed this change in their policy to an assurance from, and to a resolution of, the Congress Working Committee, whereby the Congress recognized that the Mission's proposals were unjust to the Sikhs and promised to support them in securing adequate safeguards for their protection.[181]

By this time Congress's earlier statements about the clauses concerning grouping had begun to cause serious problems for Wavell. He knew that if the Congress's demand regarding grouping was accepted the Muslim League would inevitably refuse to take part. This would hold up the constitution-making process while communal stresses in the country would get worse. Wavell further told Nehru that if the matter was referred to a Federal Court it would not lead to any substantial gains for anybody.

Writing to Lawrence on 29 August 1946, Wavell stated that the compulsory grouping was the most important part of the scheme and that they must insist on it being observed. He hoped that if His Majesty's Government would stand quite firm on the matter of grouping then the intentions of the Mission must prevail. He hoped that it would also help to bring the League into the Interim Government. Therefore, he suggested to Whitehall that it would be unwise to call the Constituent Assembly till there was a firm agreed view on the grouping question.[182] But the Labour government did not want to annoy the

Congress and directed Wavell to summon the meeting of the Constituent Assembly.[183]

According to B.R. Nanda, 'A three-tier constitution, such as the Cabinet Mission had outlined, was a delicate mechanism with numerous checks and balances. Unless the two major parties, the Congress and the League, entered the Constituent Assembly with tremendous goodwill and determination to cooperate, it was impossible to draft a workable constitution, much less to enforce it.'[184] Nehru had already indicated that the Congress would remain in that assembly as long as they thought it was good for India. In fact he was rejecting the whole basis of the Mission Plan.[185] So when Wavell summoned the Constituent Assembly on 9 December 1946 Jinnah roundly criticized the move and refused to participate. This further ignited the mutual dislike between the League and the Congress.[186] Wavell had been asking Whitehall to issue a clear statement in this regard[187]and he also persuaded the Congress leaders to accept the League's interpretations,[188] but was rewarded with secret cables and letters from Gandhi and Nehru to His Majesty's Government requesting his removal as the Viceroy.[189]

THE CONSTITUENT ASSEMBLY

The League had joined the Interim Government on 2 October to prevent the mischief flowing from the Congress domination of the Interim Government. Following this move by the League Congress felt confident that the League would soon agree to join the Constituent Assembly as well.[190]

It had gradually become clear to all the parties that the Constituent Assembly would be a farce in the absence of the Muslim League. The Congress might have conveniently framed a constitution for Section A as defined in the Cabinet Mission Plan but it could not have framed a constitution for either Section B or C or for British India as a whole. Therefore, to continue with the Constituent Assembly under such circumstances would have been provocative.

It was important for the British government to do something to allay Muslim fears with regard to the Constituent Assembly, but it did not do so. However, Wavell did state in effect that the Constituent Assembly was expected to follow the conditions laid down by the Cabinet Mission but indicated no sanctions in the event of it not doing so.[191] Additionally, Wavell was of the view that till the Congress had categorically stated its acceptance of the Mission's interpretation regarding grouping, the Constituent Assembly should not be called.[192] But he was overruled by His Majesty's Government;[193] on 20 November 1946 he announced the decision of His Majesty's Government to call the Constituent Assembly on 9 December.[194] These differences between Wavell and the Congress proved to be serious enough and led to Wavell's removal later on.

The Constituent Assembly was called to meet on 9 December, but Jinnah was strongly opposed to it. He stated categorically that no League representative would attend the opening session of the Constituent Assembly, as the League's Resolution of 29 July had not been withdrawn yet.[195]

The Congress high command started pressurising the Viceroy to force the League to join the constituent assembly.[196] The *Daily Telegraph* commenting on some of Nehru's statements in this regard characterised them as 'imitating the language of Hitler' which had caused serious damage to Hindu–Muslim relations.[197] As part of this move, he wrote in a letter dated 23 October, to the Viceroy, that the latter should clarify whether the League's willingness to join the Interim Government meant working as a team or not, and, secondly, whether the League accepted the statement of 16 May or not.[198]

Wavell tried to pressure the Congress and the League to bridge their differences but failed since Congress had so far refrained from issuing an unequivocal statement regarding grouping; the League, therefore, refused to enter the Constituent Assembly. In such circumstances Congress demanded the resignation of the League members from the Executive Council.[199]

On 23 November, Wavell told Liaquat Ali Khan, Secretary General of the Muslim League, that he would not agree to the League remaining in the Interim Government unless they accepted the long-term plan. Liaquat Ali Khan replied that the League members were prepared to resign whenever the Viceroy required them to do so but they would not accept the long-term plan unless His Majesty's Government declared that the provinces must meet in sections and that the representatives in the sections could, by a majority if necessary, frame the provincial and the group constitutions. Liaquat Ali Khan's position was, 'if His Majesty's

Government was afraid of the Congress and had not the courage or honesty to maintain their own Mission Plan, then the Muslims had been thrown to the wolves and must accept the position and do the best they could by themselves, for it was useless to expect any mercy from Congress.'[200]

LONDON CONFERENCE (DECEMBER 1946)

Faced with this intractable problem and growing disturbances in various parts of British India, Attlee invited, for discussion, two members each from the Muslim League and the Congress and a representative of the Sikhs to England.[201] For the last time, it was in an effort to save the Cabinet Mission Plan.[202]

On 1 December, Wavell, Jinnah, Liaquat Ali Khan, Nehru, and Baldev Singh, a Sikh, left for London by air. The discussions lasted for four days and efforts were made towards bridging the gap between the League and the Congress concerning the interpretation of the grouping provisions in the Mission's statement of 16 May but without any success.

After the attempt to bring the Congress and League together failed, the British government on 6 December issued a statement which made it clear that no settlement had been reached.[203] It explained that the main hurdle was the interpretation of subsections (v) and (viii) of para 19 of the Cabinet Mission's statement of 16 May relating to the meetings in sections.[204]

Before meeting these leaders, Attlee had obtained the opinion of Lord Jowitt, the Lord Chancellor, about the Congress stand on the provision of grouping of provinces. Giving his opinion, Lord Jowitt stated:

> I do not agree that it is any part of the recommendations for the constitution-making machinery that the provinces shall in the first instance make their choice as to whether or not to belong to the section in which they are placed......I therefore conclude that the recommendation involves that it is for the majority of the representatives in each section taken as a whole to decide how provincial constitutions shall be framed and to what extent, if any, they shall be grouped.[205]

Actually, the Cabinet Mission had maintained throughout that the decisions of the sections should, in the absence of an agreement to the contrary, be taken by a simple majority vote of representatives in the Sections. So, the Mission had intended that the Constituent Assembly would decide on the groupings by a single majority vote decision of the assembly, but any province which might find itself forced by the majority vote into group to which it did not wish to belong would be safeguarded by being allowed, after the first general election held under the new constitution, to withdraw from the group on the basis of a simple vote in the province's own legislature. This view of the Cabinet Mission had been accepted by the Muslim League. The Congress interpreted it differently by saying that a province like Assam could stay out of Section C from the very beginning and frame its constitution independently, and that the true meaning of the statement, read as a whole, was that the provinces had a right to decide both as to grouping and as to their own constitutions.[206]

The 6 December statement of His Majesty's Government urged the Congress to accept the view of the Cabinet Mission in order that the way might be opened for the Muslim League to reconsider its attitude. It also left the matter undecided, as it said, 'if, in spite of this re-affirmation of the intention of the Cabinet Mission, the Constituent Assembly desires that this fundamental point should be referred for the decision of the Federal Court, such reference should be made at an early date. It will then be reasonable that the meetings of the Sections of the Constituent Assembly should be postponed until the decision of the Federal Court is known.'[207] According to K.B. Sayeed, 'The League scored another victory when the British Government issued a statement on 6 December 1946, saying that the League's interpretation was correct.'[208]

The British government, however, made it clear that its interpretation was the final interpretation, and that it must be accepted by all the parties in the Constituent Assembly. His Majesty's Government's statement of 6 December was the last effective effort to bring the Congress and the League together, in framing a constitution for a united India.[209] The political changes in India had affected Attlee's thinking as well and now he stated:

There has never been any prospect of success for the Constituent Assembly, except upon the basis of an agreed procedure. Should a Constitution come to be framed by a Constituent Assembly in which a large section of the Indian population had not been represented, His Majesty's Government could not of course contemplate—as the Congress have stated they would not contemplate—forcing such a Constitution upon any unwilling parts of the country.[210]

The 6 December statement of His Majesty's Government had satisfied neither the League nor the Congress because it had failed to offer an authoritative and clear verdict about the intentions of the Cabinet Mission. Nehru's reaction was that Attlee's statement amounted to an addition to the plan and he gave the impression that the Congress might decide to withdraw from the Constituent Assembly and even perhaps from the Interim Government.[211] Attlee rejected this interpretation and told Nehru that he could not admit that any addition had been made to the statement of 16 May.[212] Sardar Patel described it as 'a betrayal'.[213]

The All-India Congress Working Committee in its meeting of 6 January accepted the statement of 6 December with some reservations:

There must be no interference whatsoever by any external authority, and no compulsion of any province or part of a province by another province. The AICC realises and appreciates the difficulties in the way of some provinces, notably Baluchistan, Assam, the N.W.F.P. and the Sikhs in the Punjab, by the British Cabinet Scheme of 16th May 1946 and more especially by the interpretation put upon it by the British Government in their statement of 6th December 1946.[214]

Wavell was not satisfied with the Congress's conditional acceptance as he feared that it would not 'be enough to bring in the Muslim League,'[215] into the Constituent Assembly. Now Congress tried to use the 6 December statement for its own ends and instead of pledging solemnly that it would abide by it, stated that it would be prepared to abide by an Indian Federal Court's ruling on the interpretation of the Grouping clause.[216] The fact was that the British Government had failed to set 'Jinnah's mind at ease or budge him from his intransigent position.'[217]

The first session of the assembly took place on 9 December and Rajendra Prasad was elected its president. Since no Muslim League member was in attendance its estrangement with the Congress increased even more. In defiance of the limits specified in the Cabinet Mission Plan, a committee on rules of procedure, with power to frame rules not only for the full Constituent Assembly but also for Sections B and C and other committees, was formed by the brute majority of the Congress members present, with Dr Ambedkar as the only dissident. On 13 December Nehru, moved the noted 'Objectives Resolution' and the session was then adjourned till 20 January 1947.

COMPULSORY GROUPING: ASSAM LEGISLATIVE ASSEMBLY RESOLUTION

Even the conditional acceptance by Congress of His Majesty's Government's statement of 6 December had upset Gandhi to the extent that he advised the representatives of Assam and Sikhs in the Constituent Assembly to refuse to go into their respectively allocated sections and he stressed the inclusion of the following paragraph in that statement:

> It must be clearly understood however that this must not involve any compulsion of a province, and that the right of the Sikhs in the Punjab should not be jeopardized. In the event of any attempt at such compulsion, the province or part of a province has a right to take such action as may be deemed necessary in order to give effect to the wishes of the people concerned.[218]

At Gandhi's and Congress's behest, therefore, the Working Committee of Assam Provincial Congress passed a resolution on 18 January 1947 in which they stated, 'The Committee reiterates that the constitution for Assam shall be framed by her own representatives only.'[219] It further complicated any understanding which might have emerged between the Congress and the League about the Cabinet Mission Plan. Assam had about 3.5 million Hindus, 3.4 million Muslims, 0.7 million Scheduled Castes, and 2.6 million tribesmen, Christians and others.[220] Later, a civil disobedience movement started which resulted in Hindu–Muslim riots in that province.[221]

All these political moves very simply meant that Congress and Gandhi had no intention of letting Jinnah get away with a Pakistan comprising of six provinces by disguising them as 'groups of provinces', in the first instance. Nehru's statements of those times that the smaller provinces like NWFP, Sindh, and Balochistan would not be happy with a big province like Punjab have deeply affected even the post-partition intra-province relations within Pakistan (West) till the present day.

WORKING OF THE CONSTITUENT ASSEMBLY

Bipen Chandra has observed, 'Nehru's approach to the communal problem proved to be a complete failure because of its very impracticability. His radicalism blocked the path of negotiations and compromise at the top which was in the end adopted with disastrous results in 1947.'[222] On 22 January, the Constituent Assembly, whose proceedings were boycotted by the Muslim League, unanimously passed a resolution declaring 'a firm and solemn resolve to proclaim India as an independent, sovereign republic.' It was a clear indication that without the League the Congress was bent upon taking unilateral decisions. Both Wavell and Maulana Azad were unhappy with this development[223] and thought that it was bound to result in a deterioration of the Congress-League relationship and ultimately the Hindu–Muslim relationship. Wavell got especially disturbed about these developments and thought that the Congress had been unwise and short-sighted in providing all the excuses for the League to abstain from attending the Constituent Assembly. In his eyes, not only had its acceptance of the statement of 6 December been unequivocal but the conduct of business in the Constituent Assembly, which met on 9 December, and again on 20 January, had been unnecessarily provocative, especially Nehru's premature resolution in favour of a republic. He also held Gandhi responsible 'for his mixing politics with prayers and chicanery with piety in his usual sanctimonious but cryptic fashion.'[224]

Even a Sikh historian, Sangat Singh said that, Congress's acceptance of the 6 December statement on 6 January 1947 was so conditional that Jinnah treated it as a repudiation of the Cabinet Mission Plan.[225] The Working Committee of the League, in its resolution of 31 January 1947 decided not to call upon the Muslim League Council to reconsider its withdrawal of acceptance of the Cabinet Mission Plan. It denounced the composition and procedure of the Constituent Assembly as null and void, invalid and illegal. The League demanded from the British government the declaration that the Cabinet Mission had failed because the Congress had not really accepted it. The Sikhs and the Scheduled Castes had also rejected it. Therefore, the League demanded the dissolution of the Constituent Assembly. The Congress ministers[226] in turn responded by demanding from Wavell on 5 February 1947 the resignation of the League members from the Interim Government. In response to this, Wavell has recorded, 'V.P. Menon, whom I saw this afternoon, usually so optimistic, was gloomy about the position and thinks that the partition of India is now inevitable. He says the League reckon on this, and expect to capture the Punjab Government soon.'[227] This was not the end of Congress's actions concerning the League's continued boycott of the Constituent Assembly because Nehru demanded the same in a letter to Wavell on 13 February.[228] Right on the following day, i.e. on 14 February, Patel threatened that the Congress members would withdraw from the Cabinet if the representatives of the League did not quit forthwith.[229]

By this time, Wavell felt deeply frustrated as his ideal of preserving a united India was being shattered. Writing to King George VI of England on 24 February 1947, he said,

> League's resolution (of 31 January 1947) seems to me to be based largely on the naval theory of "A Fleet in being". So long as they remain in the sheltering harbours or narrow waters of Sindh, Bengal and the Punjab, and do not risk the superior broadsides of the Congress in the open seas of the Constituent Assembly at Delhi, they feel that they still have a chance of securing a Pakistan of some sort.[230]

Civil Disobedience Movement (February–March 1947)

A fresh development of significant import, however, soon precipitated a fresh crisis. The province of Punjab had occupied the crux of the whole struggle for Pakistan. Although the League had captured 79 seats in the provincial Legislative Assembly out of 175 in the 1945 elections, it was denied power, and Khizar Hayat, the Unionist leader, formed a government with the support of Congress and the Sikhs. Khizar outlawed both Muslim League National Guard and Hindu extremist organisation Rashtriya Swayamsewak Sangh (RSS) to avoid any direct clashes which might have led to communal riots in the Punjab.[231] The supporters of the League defied the ban and staged protests against the decision. The Hindus organized counter demonstrations and thus communal tension mounted to its highest pitch which raised fears of a civil war between the Muslims on one hand and Hindus supported by Sikhs on the other. Consequently, Khizar had to resign on 3 March but the Muslim League was still denied the formation of a government. Even Evan Jenkins, the Governor of Punjab, expecting that the trouble could take an anti-European turn, suggested evacuation of the British from Punjab ahead of the rest of India. It was quite an anti-thesis of Wavell's Breakdown Plan.[232]

On 17 February, Liaquat Ali Khan, Finance Member in the Interim Government, stated categorically at Aligarh that only the establishment of an independent Muslim state, Pakistan, would satisfy Muslim sentiments. Three days later, on 20 February, Attlee announced the definite intention of His Majesty's Government 'to take the necessary steps to effect the transference of power into responsible Indian hands by a date not later than June 1948.' Although hesitant as to the final outcome, the players in the last act of the Indian freedom movement, had taken up their positions and India prepared for the end of the British Raj.[233]

In fact, in February 1947, there was large scale violence in Bengal and Punjab while NWFP experienced a widespread civil disobedience movement launched by the League; the food position was at the breaking point and from the British point of view the situation was intolerable. The British would have to either re-establish their authority in India or transfer responsibility immediately. Attlee decided to quit India with a new policy and with a new Viceroy.

The Cabinet Mission had intended to bring about an agreement amongst Indian leaders on the principles and procedure to be followed in framing a constitution for an independent India and they struggled hard for achievement of this goal. According to Ronald Lewin the delegation was 'not enjoined to impose, or to recommend for imposition, any solution; nor were they to be concerned with the details of a future constitutional structure. They were not principals but mediators.'[234]

Jinnah had found in the Cabinet Mission Plan the seed and substance of his demand for Pakistan and believed that it could be a reality after ten years. He had been a constitutionalist throughout his life and believed in negotiated settlements. He, therefore, was fully conscious of the growing Hindu–Muslim tension which might lead to a civil war and he wanted to avoid it all costs. Congress, on the other hand, wanted to completely disregard the Pakistan issue and preferred to focus totally on their demand for the complete freedom of India in the first place in order to grab power without caring whatsoever for the cost.

For the Congress it was vital to preserve the unity of India and it also felt that only a unitary form of government could in the long run guarantee rapid economic and industrial development. If these objects were missing, it was ready to allow the League to have a Pakistan but of its (Congress's) choice and one which could not survive for long on its own and would be soon forced to rejoin India. It considered its demand that the provinces should be given the choice to opt out from the groups as legal and genuine; this would help her include the provinces of Assam and the NWFP in 'their' Hindustan. In Jinnah's eyes, this demand was fantastic and claptrap.

R.J. Moore has recorded that the upper-most concern in official minds was that of imperial defence, and for that purpose a united India was considered to be in Britain's best interests.[235] The British could claim that they were serious about transfer of power to the Indians and in promoting an agreed solution among the political parties, thereby leaving the field open for friendly relations in the future.[236] They desired all kinds of cordial relations with an independent India but their primary concern was commerce[237] because of its importance to Britain in the post-war situation. This consideration accounts for the evident eagerness of the British government not to oppose the Congress, since they believed that it would be the Hindu India, which would control the bulk of Indian trade and industry.[238] Therefore, V.P. Menon, a Hindu secretary to Viceroy, warned, 'If we cannot rehabilitate our economy and politics, I am afraid we will be bound to have trouble next year.'[239] He advised the British government,

Congress is now exactly in the same position as the Liberals were in 1919 before the split, and if we do not support the Right Wing, which is now in office, we will be swamped by the left and we shall have to thank ourselves for it. I feel that I am like a man in an aeroplane which is going to crash and even if I know how to save it I am powerless to do so.[240]

Ayesha Jalal has recorded that 'London's deadline set the stage for an understanding between the Attlee government and the Congress high command. Both sides wanted India to have independence soon, and both wanted a constitution which gave a strong unitary centre—the British because this was the best way of assuring their economic and strategic interests in South Asia, and the Congress high command because a strong unitary centre would enable it control its provinces and discipline its followers.'[241]

According to David Blake, Wavell was a progressive and a liberal but turned conservative in his last days and opposed the termination of the British Empire and fixing a date for the British departure.[242] Though the point looks valid, it seems a somewhat unfair assessment of Wavell's thoughts as they evolved in the light of his experiences with Indian politics. In reality, there was a chain of events which had convinced him that the actions of the Congress would lead to the division of India. Wavell asked Nehru to take the League into confidence as not doing so would create administrative problems.[243] Nehru replied that the Constituent Assembly would carry on its business and 'obviously could not force a constitution on unwilling provinces.'[244]

When Wavell received a telegram from Whitehall with reference to the Congress request for the removal of the League members from the government, he thought the British government would issue the statement for the early termination of British Raj. Thus, Wavell, on 9 February 1947, while giving an appreciation of the political situation in India, strongly recommended that a final attempt should still be made to bring all parties into the Constituent Assembly before announcing a date for the withdrawal of British authority. Subsequently, he also sent a draft statement in this regard. His suggestion proves that he was sincerely determined to keep India united and wished to make a last ditch effort to help both the Congress and the League to come to terms, because he did not realise that it was already too late. But Whitehall thought that his suggestion was inconsistent with his older ideas and suggestions, so instead of following up on his latest advice, Whitehall on 20 March 1947 replaced him with Mountbatten.

It was expected that the Cabinet Mission Plan would help Wavell sidestep the division of India, preserving the rights and interests of Muslims and other minorities at the same time, but the attempt had failed. Its failure precipitated the process of transfer of power, not to a united India but to two independent and sovereign states, India and Pakistan. Although it seemed for a while as if Wavell just might succeed in achieving his goal, but neither the British government nor the Congress and the Muslim League due to their clashing interests displayed any readiness in helping him achieve it.

Wavell's main thesis about the Hindu–Muslim problem had been that formation of a coalition government of the main political parties would create a team spirit and thereby, after sharing power, they would be able to solve their problems including overcoming the demand for Pakistan. Formation of the Interim Government did provide such an opportunity but eventually that attempt also failed. The working of the Interim Government will be analyzed in the fourth chapter.

NOTES

1. The Second World War had delayed the holding of elections and so held the political process in abeyance. As a result, the claims of Congress and the League and other parties, had been judged through the results of by-elections, intelligence reports and other sources, yet these were not considered perfect yardsticks for a correct assessment of the political parties' standing among the masses. The results of the general elections could validate their demands. Muslim League under Jinnah emphatically demanded fresh general elections. But given the weak, disorganized League of 1935, with its small membership and extremely limited appeal, one is filled with wonder at the revolution in Muslim politics which the party had brought about in a decade. For details see: Z.H. Zaidi, 'Aspects of the Development of Muslim League Policy, 1937–47', in *The Partition of India: Policies and Perspectives 1935–1947*, eds., C.H. Philips and Mary Doreen Wainwright (London: George Allen & Unwin, 1970), p. 274.

2. The war ended on 15 August 1945.

3. Whitehall had been suggesting holding an election merely to sideline the Wavell Plan, but Wavell did not agree as he thought it would widen the gulf between the Muslims and the Hindus. Wavell had reason to believe that the Muslim League would not agree to a constitution-making body of this kind save on the basis of the partition of India. Many persons and agencies had been indicating the negative

implications of the elections. Contrary to these reservations, the ground reality was that the year 1945 was entirely different from the year that had preceded it. The Governors' Conference also pointed out the urgency for such a political exercise. On 10 July 1945, Clement Attlee replaced Churchill as prime minister of England. He issued a number of statements regarding India and promised to give complete freedom.

4. Wavell, though he did not like Labour's victory in the elections, was happy as the Labour government would be sympathetic towards India, and would take more interest in solving its problems.

5. Therefore, in order to determine the modalities, Wavell went to England on 24 August and returned on 16 September. He made a final announcement on 19 September 1945. Wavell to Pethick–Lawrence, 21 August 1945, Wavell Collection, MSS Eur D 977/2.

6. Wavell to Lawrence, 23 September 1945, Wavell Collection, MSS Eur D 977/2.

7. Maulana Abul Kalam Azad, then president of the Congress, wrote a letter to Wavell protesting about the announcement of elections in the country. He contemplated that it would be a glaring injustice to hold elections without first allowing the Congress to function normally, and for sufficient time, in order to organize elections. Sardar Patel thought that it was another effort on the part of the British authorities to deny Congress its right of forming governments in the provinces and at the Centre. He demanded that the Congress be allowed to form a national government right then. Azad to Wavell, 22 August 1945, Wavell's Official Correspondence with Persons in India, January to August 1946, IOR, MSS Eur D 977/15.

8. Agreeing with this Sardar Patel also believed that the Congress could not 'afford to have any truck with the League' as it was obstructing the freedom of the country which in his eyes was a sin', *Indian Annual Register*, 1945, Vol. II, p. 98.

9. Ibid.

10. Ibid.

11. *Dawn*, 21 September 1945.

12. Wavell and some other Government officials, like the Governor of Bengal, Richard Gardiner Casey, truly believed that Jinnah had not properly defined Pakistan. Casey recorded, 'I asked Nazimuddin many questions about Pakistan. Very little has been discussed or worked out by them. I said that I thought it would also be extremely difficult for Calcutta to be included and I suggested that it might be treated as a 'free port' between Pakistan and Hindustan'. But stating the Muslim League's position, Khawaja Nazimuddin had argued that the analogy of Burma regarding which a decision (to separate it from India] was taken first and then the details were worked out.' Personal Diary, R.G. Casey, Bengal 1945–1946, May 1945–February 1946, 22 August 1945, MSS EUR 048/4.

13. Ibid.

14. For details see: Governor General (War Department) to Secretary of State, 21 August 1945, *Transfer of Power*, Vol. VI, pp. 109–111.

15. Some of the senior personnel of the INA were being tried in November 1945 in the Red Fort in Delhi. The Muslim League associated itself with the defence team for

the Indian National Army's Muslim personnel but Jinnah himself stayed away from the trial.

16. In the elections, Lawrence asked Wavell to allow more freedom of expression to the leaders. He wrote that in view of importance of securing an informed public opinion in this country regarding Indian elections he would consult BBC with a view to facilities being granted to Indian leaders to give broadcast talks to the British public. Lawrence to Wavell, 14 November 1945, Wavell Collections, p. 127.

17. Sikandar Hayat, *The Charismatic Leader: Quaid-i-Azam Mohammad Ali Jinnah and the Creation of Pakistan* (Karachi: Oxford University Press, 2008), p. 237.

18. The Women's Wing of the Muslim League was founded in 1937 which became extremely active in the elections of 1945–6. Some important leaders of the Wing were Fatima Jinnah, Shaista Ikramullah, Ra'na Liaquat Ali Khan, etc. For details see: Sarfaraz Hussain Mirza, *Muslim Women's Role in the Pakistan Movement* (Lahore: Punjabi Adabi Academy, 1969); Shaista Ikramullah, *From Purdah to Parliament* (Karachi: Oxford University Press); Mohammad Noman, *Our Struggle 1857–1947: A Political Record* (Karachi: Pakistan Publications), pp. 85–100.

19. The All-India Muslim Student Union was founded in 1937 and became extremely active in the elections of 1945–46. Their active support and involvement enabled the Muslim League to win the election against the more active, organized and government backed Unionist in the Punjab and the experienced and more powerful in terms of money and resources, Congress. For details see, Sarfraz Hussain Mirza, *Youth and the Pakistan Movement* (Lahore: Nazariya-i-Pakistan Foundation, 2004); Sarfraz Mirza, *The Punjab Muslim Student Federation: 1937–1947* (Islamabad: National Institute of Historical and Cultural Research, 1991); Mukhtar Zaman, *Students' Role in the Pakistan Movement* (Karachi: Quaid-i-Azam Academy, 1978).

20. For details see Sikandar Hayat, *Aspects of Pakistan Movement* (Lahore: Progressive Publishers, 1991).

21. A detailed study could be found in David Gilmartin, *Empire and Islam*; Sarah Ansari, *The Sufis, Saints and State Power: The Pirs of Sindh* (Cambridge, 1992); H.B. Khan, *Bar-i-Sagheer Pak-O-Hind Ki Siyasat Main Ulema Ka Kirdar* (Islamabad: National Institute of History and Culture, 1985).

22. For details see: manifesto of the Muslim League, Sharifuddin Pirzada, *Foundations of Pakistan*, Vol. II.

23. However, Ian Talbot writes that during the election campaign in Punjab the Muslim League's Islamic appeals transcended 'bread and butter issue'. For details see Ian Talbot, *Khizar Tiwana, the Punjab Unionist Party and the Partition of India* (London: Curzon Press, 1996), p. 132.

24. Mushir ul Haq, *Muslim Politics in Modern India, 1857–1947* (Lahore: Book Traders, n.d.).

25. Chaudhry Khaliquzzaman, *Pathway to Pakistan* (Lahore: Brothers Publishers, 1961); S.M. Ikram, *Modern Muslim India and the Birth of Pakistan* (Lahore: Sh. Muhammad Ashraf, 1970).

26. Peter Hardy, *The Muslims of British India*, pp. 237–8.

27. Vijai Shankar Rai, *The Last Phase of the Transfer of Power in India* (New Delhi: Arnold Publishers, 1990), p. 6.

28. The Sindh Muslim League prepared for the general elections and decided to contest all the 35 Muslim seats in the Sindh Assembly. Dow Collections, MSS Eur D 670/5; *Indian Annual Register*, 1945, Vol. II, p. 10.

29. People like Mian Iftikhar-ud-din, President of the Punjab Congress branch; Khan Abdul Qayyum Khan, leader of the Congress in NWFP, etc., joined the Muslim League and strengthened its position in their respective provinces.

30. Dow Collections, MSS Eur D 670/5.

31. The election results of Sindh Assembly came out on 21 January 1946; the League secured 60.46 per cent votes. The details could be found in Khalid Shamsul Hasan, *Sindh's Fight for Pakistan* (Karachi: Shamsul Hasan Foundation for Historical Studies & Research, 1992), p. 155; G.A. Allana, *The Story of a Nation: Quaid-e-Azam Jinnah*, pp. 390–1.

32. G.A. Allana, *Quaid-e-Azam Jinnah: The Story of a Nation*, p. 392.

33. In his letter, Dow, the Governor of Sindh, writes, 'I received frantic appeals to prevent ministers influencing the elections, but took no notice of them Nichaldas has been taking round in his train...Pir Muhammad Rashdi who is opponent of the official League candidate, Yousaf Haroon. It is generally believed that Rashdi is being paid generously from Congress funds.' Dow to Wavell, 4 December 1945, Dow Collections, MSS Eur D 670/5, pp. 89–90.

34. Jinnah contested the election from Bombay Urban Constituency. His opponent was Hussain Bhai Lalji, an Ismaili who was being backed by the Congress. At the request of Rahimtoola, another Ismaili pro-League leader, Aga Khan instructed the Ismailis to vote for Jinnah. For details see, Mukhtar Zaman, Quaid-i-Azam Mohammad Ali Jinnah as a Parliamentarian,' in *Pakistani Scholars on Quaid-i-Azam Mohammad Ali Jinnah*, ed., Riaz Ahmad (Islamabad: NIPS, 1999), pp. 43–5.

35. In one of his letters to Lord Wavell, Dow writes, 'G.M. Syed continues, in league with the Congress minister Nichaldas, openly to work against the official League candidates, but as yet lacks the courage to break away from the League organization, while at the same time the L[eague] hesitates to expel him. Meanwhile rank and file of the C[ongress], realizing that Syed is at heart a fanatic communalist, look askance at Nichaldas's flirting with him, though they realize that Nichaldas has done much to ensure Congress success.' Dow to Wavell, 25 November 1945, Dow collections, MSS Eur D 670/5, p. 86.

36. Dow writes, 'Yousaf Haroon has been returned to the Central Assembly by a comfortable majority over Pir Rashdi. Political interest has now been switched over entirely to the Provincial elections, and, still Nichaldas's idea is that Rashdi should stand as an anti-League candidate against Khan Bahadur Khuhro who has a safe seat in Larkana district. Nichaldas told me that Rashdi has no chance, but the idea was to keep Khuhro enclosed in Larkana instead of having him free to stump the country on behalf of the more shaky League candidates. My Premier is very anxious to get Nichaldas out of the cabinet at once, but cannot get him to resign. He told me that in the North-West Frontier Province, Cunningham had forced one of his ministers, Abbas Khan, to resign under threat of dismissal on the ground that, he had changed his allegiance from the Congress to the Muslim League since his

appointment.' Dow to Wavell, 21 December 1945, ibid., pp. 91–3; see also Ian Talbot, *Khizar Tiwana, the Punjab Unionist Party and the Partition of India*, pp. 129–40.

37. S. Muhammad Asif Rizvi, 'Quaid-i-Azam and the Punjab: 1936–46', in Riaz Ahmad, *Pakistan Scholars on Quaid-i-Azam Mohammad Ali Jinnah*, pp. 201–21.

38. Ian Talbot, *Provincial Politics and the Pakistan Movement: The Growth of the Muslim League in North-West and North-East India 1937–47* (Karachi: Oxford University Press, 1988), pp. 98–100.

39. For details see David Gilmartin, *Empire and Islam and Demand for Pakistan*; Sarah Ansari, *The Sufis, Saints and State Power: The Pirs of Sindh*.

40. The League in conducting its election campaign had trained workers, imbued with missionary zeal to fight for the national cause. They were drawn from the poor classes and students of colleges and universities, particularly those of Aligarh, Lahore, Calcutta, and Dacca.

41. Casey reports to Wavell, 'As I believe has turned out to be the case in all other provinces, the elections have shown that the only two parties that count are Congress and League which are backed solidly (at least in Bengal) by the Hindus and Muslims respectively. The nationalist Muslims have made a poor show—having forfeited their deposits in many cases. No one seems to doubt that the Congress and the Muslim League successes will be repeated in coming provincial elections.' Casey to Wavell, 7 January 1946, Wavell official correspondence with persons in India, January to August 1946, Wavell Collections, MSS Eur D 977/15, pp. 4–6.

42. Ibid.

43. W. Norman Brown, 'India's Pakistan Issue', *Proceedings of the American Philosophical Society*, Vol. 91, No. 2 (April 1947), pp. 162–180.

44. The Congress despite its network, past organizational experience and huge resources which were provided by big industrialists like Tata and Birla failed to impress Muslim voters. Sir Francis Brown asked Sir Gregory 'what would be the attitude of Big Businessmen in the election? Gregory said they would, of course, back Congress.' Lecture from Gregory 10 September 1945, Sir Theodore Gregory Collection, MSS Eur D 1163/11.

45. The Majlis-i-Ahrar, Jamiat-i-Ulema-i-Hind, All-India Shia Conference, All-India Momin Conference, Khaksars etc., were the Muslim parties, which were against the Muslim League. These parties were rebuffed by the wave for Pakistan and lost elections by a huge margin and forfeited their surety bond in most of the cases. V.P. Menon writes that the Muslim League won almost every Muslim seat whereas the nationalist Muslims forfeited their deposits in many instances. V.P. Menon, *The Transfer of Power*, p. 226.

46. Sekhar Bandyopadhyay discusses the causes that made the 'dalit' to vote for the Congress. Among other causes the most important was the fear of the Muslim domination over the Hindus after the creation of Pakistan. It was religious fervour of Hinduism that the distinction between low-castes and the caste-Hindus overpowered. Sekhar Bandyopadhyay, 'Hindu Solidarity and Dalit identity: Discourse of Hegemony in Colonial Bengal', (Calcutta) *Prachya: A Journal of Asia: Past and Present*, No. 1, 2002, pp. 1–41.

47. There was a strong solidarity between the Congress and Hindu Mahasabha leaders against the demand for Pakistan. It needs to be investigated how and why Hindu Mahasabha merged into the Congress fold in the 1945–6 elections and almost lost its identity.

48. The communist and socialist Hindus joined the Congress and the Muslim communists like Mian Iftikhar-ud-din joined the Muslim League.

49. Some historians also tend to belittle the significance of this election. Though the electorate was heavily restricted to about 10 per cent of the population; this was interpreted as a popular mandate. However, the Hindus and the Sikhs interpreted their respective candidates' victories based on voting by almost the same percentage of Hindu and Sikh voters. Sekhar Bandyopadhyay, *From Plassey to Partition* (Hyderabad: Orient Longman Private Limited, Reprint 2004), p. 448.

50. In the recent past, attention has been focused on the exploration of the non-religious aspects, such as political, economic, and social, of the Pakistan Movement.

51. The general elections of 1945–46 turned out to be the real test for the Muslim League and its opponent Muslim parties. In the NWFP, the Khudai Khidmatgars, an ally of the Congress won 21 seats, four more than those secured by the Muslim League but in number of votes polled, the Muslim League's share was larger than that of the Congress. This election result was the peg on the basis of which Nehru and Dr Khan Sahib persuaded Mountbatten to include a plebiscite in the NWFP on the question of its joining Pakistan or India in his 3rd June Partition Plan, Qutubuddin Aziz, *Quaid-i-Azam Mohammad Ali Jinnah and the Battle for Pakistan*, pp. 73–92.

52. In the pre-election period the League had tried hard, particularly in Bengal, to strengthen its rural base by appealing to the religious sentiments of the people. This combined with the call for end of landlordism and land to the people gave the League a breakthrough in these Muslim majority areas. Bhashyam Kasturi, *Walking Alone: Gandhi and India's Partition* (New Delhi: Vision Books Ltd., 2001), p. 25.

53. Wavell feared that the Labour government might try to hand over 'India to their Congress friends as soon as possible', Sumit Sarkar, *Modern India* (New Delhi: McMillan Ltd., 1983), p. 417.

54. The breakdown of the seats won by the Muslim League province-wise is as follows: Assam 31; Bengal 113 out of 119; NWFP 17 out f 38; Bihar 34 out 40; UP 54 out of 66; and Sindh 28 out of 35. Later in the second general elections held in December 1946, the position went up to 35 out of 35 in Sindh; 30 out of 30 in Bombay; Madras 29 out of 29; CP 13 out of 14 (the remaining member later joined the Muslim League); 4 out of 4 in Orissa. The League thus won 440 out of 495 seats, i.e., approximately 88 per cent.

55. The delegation consisted of suitable members of both houses of the Parliament. The following were the members of the delegation: R. Richards (leader of the Delegation); R. Sorensen; Mrs Muriel H. Nichol; A.G. Bottomley; Major Woodrow Wyatt; Godfrey Nicholson; A.R. Low; R. Hopkins Morris (MP, labour); Earl of Munster; Lord Chorley of Kendal.

56. The Labour government had decided to send a Parliamentary Delegation, consisted of ten members, on 19 November 1945, but it arrived on 5 January 1946. Wavell

observed that 'their knowledge of India is not very comprehensive but they are keen and interested. I know four of them before—Sorensen, Low, Nicholson, and Munster.' The delegation met various political leaders including Gandhi, Azad, Nehru, and Jinnah. In his talks with the delegation, Jinnah explained the League's stand with regard to the constitutional development and made it clear that the League would take no part in an interim government without a prior declaration for accepting the principle of Pakistan.

57. On the other hand, the Muslim League maintained that this was not just a difference of opinion between the two political parties. Both parties represented two different nations. Enclosure to No. 429, *Transfer of Power*, Vol. VI, pp. 970–5.

58. Cripps to Nehru, 12 January 1946. Ibid.

59. Proshanta Nandi, 'Visions of Nationhood and Religiosity among Early Freedom Fighters in India', in *Nation and National Identity in South Asia*, eds., S.L. Sharma and T.K. Ommen, (New Delhi: Orient Longman, 2000), pp. 145–46.

60. Nehru opined that the British introduced separate electorates which had grown now to 'poison all our national life and prevent progress with the growth of national movement, the British government and its agents intensified their support of separatist tendencies. In particular they encouraged the growth of the Muslim League.' He believed that 'Pakistan' as such was hardly understood or appreciated by most members of the League; it was a sentimental slogan. He said that 'in the result there is likely to be Congress majority in 8 provinces that is in all except Sind, Punjab and Bengal. Jinnah appeared to be wholly intransigent and threatened bloodshed and rioting if any thing was done without his consent.' Nehru to Cripps, 27 January 1946, *Transfer of Power*, Vol. VII, pp. 851–59.

61. To Nehru 'the crux of the Pakistan issue is that: A Pakistan consisting of only parts of Punjab and part of Bengal, no separation at all. He suggested to establishing a federation of autonomous units with minimum list of compulsory common subjects. They would be defence, foreign affairs, communications, currency etc. this would give a maximum freedom and self-reliance to the units and a sense of functioning. Further there could be any number of safeguards for minorities and finally a supreme court would be empowered to protect the minority rights. He proposed that 'finally if a definite area expresses its will clearly in favour of separatism and this is feasible, no compulsion will be exercised to force it to remain in the Federation or Union. But it can not take other areas away with it against their will, and there must be a clear decision by plebiscite of all the adult voters of that area.'

62. Nehru said that it would be impossible to hang up everything simply because Jinnah did not agree. He tried to appeal Labour's socialist programme by suggesting that the Muslim League membership was far too reactionary (they were mostly landlord) and opposed to social change to dare to indulge in any form of direct action. He said, 'They are incapable of it, having spent their lives in soft jobs. It was very likely that there might be riots, especially in the UP probably encouraged by local officials and the police who wanted to discredit Congress.' There would be no real strength behind them even if there was some strength it was impossible to hold everything for fear of them. He warned that the other consequences were of graver import. Ibid.

63. Ibid.

64. Nehru to Cripps, 27 January 1946, *Transfer of Power*, Vol. VII, pp. 851–59.

65. In his address to the newly elected Central Legislature on 28 January 1946, Wavell revealed government's will to establish a new Executive Council composed of political leaders, and to bring about a constitution-making body or convention as soon as possible. Commenting on Wavell's speech, Jinnah said that there was no reason now to talk of any arrangements to set up an interim government; the war had come to an end and they had to tackle the main issues which would result in a permanent settlement of India's constitutional problems. He said that it was far better to expedite means of arriving at a permanent settlement in which the question of Pakistan must form a major issue. B.N. Pandey, *The Indian Nationalist Movement 1885–1947*.

66. On 28 January 1946 Wavell announced that he would establish a new Executive Council composed of the main political parties and also set up a Constitution-making body as soon as possible. His Excellency, the Viceroy's Speech to the Central Legislative Assembly, 28 January 1946, *Transfer of power*, Vol. VI, Annexure III, No. 44, pp. 1013–5.

67. I.H. Qureshi, *The Struggle For Pakistan*, p. 245.

68. Justice Syed Shameem Hussaain Kadri, *Creation of Pakistan* (Rawalpindi: Army Book Cub, 1983), pp. 327–8.

69. This pleased Gandhi as well as Nehru who became very optimist about it. Mohammad Ashraf, ed., *Cabinet Mission and After* (Lahore: Mohammad Ashraf, n.d.), p. 2.

70. Ibid., p. 3.

71. Ronald Lewin, *The Chief: Lord Wavell A Military Viceroy*, p. 237.

72. The Cabinet Delegation consisted of Lord Pethick-Lawrence, Alexander and Cripps.

73. When they came to India, the Congress, including some Muslims in their ranks, claimed to speak for All India. The Congress insisted that the sovereignty of the people must be exercised through their elected representatives in a strong central government, with powers to overrule provinces. On the other side, Jinnah claimed to speak for all Muslims. The Muslim League wanted the division of India and establishment of Pakistan on the basis of the Lahore Resolution. Both sides hoped that the British should take the initiative and decide. However, the British would not as they held to the principle that India should draft her own constitution. Jack Bazalgette, *The Captains and the Kings Depart* (Oxford: The Amate Press Ltd., 1984), IOR, MSS Eur F 226/2, part 2, Chapter 10.

74. Record of meeting of Cabinet Delegation and Wavell on 28 March 1946, ibid., pp. 24–9.

75. Statement by Lord Pethick-Lawrence and Cripps on their arrival in India 23 March 1946, ibid., pp. 1–2.

76. K.M. Munshi, *Pilgrimage to Freedom*, Vol. I, pp. 970–5.

77. On 3 April 1946, Azad as the President of the Congress met the Mission.

78. Record of Meeting between Cabinet Delegation, Wavell and Gandhi, 3 April 1946, Wavell Collections, IOR, MSS Eur D 997/18.

79. The meeting between Jinnah and the Cabinet Mission took place on 4 April and lasted for three hours. Dewan Ram Parkash, *Cabinet Mission in India* (Lahore: Tagore Memorial Publications, 1946), p. 43.
80. Jinnah said that throughout her history, from the days of Chandragupta Maurya, there had never been any Government of India in the sense of a single government. The Mughal Empire had had the largest control but even in those days the Marathas and Rajputs were not under Muslim rule. When the British came they gradually established their rule in a large part of India but, even then India was only one-third united. The big states and sovereign states are constitutionally and legally already Pakistan. Record of Meeting between Cabinet Delegation, Wavell and Jinnah, 4 April 1946, Wavell Collections, IOR, MSS Eur D 997/18.
81. Ibid.
82. Ibid.
83. He claimed that Islam and Hinduism were two entirely divergent cultures and civilizations. It would be great injustice to the Muslims if the British left a hundred million Muslims under the mercy of 250 million Hindus. This would result in the permanent rule of Hindu majority over the Muslim minority.
84. Wavell, *Viceroy's Journal*, p. 236.
85. Jamil-ud-din, *The Final Phase of the Struggle for Pakistan*, p. 36.
86. Jinnah soon realized that things were not moving in the right direction for the Muslim League. So, in order to consolidate his case for Pakistan and multiply the pressure on the Delegation, he called the convention of those Muslim League members who had been elected in the Central and Provincial assemblies. The Convention held in Delhi on 9–11 April, was attended by four hundred delegates. Huseyn Shaheed Suhrawardy moved a resolution, demanding one unified Pakistan, instead of two zones. It also demanded that there should be two-Constitution-making bodies, one for Pakistan and the other for Hindustan. A number of exciting speeches were delivered, showing strong commitment to achieve this goal. Jinnah warned the British government that no power on earth could deprive the Muslims from getting their self-determination. He said that 'Britain can only delay Pakistan, but no power on earth can deny Pakistan.' Jamil-ud-din, *The Final Phase of the Struggle for Pakistan*, pp. 34–38.
87. Pethick–Lawrence wrote to Jinnah 'Dear Jinnah, some of your public utterances which have been recently reinforced from our private sources…I gather that you feel that not only did I commit a breach of faith towards you but in addition I was guilty of personal discourtesy to you when we met at the Viceroy's House on 25 June.' Pethick–Lawrence to Jinnah, 15 August 1946, Lawrence Collections, IOR, MSS Eur.
88. When Jinnah was again interviewed on 16 April, he came up not only with a new hope, courage and faith but also support of the real representatives of the Muslims of India. It was expected that the Delegation would not deal with Jinnah in the same hostile manner as they had done before. Stanley Wolpert, *Jinnah of Pakistan*, p. 260.
89. Attlee to Cabinet Delegation and Wavell, 13 April 1946, *Transfer of Power*, Vol. VII, pp. 260–1.

90. Record of Meeting of Cabinet Delegation and Wavell, 13 April 1946, Wavell Collections, IOR, MSS Eur D 997/18.
91. Wavell to Lascelles, 13 April 1946, Wavell Collections, MSS Eur 997, pp. 119–20.
92. Wavell to Lascelles, 13 April 1946, ibid., pp. 119–20.
93. Dr Ambedkar presented the case of Scheduled Caste Hindus and denounced the Pakistan demand, and also showed dissatisfaction over the growing influence of the Caste Hindus and suggested measures to ensure the interests of his class. Record of Meeting between Cabinet Delegation, Wavell, and Dr B.R. Ambedkar, 5 April 1946, *Transfer of Power*, Vol. VII, pp. 144–46.
94. Record of Meeting between Cabinet Delegation, Wavell and Representatives of the Sikh Community, 5 April 1946, Wavell Collections, IOR, MSS Eur D 997/18.
95. Record of Meeting between Cabinet Delegation, Wavell, and Sardar Baldev Singh, 5 April 1946, ibid.
96. In their strong arguments against the division of Pakistan, the delegation and Wavell always put forward the case of the Sikhs and suggested the division of the Punjab along with the division of India. Though they never promised that Sikhs would be getting their Khalistan, they exploited Sikh fears of Muslim domination against Jinnah's demand for Pakistan.
97. Saleem M.M. Qureshi, *The Politics of Jinnah* (Karachi: Royal Book Company, 1988), p. 115.
98. Azad met the Delegation on 17 April 1946. For detail of their discussions see, Record of Meeting of Cabinet Delegation and Wavell with Azad, 17 April 1946, *Transfer of Power*, Vol. VII, pp. 294–300.
99. Cabinet Delegation to Attlee, 18 April 1946, Attlee Papers.
100. Ibid.
101. Ibid.
102. Record of Meeting of Cabinet Delegation and Wavell, 24 April 1946, Wavell Collections, IOR, MSS Eur D 997/18.
103. Eventually, on 27 April the delegation drafted a letter to be sent to Jinnah and Azad, asking them to delegate four representatives each to meet the Cabinet Mission at Simla for negotiations on a three-tier proposal as a basis for further negotiation and settlement. Record of Meeting of Cabinet Delegation and Wavell, 27 April 1946, *Transfer of Power*, Vol. VII, 147, pp. 349–50.
104. Cabinet Delegation to Attlee, 27 April 1946, *Transfer of Power*, Vol. VII, 148, pp. 350–1.
105. Maulana Azad, in his letter to the Cabinet Mission, 27 April 1946, expressed the point of view of the Congress on the proposed scheme. He said that 'The Congress has never accepted the division of India into predominately Hindu and predominantly Muslim Provinces. It however recognizes that there may be provinces which are willing to delegate to the Central Government subjects in the optional list, while others may agree to delegate only compulsory subjects like Foreign Affairs, Defence, and Communications the Congress has agreed that residuary powers are to vest in the Provinces, but the use of the term "sovereign" in that connection would tend to cause misunderstanding, I would therefore, request that the word may be taken out.'
106. *Transfer of Power*, Vol. VII, pp. 42–526.

107. Record of First Meeting of Second Simla Conference held on 5 May 1946, Wavell Collections, IOR, MSS Eur D 997/18.

108. In the second meeting on the same day, discussion started on the relationship between the Groups and Union in the absence of a Union Legislature. Jinnah agreed with Lawrence that if there was to be a Legislature, the most reasonable agreement would be for the members to be elected in equal numbers by the Group Legislatures. At the start of the third meeting, the Secretary of State explained that one must face the fact that the main reason for the Groups was to get over the communal difficulty, and to make it possible to call together a Constitution-making body. Nehru repeated the old 'theory of conspiracy' that the main problem was the independence of India from the British, and the communal problem would be solved after their departure.

109. Ibid.

110. Ibid.

111. Ibid.

112. The states should set up their own constitution-making machinery in their ways on proportionate basis. The two group Constitution-making bodies and the states' representatives would meet together to decide the constitution of the Union in respect of three subjects. All other matters would be decided in the Group Constitution-making body, both matters of common concern to the group and other matters not of common concern. There could at the outset be a joint meeting of three bodies to decide the agenda and procedure but thereafter they would meet separately except for the determination of the Union Constitution-making body in which decisions on major issues could not be reached without the majority vote of both groups and with freedom to withdraw from it. Ibid.

113. Cripps and other members of the delegation thought that the right of provinces to opt out of the group would force Jinnah to consider his inflexible stand on Pakistan and to accept the three-tier plan.

114. Lord Cripps in his speech in the House of Commons said that there are three possible forms of parity-first, between the Muslim League and Congress on party basis; secondly, between Muslims and Hindus on communal basis; third, between Muslims and Hindus other than scheduled castes. Speech of Lord Cripps, Parliamentary Debates (Hansard) House Of Commons (Official Report] Vol. 425, No. 179, London, 18 July 1946, IOR, MSS Eur F 189/15, pp. 1400–6.

115. Wavell said that we listened to an 'almost inter-mixable repetition of these two cases, stated by various degrees of skill and plausibility, hardly ever with the least originality or the least recognition of the British passion for compromise.' Wavell, Viceroy's Journal, p. 267.

116. Ibid., pp. 260–67.

117. Ibid.

118. Quaid-i-Azam Papers, File No. 20, pp. 144–9; I.H. Qureshi, The Struggle for Pakistan, p. 248; Hodson, Great Divide, pp. 146–7.

119. Wavell was one of the chief architects of the statement as it helped him sidetrack the Pakistan plan. Record of Meeting of Cabinet Delegation and Wavell on 15–16 May 1946, Transfer of Power, Vol. VII, pp. 562–72.

120. For the long-term solution the statement suggested that: (1) There should be a Union of India, embracing both British India and the states, which should deal with the following subjects: Foreign Affairs, Defence and Communications; and should have the powers necessary to raise the finances required for the above subjects. (2) The Union should have an Executive and a Legislature constituted from British India and states representatives. Any question raising a major communal issue in the Legislature should require for its decision a majority of the representatives present and voting of each of the two major communities. All subjects other than the Union subjects and all residuary powers should vest in the provinces. (3) The states will retain all subjects and powers other than those ceded to the Union. (4) The provinces should be free to form groups with executives and legislatures, and each group could determine the provincial subjects to be taken in common. (5) The constitution of the Union and of the group should contain a provision whereby any Province could, by a majority vote to its Legislative Assembly, call for reconsideration of the terms of the constitution after an initial period of ten years and ten-yearly intervals thereafter. The Mission proposed that each province would be allotted a total number of seats proportional to its population, roughly in the ratio of one to a million as the nearest substitute for representation by adult suffrage. This provincial allocation of seats would be divided between the main communities in each province in proportion to their population. The representation allocated to each community would be elected by members of that community in the Provincial Assembly. Statement by the Cabinet Delegation and Wavell on 16 May 1946, Quaid-i-Azam Papers, File No. 20, pp. 144–9.

121. Ibid.

122. Stanley Wolpert, *Jinnah of Pakistan* (Karachi: Oxford University Press, 1999), p. 267.

123. The Muslim League could achieve Pakistan if provisions relating to sections of the Constitution-making body and grouping of provinces could be implemented properly. It was clearly laid down that after a preliminary meeting of the Constitution-making body at which the general order of the business would be decided and a chairman and other officers elected, the provincial representatives would divide up into three sections, A, B, and C. These sections according to paragraph 19 (v) of the plan would 'proceed to settle the provincial constitutions for the group constitutions for the provinces included in each section and shall also decide whether any group constitution shall be set up for those provinces and if so, with what provincial subjects the Group should deal'. After the group and the provincial constitutions had been settled the three sections would reassemble with the representatives of Indian states to settle the Union Constitution.

124. Jamil-ud-din Ahmed, ed., *Speeches and Writings of Mr. Jinnah*, Vol. II, pp. 29–3.

125. Jamil-ud-din Ahmad, *The Final Phase of the Pakistan Movement*, pp. 1–56.

126. Jamil-ud-din Ahmed, ed., *Speeches and Writings of Mr. Jinnah*, Vol. II, pp. 29–3.

127. For reaction of the Muslim League see statement made by Jinnah on the Cabinet Mission Plan on 23 May, *Dawn*, 23 May 1946; Latif Ahmed Sherwani, ed., *Pakistan Resolution to Pakistan, 1940–1947*, pp. 118–21.

128. For reaction of the Congress see resolution of the Congress Working Committee on the Cabinet Mission Plan, 24 May 1946; Azad to Lawrence, 24 May 1946, *Indian Annual Register*, 1946, Vol. II, pp. 162–4.

129. V.P. Menon, *Transfer of Power*, pp. 36–55; H.V. Hodson, *The Great Divide*, pp. 151–66.

130. *Transfer of Power*, Vol. VII, pp. 917–21.

131. Note by Major Wyatt, 25 May 1946, L/P&J/10/43: ff 53–6.

132. Ibid. Liaquat Ali Khan, ed., *Resolutions of the All India Muslim League from January 1944–December 1946*, Muslim League Papers, pp. 49–51.

133. *Indian Annual Register*, 1946, Vol. II, pp. 181–2.

134. M.A.H. Ispahani, *Quaid-e-Azam as I Knew Him* (Karachi: Royal Book Company, 1976), p. 209.

135. I.H. Qureshi, *The Struggle for Pakistan*, p. 262.

136. M.A.H. Ispahani, *Quaid-e-Azam Jinnah As I Knew Him*, p. 181.

137. Ibid.

138. Ibid.

139. *Indian Annual Register*, 1946, Vol. II, pp. 181–2.

140. Hector Bolitho, *Jinnah the Creator of Pakistan* (London: John Murray, 1954), p. 160.

141. Cripps and his other colleagues continued their efforts to enlist Congress support and tried to convince them that the plan was the best solution as it offered a united India which they had been demanding for years. When the Congress got passed it resolution of 24 May, Gandhi wrote a letter to Lawrence while informing him he said 'The WC passed its resolution this evening, I call it a good resolution. So far as the Congress is concerned I am free now to leave Delhi what would you have me to do? Hoping you are not finding your labour too exacting'. Gandhi to Pethick–Lawrence, 24 May 1946, Note by Major Wyatt, 25 May 1946, L/P&J/10/43: ff 53–6.

142. According to Qazi Isa, one of the great leaders of Balochistan and founder of the Balochistan Muslim League, 'of the members of the Cabinet Mission, Mr Jinnah considered A.V. Alexander 'frank and honest; but Sir Stafford Cripps he said 'was not playing a straight game'. Though Mr Jinnah never actually used the word, he clearly implied that Cripps was dishonest.' Quoted in K.H. Khurshid, ed., *Memoirs of Jinnah* (Karachi: Oxford University Press, 1990), pp. 62–3.

143. Maulana Azad to Pethick–Lawrence, 24 May 1946, V.P. Menon, *The Transfer of Power*, p. 270.

144. Mr Gandhi's article in *Harijan*, 17 May 1946, *Transfer of Power*, Vol. VII, p. 614.

145. H.V. Hodson, *Great Divide*, p. 151.

146. Statement by the Cabinet Delegation and Wavell on 25 May 1946, L/PEJ/10.43: ff 57–60.

147. Jamil-ud-din, *The Final Phase of the Struggle for Pakistan*, pp. 46–7.

148. Gandhi in his article in *Harijan*, entitled 'Vital Defects', says that 'The three ministers have come to do what they have declared. It will be time to blame them when they go back upon British declarations and devise ways and means of perpetuating British rule. Though there is ground for fear, there is no sign on the horizon that they have said one thing and meant another.'

149. Lawrence to Attlee, 26 May 1946, L/PO/6/115: ff 66–7.
150. Ibid.
151. Interview with Gandhi and Nehru, on 11 June 1946, Interviews of Wavell, IOR, MSS Eur D 977/17, pp. 79–81.
152. Note for Wavell's talks with Nehru 26 May 1946, *Transfer of Power*, Vol. VII, pp. 698–700.
153. Resolution of the Congress Working Committee, 25 June 1946, pp. 1036–8.
154. *Hindustan Times*, 27 June 1946.
155. *The Dawn*, 27 June 1946.
156. Wavell explained to Nehru that the statement of 16 May did not make grouping compulsory. It left the decision to the elected representatives of the provinces concerned sitting together in sections. The only provision which was made was that the representatives of certain provinces should meet in sections so that they could decide whether or not they wished to form groups. Even when this had been done the individual province was still to have the liberty to opt out of the group, if they so decided. He recognized the difficulty about the Europeans who through no fault of their own, found themselves in a difficult position. He still hoped that satisfactory solution of this problem would be found. Wavell to Azad, 15 June 1946, *Cabinet Mission and Aftermath*, pp. 149–50.
157. Michael Edwards, *Nehru: A Political Biography*, p. 175.
158. Nehru's Press Conference of 10 July, Lumby Collection, India and Burma news summary, compiled from official and press sources, Vol. VI, week ending July to September 1946, Report of 18 July 1946, 2–5, MSS Eur D 1033/7; R.C. Majumdar, *History of the Freedom Movement*, Vol. III, p. 770.
159. *Transfer of Power*, Vol. VIII.
160. Moreover, Nehru believed that the Centre must control currency and credit and there must be overall authority to settle inter-provincial disputes and deal with administrative and economic breakdowns. Jamil-ud-din Ahmed, *The Final Phase of the Pakistan Movement*.
161. Maulana Azad, *India Wins Freedom*, p. 64.
162. Michael Brecher, *Nehru: A Political Biography* (London: Oxford University Press, 1959), p. 324.
163. Maulana Azad, *India Wins Freedom*, pp. 154–5.
164. Ibid.
165. Yogesh Chadha, *Rediscovering Gandhi* (London: Random House UK Ltd., 1997), p. 416.
166. A.A. Ravoof, *Meet Mr. Jinnah*, p. 204.
167. Waheed-uz-Zaman, *Quaid-i-Azam Mohammad Ali Jinnah: Myth and Reality* (Islamabad: National Institute of Historical and Cultural Research, 1985), p. 80.
168. Syed Sharifuddin Pirzada, ed., *The Foundations of Pakistan*, Vol. II, p. 547.
169. G.A. Allana, *The Pakistan Movement: Historical Documents*, p. 186.
170. Sayeda Saiyidain Hameed, *Islamic Seal On India's Independence, Abul Kalam Azad—A Fresh Look* (Karachi: Oxford University Press, 1998), p. 272.
171. Speech of Lord Cripps, 18 July 1946, Parliamentary Debates (Hansard) House Of Commons (Official Report) Vol. 425, No. 179, London, IOR, MSS Eur F 189/15, p. 1400.

172. Hopkins to his wife, Hopkins Collection, IOR, MSS Eur D 998/17.
173. Ibid.
174. Ibid., pp. 194–5.
175. Leonard Mosley, *The Last Days of the British Raj*, pp. 42–6.
176. Jack Bazalgette, *The Captains and the Kings Depart* (Oxford: The Amate Press Ltd., 1984), p. 129; IOR, MSS Eur F 226/2, part 2, Chapter 10, End of the Empire.
177. I.H. Qureshi, *The Struggle For Pakistan*, pp. 265–6.
178. Wavell to Jinnah, 27 June 1946, in Syed Sharifuddin Pirzada, ed., *Quaid's Correspondence* (Lahore: Service Book Club, 1987), p. 382.
179. Michael Edwards, *Nehru: A Political Biography*, p. 171.
180. Ibid., p. 172.
181. Wavell noted his interview with Nehru and discussed the Sikhs' response to the four seats for the Constituent Assembly. Nehru said that 'the Sikhs had been stupid about it; and that he himself had also acted foolishly in leaving it to their good sense, instead of giving them direct instruction what to do.' Wavell's interview with Nehru, 22 July 1946, Wavell Papers, Notes of Important Interviews, 1943–7, pp. 189–90.
182. Wavell to Pethick–Lawrence, 29 August 1946, R/3/1/117: f 173.
183. Pethick–Lawrence to Wavell, 30 August 1946, L/P&J/10/75: ff 368–71.
184. B. R. Nanda, *Three Statesmen, Gokhale, Gandhi, and Nehru* (New Delhi: Oxford University Press, 2004), p. 159.
185. Wavell wrote to Pethick–Lawrence, 'I have talked to Nehru about grouping without any conclusive result. I am informed that the Congress have turned down a proposals by their legal adviser, K.M. Munshi, that they should maintain that the Constituent Assembly as a whole will lay down procedure for the sections. It is believed that they will ultimately admit that the sections can decide their own procedure and if they say no now it is possible this might satisfy Jinnah. But I see no good at the moment in putting a formula to Nehru. I got the impression from him today that the Congress do not, repeat not, at present want to secure League co-operation. The members of Muslim League Working Committee are mostly in Delhi and I propose to send at once for Jinnah who is in Bombay....The difficulties about the Interim Government can be dealt with afterwards.' Wavell to Lawrence, 10 September 1946, Wavell Collections, Political Series, 28 June to 6 December 1946, Vol. IV, Part V, IOR, MSS Eur D 977/8, p. 187.
186. *Indian Annual Register*, 1946, Vol. II, p. 279.
187. Wavell wrote to Pethick–Lawrence, 'We have received the reports of Nehru's remarks at a press conference on 10 July and of Jinnah's reaction in an interview at Hyderabad on the 12 July. You have also received in my telegram No. 14 53-S of the 15 July the text of the Chancellor's letter on the subject. From the full API report which has been telegraphed today it does not (repeat not) appear that the Congress have definitely decided to disregard the procedure laid down for the Constituent Assembly or to try for instance to carry a decision on the major communal issue (such as initial grouping in Sections A, B, and C) by a bare majority, although individual passage read out of their context give the opposite impression. The C press has naturally gone farther than Nehru and both the Princes and the L have been agitated by articles suggesting that the Congress will regard the CA as

completely sovereign body, that Central subjects will be greatly expanded, etc. I recommend that a statement on the following lines should be made in the course of Parliamentary debate: 'Though some press reports might give the contrary impression, His Majesty's Government have no reason at present to suppose that the Congress will attempt to disregard the procedure laid down in Paragraph 19 of the Statement of 16th May or for instance to claim the right to pass a resolution on an issue adjourned to a major communal issue or a resolution varying the provisions of paragraph 15 without the necessary majority of each of the two major communities. All parties are undoubtedly aware that the decisions of a C proceeding on some other basis than that of the Statement of the 16th May could not be accepted or implemented by His Majesty's Government. Anxiety has been caused to the States by statements implying that the Central subjects can be expanded, without their consent, that Paramountcy will be inherited by the Union Government and so on. Such pronouncements are unfounded. The States have not yet negotiated the terms on which they are prepared to represent in the CA. it is hoped that the States Negotiating Committee at its preliminary session will be able to negotiate terms which will be acceptable.' Wavell to Lawrence, 16 July 1946, R/3/1/112: ff 15–16.

188. Leonard Mosley, *The Last Days of the British Raj*, pp. 42–6.
189. Sudhir Ghosh, *Gandhi's Emissary* (London: The Cresset Press, 1967), pp. 9–48.
190. Wavell to Lawrence, 10 September 1946, Wavell Collections, Political Series, 28 June to 6 December 1946, Vol. IV, part V, IOR, MSS Eur D 977/8, p. 187.
191. Griffiths to Lawrence, 3 September 1946, *Transfer of Power*, Vol. VIII, pp. 402–411.
192. For details see: *Transfer of Power*, Vol. VII, pp. 312, 337, 340, 368, 398, 417, 495; *Transfer of Power*, Vol. IX, pp. 91–92.
193. Ibid., p. 103.
194. Wavell stressed that 'His Majesty's Government must now make up its mind whether it will stand by the statement of the Mission or not'. He believed that it would save the Mission's plan by a definite statement on the lines proposed by the League in paragraph 3 of his No. 2459-s, which were in effect the assurances given to the League leaders by the Mission in their interview of 16 May. He assured that 'If His Majesty's Government decides to make such a statement, I should of course put it first to Jinnah and obtain a definite pledge that the League would come in on this assurance. Otherwise His Majesty's Government must recognize that it has in effect abandoned the plan drawn up by the Mission and has surrendered to Congress.' He however said that he could cannot guarantee the reaction of Congress to such a statement, but he expected that they would accept it after a great deal of preliminary bluster, and that the majority of Indians, including all sensible and moderate men, would be glad that His Majesty's Government had at last shown some firmness of purpose. He however admitted that the Congress may react by resignation for their Members at the Centre and of all Congress Government followed possibly by widespread violence. He suggested that they could face this only if they had a breakdown plan on the lines which he had proposed. It would help them to get rid of India without serious loss and with some dignity. He warned that if His Majesty's Government decides to adopt the line of surrender to the

Congress point of view, I fear that the result will be something approaching civil war leading to the eventual break-up of the Indian Army and chaos throughout India, since the Muslim League has been driven to point of desperation and will use the religious issue to stir up trouble. British troops will be involved in the suppression of civil disturbances and attack on the European community will develop'. He professed that the Mission plan would have failed since no constitution that the Assembly would frame without the Muslim League would be acceptable to the Muslims. He said that the States would also not as a whole join either side but many of them were likely to be involved in the general disorder. He emphasized that serious note of his advice should be taken and said that 'I do not think that half-measures or wishful thinking will get us further. His Majesty's Government has a clear-cut issue in front of it, either to stand by the Mission plan or to surrender to Congress, and they must make up their minds at once'. He had done his best to persuade the parties to come together into the Government and the Constituent Assembly and make it work, but he admitted that he had failed. Wavell to Lawrence, 24 November 1946, Wavell Collections, Political Series 28 June to 6 December 1946, Vol. IV, part V, IOR, MSS Eur D 977/8, pp. 127–82, 342–4.

195. Ibid., p. 135.
196. Wavell in his reply told Nehru that Jinnah had assured him that the League intended to cooperate in the government and the Constituent Assembly and had promised to call the Muslim League at an early date to rescind its resolution rejecting the Cabinet Mission's Statement of 16 May. Nehru to Wavell, 23 October 1946, *Transfer of Power*, Vol. VIII, pp. 781–85.
197. *Daily Telegraph*, 26 November 1946.
198. Nehru to Wavell, 23 October 1946, *Transfer of Power*, Vol. VIII, pp. 781–85.
199. M. Rafique Afzal, *Speeches and Statements of Quaid-i-Millat Liaquat Ali Khan, 1941–51* (Lahore: Research Society of Pakistan, 1975), p. xiv.
200. Wavell to Lawrence, 23 November 1946, R/3/1/127: ff 69–70.
201. Seervai, *Partition of India: Legend and Reality*, p. 76.
202. Hector Bolitho, *Jinnah, Creator of Pakistan*, p. 170.
203. Statement by His Majesty's Government on 6 December 1946, India Conference in London. Paper ICL (46)11, L/P&J/10/111: ff 41–4.
204. Statement by His Majesty's Government on 6 December 1946, *Transfer of Power*, Vol. IX, Appendix No. 166, pp. 295–96.
205. *Transfer of Power*, Vol. IX, pp. 239–40.
206. Statement by His Majesty's Government on 6 December 1946, India Conference in London. Paper ICL (46)11, L/P&J/10/111: ff 41–4.
207. Ibid.
208. Khalid Bin Sayeed, *Pakistan: The Formative Phase* (Karachi: Pakistan Publishing House, 1960), p. 175.
209. Seervai, *Partition of India: Legend and Reality*, pp. 67–7.
210. Statement by His Majesty's Government, 6 December 1946, L/P&J/10/111: ff 41–4.
211. Lawrence to Bevin, 6 December 1946, Telegram, R/3/1/128: ff 116–17.
212. Indian Conference in London. Paper ICL (46)12, 6 December 1946, L/P&J/10/111: ff 45–8.

213. Durgadas, ed., *Sardar Patel's Correspondence*, vol. 3, No. 326 (Ahmedabad, 1972).

214. Text of the resolution passed by All-India Congress Committee, 6 January 1947, R/3/129: ff 123–4.

215. Wavell, *Viceroy's Journal*, p. 406.

216. Michael Edwards, *Nehru: A Political Biography*.

217. Stanley Wolpert, *Jinnah of Pakistan*, p. 300.

218. Text of the resolution passed by All-India Congress Committee, 6 January 1947, R/3/129: ff 123–4.

219. Latif Ahmad Sherwani, ed., *Pakistan Resolution to Pakistan* (Karachi: National Publishing Housing Limited, 1969), p. 158.

220. Ibid., p. 10.

221. Mehmud Ali, 'My Contact with Quaid-i-Azam 1945–1948', in *Pakistani Scholars on Quaid-i-Azam Mohammad Ali Jinnah*, ed. Riaz Ahmad (Islamabad: NIPS, 1999), pp. 1–12.

222. Bipen Chandra, *Nationalism and Colonialism in Modern India* (Hyderabad: Orient Longman Pvt. Ltd., reprinted 2004), p. 277.

223. Wavell, *Viceroy's Journal*, p. 413.

224. Wavell to His Majesty the King-Emperor, 24 February 1947, Wavell Collections, MSS Eur 977/17, pp. 139–48.

225. Sangat Singh, *The Sikhs in History* (New Delhi: Uncommon Books, 1996), p. 238.

226. Nehru, Patel, Rajagopalachari, Matthai, Bhabha, Azad, Jagjivan Ram and Baldev Singh wrote a letter to Wavell on 5 February 1947. They wrote, 'We are clearly of opinion that as a consequence of the Muslim League decision it is no longer possible for members of the Muslim League to continue in the Interim Government. For them to continue to do so would mean an abandonment of the Cabinet Delegation's scheme of May 16th 1946. You will remember that prior to the inclusion of the nominees of the Muslim League in the Interim Government we had repeatedly laid emphasis on the necessity of their accepting the long-term plan of the Cabinet Mission. You told us that this was a pre-requisite to their joining the government. Immediately after entering the Government our colleagues of the Muslim League made it clear that they would not join the Constituent Assembly and that they did not consider the Interim Government as a Cabinet.... In spite of these difficulties, however, we have continued to function, though rather precariously, in the hope that the Muslim League would after sometime accept the full Scheme and enter the Constituent Assembly. This hope has now finally gone and we have to face an open defiance of the whole Cabinet Mission Scheme. The resolution of the Muslim League, which has now been reaffirmed, it is not merely for non-participation in the Constituent Assembly but for a total rejection of the Scheme...It seems impossible to us that this policy and programme can proceed side by side with membership of the Interim Government. The two are incompatible. If the Cabinet Mission' s scheme is to be worked out, as we think it must be, then those who reject it can not continue as members of the Interim Government. There is no alternative. Any change in the Interim Government at this stage, and during the Budget Session of the Central Assembly, may lead to administrative and other difficulties. We are convinced, however, that to attempt to avoid or delay these changes would result

in far graver and more harmful consequences.' Wavell Collections, Political Series, 28 June to 6 December 1946, Vol. IV, Part V, IOR, MSS Eur D 977/7, pp. 24–5.

227. Wavell, *Viceroy's Journal*, p. 418.

228. Nehru to Wavell, 13 February 1947, R/3/1/130: ff 69–70.

229. Sardar Patel to Wavell, 14 February 1947, Wavell Collections, Official Correspondence, January 1946–March 1947, p. 242.

230. Wavell to His Majesty the King-Emperor, 24 February 1947, Wavell Collections, MSS Eur 977/17, pp. 139–48.

231. Punjab Governors to Wavell, 26–27 January 1947, Wavell Collections, MSS Eur 977/16, pp. 219–24.

232. Wavell, *Viceroy's Journal*, p. 428.

233. Diana Mansergh, ed., *Independence Years: The Selected Papers of India and Commonwealth of Nicholas Mansergh* (New Delhi: Oxford University Press, 1999), p. 52.

234. Ronald Lewin, *The Chief*, p. 237.

235. R.J. Moore, *Escape from the Empire: The Attlee Government and the Indian Problem* (Oxford: Clarendon Press, 1983), pp. 63–64.

236. Shuster writes, 'The basic ideas of this note are: this is of vital importance to maintain close links between Britain and India; that in future these links must depend mainly on non-official relations (personal, cultural, educational, commercial and industrial). The note is mainly concerned with commercial and industrial relation; but it is important that these should not be considered isolation.' He also proposes to establish a society namely Friends of India. In order to work a common policy to protect British interests in India, to promote collaboration with Indians, and to establish good relations with the central and provincial and state governments, and with the big Indian financiers and industrialist, it is very desirable that in each main centre there should be a permanent chairman of the European Chamber of Commerce or of the European Association. Schuster to Short, January 29 February 1947, Short Collection, pp. 43–6.

237. Schuster wrote, 'I had a meeting yesterday with Lord Haily and General Hutto to discuss future procedure. We agreed that the question of outstanding importance today is 'how can British industrialists and traders best collaborate with Indians during the next few years, so as to give the maximum help to Indian economic development in a manner consistent with the British interests and productive capacity.' Schuster to Short, 18 February 1947, Short Collection, 67.

238. Percival Spear in his memorandum to the British government suggested that on Wavell's model of the Breakdown Plan. He says this course is 'retreat from India via the North West, British civilians should be withdrawn to the nearest ports which themselves could be held till the evacuation was complete. British civilians and officials in the north would retire to the Punjab and thence home via Karachi. British troops in the north would be concentrated on the Sutlej (or perhaps on the Jamuna) while the evacuation proceeded and while the Pakistan government of the north was taking shape. As soon as Pakistan desired it, they would be withdrawn altogether. North East Pakistan has to be abandoned.' Percival Spear, 'The British Policy in India A Memorandum', 4 February 1947, p. 151.

239. V.P. Menon to Short, 7 January 1947, Short Collection, pp. 15–6.

240. Ibid.
241. Ayesha Jalal, 'Inheriting the Raj: Jinnah and the Governor-Generalship Issue', *Modern Asian Studies*, Vol. 19, No. 1 (1985), pp. 29–53.
242. David Black, presently a curator of the British Library London, was associated as a research scholar, with the team of Roger Lumley and Penderel Moon in editing the *Transfer of Power Papers*. Interview with David Black by the author, India Office Library, London, 17 February 2005.
243. Nehru met Wavell on 1 February 1947; Wavell to Lawrence, 1 February 1947, L/PEJ/10/77: ff 443–4.
244. Wavell, *Viceroy's Journal*, pp. 416–7.

4

Wavell and the
Interim Government in India
(September 1946–March 1947)

'Interim Government' is the term applied to a political arrangement between various political groups in India and which was expected to take charge of the government from the British; it also formed the 'short-term' part of the Cabinet Mission Plan. It was supposed to function till a new constitution for India had been approved and a new government based upon that constitution had come into existence.

Wavell's hope in pursuing the formation of an Interim Government, composed overwhelmingly of leading Indian politicians, was that the joint working of the two leading political parties would foster a team spirit among them so that they would be able to tackle the country's outstanding constitutional, administrative and communal problems. This, he sincerely felt, would help to keep India united thus obviating the Muslim need for a separate homeland, Wavell's long-sought goal.

Three differing points of view dominate the writings on the failed episode of the Interim Government: First one blames the League; the second school of thought holds Wavell primarily responsible for the failure of the Interim Government; the last one holds both Nehru and Jinnah chiefly responsible for this political setback to India. However, the author of the present study feels that none of the above viewpoints can be characterized as representing the full picture; the present author has, instead, highlighted the role of the Congress which by its conscious and deliberate policy of ruling India independently and single-handedly, brought about the failure of the Interim Government. The role played by the Labour government, in extending undue support to the Congress and neglecting the other political parties, especially the League, is also put into focus.

Wavell's role, especially his failure to preserve the necessary balance between the League and the Congress, is therefore, also appropriately dealt with; Patel's role is spotlighted along with that of the big Hindu industrialists and businessmen who soon began to clamour for partition. This chapter also endeavours to investigate Wavell's earnest desire for the formation of a coalition government consisting of the two major parties; the reason Muslim League was not given an opportunity to form the government when it deserved to do so; and, lastly, the reason why Congress alone was given the right to form the Interim Government.

WAVELL'S EFFORTS FOR THE FORMATION OF THE INTERIM GOVERNMENT

Elections, which were held following the failure of the First Simla Conference (1945), furnished ample proof of the respective strengths of the Muslim League and the Congress in their respective communal backyards. This gave Wavell a fresh chance to bring about the participation of the major parties in the political setup of the country, his cherished goal.[1] His letter of 27 December 1945 to the Secretary of State clearly outlined his method of inviting both parties to join the Executive Council, his approach of assuring the League's parity with the Caste Hindus and distribution of important portfolios between the two parties.[2]

Formation of an Interim Government was an important, 'short-term' part of the Cabinet Mission Plan and Wavell carried full responsibility for such a task.[3] It obviously required a spirit of give and take and genuine cooperation between the two leading political parties of the country. An important aspect of this Plan was maintaining a balance of power between the Muslim League and the Congress.

Many important issues confronted Wavell right at the outset of his efforts for the formation of an Interim Government: Firstly, would the Governor General be able to wield his powers as per the Government of India Act of 1935; secondly, how best to resolve the dispute concerning the total number of cabinet members in the Interim Government; thirdly, Muslim League's claim to nominate all the members for the Muslim seats in the Cabinet; fourthly, party-wise distribution of the cabinet members; lastly, distribution of important portfolios amongst the various parties constituting the cabinet.

Each one of the above issues generated such bitter debates between Wavell and the Cabinet delegation on the one hand and leaders of either one or both of the two leading parties on the other, that any progress towards the formation of the Interim Government became a Herculean task for Wavell to carry through.

REACTION OF THE CONGRESS

In the early stages, Congress was preoccupied by two main issues: firstly, the composition and status of the Interim Government, and, secondly, its responsibilities. It demanded that the Viceroy should function as a constitutional head of the government only, and in practice the Interim Government should have the same powers as those of a cabinet of the dominions with responsibility only to the central legislature.[4]

Contrary to Wavell's expectations, Congress proposed that the Interim Government should be formed by inviting eleven provincial governments to nominate one representative each.[5] By this procedure Congress expected to dominate the council by limiting the Muslim League representation to no more than two or three representatives in a council of fifteen. Although Maulana Azad wanted to include up to four Muslim League representatives,[6] he was not hopeful of League's parity with the Congress.[7]

Wavell stated at this time that though His Majesty's Government was serious in handing over power to Indians in a united India, it did not consider Congress as the sole representative of all Indians.[8] Although Wavell and the British government refused to go along with interpretations put forth by the Congress[9] they also were conscious of not giving Jinnah a veto power by default.[10] At the same time discussions continued between the parties concerned on the relevance of the 1935 Act to the existing situation.[11]

Muslim League's Response

Two issues confronted Wavell and Jinnah: Firstly, whom to include in the government, and, secondly, relative representation of the Muslim League and the Congress in that government. Concerning the first issue Wavell had assured Jinnah that the parties accepting the 16 May statement would be invited to take part in the government. Regarding the principle of relative representation the League demanded a 'parity of representation' between the League and the Congress in the Cabinet which, however, Wavell disagreed with.[12] Another issue which troubled Wavell's negotiations with both the parties was the size of the Cabinet.[13] After a lot of back and forth between all concerned, Wavell finalised the Cabinet strength at fourteen,[14] basing his decision on a 6:5:3 formula.

Statement of 16 June

It appeared from the negotiations and correspondence between the parties concerned that the divergence in their views would prevent them from arriving at a settlement. Neither the Congress nor the League agreed on the strength and composition of the Interim Government,[15] despite all efforts to convince them. Thus, Wavell and the Delegation gave their own Statement on 16 June.[16]

This statement proposed setting up an Executive Council of 14 members, 6 from the Congress, excluding a nationalist Muslim but including a member of the Scheduled Castes, 5 belonging to the League, besides 1 Sikh, 1 Indian Christian and 1 Parsee.[17] The portfolios would be arranged by the Viceroy in consultation with the leaders of the two leading parties. Wavell and the delegation clarified that the composition of the Interim Government was not to be treated as a precedent for the solution of any other communal question. It was made clear that:

> In the event of the two major parties or either of them proving unwilling to join in the setting up of a coalition Government on the above lines, it is the intention of the Viceroy to proceed with the formation of an interim Government which will be as representative as possible of those willing to accept the Statement of May 16th.[18]

From the above-mentioned statement, it seemed that every effort had been made to accommodate the desires and demands of both the parties, particularly the Congress. Learning from experience and in a determined attempt to reach an agreement Wavell had side-stepped the principle of parity for the parties as well as the question of relative Muslim/Hindu representation.[19] Regarding the Indians' demand for a dominion status the Delegation had already announced that the Interim Government, in reality if not in theory, would be treated as the Dominion Cabinet.[20]

Jinnah was shocked when Wavell informed him that the composition of the Interim Government was changed to the ratio of 6:5:3 instead of the 5:5:3 which Wavell had communicated to him on 13 June. Jinnah said that the new formula was against the promise made by the Viceroy regarding the principle of parity.[21] Jinnah placed the statement of 16 June before the Muslim League Working Committee which held its meeting on 25 June. After careful consideration the committee came to the following conclusions:

1. The League was surprised that invitation had been issued to five Muslim Leaguers to join the Interim Government without calling for a list from the Leader of the Muslim League.[22]

2. It was also unacceptable for the Muslim League that the parity between the two major parties, the Congress and the League, had been abandoned. Besides, the selection of Jagjivan Ram, Scheduled Caste and a member of the Congress party, provided an additional seat to the Congress.

3. The inclusion of a fourth representative of the minorities, namely, N.P. Engineer, without consultation with the League president was against the method and understanding given to Jinnah.

4. The modifications which had been made in the original formula for the Interim Government had already adversely affected the proportion of the Muslims in the Interim Government as a whole and the Congress as a single party, because it got 6 seats rather than 5.

5. In view of the serious changes which had from time to time been made to satisfy the Congress, it was not possible for the Working Committee to arrive at any decision in the matter of the formation

of the Interim Government so long as the Congress did not finally convey its decision on the proposals.

6. The League also thought that the question of distribution of portfolios had not been finally decided which might create a hitch.[23]

Even then, the League wished to benefit from the statement if the Viceroy made some clarifications regarding their reservations. Wavell, ever eager to enlist support for the proposals, was ready to explain what had been demanded but not without prior discussions with and approval of the Cabinet Delegation.[24] Wavell assured Jinnah that no decision on a major communal issue could be taken by the Interim Government if the majority of either of the two main parties was opposed to it.[25] He stated that it would not be possible for him or the Cabinet Mission to accept a request from the League for the exclusion of a Muslim nominated by the Congress from its quota. Nevertheless, Jinnah got satisfactory answers on a number of points; therefore, the Muslim League resolved to join the Interim Government on the basis of the statement of 16 June and clarifications and assurances subsequently given by the Viceroy.[26]

To consider the Cabinet Mission's latest proposals, the Congress Working Committee was in almost permanent session from 20–25 June. Congress raised two objections: Firstly, it wanted the Cabinet strength to be fifteen instead of the suggested fourteen with the additional member being a Muslim nominated by the Congress.

On 25 June the Congress Working Committee rejected the proposals for an Interim Government but decided that the Congress should join the proposed Constituent Assembly with a view to framing the Constitution of a free, united and democratic India.[27]

To Jinnah's surprise,[28] Wavell informed him on 25 June that the Congress had accepted the statement of 16 May while refusing to take part in the Interim Government proposed in the statement of 16 June. He said, because of that, the whole scheme had broken down and he could not give effect to the scheme of 16 June but promised that he would be willing to reopen the negotiations after a short interval.[29]

Congress's rejection had placed Wavell in a dilemma. He could neither fulfil the assurances given to Jinnah by the British government nor could he accept responsibility for its failure. He failed to understand the reasons which led the Congress to create such a deadlock. He opined, 'This ability of Congress to twist words and phrases and to take advantage of any slip is what Jinnah all along feared.'[30] Wavell, in one of his secret meetings with the Cabinet Delegation, frankly conveyed to them that they had made a mistake in para 8 of the 16 June statement which referred to formation of an Interim Government by anyone who would accept the statement of 16 May, and because of which a sticky situation had now arisen. In fact, now, they were unwilling to risk the formation of an Interim Government by the League lest the Congress react in such a hostile manner as to precipitate either a civil war or a repetition of the 1942 rebellion. Wavell believed that the last chance of securing a genuine coalition government for India had gone, for a long time at any rate.[31] Though Wavell was sure that it was upon Cripps's and Pethick-Lawrence's advice that Congress had eventually accepted the Mission's statement of 16 May, thus preventing paragraph 8 of the 16 June statement being operated in the League's favour,[32] he and his colleagues decided to form a caretaker government composed of government officials.[33] At the same time, he promised to make arrangements for the elections and summoning of the Constituent Assembly according to the 16 May plan.[34]

In Jinnah's view, Wavell's decision to postpone indefinitely the formation of the Interim Government was contrary to the pledge given to him, viz., in case one party refused to co-operate the Viceroy would proceed with the formation of the Interim Government with the help of the party which had accepted the statement of 16 June.[35] He felt let down badly by Wavell and the delegation.[36] As the Congress had refused and the Muslim League had accepted the statement, it was a breach of promise of the Provision I, Paragraph (8), of the Statement of 16 June.[37] To cover up the situation they had created, the delegation announced that new elections would take place for the Constituent Assembly and it would probably be better to get over them first.[38]

Jinnah suffered from a great disadvantage because the Government was not ready to ignore the 'majority party', Congress.[39] According to Victoria Schofield, 'Jinnah was outraged at what he termed a "betrayal"; he asserted that the Mission were "in honour bound to go ahead" on the basis of paragraph 8, and that by not doing so, they had revoked "their plighted word"'.[40] Therefore, he called a meeting of the League's highest executive body in order to take them into confidence. He told its members that the Viceroy had earlier promised to form an Interim Government even if it excluded the Congress but now he had chewed his words and refused.[41] He accused the Viceroy and the Mission of a breach of faith and demanded the postponement of the elections for the Constituent Assembly, a demand the Viceroy refused.[42]

In the meanwhile, the Cabinet Delegation left India on 26 June under the impression that, despite everything, a Constituent Assembly at least would come into being. Both Cripps and Lawrence claimed in the Parliament that the Mission had been a success[43] although it had failed to bring about a change in the attitude of the two main parties. As a matter of fact, Congress was still not prepared to move an inch from its position that power to Indians must be transferred only on the basis of a united India, while the League had its sights set only on the achievement of Pakistan.

Wavell's decision to postpone the formation of the Interim Government had exposed him to valid criticism. Victoria Schofield has recorded, 'The Mission's actions appeared so contrary to their earlier statement that even the English language press in India—normally favourable to the British government—was critical.'[44] Even Percival Joseph Griffiths, leader of the European group in the Legislative Assembly, was severely critical of Wavell's explanations.[45]

The following points make it significantly clear that Wavell's refusal to go ahead without the Congress left considerable negative effects on later political developments: 'A majority of the political opinion concluded that by backtracking on their promise both His Majesty's Government and the Viceroy, had lost credibility in the eyes of the Muslims, who simply felt cheated and deceived by such a one-sided decision.'[46]

Congress, as the dominant party, had been able to raise its stature in the eyes of the British[47] and this had the effect of making it even more intransigent in its dealings with the British government.[48] As a result, Muslims, in order to counter their reduced[49] political stature in the eyes of the British, chose a new tactic they termed 'Direct Action',[50] as per Bolitho, to 'force the cause of Pakistan.'[51]

1. Communal friction gained in intensity and Wavell became convinced that unless some agreement was effected soon between the Congress and the League, the fearful Calcutta disorders could be repeated in other parts of India.
2. Wavell's role as an effective negotiator and coordinator was considerably weakened. Wavell's relations with Whitehall also experienced a setback.
3. Wavell believed that the Cabinet Delegation, members of its staff and persons like Agatha Harrison[52] and Horace Alexander[53] were responsible for the Delegation's failure to reach any settlement because of their openly pro-Congress stance.[54]
4. Wavell became convinced that Congress was quite capable of creating a political deadlock. Therefore, he vigorously stressed the implementation of the 'Breakdown Plan'.

While *Hindustan Times*, a Congress supporter, in its writing on 27 June 1946 praised the Mission's actions,[55] the *Dawn*, a Muslim League supporter, in a differing opinion on 27 June, bitterly criticized the declaration that the League would not be permitted to form the government and suspected that it was a first step towards a double-cross on the Muslim League and the Muslim nation. It feared for the peace of India[56] and added that the fears of the Muslim League leaders and its press were not groundless.[57]

As discussed in Chapter 3 that Nehru, as the new Congress president, issued an explosive statement on 10 July which many people regard as having changed the course of history. He had out-rightly rejected the compulsory grouping part of the long-term plan and stated that the constitution would only be framed for a united India.[58] In these circumstances the Muslim League Council in its Bombay session of 27–29 July 1946 decided to withdraw its previous acceptance of the Cabinet Mission Plan 'due to the intransigence of the Congress and the breach of faith with the Muslims by the British.'[59] Thereafter the Muslim League adopted a strategy to achieve Pakistan with or without constitutional means relying solely on its own strength. The result of all this politics was its call for a 'Direct Action Day' to be observed throughout India on 16 August which produced catastrophic results in Calcutta.

Wavell, under pressure from the British government, thought of new ways to restart the negotiation process.[60] This time he wanted to initiate secret negotiations and start with the Congress as he was extremely unhappy about the criticism which he had received from the League and Jinnah. He had also received a secret report that the Congress was ready to create an atmosphere of chaos, disorder and a revolution in the country.[61]

At this point, the League's claim that 6:5:3 was not the right formula for an agreement, was rejected.[62] Lastly, they decided, that Congress had the right, contested by the League, to nominate a Muslim.[63] If the Muslim League decided to stay out of the Interim Government, they wanted to fill the Muslim League quota of places with other Muslims.[64] Wavell's identical letters of 22 July to Jinnah and Nehru contained the details of this offer to form a government and pointed out that there would be an equitable distribution of important portfolios.[65] Excepting one point, right of Congress to nominate a Muslim, Wavell's latest plan was identical to the one offered in the Statement of 16 June.[66]

On 27 July the Muslim League reversed its earlier decision of accepting the 16 May and 16 June statements[67] and Jinnah also declined Wavell's invitation of 22 July.[68]

Congress, meanwhile, did not change its strategy in spite of Wavell's latest offer. Maulana Azad in his letter to Cripps on 22 July 1946 stated that if an Interim Government was not set up quickly, the deteriorating internal situation of the country may destroy the possibility of a peaceful settlement,[69] while Nehru stressed the need for giving 'independence in action' to government by treating the Viceroy as a constitutional head.[70] This argument of Nehru's was rejected by Wavell, who thought, 'I had not anticipated that the showdown with Congress would come quite so soon.'[71] And to clarify His Majesty's Government's policy he stated that the British government would decide their policy in the event of a direct challenge by the Congress.[72] Additionally, Nehru replaced Azad as the Congress president because he was acceptable to the non-Hindu elements of the party as well.[73] In the event of a deadlock, Pethick–Lawrence wished that Wavell should come to London to participate in the conversations along with the League and Congress leaders.[74]

Regarding the League's decision to withdraw its earlier support of the Plan, Wavell offered a number of explanations. He stated, 'Thanks to the Mission living in the pocket of Congress while out here, dishonesty of Cripps, my stupidity and weakness in not spotting his dishonesty earlier and standing up to it.'[75]

He further criticized the dishonesty of Cripps and Pethick–Lawrence in instigating Congress's insincere acceptance of the 16 May statement.[76] Not sparing Nehru he criticized him for making unwanted and harsh statements regarding the Cabinet Mission Plan.[77]

As labour trouble, instigated by the Congress's left-wing, spread, Wavell decided to invite the Congress to form the Interim Government with or without the League.[78] Wavell was so keen to bring the Congress into the Interim Government at the earliest possible moment that he was willing to overlook any meeting with Jinnah aimed at inducing him to join a coalition government.[79] He wrote thus to Pethick–Lawrence, 'I should propose to leave Jinnah alone for the moment.'[80] Pethick–Lawrence wrote back on 2 August that 'We accept your view that it would not for the reasons you give be desirable to see Jinnah immediately.'[81]

Reflecting the Hindu bureaucracy's view, V.P. Menon suggested that His Majesty's Government should proceed to form an Interim Government with the help of the Congress. He believed that a lasting settlement between India and Great Britain could only be arrived at by the active support of the majority party, which was the Congress.[82]

Wavell also stated in frustration, 'We ought to hand over power to one or other of the parties and that no progress would be made by negotiating with both.'[83] Therefore, both Wavell[84] and Pethick–Lawrence[85] deemed it expedient to leave the Muslim League aside while inviting the Congress to form the Interim Government. On 6 August 1946, Wavell invited Nehru to form an Interim Government, 'On the basis of assurances given in my letter of the 30 May to Maulana Azad.'[86] Wavell did so on the plea that the Congress had accepted the plan, although it had done so with reservations, and it became entitled to form an Interim Government under Para 8 of the delegation's statement of 16 June. The aim of all this political manoeuvring, it seems, was to somehow force Jinnah into a repudiation of the League's former acceptance of the Cabinet Mission Plan thus leaving the field clear for the Congress to form a one-party dominated government at the centre.

It is stated that Mr Patel influenced his party's decision to join the government.[87] However, it seems that Mr Gandhi, by urging the Congress leadership to use common sense and sense of duty to cope with the problems,[88] was mostly responsible for this decision. Actually, Gandhi was so eager for Congress to acquire power at that time that he was ready to say goodbye to his creed of non-violence.[89] In his meeting with Wavell, he suggested that 'force should be used against the Muslims if they resisted a Congress Government.'[90] Therefore, it had become obvious that the Congress Working Committee would accept the offer.[91] The committee emphasized the sovereign character of the Constituent Assembly, namely the right to function and draw up the Constitution of India without interference of any external power or authority.[92] Thus by his letter of 10 August 1946, Nehru accepted Wavell's invitation for the formation of an Interim Government but since he was against inviting the League to join the government he added, 'Any premature attempt to induce them (Muslim League) to do so might produce a contrary result. Such an attempt will inevitably become public and result in communal controversy and further delay which you deprecate.'[93]

Following Nehru's acceptance of the Viceroy's invitation of 6 August to form a new government, Wavell persuaded him on 13 August to write to Jinnah, inviting his cooperation in the task of forming the Interim Government.[94] Jinnah in his reply on 15 August enquired about a number of items and ended by stating, 'If this means the Viceroy has commissioned you to form an Executive Council of the Governor General, and has already agreed to accept and act upon your advice, and proceed to constitute his Executive Council accordingly, it is not possible for me to accept such a position on that basis.'[95]

The next day, following a Jinnah–Nehru meeting on 15 August to heal the rift, Nehru announced during a press conference the next day that Jinnah had declined to accept his request for cooperating with the Congress in the formation of the provisional national government. Jinnah in fact had always disagreed with Nehru's personal interpretations of the Cabinet Mission Plan which the latter had kept issuing, especially about the status and powers of the Constituent Assembly, so he declined Nehru's invitation to cooperate on his terms.[96] While briefing Wavell about the outcome of his negotiations with Jinnah Nehru said, 'Jinnah's only proposal was apparently that all action should be held up for six months. Nehru said that his impression was that Jinnah had gone farther than he had intended and was at a loss how to get out.'[97] Wavell was pretty sure that these negotiations would fail, as he thought, 'Nehru's message which I repeated to you was I think fairly satisfactory, in that he is prepared to try for a coalition government. But even if the terms are reasonable, I doubt very much if Jinnah will be able to swallow his pride and enter the Interim Government.'[98]

However, Wavell was happy the way things were moving until he experienced the true colour of Nehru and his colleagues. Nehru, once assured of ruling India without an opposition party, now assumed he had become the unchallenged and full-fledged 'Prime Minister' of India.[99] Right from the outset, he began to dictate the terms, and proposed to Wavell that he wanted the Interim Government to consist of fifteen members instead of thirteen, including one Anglo-Indian, if the League refused to come in.[100]

Wavell thought that the main difficulty regarding Congress's proposal was the question of seats. The names Nehru proposed as replacements for the Muslim League quota were mostly nonentities and to include them in the Interim Government, Wavell thought, would probably destroy the last chance for Jinnah to come in. Personally, he would have liked to leave five Muslim League seats vacant, for say one month, to give the League an opportunity of coming in, and carry on for that month with an Executive Council of nine. However, if the deadlock continued for longer than a month, he was ready to fill the remaining five places and redistribute the portfolios. But he decided to recommend only one non-League Muslim and one Anglo–Indian in place of five Muslim League seats and 'remainder would be left vacant rather than filled by 'stooge' Muslims.'[101] Interestingly, for the list of names reserved for the Muslim quota Nehru proposed the names of Asif Ali (Congress leader), Maula Bux of Sindh, Ali Zaheer (president All-India Shia Conference) and Zaheeruddin (president of Momin Conference), all of whom in Wavell's eyes, were not up to par, and whose nomination just might provoke the Muslim League into direct action against them.[102] Wavell did not like to propose names of Muslims like Fazlul Haq, Syed

Ali Zaheer and Shafat Ahmed Khan as they were poor specimens in his eyes.[103]

Wavell asked Nehru why Matthai had been preferred to Rajagopalachari for the finance portfolio and Nehru replied that Rajagopalachari had refused to accept that portfolio. Both Wavell and Nehru agreed that the portfolio of the war member would be known as the defence portfolio.[104] Wavell also told Nehru that the government would be known as the Interim Government, not the provisional national government.[105]

Nehru's next step was to write a letter to the Viceroy on 22 August stating that although he was anxious to form a coalition with the Muslim League, but as he pointed out, he wanted a strong, virile, active and stable government and not a weak, disjointed, apologetic government which could easily be bullied or frightened and which dared not take any step for fear of possible consequences.[106] He argued that he would not allow the Muslim League to undermine the prestige and authority of the government.[107]

On 24 August, Wavell, in his broadcast speech to the Indians, announced the formation of an Interim Government.[108] He continued that the offer of five seats in the Interim Government made to the Muslim League, and rejected by it, was still open.[109] Contrary to the delight of the Congress Party and the British leaders,[110] the Muslim League expressed disappointment and bewilderment over this development because it had not been taken into confidence when negotiations and discussions between the Congress leaders and Wavell regarding the Interim Government were taking place.[111] Jinnah, while condemning Wavell's announcement, said that (Wavell) for 'nearly a week carried on discussions and negotiations behind my back and without any information being furnished to me, except the communiqué that was issued last night announcing the formation of the Interim Government.'[112] Commenting on the idea of referring the case to the federal courts in case of a dispute in interpretation, Jinnah stated, 'Are we going to commence the proceedings of the Constituent Assembly with litigation and law suits in the Federal Court? This kind of spirit in which the future constitution would be framed was unwanted by the Muslim League.'[113] He said that insult had been added to injury by the nomination of three Muslims who commanded neither the respect nor the confidence of Muslim India.[114]

The Congress took office on 2 September.[115] There were twelve members of whom eight belonged to the Congress. Three of the members were Muslims but none of them represented the Muslim League and neither did anyone belong to any of the Muslim-majority provinces including the NWFP. Hearing of the Congress party's launch in the Interim Government, the Muslims felt that 'a Hindu government is set up without the consent and collaboration of the Muslim League.'[116] On Nehru's assumption of office, Jinnah remarked that Congress had proved it was the King's party and that it was helping the imperialistic British government to prolong its stay in India.[117]

The Muslim League decided to declare 2 September, the day the Congress-led Interim Government started its tenure, as a day of mourning and Jinnah instructed the Muslims to display black flags, which led to communal riots in Bombay, Punjab, Bengal and Bihar. Jinnah's response to Nehru's broadcast was a bitter attack on the Congress and the British Cabinet.[118]

Wavell knew that Congress controlled three-fourths of British India. In the Congress-majority provinces the party had almost a monopoly of power. They could, if they wished, make government functioning impossible. But he was equally conscious of the rights of other communities and did not want the Congress to demolish his ideal of Indian unity because without the cooperation of the Muslim League it was impossible to preserve it. He said:

I said that in my opinion it was far more in the interests of Congress to get the League into the Constituent Assembly and Central Government than it was for the League to come in; it seemed to me in fact to be absolutely vital for the Congress, if they wished a united India and a peaceful transfer of power. I said in fact that I thought they ought to try and get them in, for their own sake, on almost any terms, and that it was well worth their while to go a long way to reassure the League. I said that I thought it was the only hope for a united India and for the peace required to enable India to make progress and raise her standard of living. I said that if there was no agreement, I was quite certain that the Muslims would resist fanatically any attempt at domination and would make the goal of a united India impossible; the Army would break up, the tribes on the N.W. Frontier would go out of control; and there might even be danger of Russia stepping in. I said that the British were certainly not going to stay in India to enable the Congress to put down the Muslims. (Patel nodded here and said 'Of course not').[119]

After the failure of the Nehru–Jinnah talks he decided to see Jinnah but when the latter's strong criticism of Wavell and His Majesty's Government became public, he dropped the idea.[120]

The Calcutta killings, as observed by Jaswant Singh, 'was not a massacre alone but the response to it of the Indian politicians, of all those who were then engaged in fighting this "war of succession" in India, that was so inexpressibly tragic, also unforgivable.'[121] However, the Calcutta killings of August 1946 had a dramatic effect on Wavell. He thought that it was not so much the actual loss of life and property which mattered, but the growing spirit of mutual rivalry and challenge which threatened to plunge the country into civil war and bloodshed.[122] He called Nehru and Gandhi on 27 August for a meeting over the prospect of getting the League to join the Interim Government. He told them about his visit to Calcutta and suggested that the only way to avoid similar trouble all over India on an even larger scale was by lessening of communal tension and bringing about of a settlement between the Hindus and the Muslims. He underlined the importance of forming coalition governments, both in Bengal and at the Centre. He also presented them with a draft of a statement, which he suggested, they should make, as follows,

> The Congress are prepared in the interest of communal harmony to accept the intention of the Statement of May 16 that Provinces cannot exercise any option affecting their membership of the Section or of the Groups if formed until the decision contemplated in paragraph 19(viii) of the Statement of the May 16 is taken by the new Legislature after the new constitutional arrangements have come into operation and the first general elections have been held.[123]

Wavell said that since the Congress had agreed to abide by the statement of 16 May, he took it as their acceptance of the grouping arrangements as well. Instead, Wavell was very shocked to hear from Gandhi that 'if a bloodbath was necessary, it would come about in spite of non-violence.'[124] However, most disturbing for Gandhi was Wavell's threat not to convene the Constituent Assembly if the formula he had placed before them was not accepted by the Congress. Nehru repeated[125] the same argument stated earlier by Gandhi regarding the summoning of the Constituent Assembly.[126]

Wavell was disappointed with such reactions of the Congress leaders to his proposals regarding the coalition government. He thought that this, of course, had been Gandhi's objective and of the majority of Congress, from the beginning to establish them at the Centre, and to suppress, cajole or buy over the Muslims, and then impose a Constitution at their leisure. Writing to Pethick–Lawrence, Wavell said that the reaction of Gandhi to his suggestion that the Congress should clearly state their position about the grouping showed how justified Jinnah was in doubting the Congress's previous assurances on the subject. Therefore, Wavell became further convinced that Congress had always meant to use their position in the Interim Government to try to break up the Muslim League, and in the Constituent Assembly to destroy the grouping scheme which was the one effective safeguard for the Muslims. He argued that Calcutta with its 4400 dead, 16,000 injured and over 100,000 homeless showed that one party government at the centre was likely to cause fierce disorders everywhere.[127] If the Congress's intention were as Gandhi's letter of 28 August 1946 suggested, he believed that the only result of their being in power could be a state of virtual civil war in many parts of India. He proposed that if the Congress Working Committee refused to join the Interim Government as a protest against his proposal, he would like to carry on with the caretaker government.[128] But he was directed by Lawrence to let the Congress form the Interim Government, despite all its loose talk and irresponsible statements.[129]

MUSLIM LEAGUE JOINS THE INTERIM GOVERNMENT (26 OCTOBER)

Though Wavell was initially slow to remove the League's apprehensions following the formation of the Interim Government, he did eventually develop communication with leaders, other than Jinnah, of the League. In this regard, Mr Scott, deputy private secretary to the viceroy, met Liaquat Ali Khan, general secretary of the League. During their meeting Liaquat Ali Khan suggested that the Union Assembly will have no power to alter group constitutions (if any) or provincial constitutions. He demanded that the division of portfolios should be 'equal' not 'equitable; and the selection of minority representatives should be done with the joint advice of the Congress and the League.[130] Wavell could not accept Jinnah's claim that no Muslim except a member of the League could take part in a government.[131] He failed to see what harm it could do to Jinnah if the Muslim came out of the Congress quota, since Wavell was quite sure that every Muslim would support the Muslim thesis on any vital matter of Muslim interest.[132]

Delay in forming a coalition government was making Wavell's dream of preserving Indian unity ever more difficult. He was determined to secure a coalition of the Congress and the League. According to Ghulam Kibria, 'Jawaharlal, not being as great as his followers thought he was, perhaps did not even have the political sagacity to realize the extremely serious import and was happy keeping the League away from his government and running it with the help of so-called nationalist Muslims with negative mandate from the Muslim masses.'[133]

Although publicly the Congress leaders, particularly Nehru, had repeatedly expressed their desire to seek co-operation with the League, in reality, however, they left no stone unturned to keep the League from the Interim Government.[134] As Wavell said, 'I got the impression from him (Nehru) today that the Congress do not (repeat not) at present want to secure League cooperation.'[135]

While writing to Pethick–Lawrence on 10 September 1946 he informed him that there were indications that the League wanted an accommodation.[136] Writing to Attlee on 10 September 1946 Pethick–Lawrence said, 'It may be that the Congress will dislike Jinnah being seen by the Viceroy, but in any case we must resist any attempt to restrict the Viceroy's discretion to see leading politicians of any party.'[137] Wavell believed that the Congress leadership, particularly Nehru and Rajagopalachari, having accepted the Viceroy's offer of forming the Interim Government would have much preferred to do so by themselves only, but after Calcutta Wavell stated that 'we must make another determined effort to get the League in' to avoid a civil war.[138]

On failing to stop Wavell's efforts to bring the League into the Interim Government, after Congress had already joined it, Nehru wrote a letter to Cripps to obtain his support against Wavell's efforts, in which he stated,

> As a matter of fact within a few days of our taking office, fresh attempts were made, without our concurrence, to reopen old issues and to go back to where we were months ago. This is very unsettling both for us and the public. The Interim Government can either function as Govt or not at all. There is no middle position. I do not wish to trouble you about these matters but thought it better to indicate to you that we are not at all happy at the developments.[139]

At quite an early stage of Wavell's insistence for a coalition government, Gandhi came out with the idea that Wavell had been unnerved by the Bengal tragedy.[140] Sudhir Ghosh conveyed this feeling of Gandhi's and other top Congress leadership to the Labour leaders that the Viceroy was not the right man in the right place.[141] Nehru's idea of what a coalition government's composition and goals ought to be, in 1946, to tackle any of the urgent problems facing the country was at variance from that of Wavell's. His remedy was:

> The country needs a strong, virile, active and stable Government which knows its mind and has the courage to go ahead, not a weak, disjointed, apologetic Government which can easily be bullied or frightened and which dare not take any step for fear of possible consequences. To give an impression to the country and our people that we are merely a casual and temporary Government waiting for the favour of the Muslim League is to undermine the prestige and authority of the Government. That way will not lead to the coalition we hope for. It will lead to renewed attempts to bully and coerce, which again produce like reactions on the other side, as we have seen in Calcutta. The only proper approach is to make clear that while we shall always welcome co-operation we propose to carry firmly on even if this is denied....But do not believe that co-operation will come out of appeasement of wrong-doing. Hence my dislike of approaches, direct or indirect, which have an appearance of this type of appeasement and are always likely to be misunderstood. The time will surely come when all of us, or most of us, will cooperate together. It will be retarded by wrong tactics and approaches. We may have rough weather ahead. We must have a strong and stable ship if are to face it with confidence.[142]

Wavell, as overall head of the administration, however, knew and felt, that without the cooperation of the League there would be no chance of a united India or for a peaceful transfer of power. His fears increased when leaders like Liaquat Ali Khan accused the British of alliance with the Congress against the Muslims. Liaquat Ali Khan warned that failing a settlement, communal disturbances in future were going to be quite different from the Congress movement of 1942 with an increased frequency of clashes.[143]

Hugh Tinker points out, 'Was Jinnah prepared for any solution other than the oft-declared formula of a full five provinces Pakistan? London, the Viceroy and the Congress were united in refusing to entertain this.'[144]

By the end of September 1946 Wavell realized that his policy of trying to induce the League's participation in the Interim Government via indirect contacts had failed to produce any positive results. To avoid further delay, Wavell engaged in an attempt to bring around Jinnah through a direct contact with him. Therefore, in his meeting with Jinnah on 2 October, Wavell tried to secure Jinnah's confidence.[145] The positive outcome of the negotiation was that Jinnah agreed to summon the League's Working Committee to discuss outstanding points about the Interim Government.[146] At this stage, Gandhi came out of the wilderness and according to Seervai, 'As Wavell went ahead with his efforts to see Jinnah and bring the League into the Interim Government, and since neither Pethick-Lawrence nor Cripps would stop Wavell from making those efforts, Gandhi made a fresh attempt to side-step Wavell.'[147]

Now, therefore, Gandhi tried to remove Jinnah's objection to the nomination of a nationalist Muslim by agreeing, on 4 October 1946, upon a formula with him to deal with his complaint.[148] The formula accepted Jinnah's contention that the League had the sole right to nominate any and all Muslims and in return the League accepted the right of the Congress to nominate any of its members for inclusion in the Interim Government. However, Nehru and Patel were angry with Gandhi because as Bhashyam Kasturi points out, 'Only when this suggested change was brought to his notice that Gandhi realized his mistake. He had not read the document carefully and had signed it. To err is human, but at times it can be dangerous.'[149] As a result he was sidelined by Nehru and Patel as Rajagopalachari and Desai had been in the past.

Wavell wanted to bring the League into the coalition government at the earliest because he knew that success of democracy in a country like India depended primarily upon the multi-party system and, therefore, believed that one party rule was not only unfair but fraught with dangers.[150] So he pushed ahead and even disagreed with the secretary of state whose advice was to allow the Congress to continue in office. At this moment he received information that Jinnah would be ready to accept the offer.[151] According to Ayesha Jalal here was a welcome opportunity for Jinnah to rebuff the Congress and foreclose with the government.[152]

Jinnah in an interview with Wavell on 12 October reiterated his objections to joining the Constituent Assembly. He also suggested that the vice-presidentship should be held in rotation.[153] More meetings and exchanges of letters followed and in the end Wavell asked Jinnah to submit names of five of his nominees to his office.[154]

Eventually, on 13 October Jinnah informed Wavell that:

> ...my Committee have, for various reasons, come to the conclusion that in the interests of Mussulmans and other communities it will be fatal to leave the entire field of administration of the Central Government in the hands of the Congress...we have decided to nominate five (members) on behalf of the Muslim League in terms of your broadcast dated August 24, 1946 and your two letters to me dated 4th October, 1946 and 12th October, respectively, embodying clarifications and assurances.[155]

In fact, the Muslim League reversing its previous stand was now prepared to join the Interim Government. Ayesha Jalal has recorded that, 'The only area where the League could give the Congress an effective opposition was the Interim Government. It could not do this in the streets, in the countryside or the Constituent Assembly.'[156] Though Jinnah believed it was not an equitable distribution, he decided to nominate five members from the League's ranks for joining the Interim Government.[157]

Now a new problem suddenly arose and stared Wavell in the face. This one concerned the division of portfolios. Wavell had previously heard that Congress leaders had a habit of twisting words and breaking promises but now he himself was experiencing this on a regular basis. Nehru had assumed power with the promise that he would be ready to surrender two important portfolios to the League, but now, inexplicably, he retreated from his earlier position.[158] He was not even ready to surrender the portfolio of Matthai and threatened resignation along with bringing their Labourite friends into the dispute.[159] But this time Wavell neither accepted the direction from Whitehall[160]nor bowed to Nehru's threat of resignation.[161]

With the prior understanding and agreement of Nehru, Wavell stated that he was prepared to offer the deputy chairmanship of the Cabinet Co-ordination Committee (CCC) to a representative of the Muslim League in the Cabinet. Nehru suggested that apart from Wavell and himself the following persons should form the CCC: Patel, Matthai, Rajagopalachari, Liaquat and one other representative from the Muslim League.[162] Wavell categorically rejected his contention and said that he must give the deputy chairmanship of the CCC to one of the League representatives. He held that it was right based on the merit and he had committed to it. [163]

In an attempt to work harmoniously and for achieving a peaceful transfer of power, Liaquat Ali Khan was so careful in his statements and remarks when he entered as the finance minister in the Executive Council that he did not mention the demand for Pakistan. He said that the 'League had come into the government with the intention of working in harmony with our other colleagues.'[164] It was a good beginning in Pethick–Lawrence's eyes to forge unity and 'solidarity of the Muslims and other Minorities within united India as opposed to a separate sovereign Muslim state.'[165]

Ayesha Jalal points out the real intentions and course of actions of the Congress concerning the Interim Government, 'With the Viceroy facing a dismissal and Jinnah's world collapsing, Congress began to build its new order.'[166] It decided to take the League's entry into the Interim Government as a declaration of war. As Wavell had ridiculed the panel of ministers which Congress had presented to him, the latter in its turn criticized the League for the 'poor quality of its men.'[167] Pethick-Lawrence commented that he felt that Liaquat was not very appropriately placed in the finance portfolio but he hoped that he would perform adequately.[168]

Right from the outset, the Interim Government suffered from controversies, mutual distrust and jealousies.[169] Wavell also decided at this time that at least the home portfolio should be given to the Muslim League as part of his earlier thinking but Patel, who was the home minister, refused to give up his portfolio. Patel who wished to have command and control of internal security during the apparent 'war of succession' declined to leave the post. Nehru informed Wavell that Sardar Patel had threatened to resign from the government if his portfolio was changed.[170] Thereupon, Congress offered the finance portfolio to the Muslim League. The Congress leaders expected that because of the technical nature of the subject, the League would refuse the offer of the finance chair and if this happened the Congress would lose nothing; if on the other hand the League nominee did accept the finance portfolio, he would soon make a fool of himself.[171] Either way the Congress would stand to gain.[172] These were its 'noble' sentiments in offering the finance portfolio to the Muslim League. Jinnah was more interested in the foreign and defence portfolios but Chaudhri Muhammad Ali suggested to him to accept the finance portfolio as it could permit the League to influence the policies of the government.[173]

Thus, the first full-fledged, Indian-dominated, Interim Government was inaugurated on 26 October 1946 on the stormy seas of mutual distrust and contrary aims.[174] Congress had tried to keep the League away from the Interim Government but having failed in doing so, they resolved to give the impression that the League had not entered the government to cooperate with the Congress but to prove otherwise. Liaquat Ali Khan on his part refused to accept the leadership of Nehru in the Interim Government stating that Nehru was nobody else's leader but only of the Congress bloc in the government.[175] Rajendra Prasad writes,

Before the members of the League joined the Interim Government the other members had acted as a team and a Cabinet. The Viceroy, too, had recognized the Interim Government as a Cabinet, and in all papers the word 'Cabinet' had officially begun to be used, presumably under the instructions of the Viceroy. In our deliberations also we acted like a Cabinet. The League members, however, were not prepared to accept the Interim Government as a Cabinet, but only as an Executive Council under the government of India

Act, in which each member was more or less the head of a department and had no responsibility to anyone except the Viceroy.[176]

But the discord within the government was merely a sign of the turmoil raging in the country.[177]

Nehru wanted to be treated as a *de facto* prime minister but Liaquat Ali Khan resisted this claim. Secondly, another matter which caused friction between them was the Congress's claim that the League came into the Interim Government on the understanding that the League would revoke its resolution of 29 July withdrawing its acceptance of the plan. Thirdly, violence in Bengal had not ceased. In Bengal there was a League ministry and both Patel and Nehru suggested to Wavell that the Centre should take over the affected areas.[178] Lastly, the League, in its turn, also demanded the same kind of treatment for the UP government where there was a Congress Ministry and complaints about outbreaks of violence, in which Hindu extremists had butchered numerous men, women and children, had been pouring in.[179]

Wavell stuck to his conviction that the two parties might soon come to realize that the British presence in India was necessary and hence would accept guidance, if not actual direction, in the administration of the three central subjects.[180]

All the correspondence and the exchange of views at the personal level, make it quite clear that all the three parties, the Congress, the Muslim League, and the British, were living during those days in a world of false expectations. The aims and objects of each of the three political players were quite different from those of the others. On the one hand, Congress was unwilling to permit the League to have its fair and just share in the Interim Government, and on the other, the League wanted 'to get a foothold for its cherished goal of Pakistan.'[181] The rivalry between the League and the Congress created disharmony, disunity and as a result there was no coordination and cooperation among the ministers. It appeared that each party was working for its respective communal interests which led to an open confrontation between them.[182]

Wavell's main purpose in forming the Interim Government was to make the participants work constructively as a team but the Indian membership of the Interim Government did not share his optimism and high faith in his mission, as a result of which the Council stood divided into two rival camps. This was a turning point in the history of Interim Government, for it proved advantageous for the Muslims' struggle for the cause of Pakistan. Hugh Tinker has recorded that 'pressed by the Viceroy, at the suggestion of the tough Sardar Patel, they agreed to hand over Finance to a Leaguer, confident that any Muslim would 'make a fool of himself'. Liaquat Ali Khan, the new Finance Minister, proceeded to make fools of his Congress colleagues.'[183] The Finance Ministry under the able leadership of Liaquat Ali Khan proved extremely successful and all the assumptions and computations of the Congress and its supporters were proved incorrect.[184] Indeed, the League's control over the finances forced every other government department into submission.[185] According to Maulana Azad, 'the Congress soon realized that it had committed a great blunder in handing over Finance to the Muslim League.'[186]

The formation of the Interim Government truly exposed the Congress and the League as two hostile and irreconcilable parties with totally divergent ideas and methods to deal with the political problems of India at the end of the British rule in India. The more they tried to work together the greater became their mutual bitterness, animosity and clash of interests.[187] Asim Roy has written, 'The Congress steadily and deliberately worked itself up to a position where Jinnah was forced to take Pakistan and leave the scene for good.'[188]

Meanwhile, Jinnah had not committed, so far, to Wavell about the withdrawal of the Muslim League Council's resolution rejecting the Cabinet Mission's statement of 16 May. So Nehru had been insisting upon Wavell to clear up this point with the League and ascertain whether the League's willingness to join the Interim Government meant working as a team or not.[189] Wavell told him that Jinnah had promised to call a meeting of the Muslim League at an early date to rescind its resolution rejecting the Cabinet Mission's statement of 16 May.[190] No doubt, deteriorating internal conditions in the country and fear of a communal civil war had made Wavell so anxious to bring Jinnah into the Interim Government that he had not insisted upon the fulfilment of other conditions.

A number of attempts failed to induce the Muslim League to issue a statement accepting the Mission's plan and, consequently, to begin to participate in the work of the Constituent Assembly. Finally, on 23 November, Wavell told Liaquat Ali Khan that he would not agree to the League remaining in the coalition without accepting the long-term plan. Liaquat Ali Khan replied that the League members were prepared to resign whenever the Viceroy required them to do so but they would not accept the long-term plan unless His Majesty's Government declared that the provinces must meet in sections, and that the representatives in the sections would, by a majority, frame the provincial and the group constitutions. Wavell's arguments failed to convince Liaquat Ali Khan to accept the plan. Liaquat Ali Khan's position was that 'if HMG was afraid of the Congress and had not the courage or honesty to maintain their own Mission Plan, then the Muslims had been thrown to the wolves and must accept the position and do the best they could themselves, for it was useless to expect any mercy from Congress.'[191] The British government made it clear that as far as it was concerned, the British government's interpretation was the official interpretation, and that it must be accepted by all parties in the Constituent Assembly. The statement of 6 December was the last effective effort to bring the Congress and the League together, in framing a constitution for a united India.[192] Unfortunately, it satisfied neither the League nor the Congress. It failed to clarify anything and did not give an authoritative and clear verdict about the intentions of the Cabinet Mission either.[193] The fact was that the British Government had failed to set, as Stanley Wolpert has observed, 'Jinnah's mind at ease or budge him from his intransigent position.'[194]

LIAQUAT'S 'POOR MAN'S BUDGET' OF 1947

Liaquat's most remarkable achievement as the finance minister of the Interim Government was the preparation and presentation of the national budget for 1947–48. According to Muhammad Reza Kazimi, the underlying principle of the budget was 'social justice' which had the potential of uniting the poor masses of both the major communities.[195] The main principles of the budget had been discussed by Liaquat Ali Khan with the Congress representatives, prior to its presentation in the Cabinet, and they had agreed with him on 'general grounds.' Liaquat Ali Khan's memorable Budget speech is 'one of the most brilliant chapters of the Pakistan Movement'.[196] He presented the budget on 28 February 1947. The budget, as it was presented by the first non-British finance minister, was acclaimed as the 'first national budget' and a 'poor man's budget'. In fact both the Congress and the League members cheered him (Liaquat Ali Khan). However, opposition soon arose from the Congress circles. Dishonest intentions were attributed to Liaquat Ali Khan, it was said that he had brought up these proposals 'to ruin the economic life of the country and then to go to Pakistan.'[197]

It is worth mentioning that the Congress had all along been financed by the Hindu capitalists who were especially hit hard by these proposals. Though it was not easy for men who called themselves Socialists, like Nehru, to oppose such a budget but they did not mind totally forgetting their slogans of socialism. According to V.P. Menon, 'This was interpreted in Congress circles as an attempt to penalize the Hindu capitalists (who largely financed the Congress) and to bring about dissension between the right wing and the socialist group within the Congress Party.'[198] With all the other worries, however, as has been observed by V.P. Menon, sharp debates over the budget only added to Wavell's worries as his dream for Hindu–Muslim unity began to mutate into an unattainable illusion.[199]

It was in such an atmosphere of mutual recriminations and impending civil war in India that Prime Minister Attlee, in a statement in the British Parliament on 20 February 1947, stated that His Majesty's Government wished to transfer power to responsible Indian hands not later than June 1948 and if an agreed constitution was not worked out, the government would consider to whom the power of the central government should be handed over; and, in a dramatic move, Wavell was replaced by Lord Mountbatten.[200]

To the Labour government in England, Wavell seemed tired and weighed down by a feeling of frustration; his outlook, inflexible. At the Cabinet meetings during the Interim Government, his strong but silent personality was unequal to the very formidable task of bridging the gulf between divided representatives of the two major communities. Although he had been viceroy for a comparatively short time if one thinks in terms of years only, in a political sense he had been through a long and exacting period. It is argued that his successor Mountbatten's diplomacy and understanding brought about a quick change. Diana

Mansergh has observed that where Mountbatten 'diplomatically guided', Wavell correctly presided.[201] But she overlooks the fact that it was the 'guidance' that caused the murder of impartiality, fair-play and honesty after Wavell's departure. The balance of power also shifted totally to the side of the Congress.

Though it did not meet all of the League's demands Jinnah had accepted the statement of 16 June with a view to a peaceful and constitutional attainment for his goal, but Congress rejected it. The British government went back on its word and Jinnah was not allowed to form the Interim Government. Wavell failed to deliver the goods and his integrity and prestige suffered tremendously in the eyes of the Muslim League. The Congress stock grew higher and it began to assert its position and threatened to create a deadlock. The British could not ignore it as it was a majority party of 70 per cent of the Hindu population of India and was believed to be quite capable of starting a vicious civil war.

Wavell's fair play, impartiality and sense of justice were put to test and he failed to deliver. Wavell knew that the sole purpose of the Congress leaders was to seize power at the Centre and destroy the Muslim League. He believed that the Congress would not like a coalition government, due to its authoritative attitude. Why then did he break his pledge to the League but allow the Congress to form the Interim Government without the League almost on the same terms and condition which the Congress had rejected earlier?

Later, through Wavell's efforts the League did join the Interim Government, however, that caused more harm than good to his dream of a united India because divisions between the two groups had become so acute that any chance of reconciliation had all but disappeared. He believed that the Congress had committed a blunder in 1937 by not forming coalition governments in the provinces, causing thereby, great damage to the communal harmony and leading directly to the Lahore Resolution of 1940. Therefore, Wavell felt that learning from its past experience Congress would avoid a repetition of such acts. However, he was proved entirely wrong in his assessment of the Congress mindset.

In fact, the Congress high command and the leading members of its working committee had always aimed at establishing a unitary form of government, which they succeeded in doing, but only after the partition of India in 1947.

The working of the Interim Government clearly exposed the hidden communal feelings and real political and communal character of both the Congress and the League. Wavell did not allow the Congress to act unilaterally, frustrating its designs to the extent that it demanded his dismissal.

Liaquat Ali Khan as finance member of the interim government was accused of creating problems for the Congress leadership. Congress's dream of having a strong centre with the least possible provincial autonomy began to shatter when League joined the Interim Government and began to share power. It was not Patel who is believed to have spearheaded the Congress demand after the experience of the Interim Government; it was in fact its shattered dreams which forced the Congress to demand a division of India.[202]

Wavell wanted to keep India united and sidetrack the demand for Pakistan; therefore, he believed that a coalition government consisting of the Congress and the League, if established, would solve communal, political, administrative and constitutional problems of India. Wavell's vision of a cooperative coalition government of the two major political parties, however, began to unravel the moment it started to form.

While the Congress had been demanding Wavell's dismissal since August 1946, the Labour Party had begun to think of him as a spent force. In fact, Wavell had become unacceptable both to the Congress and the British government, because in their eyes he had begun to lean towards the League. This led to his dismissal in the end. As we shall analyze in the next chapter, Wavell was, actually, hamstrung by Whitehall for trying to implement his plans.

NOTES

1. Wavell to Pethick–Lawrence, 27 December 1945, *Transfer of Power*, Vol. VI, 315, pp. 686–99.
2. Wavell once again chalked out a plan to cope with the new situation. In his letter of 27 December 1945 to the Secretary of State. He suggested forming a new Central Executive Council as early as the first week of April, for then the results of the elections in the Punjab would be known and these would show the measure of the League's success. This time, he did not want to have a conference on the lines of the Simla Conference and wished to see only the presidents of the League and the

Congress and ask them to let him know the names of panels from which he would choose the League and the Congress members of the Executive Council. He would, if necessary, make it clear to them that if any party refused to co-operate he would go ahead and form an Executive Council without it. He thought if the elections in the Punjab went well for the Muslim League, he intended to assure Jinnah that the Muslims would have parity with the Caste Hindus in the Executive Council, and that the Muslim League could have two of the four key portfolios of External Affairs, Home, Finance and Defence. Although, he visualized the council as consisting of fourteen members, viz, 5 Muslims, 5 Caste Hindus, 2 Scheduled Castes, 1 Sikh and 1 Indian Christian, but he would have preferred it to have only 12 which would include 5 Caste Hindus, 1 Scheduled Caste, 5 Muslims, and 1 Sikh. Ibid.

3. Wavell had always shown great interest in forming the Interim Government and this was evident even immediately after the Cabinet Mission Plan was announced. He believed that if the Congress and the League decided to join the Interim Government, the need for them to work together harmoniously for solving pressing post-war problems would produce a friendly atmosphere which would make the working of the Constituent Assembly smoother and easier. No doubt, he required goodwill on the part of Congress and League not only for the temporary settlement of the issue but also for the peaceful transfer of power to the Indians. But things did not happen according to his wishes as the main political parties had clashing views and contradictory claims.

4. In this connection, Maulana Azad, president of the Congress, stated that though the existing law did not permit an executive to be dependent on the central legislature, however, a convention could be created by which its tenure of office would depend on its enjoyment of such confidence. For the moment, Wavell did not bother to chalk out details regarding the composition of the Interim cabinet, for it would all depend upon the satisfactory solution. Resolution passed by the Congress Working Committee on 24 May 1946, *Transfer of Power*, Vol. VII, Enclosure 370, pp. 679–82.

5. Sarat Chandra Bose, a prominent Congress leader from Bengal, suggested that the Viceroy should first of all invite the provincial governments to submit names of persons suitable for appointment to the Executive Council. He thought that all the provinces except Bengal would comply. The Central Legislature would also have to be asked whether they had any names to put forward. The formation of an Interim Government on these lines would be a first step which would bring everyone face to face with reality and enable the country to get down to the economic and other problems which demanded urgent attention. He thought that the composition of the Interim Government would for the greater part be based on the recommendations of the provincial governments. In this procedure, he contemplated a Congress majority of 8 to 3 in the Interim Government.

6. Lawrence to Attlee, 7 April 1946, *Transfer of Power*, Vol. VII, Annexure to No. 114, pp. 276–78.

7. Contrary to Maulana Azad, Gandhi suggested that members of the Central Legislature should nominate the members of the Executive Council. Nominated members of the official block must be left out of picture. If the Central Legislature

nominated people who were not its members then seats would have to be found for them in the Central Legislature. Gandhi said that he would urge on the Congress that they should offer seats on the Executive Council to the Muslim League. If the British government did not wish to accept the nominations of the Congress then they should accept the nominations of the Muslim League. Note by Major Wyatt of Conversation with Gandhi, 13 April 1946, *Transfer of Power*, Vol. VII, pp. 261–63.

8.   Wavell to Pethick–Lawrence, 18 March 1946, *Transfer of Power*, Vol. VII, pp. 114–5.

9.   Wavell in his reply to Maulana Azad on 30 May said that they had discussed many times before the definition of the powers of the Interim Government and he had never stated that the Interim Government would have the same powers as a Dominion Cabinet. He admitted that His Majesty's Government would treat the new Interim Government with the same close consultation and consideration as a Dominion Government. His Majesty's Government had already stated that it would grant the Interim Government in India the greatest freedom in the exercise of the day-to-day administration of the country and it was his intention to carry out that undertaking faithfully. Further, he was quite sure that the spirit in which the government would work would be of much greater importance than any formal document and guarantee. He said that if the Congress trusted him they should be able to co-operate in a manner which would give India a sense of freedom from external control and this could be a first step for complete freedom when the new constitution was drawn up. He hoped that the Congress would accept these assurances and would have no further hesitation in accepting his offer. Wavell to Azad, 30 May 1946, L/P&J/5/337, pp. 379–80.

10.   Agreeing with Wavell's proposition the British government stated that they could not go beyond the position taken in his letter to Maulana Azad of 30 May 1946. They approved of Wavell's approach but they wished to omit the last sentence of Para 3, 'Because though this must be substantially our position, the enunciation of it as a principle might result in giving Jinnah an absolute veto.' For details see Wavell to Maulana Azad, 30 May 1946, *Transfer of Power*, Vol. VII, Enclosure to 405, pp. 728–29; V.P. Menon suggested to Wavell that he should negotiate with the parties regarding the Interim Government but it would be appropriate that there was nothing to be said for leaving the position fluid and adjusting their course to the circumstances as they went along.

11.   Maulana Azad, in his letter to Wavell on 25 May, demanded that there must be legal and constitutional changes in order to give the status of a truly national government which would not only create a consciousness of freedom but also for the peaceful settlement of the Indian problem. Though the existing Act of 1935 did not permit an Executive responsible to the Central Legislature, Congress believed that the Interim Government on its own accord would make a declaration that it would remain in office only so long as it enjoyed the confidence of the assembly. Ibid.

12.   In his reply to Nehru's letter of 15 June, Wavell stated that he had never believed that his discussions with him and Maulana Azad with regard to the Interim Government had been on the basis of political parties and not communities. In the proposed Interim Government of himself and 13 others, there would be 6

Congressmen and 5 Muslim Leaguers. He did not see how this could be called parity. Nor was there parity between Hindus and Muslims, there being 6 Hindus to 5 Muslims. Wavell to Maulana Azad, 15 June 1946, Mohammad Ashraf, *Cabinet Mission and After*, pp. 149–50.

13. Wavell's approach was that it would bring some positive results if both the leaders met him together and it all seemed headed in the right direction. But quite surprisingly, on the same day, Gandhi in his talk with Lawrence alleged that Jinnah had said that he would use his position in the Interim Government to 'water the seed of Pakistan. His allegation caused enough dent to Wavell's efforts as Nehru felt compelled not to see him along with Jinnah. Wavell in his letter to Nehru invited him together with Jinnah for consultation on how best he could fill the various posts in the Interim Government. He made it clear that he would not discuss any question of principle such as parity or otherwise, but concentrate upon the common objective, that was to get the best possible Interim Government drawn from the two major parties and some of the minorities. Wavell to Nehru, 12 June, Quaid-i-Azam Papers, File No. 14, p. 4.

14. In this connection, Wavell wrote a letter to Jinnah and Nehru on 12 June in which he explained that he did not want to discuss any question of principle such as 'parity' or otherwise but to get the best possible Interim Government drawn from the two major parties and some minorities, and to approach this decision by a consideration of what the portfolio should be and how each one could best be filled. However, to ensure consent of the Congress and the success of the formation of the Interim Government, Wavell put up an altered plan which was based on a ratio of 5:5:3. Note of Pethick–Lawrence's interview with Gandhi on 12 June 1946, *Transfer of Power*, Vol. VII, pp. 888–89.

15. On 15 June he rejected Maulana Azad's proposal to continue his attempt to negotiate an agreement between the two major parties on the composition of the Interim Government. He then informed Maulana Azad the decision of the Cabinet Delegation that the next day they would issue a statement regarding the short-term plan. Tara Chand, *History of the Freedom Movement in India*, Vol. IV (Lahore: Book Traders, 1972), p. 473.

16. It was stated that the Viceroy in consultation with the members of the Cabinet Mission had for some time been exploring the possibilities of a coalition government drawn from the two major parties as well as certain minorities. The discussion had revealed the difficulties which existed between the two main parties in arriving at any basis for the formation of the government. Therefore, they thought that no useful purpose would be served by prolonging these discussions. They held that it was urgently necessary that a strong and representative Interim Government be set up to conduct the pending important business that had to be carried forward. Statement by the Cabinet Delegation and Wavell on 16 June 1946, *Transfer of Power*, Vol. VII, pp. 954–55.

17. These were the proposed names: Jinnah, Nishtar, Liaquat Ali Khan, Nawab Muhammad Ismael Khan, Khawaja Nazimuddin (Muslim League) Sardar Baldev Singh (Sikh), Dr John Matthai (Indian Christian), Sir N.P. Engineer (Parsee), Jagjivan Ram (Scheduled Caste from Congress), Nehru, Rajagopalachari, Dr Rajendra Prasad, H.M. Mahtab, Sardar Patel (Congress).

18. Statement by the Cabinet Delegation and Wavell on 16 June 1946, *Transfer of Power*, Vol. VII, pp. 954–55.

19. H.M. Seervai, *Partition of India: Legend and Reality* (Rawalpindi: Services Book Club, 1991), pp. 61–2.

20. Maulana Azad in his reply on 16 June to Wavell conceded that the parity, between Caste Hindus and Muslims, which they had accepted in the First Muslim League Conference, was only owing to the stress of war and other conditions then existing. He argued that in this context and in present circumstances, they considered this kind of parity as unfair and likely to lead to difficulties. On the one hand, he thought the whole scheme proposed by the British in the statement of May 16 was based on absence of weightage, and on the other, he maintained that 'in the proposed provisional government, there is this weightage, in addition to other far-reaching communal safeguards.' Therefore, these proposals had thus far been unacceptable to the Congress. Ibid.

21. Interview of Wavell with Jinnah, 13 June 1946, Wavell Collection, MSS EUR 997/17.

22. Liaquat Ali Khan in his reply to Wavell's offer to join the Interim Government, said that 'President of the Muslim League had not submitted any list of names to be included in the Interim Government as representatives of the Muslim League I am unable to accept Your Excellency's invitation without the approval and consent of the President of the All India Muslim League.' Liaquat Ali Khan to Wavell, 19 June 1946, R/3/1/114: f 351.

23. Resolution of Muslim League Working Committee on 25 June 1946, Quaid-i-Azam Papers, File No. 14, p. 43.

24. Wavell put forward Jinnah's letter of 19 June before the meeting and sought their opinion. Thus a reply was drafted in the light of the suggestions of the members. The Record of Meeting of Cabinet Delegation and Wavell on 20 June, L/PEJ/5/337, pp. 472–3.

25. Wavell elucidated that until he had received acceptance from those invited to take office in the Interim Government, the names in the statement could not be regarded as final and no change in principle would be made in the statement without the consent of the two major parties. Also no change in the number of 14 members of the Interim Government would be made without the agreement of two major parties. He said that if any vacancy occurred among the seats at present allotted to representatives of the minorities, he would naturally consult both the main parties before filling it. The proportion of members of communities would also be changed with the approval of both the parties. Wavell to Jinnah, 20 June 1946, Quaid-i-Azam Papers, File No. 14, pp. 33–34.

26. Resolution of Muslim League Working Committee on 25 June 1946, Jinnah to Wavell, *Transfer of Power*, Vol. VII, Enclosure to No. 611, pp. 1049–50.

27. They thought that replacement of Sarat Chandra Bose by Mahtab was unjustified. They wished to have Sarat Bose in the Interim Government as he was the leader of the Congress Party in the Central legislature, to control the left wing of their party, and to give representation to Bengal. Mahtab in their eyes was no substitute for Bose as well, was too young for the post and could not be separated from the affairs

of Orissa. The Congress was also opposed to the inclusion of Sardar Abdur Rab Nishtar because of objection. Ibid.

28. Jinnah to Wavell, 26 June 1946, Quaid-i-Azam Papers, File No. 14, p. 46.

29. Wavell to Jinnah, 25 June 1946, L/PEJ/5/337, p. 516.

30. Note by Wavell, 25 June 1946, *Transfer of Power*, Vol. VII, Enclosure to No. 604, pp. 1038–4.

31. Note by Wavell, 25 June 1946, *Transfer of Power*, Vol. VII, Enclosure to No.604, pp. 1039–40.

32. Wavell, *Viceroy's Journal*, pp. 313–4.

33. Besides Viceroy, Sir E. Coats, Sir E. Conran Smith, Sir A. Hydari, Sir R. Hutchings, Sir A. Waugh, Sir Gurunath Bewoor, and Sir George Spence. Wavell to Henderson, 27 June 1946, *Transfer of Power*, Vol. VII, pp. 1059–60.

34. Michael Edwards, *Nehru: A Political Biography*, p. 171.

35. Statement by Jinnah on 27 June, L/PEJ/5/337, pp. 529–34.

36. Record of Meeting of Cabinet Delegation and Wavell on 26 June 1946, *Transfer of Power*, Vol. VII, pp 1060–62.

37. Tara Chand, *History of the Freedom Movement in India*, Vol. IV, pp. 473–4.

38. Wavell to Jinnah 27 June 1946, L/PEJ/5/337: p. 528.

39. S.M. Burke, *Landmarks of the Pakistan Movement* (Lahore: Research Society of Pakistan, 2001), pp. 370–76.

40. Victoria Schofield, *Wavell: Soldier & Statesman*, p. 356.

41. Resolution of Muslim League Working Committee, 25 June 1946, Quaid-i-Azam Papers, File No. 14, p. 43.

42. Wavell to Jinnah, 27 June 1946, L/PEJ/5/337, p. 528.

43. G. Allana, *Quaid-e-Azam Jinnah: The Story of a Nation* (Lahore: Ferozesons Pvt Ltd., reprint 1996), pp. 11–2.

44. Victoria Schofield, *Wavell: Soldier & Statesman*, p. 356.

45. Griffiths to Lawrence, 3 September 1946, L/PEJ/7/10500: ff 8–10.

46. Record of Meeting of Cabinet Delegation and Wavell on 26 June 1946, *Transfer of Power*, Vol. VII, pp. 1060–62.

47. Wavell said that 'In view, however, of the long negotiations which have already taken place, and since we all have other work to do, we feel that it will be better to have a short interval before proceeding with further negotiations for the formation of an Interim Government'. Wavell to Jinnah, 25 June 1946, L/PEJ/5/337, p. 516.

48. Wavell recorded, 'The result has been that I have had to deal for the rest of the year with an arrogant Congress, convinced that it had H.M.G. in its pocket; a suspicious and resentful Muslim League, feeling it had been betrayed'. Wavell, *Viceroy's Journal*, p. 402.

49. Yogesh Chadha, *Rediscovering Gandhi*, pp. 412–3.

50. Though the author of this study believes that there were many other important factors, (already discussed) that made Jinnah and the League popular with the Muslims in the Muslim-majority provinces but Ayesha Jalal writes that: 'The fear of a powerful centre dominated by the Congress had been the main reason why the Muslim-majority province politicians had rallied behind Jinnah and the League. Nehru's statements seemed to suggest that the Congress High Command intended

to deploy central authority to restrict their freedom of action in their provincial domains'. Ayesha Jalal, *The Sole Spokesman*, p. 210.

51. Hector Bolitho, *Jinnah, Creator of Pakistan*, p. 165.

52. Agatha Harrison was Secretary of Indian Conciliation Group formed in 1931.

53. Horace Gundry Alexander was a leader of the Friends' Ambulance Unit in India and Lecturer at Wood Brooke College, Birmingham.

54. Wavell, *Viceroy's Journal*, pp. 309–15.

55. *Hindustan Times*, 27 June 1946.

56. *Dawn*, Delhi, 27 June 1946.

57. As we discussed earlier that if there was any doubt about the Congress's real intention and attitude with regard to the Cabinet Mission Plan, it was effectively set at rest by the speeches and the statements of Nehru after he had taken over as president of the Congress in July 1946. Whether on purpose or unconsciously, Nehru's statements and speeches, along with Gandhi's already stated ideas about the Cabinet Mission Plan did great damage to the success of the Cabinet Mission Plan. These statements convinced Jinnah and the Muslim League more strongly than ever before that Congress, with its brute majority in the Constituent Assembly, had the sole intention of establishing a 'Hindu' Raj in India. Though the Cabinet Mission, in its distress and disappointment, was prepared to clutch at any convenient straw, it was the equivocal and pusillanimous attitude of the British government which encouraged the Congress to persist in its unjustified and wrong claims. This passive encouragement of the Congress by the British government made them even more arrogant, thereby rupturing India's unity. Wavell explained to Nehru that the statement of 16 May did not make grouping compulsory. It left the decision to the elected representatives of the provinces concerned sitting together in sections. The only provision which was made was that the representatives of certain provinces should meet in sections so that they could decide whether or not they wished to form groups. Even when this had been done the individual province was still to have the liberty to opt out of the group, if they so decided. Wavell to Maulana Azad, 15 June 1946; Sh. Muhammad Ashraf, *Cabinet Mission and Aftermath*, pp. 149–50.

58. Waheed-uz-Zaman, *Quaid-i-Azam Mohammad Ali Jinnah: Myth and Reality* (Islamabad: National Institute of Historical and Cultural Research, 1985), p. 80.

59. Syed Sharifuddin Pirzada, ed., *The Foundations of Pakistan*, Vol. II, p. 547.

60. Wavell wrote to the Governor of Bengal that 'The Muslim League is clearly very sore about the decision not to proceed with the Interim Government after the rejection by Congress of the scheme of the 16th June. Paragraph 8 of the Statement of the 16th June was put in deliberately to safeguard the Muslim League since Congress had stated in writing that they considered the two plans to hang together and that they would either accept or reject both. When the Congress turned around and accepted the long-term scheme of May 16th while rejecting the proposals for the Interim Government in the Statement of June 16th we found ourselves compelled by paragraph 8 in the Statement of June 16th to make a fresh attempt to negotiate agreement with both the major parties about an Interim Government. I do not think there can be two opinions about the meaning of paragraph 8 of the 16th June, and it compelled us to consult both main parties in any fresh attempt

when both had accepted the Statement of May 16th. Perhaps we ought to have put out more publicity in the first day or two since people got an entirely wrong idea of situation. Jinnah concealed the fact that he had been told (before over his Working Committee met to consider the proposals for the 16th June) that in effect the offer was no longer open since the Congress had turned it down. It was only when the correspondence was published that it became clear to the public that Jinnah knew the position when he went to his Working Committee and got them accept the scheme for the Interim Government. I shall hope to have it out with Jinnah some time but with his known obstinacy I doubt if I shall convince him that his allegations were unjustified. I put in great deal of hard work and had some acrimonious discussion at times to get the best possible deal for the League; and it was very largely Jinnah's own fault that we did not succeed in getting an Interim Government on what would have been very good terms of the League. So I feel a little sore myself at line Jinnah and League have since taken.' Wavell to Sir F. Burrows (Bengal), 19 July 1946, R/3/1/123: ff 168–70.

61. This was reported in the report that 'Sarat Bose and Surendra Mohan Ghose have been trying to convince all that the Congress policy to accept the proposals is part and parcel of the freedom movement. They say that simultaneously with the formation of the Constituent A, there would be a demand by the Congress for the substitution of the Care-Taker Government by Nationalist Interim Government with a Nationalist Muslim on it. At the same time, the demand for recognition of the right of provinces to opt out, if they so desired, would be revived by the Congress. these would constitute a direct challenge to both the Muslim League and the British Government. In this context, Surendra Mohan Ghose and the Bengal Congress particularly the Jagantar Group, feels that these two demands would be acquiesced in the British Government even if that forces the Muslim League out of the Constituent Assembly. But Surat Bose says that the Congress High Command is of the opinion that in that eventuality the British Government would back out and declare the Constituent Assembly null and void. This will be the turning point in the present negotiations and the Congress will declare the Constituent Assembly to be the real national Government. This government will continue to function irrespective of opposition and repression the Congress will marshal the different leftist forces to run the Constituent Assembly as parallel government with a country-wide network of panchayats. Meanwhile, the disbanded Indian Army personnel, the INA and the 9th-Augusters will constitute the front-rank fighters, behind whom the Congress civil administration will function'. Intelligence Bureau, Home Department, Report by P.E.S. Finey, Deputy Director, 8 July 1946.

62. Syed Sharifuddin Pirzada, ed., *The Foundations of Pakistan*, Vol. II, p. 547.

63. Wavell had formed a new caretaker government, which was sworn-in on 4 July. But in view of the internal condition of the country especial worsening communal tension, he realized the immediate need for installing a popular government consisting of leaders of the political parties. Wavell decided to reopen negotiations for an Interim Government with Jinnah and Nehru on 16 July and a final draft of letters was approved by His Majesty's Government. Pethick–Lawrence agreed with his proposal to go ahead without the League if it refused to accept that Congress

nominees could include a Muslim. Lawrence to Wavell, 18 July 1946, L/PEJ/10/73: ff 217–18.

64. Pethick–Lawrence directed Wavell that 'If Muslim stays out of Interim Government our intention is that you should fill the Muslim League quota of places so far as possible with other Muslims'. Ibid.

65. Wavell to Maulana Azad and Jinnah on 22 July 1946, R/3/1/116: ff 61–3.

66. Wavell, *Viceroy's Journal*, p. 320.

67. Text of two resolutions passed by the All-India Muslim League Council at Bombay on 29 July 1946, Quaid-i-Azam Papers, File No. 20, pp. 140–43.

68. Sher Muhammad Garewal, *Jinnah–Gandhi Correspondence*, p. 81.

69. Maulana Azad to Cripps 22 July 1946, L/PO/6/115: f 1.

70. Nehru to Wavell, 23 July 1946, R/3/116: ff 65–6.

71. Wavell, *Viceroy's Journal*, p. 320.

72. Wavell to Lawrence, 24 July 1946, R/3/1/116: ff 75–6.

73. As pointed out earlier the extremist wing of the party wanted Sardar Patel to be the president of the Congress, for they wanted strong and inflexible policy to be carried out in the final phase of the freedom struggle. As Michael Edwards has recorded that Nehru was elected the new president of the Congress at the persuasion of Gandhi, who had been still influential in Congress because the real power in the Congress rested with the right wing which dominated the organization and with Gandhi. Above all, Gandhi seemed to be convinced that Nehru would be more acceptable to the Labour party in London. Michael Edwards, *Nehru: A Political Biography*, p. 175.

74. Lawrence to Wavell, 26 July 1946, L/PEJ/10/73: ff 157–61.

75. Wavell, *Viceroy's Journal*, p. 324.

76. Ibid.

77. An account of Wavell's Interview with Nehru on 30 July 1946. Notes of Important Interviews, 1943–7, Wavell Collection, pp. 192–3.

78. V.P. Menon, *Transfer of Power in India*, p. 238.

79. Wavell to Lawrence, 1 August 1946, R/3/1/116: f 105.

80. Ibid.

81. Lawrence to Wavell, 2 August 1946, L/PEJ/10/73: ff 104–5.

82. Menon said that the British government was committed to this course (vide paragraph 8 of the statement of 16 June) since the only party which had now accepted the statement of 16 May was the Congress. He held that political considerations also pointed to the same conclusion. To him, defection of the League had added to the political confusion; strikes were becoming more frequent and widespread than ever before and were no longer confined to industrial workers. There were vast administrative problems waiting to be tackled and he held that the situation could be more adequately tackled by the Congress than by the present caretaker government with its backing by nine provincial governments. He told them that apart from the question of administrative efficiency, question of future Indo-British relationship was also important. It seemed reasonable to expect that the majority party installed in power with the help of the British Government would be inclined to help in reaching an amicable settlement. Note by V.P. Menon, undated, *Transfer of Power*, Vol. VIII, pp. 180–82.

83. Note of Proceeding of the Special meeting of the Executive Council held on 4 August 1946, R/3/1/116: ff 120–6.
84. Wavell to Lawrence, 4 August 1946, R/3/1/116: f 128.
85. Lawrence to Wavell, 5 August 1946, L/PEJ/10/73: ff 98–100.
86. Note of Proceeding of the Special meeting of the Executive Council held on 4 August 1946, *Transfer of Power*, Vol. VIII, pp. 182–87.
87. Wavell to Pethick–Lawrence, 4 August 1946, ibid., p. 188.
88. Pethick–Lawrence to Wavell, 5 August 1946, *Transfer of Power*, Vol. VIII, p. 190.
89. Wavell recorded, 'Gandhi at the end exposed Congress policy of domination more nakedly than ever before. The more I see that old man, the more I regard him as an unscrupulous old hypocrite; he would shrink from no violence and blood-letting to achieve his ends though he would naturally prefer to do so by chicanery and false show of mildness and friendship'. Wavell, *Viceroy's Journal*, p. 353.
90. Ibid., p. 336.
91. Congress Working Committee Resolution of 10 August 1946, Political Series, June–December 1946, Wavell Collections, pp. 95–96.
92. Lal Bahadur, ed., *Struggle for Pakistan: Tragedy of the Triumph of Muslim Communalism in India* (New Delhi: Sterling Publishers Pvt. Ltd., 1988), p. 254.
93. Nehru to Wavell, 10 August 1946, R/3/1/116: f 167.
94. Correspondence between Jinnah and Nehru, *Transfer of Power*, Vol. VIII, pp. 237–9.
95. Jinnah to Nehru, 15 August 1946, ibid.
96. Tara Chand, *History of the Freedom Movement in India*, Vol. IV, p. 482.
97. Wavell to Lawrence, 18 August 1946, R/3/1/117: ff 18–19.
98. Wavell to Lawrence, 13 August 1946, L/PO/10/23.
99. B.N. Sharma, *India Betrayed: The Role of Nehru* (New Delhi: Manas Publications, 1997), pp. 131–3.
100. Note of interview with Nehru by Wavell, 18 August 1946, R/3/1/117: ff 31–2.
101. Wavell to Lawrence, 19 August 1946, R/3/1/117: ff 34–5.
102. Note of interview with Nehru by Wavell, 18 August 1946, R/3/1/117: ff 31–2.
103. Wavell to Pethick–Lawrence, 21 August 1946, R/3/1/117: f 64.
104. Note by Wavell, 22 August 1946, R/3/1/117: ff 80–4.
105. Ibid.
106. Nehru to Wavell, 22 August 1946, R/3/1/117: ff 93–4.
107. Ibid.
108. Text of Wavell's Broadcast on 24 August 1946, R/3/1/117: f 120.
109. Ibid.
110. Pethick–Lawrence wrote to Wavell that Press reaction here in England has been well received even in such right wing organs as the *Daily Telegraph*, Lawrence to Wavell, 28 August 1946, L/PO/10/23.
111. Nyle, Governor of Bengal to Wavell, 26 August 1946, L/PEJ/5/209: f 43.
112. *Hindustan Times*, 27 August 1946.
113. Ibid.
114. Nehru handed over the list of these men indicating how portfolios should be allotted to the members of the Provisional Government. Nehru, Baldev, Patel, Dr John Matthai, Asif Ali, Rajendra Prasad, Jagjivan Ram, Dr Shafat Ahmad Khan,

Syed Ali Zaheer Rajagopalachari, Sarat Chandra Bose, C.H. Bhabha, Nehru to Wavell, 1 September 1946, R/3/1/117: ff 218–19.

115. The Interim Government took office and seven out of the 12 members were sworn in at a ceremony which took place in the Viceroy's House. *Indian Annual Register*, Vol. 11, 1946, p. 23.

116. Ibid.

117. *The Statesman*, 26 November 1946.

118. Tara Chand, *Freedom Movement in India*, Vol. 4, p. 486.

119. Wavell's interview with Sardar Patel, 5 September 1946, Wavell Papers, Notes of Important Interviews, 1943–7, pp. 223–5.

120. Wavell writing to Nehru said, 'I have read the statement by Mr Jinnah in today's papers and in present circumstances I agree that there would be no use in my sending for him'. Wavell to Nehru, 19 August 1946, R/3/1/117: f 38.

121. Jaswant Singh, *Jinnah India-Partition-Independence* (New Delhi: Rupa & Co., 2009), p. 385.

122. Mazhar Kibriya, *Gandhi and Indian Freedom Struggle* (New Delhi: APH Publishing Corporation, 1999), pp. 339–40.

123. Note by Wavell of Interview with Nehru and Gandhi on 27 August 1946, R/3/1/117: f 139.

124. Ibid.

125. Nehru to Wavell 28 August 1946, R/3/1/117: ff 164–5.

126. Gandhi to Wavell, 28 August 1948, R/3/1/117: f 142.

127. Lt.-Gen. F.R.R. Bucher, Army Commander met Wavell on 31 October 1946 and briefed him about the Bengal riots. Both Bucher and Wavell agreed the only hope of peace was if the two communities came together, but said that there was no sign of an approach towards communal harmony; on the contrary both sides were arming and organizing for struggle; Hindus were determined to show the incapability of the Bengal government and to cause a breakdown. They referred to the threat of general strike, but said that they were told that Gandhi had declared against it. They agreed that loss of life, or suffering, did not have any sobering effect compared with obtaining party advantage from such suffering. Notes of Important interviews by Wavell, Wavell Collections, MSS Eur D 997/17.

128. Wavell to Lawrence 28 August 1946, R/3/1/117: f 145.

129. Lawrence to Wavell 28 August 1946, L/PEJ/10/75: ff 394–5.

130. Scott to Abel, 2 September 1946, R/3/1/117: f 232.

131. Note by Wavell, 2 September 1946, Wavell Papers, Notes of Important Interviews, 1943–7, pp. 256–7.

132. Ibid.

133. Ghulam Kibria, *Pre-Independence Indian Muslim Mindset* (Karachi: City Press Bookshop, 2001), p. 98.

134. In this reference, Nehru appears to have written to Cripps on this topic, and Cripps forwarded Nehru's letter to Pethick–Lawrence. This is clear from the letter of 30 September 1946 addressed by Pethick–Lawrence to Cripps, *Transfer of Power*, Vol. VIII, pp. 629–30.

135. Wavell in a secret telegram to Lawrence wrote that 'I have informed you by telegram of the indications that the Muslim League would like a settlement, but I have a

definite feeling now that the Congress are not inclined to go out of their way to settle with the League. I am afraid that the Congress policy is to consolidate itself in power, to use British assistance in putting down riots from day to day, and perhaps if necessary to buy off the Muslims at a lower price when we finally go. I am quite clear that we must not allow Congress virtually to monopolize power under the protection of the British regime, and we must continue our efforts to get a coalition. Perhaps by the time you get this shall have decided what next move should be'. Wavell to Pethick–Lawrence, 10 September 1946, Wavell Collections, Political Series, 28 June to 6 December 1946, Vol. IV, part V, IOR MSS Eur D977/8, pp. 186–7.

136. Wavell to Lawrence, 10 September 1946, L/PO/10/23.
137. Lawrence to Attlee, 10 September 1946, R/30/1/8: ff 53–5.
138. Note by Wavell of interview with Rajagopalachari on 13 August 1946.
139. Nehru to Cripps, 20 September 1946, *Transfer of Power*, Vol. VIII, p. 340.
140. S.M. Burke and Salim Al-Din Quraishi, *Quaid-i-Azam Mohammad Ali Jinnah: His Personality and His Politics* (Karachi: Oxford University Press, 1997), p. 310.
141. Mrs Ghosh to Mr Ghosh, 27 August 1946, *Transfer of Power*, Vol. VIII, Enclosure to 272, p. 438.
142. Nehru to Wavell, 22 August 1946, R/3/1/117: ff 93–4.
143. Scott to Abell, 2 September 1946, R/3/1/117: f 232.
144. Hugh Tinker, *Men Who Overturned Empires*, p. 60.
145. Note of Interview with Jinnah by Wavell on 2 October 1946, Wavell Collection, MSS Eur 997/17, pp. 643–44.
146. Ibid.
147. Seervai, *Partition of India: Legend or Reality*, p. 65.
148. Ibid.
149. Bhashyam Kasturi, *Walking Alone Gandhi and India's Partition* (Delhi: Vision Books Pvt. Ltd., 2001), p. 42.
150. Tara Chand, *History of the Freedom Movement in India*, Vol. IV, p. 486.
151. Wavell wrote to Pethick–Lawrence that Jinnah stated yesterday to a *Daily Mail* representative that if His Majesty's Government were to invite him to London to start a new series of conferences on an equal footing with other negotiators he would accept. Suhrawardy also said in Delhi that if Jinnah felt there was a spirit of co-operation on the Congress side he would less than his present demands. Wavell said that he was sure that now was the time to send for Jinnah and try to get a settlement especially as the Congress seem to aim at consolidating their power and disregarding the League altogether. He held that 'the longer we wait the more difficult a settlement is likely to be'. Wavell to Lawrence, 10 September 1946, Wavell Collections, Political Series, 28 June to 6 December 1946, Vol. IV, part V, MSS Eur D977/8, pp. 187–8.
152. Ayesha Jalal, *The Sole Spokesman*, pp. 208–40.
153. Note of Wavell's Interview with Jinnah, 12 October 1946, Wavell Collection, MSS Eur 997/17, pp. 703–5.
154. Wavell to Jinnah, 13 October 1946, R/3/1/118: f 137.
155. Jinnah to Wavell, 13 October 1946, Quaid-i-Azam Papers, File No. 20, p. 68.
156. Ayesha Jalal, *The Sole Spokesman*, p. 231.

157. Those were Liaquat Ali Khan, I.I. Chundrigar, Sardar Abdur Rab Nishtar, Ghazanfar Ali Khan, and Jogendar Nath Mandal.

158. Wavell wrote to Nehru that he should fulfil his promise and said that 'I am afraid I cannot accept the position stated in your letter, dated 15 October, that the minority representatives must all continue to hold their portfolios and that the most important portfolios held by the Congress nominees must also remain with him. It is, I think, inevitable that I should ask that one of the following portfolios should be made available to the Muslim League—External Affair, Home, and Defence. Similarly I think the Muslim League must have either Industries and Civil Supplies or Commerce. I should like to discuss this matter with you today and perhaps you would be good enough to let me know when you could conveniently come. In order to get a quick decision I suggest that you should come with full authority to settle the matter so far as the Congress are concerned.' Wavell to Nehru, 22 October 1946, Wavell Collections, Political Series, 28 June to 6 December 1946, Vol. IV, part V, IOR, MSS Eur D 997/8, p. 274.

159. Nehru informed Wavell that 'we cannot continue in the Government if a decision is imposed upon us against our will, as suggested by you. We would not have attached importance to the allocation of portfolios but for the implication and circumstances which I have already mentioned and which compel us to do so. Two months ago I was asked to form the Interim Government and I undertook that responsibility. This was done as a result of all the talks and negotiations which preceded it with concurrence of His Majesty's Government. Now that a crisis has arisen which is leading to our resignation and the termination of this Government, I think His Majesty's Government should fully know the background of events here. I am glad therefore that you are referring the matter to them. I have tried to explain our position to you in my two letters, dated 23 October. These letters may be sent on to His Majesty's Government.' Nehru to Wavell, 24 October 1946, Wavell Collections, Political Series, 28 June to 6 December 1946, Vol. IV, part V, IOR, MSS Eur D997/17, p. 286.

160. Pethick–Lawrence wrote to Wavell that 'Though Jinnah's statement as it appears in *Times* of today is not encouraging I should welcome your proposal to have a discussion with Jinnah. But leave it to your discretion. As to your paragraph 5, 6 and 7, I agree with you that it would be better not to fill seats with "stooge" Muslims and thereby further exacerbate Muslim League feeling. You will no doubt consult us again before finally breaking with Nehru on the issue.' Lawrence to Wavell, 19 August 1946, Wavell Collections, Political Series, 28 June to 6 December 1946, Vol. IV, part V, IOR, MSS Eur D997/7, p. 118.

161. Nehru quite frankly conceded that 'your new proposal would change the whole approach to the problem and put an end to the responsibility which, at your suggestion, we had undertaken. We are now asked to revert to the previous stage which, we had thought, had finally ended after months of fruitless effort. It puts us in an embarrassing and unenviable position, and the difficulties inherent in the situation are likely to be considered increased. In view of recent happenings, especially in Calcutta, such a step, far from leading to harmony, will be construed and lead to a contrary result. We feel, therefore, that we are quite unable to agree to your new proposal. We have come to Delhi for a specific purpose and on an

urgent errand. If that purpose does not hold, then there appears to be no necessity for us to stay on here.' Nehru to Wavell, 19 August 1946, Wavell Collections, Political Series, 28 June to 6 December 1946, Vol. IV, part V, IOR, MSS Eur D997/7, pp. 115–6.

162. Nehru to Wavell, 30 October 1946, Wavell Collections, Political Series, 28 June to 6 December 1946, Vol. IV, part V, IOR, MSS Eur D997/8, pp. 298–9.

163. Wavell to Nehru, 30 October 1946, Wavell Collections, Political Series, 28 June to 6 December 1946, Vol. IV, part V, IOR, MSS Eur D977/8, pp. 299–300.

164. *The Statesman*, 27 October 1947.

165. Pethick–Lawrence wrote to Wavell, 'I agree that Liaquat's statement to the Press is not too bad. It is interesting that he made no reference to Pakistan until a question was put to him on the subject and then he tried to elevate Pakistan into a sort of philosophical conception as meaning freedom for Hindus and Muslims and security and justice for the minorities. I should like to think that this was an indication that the League leaders were going in for a policy more akin to that of Muslim before 1939, i.e., solidarity of the Muslims and other minorities within united India as opposed to a separate sovereign Muslim State. But this is probably too good to be true though there may be a section of Jinnah's followers who favour a return to this policy, or at any rate giving it a trial in the interim period. But even if it is merely a conciliatory gestures by Liaquat it is to be welcomed.' Pethick–Lawrence to Wavell, 8 November 1946, L/PO/10/23, pp. 308–9.

166. Ayesha Jalal, *The Sole Spokesman*, p. 218.

167. Wavell observed that 'The main difficulty about the Congress proposals is the question of seats for Muslims. I cannot recommend this proposal I feel to include them would probably destroy the last chance of Jinnah coming in. Also I think it is likely that neutral Muslim may refuse as Zakir Hussain has done, to avoid being boycotted or prosecuted by other Muslims. It would be undignified to have to tout round to get unimpressive Muslims simply to fill up the places: and it would not conduce to efficiency.' Note by Wavell, 18 August 1946, R/3/1/117: f 21.

168. Pethick–Lawrence to Wavell, 1 November1946, Wavell Collections, Political Series, 28 June to 6 December 1946, Vol. IV, part V, IOR, MSS EUR D977/8, p. 302.

169. Writing to Lawrence, Wavell said, 'before this reaches you I expect you will have heard how the negotiations for the redistribution of the portfolios have gone. I expect there may be difficulties. The Congress have already stated their maximum claim, and indicated that they think their leading members (Nehru and Patel) nor Baldev Singh, Matthai or Bhabha should be disturbed. This would leave the Muslim League without any of the most important portfolios and I have told Nehru that League must have either External Affairs or Home or Defence, and also one of the two main portfolios, Commerce and Industries and Supplies. They will not like it. They believed that there is no genuine intention on the part of the League to make the Coalition work.' Wavell to Lawrence, 22 October 1946, Wavell Collection, MSS Eur D997/17, p. 272.

170. Nehru throughout negotiations for the coalition government had been very divided and confused as his own ministers were not ready to leave the office which he had promised Wavell. He informed Wavell that 'I hasten to write to you and tell you that your decision to take away the Home portfolio from Sardar Patel and give it

to the Muslim League is one, which will lead to certain consequences, which I already have indicated to you. Sardar Patel told you personally and has told us that he would in that event resign from the Government. I take it that it is with full knowledge of this that you have taken your decision. We are in full agreement with Sardar Patel in this matter and we cannot continue in government without him.' Nehru to Wavell 24 October, Wavell Collection, MSS Eur D997/17, pp. 284–5.

171. Hugh Tinker, *India and Pakistan* (London, 1962), p. 35.

172. Maulana Azad, *India Wins Freedom*, p. 166.

173. Chaudhri Muhammad Ali, *The Emergence of Pakistan* (Lahore: Research Society of the Pakistan Punjab University, 1967), p. 84.

174. *The Indian Annual Register*, Vol. II, p. 40.

175. Muhammad Ashraf, *Cabinet Mission Plan and After*, pp. 429–30.

176. Rajendra Prasad, *India Divided* (Lahore: Book Traders, 1988), p. 412.

177. Ibid.

178. Wavell wrote that 'I made a short address to the new Cabinet Before the meeting it looked as though there might be another crisis. Patel sent to me late last night a proposal that the law and order situation in Bengal should be discussed in Cabinet today and said that he and his colleagues whom he had consulted were emphatically of the opinion that Government of India should authorize, if necessary by ordinance, special officers assisted by adequate staff and military support to proceed to and function in the areas affected, arrest, and detain offenders, and take all other steps necessary to restore order. Secondly, that I should exercise my special powers and take over law and order in the affected areas if not in the whole of Bengal, from the hands of the present Bengal government. A discussion of this proposal would probably have broken the coalition at the first meeting. It was also not constitutionally a subject for the Cabinet, unless I chose to consult them. I talked to Nehru and others and refused to discuss it. They were obviously being very strongly pressed from the outside on the line that it is useless to have Congress in a national government unless it can protect Hindus from Muslims.' Wavell to Lawrence, 26 October 1946, R/3/1/119A: ff 65–6.

179. Sir Francis Tuker, *While Memory Serves* (London: Cassel, 1950), pp. 196–201.

180. Tara Chand, *History of the Freedom Movement in India*, Vol. 4, p. 488.

181. Speech of Ghazanfar Ali Khan, *Indian Annual Register*, 1946, Vol. II, p. 271.

182. Chaudhri Muhammad Ali, *The Emergence of Pakistan*, pp. 82–102.

183. Hugh Tinker, *India and Pakistan A Short Political Guide* (London: Pall Mall Press Limited, 1962), pp. 35–6.

184. The Congress deliberately handed over the Finance department to the League as they had expected that the League would not be able to handle it, for it had no experience to deal with finances. It was argued in the Congress circle that 'because of the technical nature of the subject, the league would refuse the offer. If this happened, the Congress would lose nothing. If, on the other hand, the League nominee accepted the Finance portfolio, he would soon make a fool of himself. Either way Congress would stand to gain.'

185. Altaf Hussain, the editor of *Dawn*, somehow came to know the details of the large amount of money spent on the renovation of Patel's bungalow and published it in the *Dawn*. When the Information Department denied the charge, *Dawn* published

the facsimile of the expenditure sheets which further humiliated Patel, the iron man of the Congress. This was not all as the 'tough man', as Sardar Patel was known, could not recruit even a peon without the prior permission of the finance minister.

186. Maulana Azad, *India Wins Freedom*, p. 167.

187. Wavell wrote to Pethick–Lawrence that 'I had an interview with Nehru and Liaquat yesterday evening. I urged on them the necessity for three measures to deal with the present dangerous situation. An effective control of Press, B support by provincial ministries of officials and police in place of constant criticism, Congress formation of coalition ministries in provinces. At mention of coalition in provinces, Nehru suddenly blew up in characteristic fashion and denied the existence of a coalition at the Centre since the Muslim League members declined to recognize him as de facto Premier or to attend his daily "Cabinet meetings". I reminded him of the constitutional position, whereupon he proffered his resignation. I took no notice of this or of its subsequent repetition and told him that I was quite willing that my colleagues should meet outside the Cabinet for informal discussion as and when they liked but I could not recognize such meetings as official or his position as Vice-President as being that of a Premier. I pointed out the existence of Committees of Cabinet for discussion of business concerning several departments and suggested that they should be used. Liaquat remained calm and said that Muslim League members had every intention of co-operating in the Central Cabinet and the League was quite prepared to discuss coalitions in the provinces provided that it was general. But League members did not recognize Nehru as Premier and had come in to work existing constitution. Nehru eventually calmed down. I cannot tell yet whether the present disturbance will die down or spread but the whole country is in a highly inflammable state and we must be prepared for further trouble. It is therefore essential that His Majesty's Government should make up its mind on policy in event of Breakdown.' Wavell to Pethick–Lawrence, 11 November 1946, R/3/1/119A: f 124.

188. It was clear that the Constituent Assembly would be a solemn and perhaps dangerous farce if the Muslim League continued to boycott it. The Congress might conveniently frame a constitution for section A as defined in the Cabinet Mission Plan. But it could not frame a constitution either for Section B and C or for the British India as a whole. Therefore, to continue with the Constituent Assembly under such circumstances would be provocative. Asim Roy, 'The High Politics of India' Partition: The Revisionist Perspective', quoted in, *Themes in Indian History: India's Partition Process, Strategy and Mobilization*, edited by Mushirul Hasan (New Delhi: Oxford University Press, 1993), p. 40.

189. Nehru to Wavell, 23 October 1946, R/3/1/119A: ff 9–13.

190. Wavell to Nehru, 24 October 1946.

191. Wavell to Lawrence, 23 November 1946, R/3/1/127: ff 69–70.

192. Seervai, *Partition of India: Legend and Reality*, pp. 67–7.

193. No wonder, this interpretation had not been acceptable to Congress, which wanted each province to decide independently whether to join a group or not. Now Congress used this statement for its own end and instead of giving a solemn pledge that it would abide by the official statement of the British government, it said that

it would be prepared to abide by an Indian Federal Court ruling on its interpretation of the grouping clause.

194. Stanley Wolpert, *Jinnah of Pakistan*, p. 300.

195. Muhammad Reza Kazimi, *Liaquat Ali Khan: His Life and Work* (Karachi: Oxford University Press, 2003), p. 220.

196. For details see: Roger D. Long, ed., *Dear Mr Jinnah' Selected Correspondence and Speeches of Liaquat Ali Khan, 1937–1947* (Karachi: Oxford University Press, 2004), pp. 296–304.

197. These accusations were imposed on Liaquat Ali Khan by Mohan Lal Saksena, a member of the assembly. For details see: Liaquat Ali Khan's speech on the Indian Finance Bill on 27 March 1947, *Indian Annual Register*, Vol. 1, 1947; Rafique Afzal, *Speeches and Statements of Quaid-i-Millat Liaquat Ali Khan*, pp. 99–114.

198. V.P. Menon, *The Transfer of Power in India*, p. 348.

199. Ibid., p. 348.

200. *The Indian Annual Register 1947*, Vol. I, p. 38.

201. Diana Mansergh, ed., *Independence years: The Selected Papers of Indian and Commonwealth of Nicholas Mansergh* (New Delhi: Oxford University Press, 1999), p. 53.

202. P.N. Chopra, ed., *The Collected Works of Sardar Vallabhbhai Patel*, Vol. XI (Delhi: Konark Publishers Pvt. Ltd, 1997), p. x.

5

Wavell and His Majesty's Government

This chapter attempts to investigate the relationship between the British government in India and His Majesty's Government in London during Wavell's viceroyalty of India. It discusses the differences in ideas, approaches and plans of Wavell with the British political leaders and bureaucrats such as Winston Churchill, Sir Stafford Cripps, Leopold Amery, Lord Pethick–Lawrence and Clement Attlee, and examines their actions because they shaped the policies of the British government towards British India.

Wavell's appointment was an obvious attempt to maintain a political status quo in India for the duration of the war, but he also displayed a keen interest in resolving the constitutional and political deadlock then prevailing in India. His views and opinions collided with those of the politicians and bureaucrats in London. For example, where he advocated an early transfer of power to the Indians his bosses back in London were totally opposed to such a course of action. Such views made him unpopular with the Conservative as well as Labour governments.

As we have discussed earlier, Wavell believed in the geographical unity of India, therefore, he was against the demand for Pakistan. In order to achieve his aims he floated a number of ideas and plans such as the Wavell Plan, the Cabinet Mission Plan and the Breakdown Plan but he was prevented from implementing them by His Majesty's Government. Eventually he was dismissed because he was so sure of the correctness of his plans that he kept insisting on their implementation.

WAVELL AND THE CONSERVATIVE PARTY

Wavell's relationship with Churchill had never been cordial but it worsened soon after Wavell became the Viceroy of India because the

British War Cabinet under Churchill realized, owing to their divergent ideas with Wavell that they had chosen the wrong person at the wrong time and for the wrong place. Firstly, the War Cabinet had appointed Wavell as no suitable replacement to Linlithgow was available. Secondly, Whitehall wanted to preserve law and order in the country and did not want to touch upon the political and constitutional problems of the country. Amery wrote in his diary, 'Winston would not have been as keen about Wavell as Viceroy if he had realized how thoroughly Wavell backs up Allenby's policy of sympathy with Egyptian nationalism'.[1] Amery opined that he would not be at all surprised if Wavell went a long way in trying to find a solution to the Indian problem.[2]

Wavell, of whom Churchill thought of 'in cricketing terms as a "night watchman" inserted to stonewall until the end of the war offered fresh options,'[3] on the contrary was a politically savvy military officer who started making plans for political changes in India even before he had assumed the top office in India. His first plan is known to history as the 'Wavell Plan'. He was concerned about the tense political relationship then existing between the British government and the Indians and wanted to change that with a proactive approach.

The War Cabinet[4] issued a draft directive to the viceroy, originally suggested by Cripps on 29 September 1943 and then approved it so that the new viceroy should be able to approach the political leaders in India as and when he considers it desirable. But it was amended on 4 October in a more restrictive sense with the addition of the words 'but should consult the War Cabinet about the time and form of any invitation to be issued.'[5] The British Cabinet's instructions exhorted Wavell to give top priority first to the defence of India and he was warned to 'beware above all things' of raising political issues that might prejudice India's war effort.[6] All this meant in other words that he should simply forget about the political situation in India.[7]

Thus, not only did the Wavell Plan go into cold storage, the course of action proposed and endorsed by a majority of the India committee was also ruled out.[8] Wavell also gathered from his private discussions[9] with Churchill that the latter feared a split in the Conservative Party and some kind of a parliamentary trouble in case of any fresh step regarding political reforms in India. Churchill was not ready to take this risk and was determined to block it as long as he was in power.[10]

Churchill never wished to see his new viceroy taking initiatives on the political front in India.[11] He was so annoyed with Wavell's political views and his insistence on pursuing them that he even refused to attend Wavell's farewell party when he was leaving for India as the viceroy-designate.[12] On 7 October 1943, Amery recorded in his diary,

> Winston who seems to have been rather on the rampage at first and more or less accused Wavell of playing for his hand and trying to do a public stunt to which Wavell seems to have said that he had no desire to go to India and was quite willing to resign if the PM did not trust him.[13]

Wavell, in spite of all these impediments did introduce some confidence building measures in India like his determined efforts to help the victims of the Bengal famine.

At the beginning of his viceroyalty Wavell had a high opinion of Gandhi, thinking that he would help in resolution of the political deadlock in India. In spite of Whitehall's reluctance Wavell released him from prison in 1944 as he had been seriously ill for some time. Wavell also wrote many letters to Whitehall concerning Gandhi's demand that he wanted to talk to the Viceroy concerning the formation of a national government. Amery wired back to Wavell on 4 October in which he stated that the entire Cabinet was perturbed over his contacts with Gandhi.[14] They considered Gandhi a 'political dead-horse' and believed that Wavell's reopening of negotiations with him would revive his political career.

Wavell's actions on behalf of Gandhi led to severe disagreements with the people in London[15] including an exchange of messages between the viceroy and the British Cabinet which created a row with Prime Minister Churchill, who wanted no part of negotiations with Gandhi.[16] The debate gathered momentum over the next few days.[17] Amery maintained that the viceroy should have 'avoided a direct collision with the PM and the Cabinet on an issue, not of substance, but of tone and wording.'[18] Amery lent his dissent to the War Cabinet's decision at its meeting on 14 August, recorded in the minutes, that 'on the ground that in a matter not of broad policy, but of wording and tone, the earnest and repeatedly expressed opinion of the viceroy should not be overridden.'[19]

Wavell nearly resigned over his stand concerning Gandhi's release from prison but he withdrew from his earlier determination to do so. There was a strong Indian reaction to His Majesty's Government's decision of not having parleys with Gandhi.[20] Wavell complained to Amery of an 'obviously hostile Cabinet who seems to have no confidence in my judgement on any matter,' and justified his complaint by reference to the previous incidents. Indian reactions to Wavell's reply had been strong and Wavell rightly suggested that 'the Cabinet has destroyed at one blow my reputation for fairness and good temper in my correspondence with Gandhi.'[21] In his protesting letter to Amery, Wavell wrote, 'They have now turned down my recommendations for (a) Indian Finance Minister; (b) Section 93 in Bengal at the beginning of the year; (c) Bajpai's status; (d) the form of my reply to Mr Gandhi; and (e) my requests for food imports, of which my great persistence has produced an inadequate amount.'[22] He warned Amery that 'His Majesty's Government must really give up trying to treat the Government of India as a naughty and tiresome child whose bottom they can smack whenever they feel like it.'[23]

Future interaction between Wavell and Whitehall suffered immensely due to this episode. It substantially weakened Wavell's position in the eyes of the Indians and he feared that there might be a Congress–League coalition against the British government.[24]

In the meantime, a further clash between Churchill and Wavell occurred when Whitehall suddenly announced that the pay and allowances of the British forces serving in the Far East were to be increased. Despite the fact that under the rules of defence expenditure the costs would mainly fall on India and would almost inevitably involve a corresponding increase in the pay of Indian forces and result in increased inflation in India, the Delhi government was not consulted. Wavell did not like such decisions being made in London without even consulting Delhi.[25]

In one of his private telegrams of protest to Amery which was imprudently permitted to come to the notice of Churchill, Wavell feared that the 'Council will take the line that if His Majesty's Government has to bribe the British forces to fight in the Far East, they should pay the bill.'[26] Wavell's use of such flagrant language against him and Whitehall was more than insubordination and highly treasonable in the eyes of

Churchill, who condemned Wavell's seditious language and 'accused him of insulting the British soldier'.[27] Wavell noted in his diary that this exchange of letters and controversy would neither improve Churchill's mindset about India nor would it improve personal relations between the two.[28]

He visualized right at the outset that if the British government did not take the initiative to break political and constitutional deadlock in India, it would result in chaos, civil war and partition of India. By middle of 1944 Wavell once again stressed upon the home government to reconsider his earlier 'Wavell Plan', which had been turned down in 1943.[29] He was also conscious of the fact that India's services in the war must be recognised along with other contributions which India had made towards turning the tide of war.

Amery had been keenly observing these developments and formulated a new approach to the Indian problem. In his letter of 3 October 1944 to Wavell, he explained his plan in detail stating that India's main grievance and source of bitterness was not the existing Government of India but Downing Street and the House of Commons. He further added that Indians constantly felt discriminated in all spheres of life by decisions taken by outsiders.

Based on his own soul-searching Amery suggested to Wavell that he should announce that India would enjoy dominion status. He also visualized that the viceroy would be more powerful and would exercise the power to override his council or dismiss it with his own judgement and without any prior approval from the secretary of state for India or Whitehall.

Amery was not only interested in seeing the Delhi government rid of the 'remote' control from Whitehall but also wanted to sideline the demand for Pakistan. He wanted to ensure:

> This continuance of the unity of India under the present Government does not preclude an eventual Pakistan, though I believe that in fact it would create an atmosphere in which at any rate the extreme Pakistan demand would no longer make the same appeal, and more practical considerations get the upper hand.[30]

He chalked out a programme in which the Congress would be empowered to impede the Pakistan demand. Therefore, he thought the essence of the idea in fact would be to release the Congress internees and to send an invitation to them to take part in coalition governments in the provinces and to participate in planning the future constitution at leisure.[31]

Amery feared that the division in Indian society was so obvious that the proposed Wavell Plan would result in further division among them.[32] Similarly, after the failure of Gandhi–Jinnah talks, Amery suggested that, since the two main organized parties were incapable of finding a solution, both should be excluded from, or sparsely represented on, the contemplated constitution-making body.[33] To him, the best remedy was to avoid establishing a council proposed in the Wavell Plan and set up a council consisting of non-political elements instead. It would form a very suitable nucleus, partly because it would already include representatives of the princes.[34]

On 6 December 1944, India committee met to discuss the Wavell and Amery plans.[35] The Wavell Plan was bitterly criticized by its members including Amery who put forward his own alternate scheme. He explained that what he had in mind was a body of some 40 to 50 persons, thoroughly representatives of all sections, parties and interest groups and in particular the martial races of the Punjab. However, his idea was dropped and Wavell's proposals were postponed for another six months.[36]

However, neither the British Parliament could be bypassed nor could the two major political parties of India be ignored as proposed by Amery. Wavell was of the view that Amery 'has a curious capacity for getting hold of the right stick but practically always the wrong end of it.'[37]

As Wavell did not appreciate[38] the response from the India committee[39] he decided to write directly to the prime minister. After complaining of the various grievances of the Delhi government against London, he informed Churchill that the current Government of India could not continue indefinitely, or even for long—the British Civil Service, on which the good government of the country had up till then depended, might almost be described as moribund, the senior members being tired and disheartened. He said that with the approaching end of the Japanese war, political prisoners would have to be released and they would find a fertile field for agitation in food shortages and unemployment, following the closure of war factories, unless their energies had previously been diverted in trying to solve the constitutional problem.

Wavell, recommending an approach to Gandhi and Jinnah and their followers, said, 'But the Congress and the League are the dominant parties in Hindu and Muslim India and will remain so. They control the Press, the electoral machine, the moneybags, and have the prestige of established parties.'[40] He held that even if Gandhi and Jinnah disappeared tomorrow, he could see no prospect of having more reasonable people to deal with.[41] He insisted on consideration of his plan, because the commander-in-chief, governors of all eleven provinces, and the senior members of the services supported his plan.[42]

Churchill's response on 26 November 1944 clearly showed that he disagreed over the urgency of the matter. He held that 'these large problems require to be considered at leisure and best of all in victorious peace.'[43] Wavell was anxious to write another letter to convince the prime minister of the urgency of the moment and to inform him of the psychological advantage,[44] but was restrained by Amery's advice.[45] Amery suggested to him to refrain from a direct communiqué to the prime minister and promised to influence the members of the War Cabinet 'to get the matter referred to the Cabinet India Committee.'[46]

The India committee in its meeting of 6 December disagreed with the vitals of the Wavell Plan but did invite him to London for a face to face meeting where he could justify the details of his plan.[47]

Wavell thought that 'it would be a grave mistake' to postpone, because of Sir Tej Bahadur Sapru's non-party conference, as that would produce no proposals of value; and he proposed that he should reach London about 15 January. Now, Churchill directed Amery to place before the Cabinet the question of whether Wavell should come home at all at this juncture. He feared, 'I expect he is going to make trouble and stage a scene for resignation.'[48]

But Wavell was quite conscious of the urgency for getting both the parties to work together in the coalition government and this would, he expected, generate team spirit. Their cooperation would also help to sideline the Pakistan issue. He met with Jinnah on 6 December 1944 and got his opinion. Writing to Amery on 12 December 1944, Wavell told him:

Jinnah was prepared to accept the unity of India as an ideal, but an ideal quite unattainable in present conditions. He said that the Muslims had been led by their experience of Congress domination to regard Pakistan as the only possible solution. I put it to him that if in the critical post-war years, on which the whole future of India may depend, we were busy cutting up the country, all parties would suffer, and that it would be very much better to hold India together for the time being at least and to undertake partition only if the Hindus and Muslims found in practice that they could not carry on.[49]

Wavell thought that Jinnah would cooperate if an Executive Council was constituted under the present constitution.[50]

Wavell arrived in England on 23 March and his first meeting with the India Committee[51] took place on 26 March.[52] Attlee, who chaired the meeting, was horrified at the thought of a rule by the 'brown oligarchy'.[53] Attlee declared, 'he was dismayed that we should hand over the people of India to a few very rich individuals who would control the caucuses without responsibility to any one.'[54] Wavell noted in his diary on 18 April that 'Attlee started attacking me at once...John Anderson complained that I would not admit that I was making a radical change in the constitution. Cripps was absent; Grigg and Simon were definitely hostile.'[55]

India Committee showed a lack of concern about the Indian problem and tried to avoid the Wavell Plan. They did not want to go beyond the Cripps offer of 1942. Churchill, like Attlee, also disapproved of the Wavell plan.[56] At that moment, Wavell realized, 'Now I think we have missed the bus in any case. The sudden collapse of the Germans and the approaching reoccupation of the whole of Burma will make Indian politicians less accommodating than a few months ago. If I got my own way now, I feel it would be too late.'[57] Wavell's repeated requests[58] annoyed Churchill who gave an ungracious reply to him and said, 'I do not consider that your visit to this country was necessary at the present time.'[59]

In the meantime, War Cabinet had been the replaced by a 'caretaker' Conservative Cabinet in June 1945. However, this time both the India committee and the Cabinet accepted the Wavell Plan but not in its entirety. Thus Wavell called the Simla Conference in June 1945 which, however, failed to produce any results.

One of the main reasons for Churchill's continued tense relations with Wavell was that the former was vehemently opposed to granting of freedom to India. Wavell rightly wrote to Churchill, 'I know you have often found me a difficult and troublesome subordinate; I have not always found you an easy master to serve.'[60] Wavell got nothing from Churchill which could have made him popular in India. Amery much later conceded that the failure of the Simla Conference in 1945 was due to Churchill's obstinacy.[61] Churchill never wanted Wavell to succeed in his political plans for India and it can be rightly said that it was he, not Wavell, who was responsible for the failure of the Simla Conference.[62]

Wavell and the Labour Government

With Labour Party's victory at the polls[63] in July 1945, Attlee, as the new prime minister,[64] continued his opposition to Wavell's proposed policies for India. According to Irail Glynn the Labour Party also preferred, like its predecessor, that men in Whitehall be the final judges of the policies to be adopted in India. Wavell was thus kept in the dark by his own superiors resulting eventually in his failure to deal with the Indians in an atmosphere of mutual trust and to prevent the Pakistan plan from emerging in the near future.[65]

Labour Party had been a strong supporter of the Congress and a big proponent of self-government in India for years. Above all, during the recent election campaign it had promised that 'if Labour is returned we would close the India Office and transfer Indian business to the Dominions Office.... This act would give them confidence that they are no longer governed from Whitehall'.[66] At the start of the new parliament on 21 August 1945, Attlee replied to a question by Woodrow Wyatt about transferring Indian affairs to the dominions office by declaring that he had 'no statement to make.'[67]

The Labour government on 13 August 1945 undertook three important steps: release of the Congress prisoners, removal of ban on Congress and immediate ordering of the general elections in India.[68] Wavell was called to London immediately in this regard and he gave his briefing about the problems of the Indian political scene.[69] But ground realities were different as the Hindu–Muslim conflict had reached such a point that in the opinion of David McIntyre, 'Only one week before the Victory Parade, Wavell was predicting possibility of violent uprising, requested orders as to whether he should plan to scuttle or to stay.[70]

It had become clear after the Governors' Conference on 2 August 1945 that elections to verify the claims of the Congress and the League should be held before the formation of the central and provincial ministries. Secondly, the Pakistan issue must be dealt with and its drawbacks brought to the notice of all parties, especially the Muslims.[71] Wavell went to England with this frame of mind but was taken aback, for Whitehall had a diametrically opposite understanding of, and consequently, a different stance concerning the Indian problem.

Although the Cripps Proposals had been rejected by both the Muslim League and the Congress, they had remained the only outstanding offer of the British government during the Second World War. R.J. Moore is right in suggesting that 'the irony is that by the time Labour achieved office, its scheme for the transfer of power (Cripps Proposals) was no longer feasible.'[72]

The secretary of state for India, Lord Pethick–Lawrence, in his briefing to the India committee suggested that the best guarantor of political progress in India were still the Cripps Proposals. He said that while the constitutional issue was being settled there would presumably be a time lag during which the business of India had to be carried on. He also suggested means for forming a provisional Executive Council from a provincial panel.[73]

Wavell demanded two things during his talks in London: that the Pakistan issue be tackled, and the elections take place for the Constituent and the Provincial assemblies.

The implementation of the Cripps offer was deferred and Wavell was directed to hold the elections and after the elections set up provincial governments and a Constituent Assembly.

The general elections which were held in 1945–46 witnessed that the Muslim voters gave an overwhelming mandate in favour of Pakistan while the Hindus on the whole voted for the Congress which stood for a united India.[74] This most visible victory of the League, however, was not accepted by the Congress and the British as a complete and wholehearted mandate of Muslims for Pakistan. Durga Das has recorded his meeting with Attlee in 1945 and writes,

Attlee did not conceal his deep agitation over the Muslim demand for Pakistan and agreed with my plea that a minority should not be allowed to hold up progress of the majority to self-rule. He added that his intention was to promote in India a structure that would give her federal unity...He considered the Congress as a party which was the true advocate for freedom and the League a disruptionist one and expressed the hope that in the impending elections the League candidates in Punjab, Sind and North West Frontier would be defeated. That would help preserve the unity of India.[75]

However, contrary to the desires of Attlee and many other well-known political pundits the results of elections to the Central Assembly and the provincial seats forcefully strengthened the case for Pakistan. Even then, Wavell was not ready to accept ground realities and thought that it was time for the British government to make a clear statement regarding its intentions for acceptance or rejection of the Pakistan demand.[76] He held that the Congress and the League would be unable to settle arrive at any agreement about the Pakistan issue and this would result in a political deadlock. He thought that His Majesty's Government should not allow another deadlock in the event of parties failing to come to terms and, therefore, must be ready to offer its own plan.[77]

The Labour government, though it agreed with the seriousness of the demand for Pakistan, wanted to find out for itself whether it could be dealt with effectively by some other means. They decided to send a fact finding mission consisting of members of the Parliament to India. Wavell welcomed this proposal and rejected the other one according to which the two main leaders from the Congress and the League should go to London for talks. The Parliamentary delegation was able to confirm that Jinnah was firm on his stand. It also concluded that the demand for Pakistan was not a bargaining counter on the part of Jinnah, therefore, it had to be faced and tackled by appropriate political means.[78]

WAVELL AND THE CABINET MISSION

The British government decided, 'The foundation of a provisional constitution for India must be based upon the 1935 Act and such a constitution must continue to provide a unitary framework but within it means of satisfying, to the greatest degree compatible with preservation of India as a single state, the aspirations of Indian Moslems for self-rule.'[79] This was the game plan of the India Office as conveyed to the Cabinet Mission on its departure for India.[80]

According to Philip Ziegler, 'Lord Pethick–Lawrence was technically to be in charge of whatever negotiations were necessary; but in fact Cripps and the Prime Minister, Clement Attlee, took over responsibility.'[81] The Cabinet Mission, which came to negotiate with Indians about the formula and modus operandi of the transfer of power, did not wish to include Wavell, the governor-general, during its workings in India. Probably they thought that they knew more than him, therefore, they thought of him as less than useful. The Labour government, however, included him after his note of protest. Though they decided to include Wavell as one of the negotiators, he was not taken into confidence about their game plan.[82] Wavell rightly observed, 'I may be left with all the loose and awkward ends to tie up, and perhaps to implement a policy with which I do not agree.'[83] He, therefore, made it clear that he should not be treated as a communicator but negotiator and mediator and 'if it is the wish of HMG that I should be responsible for implementing in India any settlement to be negotiated, I must really and genuinely be consulted.'[84]

Wavell's relationship with Cripps had never been cordial and it worsened with time. Wavell thought that Cripps could not be an honest and impartial negotiator because 'He is sold to the Congress point of view.'[85] Wavell deplored that both Cripps and Pethick–Lawrence failed to maintain high standards of impartiality, fair play and justice while they were dealing with the Hindu–Muslim problem. He complained to the prime minister that 'the late Cabinet Mission had too many unofficial advisers and indirect contacts,'[86] which had made his job and the job of the Mission more difficult in settling disputes. Further, he said, 'I thought it was a mistake that the Mission should have had, outside the official discussions, such a continuous and close touch with one of the two main parties, the Congress.'[87] This naturally aroused the deep suspicions of the Muslim League about the intentions of the Cabinet ministers.

Wavell was dissatisfied with the tactics of double-cross and underhanded dealings adopted by the Cabinet delegation during their negotiations with the Indian leaders.[88] Cripps' methods created suspicion and confusion as Wavell thought that Abul Kalam Azad and Jinnah were being presented with different propositions. According to Patrick French, 'in the end the Delegation created more problems than they solved, and the last chance to retain a united India disappeared.'[89]

The Cabinet Mission Plan had pleased neither the League nor the Congress. The Cabinet delegation, especially Cripps and Pethick–Lawrence, knew that without Congress's support of the plan, a government of a united India, though with a weak centre, could not be formed. Cripps, especially, wanting to avoid the formation of a government by Jinnah at all costs, persuaded the Congress to at least, accept the long-term part of the plan. Wavell wrote on 25 June 1946:

> The worst day yet, I think. Congress has accepted the Statement of May 16, though with reservations on its interpretation. They did not intend to do so, having always said they would not accept the long-term policy unless they accepted the short-term one, Interim Government. Now Cripps, having assured me categorically that Congress would never accept the Statement of May 16, instigated Congress to do so by pointing out the tactical advantage they would gain as regards the Interim Government. So did the Secretary of State. When I talked to him on this, he defended on the grounds that to get the Congress into the Constituent Assembly was such a gain that he considered it justified. It has left me in an impossible position vis-à-vis Jinnah.[90]

Describing the delegation members' underhand dealings with the Congress Sudhir Ghosh has written:

> This 'parity' between the majority and minority, between the Muslim League and the Congress, was of course wholly unacceptable to the majority party. In giving Mr Jinnah such an indication the Viceroy had seriously slipped up and the Secretary of State was disturbed about it. He sent for me on 12th June and told me how upset he was about it all. Was there no way of persuading Gandhiji to find a way out of this tangle? I told the Secretary of State that only thing to do was to have a heart-to-heart talk with Gandhiji and to appeal to him for help. So he asked me if I could not fetch Gandhiji to his house for a talk that evening…[91]

As we have discussed earlier it was because of Gandhi's influence that the Congress accepted the long-term part of the plan only on 25 June.

Pethick–Lawrence and Cripps were partly successful in trying to clear up the mess created by Wavell's assurances to Jinnah because he had refused to allow the Muslim League to form the Interim Government without the Congress contrary to his earlier assurances.[92]

Wavell's justice, fair play and honesty were now put to the test. He told Alexander, 'I should normally ask to be relieved of my appointment after what had happened; that I thought I had been placed in an impossible position with the M.L. (Muslim League) and that Cripps had not been quite straight.'[93] He thought of resigning but soon dropped the idea, reasoning that his resignation would badly expose the conduct of the three Ministers and His Majesty's Government and he did not want to embarrass either of them.[94]

Though Wavell regretted for a short while the failure of not forming the Interim Government, he still believed, 'We must try to leave India united; and we must secure the cooperation of the Congress which represents the great majority of Indian political opinion whatever our views on the past record of that party.'[95] Besides, he held that too much dependence on the shifting views and actions of a set of inexperienced, shortsighted and sometimes malevolent politicians had caused the failure.

According to Kevin Jeffreys, 'Certainly, in assessing the record of the post-war Labour government, historians are agreed that Attlee's party made only limited advances towards its stated aim in 1945—the creation of a socialist commonwealth. In some policy areas, continuity with war-time practice was undeniable. Under Ernest Bevin, for example, the surprising choice as Foreign Secretary, hopes of a 'socialist foreign policy' soon disappeared as the Cold War got underway,[96] but in case of India it seems oversimplification of the facts. The Labour government had high regard and respect for Congress and wanted to quickly transfer power to their so-called socialist brothers. This state of mind led the delegation to appease the Congress at all costs during the negotiations and they used all means, moral or otherwise to enlist its leaders' support for keeping India united.

Meanwhile, Cripps and Pethick–Lawrence continued their daily secret meetings with the Congress leaders. Lawrence took daily walks, with Agatha Harrison (Secretary, India Conciliation Group), a friend of C.F. Andrews, who was himself an associate of Gandhi which prompted concerns about their integrity in Wavell's mind. He thought, 'But far more unfortunate than these was the presence of Agatha Harrison and Horace Alexander,[97] who lived in the Congress camp, were completely sold to Gandhi, and saw the S. of S. almost daily.'[98] According to Sudhir Ghosh:

Why Cripps and Pethick–Lawrence, at moments of crisis in the India-Britain negotiations, chose to meet Gandhiji secretly in the garden at the back of the Viceroy's House in New Delhi without the knowledge either of the British Viceroy or of the Indian political leaders in a struggle to hand over power to an undivided India is, I see now many years later, a poignant as well as a dramatic story.[99]

While saluting the services of these English leaders for the Congress, B.R. Nanda a biographer of Gandhi, quite frankly admits:

Not merely the compulsion of events, but a measure of idealism went into the policy which Prime Minister Attlee initiated and carried through during the years 1946–47. And in so far as the British Government was impelled by this idealism, by a desire to open a fresh chapter in Indo-British relations, it was a victory for Gandhi, who had pleaded for thirty years for transformation of a relationship between the two countries. Among the advocates of this transformation were several English men and women, Hume and Wedderburn, C.F. Andrews and Horace Alexander, Brailsford and Brockway, Laski and Carl Heath, Mauri Lester and Agatha Harrison, who never wavered in their sympathy for the Indian cause in their own day they represented a tiny and not-too-influential minority, but in the fullness of time their opinions became the national policies of their country.[100]

Even Cripps and Pethick–Lawrence quite frankly admitted that they had contacts with the Congress leaders about the nature of which Wavell was unclear. Lawrence admitted that he wrote a secret letter to Nehru while he was in Simla. However, even such favours failed to win Congress's support as it kept raising the bar. Even, Pethick–Lawrence later on conceded,

We think you will agree that it was our experience that it is the consistent practice of Indian parties to take up a bargaining position well in advance of what they expect to get and we feel that it would be fatal to deal with

Nehru's letter on assumption that it is final challenge under threat of a direct breach with Congress. We regard it rather as another attempt, such as was constantly made during Mission's negotiations, to squeeze some further concessions out of H.M.G.[101]

The Labour Party did not mind letting Jinnah down while trying to appease the Congress.[102] It cared the least for upholding any moral standards while dealing with him. And the Cabinet delegation also decided to blame him for its failure. Lawrence went to the extent of using provocative language and even passed irresponsible remarks about Jinnah.[103]

Wavell, before offering the formation of the government to the Congress, wanted some clarifications. He wanted to make it clear to the Congress that it must first accept the statement of 16 May fully and sincerely on the lines laid down by the Mission.[104] Besides, he did not want any reduction in the powers of the governor-general unless both parties agreed to it. He also requested the Whitehall to stand firm against any blackmailing by the Congress. He wanted to correct the Congress's impression that they had got the British 'on the run'.[105]

But the prime minister told him to carry on with what he had been directed to do. But perhaps the greatest of all the impediments to a solution was the state of mutual mistrust amongst the various political actors. According to Leonard Mosley,

Jinnah and the Muslim League mistrusted the Congress and Congress mistrusted the Viceroy; Wavell mistrusted the Labour Government; Attlee did not necessarily mistrust Wavell but he had certainly lost faith in him.[106]

Attlee asked Wavell to accept Sir Maurice Gwyer[107] as political adviser. Wavell felt very bad about it and thought that the prime minister and his Labour government did not trust his political wisdom because it was 'not sufficiently pro-Congress.' He wrote,

I had a letter from the P.M., pressing on me again Maurice Gwyer as Political Adviser. He has obviously been told that I receive nothing but official I.C.S. advice and that my political judgement is therefore unsound, i.e., not sufficiently pro-Congress. I think my judgement is better than H.M.G.'s and

shall say so; and tell him that if H.M.G. don't like it their duty is to find
another Viceroy, as I will not be a figure-head.[108]

Nonetheless, he acted upon the directions and started negotiations with
Nehru. Nehru, sensing the weak and awkward position of the governor-
general vis-à-vis his own government in London, as stated earlier, began
to behave as if he had already become the 'Prime Minister' of India and
expected Wavell to act accordingly.[109] Wavell, under the circumstances,
was forced to accept his suggestions.

Wavell was convinced that a coalition government would not only
help to bypass the demand for Pakistan but help avoid a civil war as
well. However, Nehru and Gandhi did not share his feelings and insisted
that the Congress party should solely be allowed to form the Interim
Government regardless of the consequences. When Wavell warned that
one party rule would lead to a certain civil war, as was obvious from
the carnage on the 'Direct Action Day',[110] Gandhi pounded the table and
said, 'If a bloodbath was necessary it would come about in spite of non-
violence.'[111] Gandhi in his letter on 28 August told Wavell that Congress
would not bend itself and adopt what it considered a wrong course
because of the 'brutal exhibition recently witnessed in Bengal. Such
submissions would itself lead to an encouragement and repetition of
such tragedies.'[112] Therefore, he advised Wavell to wholly trust the
Congress concerning the formation of the Interim Government.[113]

Wavell, aware of the repercussion and the backlash it would bring to
induct one party rule in a multi-religious country with hostile feelings,
three days before induction of the Nehru's government, again asked His
Majesty's Government to declare that 'Grouping' was a mandatory part
of the Cabinet Mission Plan. To him, it was not a matter of legal niceties
but of practical considerations and also because it would put the full
weight of His Majesty's Government behind that important part of the
Cabinet Mission Plan. Wavell wrote:

> Though the consequences may be serious I think it is as well that things have
> come to a head. Calcutta with its 4,400 dead, 16,000 injured and over
> 100,000 homeless showed that a one-party government at the Centre was
> likely to cause fierce disorders everywhere. Far from having any sobering
> effects, it had increased communal hatred and intransigence. If Congress
> intentions are as Gandhi's letter suggests the result of their being in power

can only be a state of virtual civil war in many parts of India while you and I are responsible to Parliament.[114]

But Pethick–Lawrence did not agree with Wavell's statement that 'Congress always meant to use their position in the Interim Government to break up Muslim League and in the Constituent Assembly to destroy the grouping scheme.'[115] In response to him he advised Wavell, 'We should therefore like you to avoid pressing the grouping question to a final issue before the Interim Government takes over and has had a period of office.'[116] Thus Wavell was left with no choice but to invite the Congress to form a new government in September 1946.

But Jinnah was not ready to yield to such pressure tactics on his principled stand for Pakistan, referring to which, Ayesha Jalal has written, 'Here were already signs of London's willingness to resort to ruthless squeeze play if this could break Jinnah's intransigence. One clue to Jinnah's remarkable resilience in the face of grave political setbacks, overwhelming odds, and unremitting squeeze play, was his extraordinary capacity to fight when all would appear lost to lesser men.'[117]

Not to be outwitted and without wasting further time, Jinnah accepted Wavell's offer of joining the Interim Government on 13 October 1946. Wavell had made this offer despite opposition from Nehru and His Majesty's Government. His aim of bringing the two parties together was an attempt to try to solve the major constitutional and political issues, especially those related to 'Pakistan' but it seems that enough time had already been wasted and now only the adoption of the Cabinet Mission Plan in its entirety could have ensured the unity of India. Such delays had already created doubts in Wavell's mind that things were moving too fast to be contained simply by bringing the two parties together.

Wavell sincerely believed that the Congress's objection to the Grouping clause was contrary to the Cabinet Mission's interpretation, therefore, he showed reluctance to call the meeting of the Constituent Assembly unless the Congress accepted the Cabinet Mission Plan in its entirety. He maintained that the 'Compulsory Grouping' part was the crux of the Cabinet Mission Plan whereas the Congress leaders believed that accepting that part would result in 'Balkanisation' of India. In fact, at this stage a difference of opinion between the Viceroy and the London authorities was noticed. Attlee and Pethick–Lawrence not only regretted Wavell's intimation to Congress that he would not call the Constituent Assembly until the point about grouping was cleared up, but also asked the Viceroy not to take any steps which were likely to result in a breach with the Congress.[118]

Now Wavell pressured the Muslim League that it must either attend the Constituent Assembly meetings or otherwise resign from the Interim Government to which, Liaquat Ali Khan[119] responded that the League members would be ready to resign whenever required, but they would not accept the long-term plan unless His Majesty's Government declared that the provinces must meet in Sections.[120] Wavell did not try again as he himself was convinced that the League's stand was right. He also knew of the growing risk of a civil war in case of the League's resignation from the government which might put the life, property and interests of the British imperialists in jeopardy.[121] He was equally aware of the growing tendency towards militancy in the League circles which he himself conceded was because of a lack of firmness and honesty on the part of the British government.[122]

Failing to convince Whitehall to make an unequivocal statement regarding the Cabinet Mission Plan, Wavell on 20 November 1946 announced the decision of His Majesty's Government to call the Constituent Assembly on 9 December.[123] In fact, the Labour government itself had been under extreme pressure from Congress leaders like Nehru and Patel who had twice threatened to resign from the Interim Government if their demand for dismissal of the League ministers from the Interim Government was not met. Thus, in order to break the deadlock and to bring about a settlement on the issue of the Constituent Assembly, Whitehall invited two representatives each from the Congress and the Muslim League along with one Sikh to fly at once to London for discussions.

On 2 December 1946 in London, Wavell apprised His Majesty's Government:

The Muslim League leaders raised the cries of Pakistan and Islam in danger originally to enhance their prestige and power and thus their bargaining value as a political party. They have now so inflamed their ignorant and impressionable followers with the idea of Pakistan as a new Prophet's Paradise on earth and as their only means of protection against Hindu domination, that it will be very difficult to satisfy them with anything else. I think Jinnah is honest in saying that he had great difficulty in putting across the Mission Plan with his party, though he was probably wise enough to recognize it as a reasonable compromise worth trying at least for a period.[124]

He recommended to the British government to make the fullest use of the present discussions to try and restore the Mission's plan to its originally intended form. He feared that it would be impossible to carry out the present negotiations with any hope of success, unless the Labour government made up their mind 'whether or not they are prepared to stand up to the Congress.'[125] On their part the British government thought that Wavell had outlived his usefulness in his present position so did not heed his advice and decided to remove him. The immediate reason for his removal, however, was his insistence upon implementing his 'Breakdown Plan' in case of a political deadlock which he felt was imminent.

WAVELL'S BREAKDOWN PLAN

The present author, disagreeing with some recent historians, has tried to prove clearly that the acceptance and implementation of Wavell's Breakdown Plan in no way implied the acceptance of the demand for Pakistan.[126]

This plan had gradually evolved in Wavell's mind because he had realised, especially after the failure of the Simla Conference (1945), that some kind of a well thought through scheme was required for implementation by the British government in India. Such a scheme should aim to preserve India's geographical unity, law and order as well because he foresaw future trouble looming on the horizon.

Ian Stephens has written that Wavell contemplated a date for the final British withdrawal from India and, therefore, 'in fact, at any rate during that crucial December of 1946, his thoughts were evidently more progressive on this point than the Cabinet's.'[127] H.M. Close has written about Wavell that 'consciously or sub-consciously, was not willing to promote a plan for partition on equality with a plan for unity, and therefore downgraded it with the unattractive name of "Breakdown".[128]

Based on a rough mental sketch of his 'Breakdown Plan' he directed his advisers Evan Jenkins, V.P. Menon and B.N. Rau to chalk out the details of the plan. Jenkins suggested on 10 November 1945 the establishment of an Indian union—he named his suggestions the 'reserve plan'—with the right of a province(s) to secede from the Indian union and form a separate union of their own. In case the Muslim-majority provinces opted to form their separate union, he suggested partitioning the Punjab, Bengal and Assam to make Pakistan small, weak and unattractive for Jinnah. He believed, 'In the long run I think that the Punjab and probably Bengal might join the original Federal Union on terms—the prospect of partition would be less attractive when it became imminent.'[129] However, he asked V.P. Menon to chalk out further details.

Abell's input into the breakdown plan was that

> Pakistan Provinces would be offered to continue for the time being under the present constitution with the British support they have now. They could watch the formation of Hindustan and they could decide later (by an unspecified procedure) to join the Federation or stay out. It would be made clear that H.M.G. would be ready to grant Dominion Status as under the Cripps Plan to the Pakistan Provinces if they wanted.[130]

However, B.N. Rau agreed with the 'reserve plan' and suggested that it would be necessary to give large territorial units in the Pakistan Provinces the option of merging themselves into the neighbouring federating provinces of 'Hindustan'. He thought that 'this is the right sort of reserve plan and that it might be acceptable to the Congress.'[131]

V.P. Menon believed that the bitter racial and religious feelings, mutual suspicion and distrust between Hindus and the Muslims reminded him of the Canadian situation before the formation of Canadian Federation and, therefore, he suggested constituting the Indian federation on the same lines to avoid any break-up. He stressed the need for the establishment of a coalition government pledged to assist in the revision of the Constitution at the earliest possible moment. He also proposed following a timetable, so that everybody may see that His Majesty's Government meant business. He disagreed with imposing a constitution, suggesting instead convening a convention of important political parties, communities and representatives which would prepare a constitution. He opined that under the existing plan there was a hope of setting at least one union by the people themselves (as Nehru had suggested that if the government did not take steps the initiative would be shifted to others meaning Hindu-dominated provinces). Having got the union, he suggested that they would be in a position to know which units stand out and to deal with them.[132]

The elections (1945–46) had electrified the political atmosphere in India causing the political parties to grow further apart. Pethick–Lawrence inquired of Wavell the actions that would be necessary in the event of their finding it impossible to bring agreement between the parties during the coming summer. Wavell informed him on 5 December that he and his staff had been considering the 'breakdown plan' for some time but had not finalized it as yet.[133] Further Wavell requested him to send David Monteath to India to chalk out details with his own staff but Pethick–Lawrence refused this request because of the under-secretary's busy schedule in England.

In the meantime Jinnah had expressed his willingness to accept 'frontier adjustments where primarily Hindu and Muslim lands were contiguous to the Hindustan or Pakistan States, as the case may be.'[134] But Wavell feared that Jinnah's contemplated adjustments could be minor ones as compared with the adjustments expected by the Congress. Wavell saw an opening in Jinnah's statement and believed that now he 'may not refuse to negotiate, and that at least is satisfactory.' [135]

Wavell believed that if Jinnah knew that he would only get Pakistan on the basis of the Lahore Resolution but with Punjab and Bengal divided on a communal basis, he would refuse to accept it. According to Wavell's calculations, this partition plan would affect at least two divisions (Ambala and Jullundur) of the Punjab and almost the whole of Western Bengal, including Calcutta, which could only be joined with the Indian Union. Wavell believed that adoption of such policy by Whitehall would diminish the attractiveness of Pakistan to Jinnah. According to Wavell 'only the husk', to quote Jinnah, would remain.[136] He expected that Jinnah faced with such a statement on behalf of His Majesty's Government would consider his position very carefully and, further, his bargaining power vis-à-vis Congress would be drastically reduced. There would thus be a chance that Jinnah would then try to secure the best possible terms for the Muslims within the Union.[137] Wavell believed, 'No-one believes that Pakistan is in the best interests of India from the practical point of view, and no-one knows where the partition of India, once it starts, will end, short of Balkanisation.'[138]

Wavell, on his part, wanted to remove the bargaining power of the Muslim League. He had no doubt that his award would force the Congress and the League to come to terms, but the best panacea was that 'the Constitution would be made sufficiently attractive to the Muslims to induce them to remain in the Federation from the start.'[139] It appears that Wavell, quite skilfully, had drafted a plan which would be unacceptable to the Muslims and Hindus, and violently opposed by the Sikhs.

But the Labour Party had a number of reservations about Wavell's Breakdown Plan. They felt that it would greatly weaken any possibility of compromise on the basis of even a very loose federation. Further, how could they enforce it without an agreement between the two leading parties?[140] They wanted to adopt measures which would be most helpful in securing a united India. Since Wavell's plan was not considered as well prepared for the breakdown purposes, therefore, Wavell, along with David Monteath's Committee, was entrusted the duty to chalk out the details of his Breakdown Plan.[141]

Therefore, he pointed out to Whitehall that they must be ready with a plan which could be put into effect if Congress and League failed to reach an agreement or in case both rejected the Mission's Proposals.[142]

But the Cabinet Mission Plan was the united effort of Wavell and the Delegation under the circumstances existing at that time. In Wavell's eyes it was the best plan which would retain the Indian unity besides providing adequate safeguards for the Muslims. But even then, he was not optimistic about the success of the Plan and therefore expected a sudden outbreak of violence, owing to disagreements among the leading parties of India. Therefore, he suggested to Whitehall an adequate consideration of his 'Breakdown Plan' as well.

As per Wavell, the better course of action to follow, in case they were forced into an extreme position, was to hand over the Hindu majority provinces of Bombay, Madras, CP, UP, Bihar and Orissa, by agreement and as peaceably as possible, to the Congress. This was to be followed by withdrawal of troops, officials, and European nationals in an orderly manner from these provinces.

Wavell was aware of the flaws in his Breakdown Plan and, therefore, suggested means to deal with them. Firstly, he thought that the Muslim League might decline the British offer. Secondly, if the Muslim League accepted the plan it would result in a division of the Indian army; even then, he held that the military position of the British in the Muslim majority areas of the northwest and northeast of India would not be weak. Thirdly, the actual military operation of withdrawal from Hindustan into Pakistan could be difficult and possibly dangerous. Fourthly, it was an equally grave problem to deal with the large minorities, Hindus and Sikh, in the Muslim provinces. Even at that stage, he suggested that there should be maximum effort to bring about a union of India on the best terms possible and then withdraw altogether.

On 6 June 1946 a Cabinet meeting was held at London under the chair of Attlee. They discussed Wavell's Breakdown Plan, at length. It disapproved the idea of withdrawal from India by a specific date. The Cabinet remarked:

> We are anxious to give India her independence and have put forward plans for achieving it. Unfortunately the Leaders of the political parties of India cannot agree among themselves on a plan for independence. We cannot in these circumstances allow a situation to develop in which there will be a chaos and famine. Accordingly we must maintain our responsibilities until the Indian leaders can find a basis for accepting our offer of independence. Our proposals still remain open.[143]

By now, due to the obstructions facing the ongoing Cabinet delegation's proposals, Wavell had developed serious reservations regarding Congress's ability to follow a statesmanlike and generous course of action for maintaining the unity of India.[144] Of great concern to him was the fact that the pool of members of the central services on which British control of India had depended was rapidly running down due to depletion and Indianization. The cohesion and discipline in the Indian army had also suffered due to the communal conflicts. It was in such circumstances that Wavell once again reiterated the implementation of his Breakdown Plan.[145]

As differences widened between the Congress and the League over the interpretation of the Cabinet Mission Plan, Wavell, along with the top Indian leadership, was invited to London for talks with the His Majesty's Government in December 1946. During his private talks with the leadership of His Majesty's Government and Whitehall Wavell insisted upon implementing his proposals for the 'Breakdown Plan' or else face serious consequences.[146] He had reached this conclusion because, firstly, Congress had not accepted the Cabinet Mission Plan in full. Secondly, His Majesty's Government by failing to emphasize in strong terms its position regarding the 'Grouping Clause' had allowed the political deadlock to continue with the resultant increase in communal tensions. Therefore, he felt that the Cabinet Mission Plan had lost its efficacy and it was time to look for alternate solutions.[147] He stated that 'The Muslim League leaders raised the cries of Pakistan and Islam in danger originally to enhance their prestige and power and thus their bargaining value as a political power.'[148]

Wavell reiterated that his Breakdown Plan was intended for use not merely in case of a widespread administrative deadlock but also in the event of a political breakdown. He believed that the plan would enable the government to take a firm line with Congress, since it had a reasonable alternative on which to fall back; such a course of action might enable it to avert a political breakdown.

Wavell's Breakdown Plan was referred to the India and Burma Committee for its consideration where on 5 December 1946 Wavell pleaded his case. Attlee emphasized the difficulty of putting the Breakdown Plan into operation since legislation in parliament would be necessary before the announcement. Wavell observed that the prime minister seemed prepared to accept it in principle and the ministers were at least beginning to realize the necessity of having such a plan. Still it did not get the wholehearted approval Wavell thought it deserved.[149]

It was again discussed at 10 Downing Street on 11 December 1946. However, the discussions about the Cabinet Mission Plan, contrary to Wavell's expectations, dominated the proceedings, concerning which it was decided that if either of the two communities refused to cooperate in carrying out the Mission's Plan, then a situation would arise which would justify and necessitate a fresh statement of policy by the government.

Wavell held that if the League refused to participate in the Constituent Assembly, the government would be ready to accept a constitution, drawn up by the present Constituent Assembly, as valid for the Hindu majority provinces only. He pointed out that an announcement by the government favouring the establishment of Pakistan would at once arouse great opposition on the part of Congress. On the other hand, he hoped that 'if they realised that continued intransigence on their part would lead to the establishment of Pakistan, the Congress leaders might become more reasonable.'[150]

Wavell explained that under his 'Breakdown Plan' the Hindu provinces of Bihar and the United Provinces would not be handed over to the Congress in the first stage. Although, politically, they were the most difficult provinces, he had the full concurrence of the commander-in-chief on this matter and proposed their retention so as to avoid giving any impression that they were only retaining hold on the Muslim provinces. In the end, Wavell's Breakdown Plan, failed to bypass the Pakistan issue completely but only succeeded in postponing it for a while.[151]

In later discussions of Wavell's Breakdown Plan the following points were raised. Pethick–Lawrence showed great concern about the minority problem in Muslim-majority provinces as a very large minority of the population—some 40 per cent in certain cases—belonged to the Hindu or other minorities.[152] They had not obtained guarantee for the minorities in the Muslim provinces which the government had always termed as a crucial point of its policy. The legal difficulties of a province by province transfer of power would be considerable. British sovereignty must be handed over to a specific body or bodies with whom treaties would have to be negotiated.

The army would remain under the control of the central government in the first stage, it could presumably only act in the provinces at the request of the provincial government. There would thus be a very awkward division of responsibilities. At a later stage control of the Indian army would have to pass under the command of some specified authority. If no central authority for the whole of India came into being they could not hand all of it over to a government for the Hindu provinces only; therefore, they would be compelled to divide it.[153]

They remained unclear about the future of the princely states. They would not decide what action was proposed in regard to the states adjoining the provinces in which sovereignty was to be handed over. At what stage Paramountcy in respect of those states would be surrendered? There would be political difficulties in Britain in giving effect to the plan. Legislation from the British parliament would be required. They would be pressed to show that they had a well thought out plan, which would achieve its objective without causing chaos and would enable them to secure protection for the minorities.[154]

Wavell emphasised the importance in announcing very soon in fixed and unequivocal terms the decision to leave India by a specified date. He believed this would make leading political parties come to terms. He said that this announcement might be of value in inducing a sense of responsibility in their minds to avoid violence. Still, they had the realization that in the last resort the British would always be there to maintain law and order.[155]

Therefore, the British ministers forwarded their own line of action. They suggested that most of the objections raised were due to the suggestion that there should be a formal transfer of power to the provinces. The 'constitution' of India could be preserved intact until the later stages. The first stage would consist in the removal of the remaining officers of the secretary of state services in the four southern provinces and the withdrawal of all British troops from there. The British governors could also be recalled unless the provincial governments specially asked for their retention and Indian governors were appointed in their place on the advice of the provincial ministers. There would thus be a complete and absolute Indianization of the services in the provinces, and the existing constitution and relationship with the central government would continue. The troops of the Indian army should remain in the provinces to help avoid the division of India into separate units. Similarly, the termination of Paramountcy of Indian States could also be avoided.

The third sitting of the India and Burma committee took place on 19 December. Now, Wavell put forward a different version of his Breakdown Plan. He proposed that it should immediately become clear that if the Muslim League were not be represented in the Constituent assembly, government should withdraw the governors, secretary of states services and British troops from the provinces of Orissa, the Central Provinces, Bombay and Madras within a period of three or four months. The present status of central government and the constitution should be maintained but fresh governors would be appointed on the advice of ministries. In his concluding remarks in favour of the Plan, he said that it would enable him to concentrate his administrative forces and limit his responsibilities. It would cause a psychological effect on the two communities and they might go for some form of cooperation.[156]

The India and Burma committee considered the revised Wavell Plan and held that legislation would be necessary because it completely disregarded the Government of India Act 1935. The secretary of state and the viceroy could not rid themselves of their responsibilities under that act without an act of parliament. It was, however, desirable to avoid legislation before the final transfer of sovereignty. They thought that such legislation would be difficult to get through the parliament and, therefore, it might be possible to use the 'convention' that governors would always accept the advice of their ministers. Alternatively, it might be possible to obtain the approval of the parliament to some 'blanket resolution' which would give the government sufficient authority to act. Without such authority they might be charged with abandoning their responsibilities towards the minorities and neighbouring states.

It was feared that Congress might regard the British withdrawal from southern provinces as implying a tilt in favour of Pakistan. The retention of Bihar and the United Provinces would not necessarily dispose of this misconception as it might be construed as a sign that they favoured Pakistan. To avoid this misconception, the proposed statement announcing the introduction of the Breakdown Plan, must be carefully worded. It was felt possible to obtain the cooperation of Congress concerning withdrawal from the southern provinces. The present constitutional structure could also be preserved. Congress leaders would wish to show that the Congress ministries were worthy of their new duties. The probability was that following the British withdrawal, southern provinces would continue to hand over to the central government the taxes necessary for financing the essential services.

The India and Burma committee resumed its discussion of Wavell's Breakdown Plan on 20 December. Meanwhile, the provincial prime ministers of the southern states had requested that the secretary of state services be wound up quickly. There were about 500 men in the Indian Civil Service and 500 in the Indian police service, two or three hundred of whom were in the southern provinces. Wavell recalled that if a definite date for British departure was announced, this point would not be pressed unduly. The ministers would be hard pressed to maintain their administration if all members of the services were withdrawn from those provinces. There was evidence that they would be willing to retain a number of them and also that Congress favoured forming a new central service.

The committee also discussed the steps to be taken after withdrawal from four southern provinces. They held that they might have to withdraw one by one from additional provinces. Finally, there would be the question of termination of the British authority. They were not clear to whom, barring an agreement between the Indian political parties, this central power would be transferred particularly after the announcement of the final date of their withdrawal. It seemed probable that eight of the eleven provinces, by then, would have accepted a constitution drafted by a constituent assembly under Congress domination. Therefore, they had to hand over the central powers in respect of those provinces to a Congress-run central government. The corollary would be to hand over the central powers in respect of other provinces either to those individually or to a separate central government for them. It would also result in splitting the Indian army.

After the aforesaid considerations the committee agreed, and decided to recommend in the House of Commons that a statement be issued on the indicated lines in which it was intended that the British would withdraw their authority by 31 March 1948.

The British Cabinet met on 31 December 1946 to discuss Wavell's Breakdown Plan.[157] It was considered that an announcement in terms of the proposed draft that might be regarded as the beginning of the liquidation of the British Empire should be made.[158]

The India and Burma committee met again on 3 January 1947 to discuss future policy concerning India. Though, no clear agreement was reached on the draft statement one thing was very clear, that they had rejected Wavell's Breakdown plan. The ministers held that

> it was wrong to press too far the analogy of a military withdrawal. The operation now to be begun was not so much a military withdrawal as a political operation of great delicacy. It must be regarded not as a withdrawal under pressure but as a voluntary transfer of power to a democratic government. To an increasing degree the Viceroy would assume the position of a constitutional ruler and he and the British officials would act in conformity with the policy of that Government.[159]

All this was, however, not conveyed to Wavell before his departure for India.

The next meeting of the India and Burma committee took place on 6 January 1947. They had before them a memorandum by the secretary of state for India in which he had set out the points at issue. The viceroy had returned to India with the understanding that he would be authorized to take steps as soon as the proposed statement of policy regarding formal withdrawal from the southern states had been made.[160]

Although the committee showed appreciation of the fact that the area under the control of the viceroy would be lessened, thereby reducing his risks, they however, disagreed with Wavell's argument that he would remain unaffected. They felt that his argument was not conclusive enough.

The second argument that the Breakdown Plan would need to be implemented in case a law and order situation arose was also rejected on the ground that the committee's plan for vacating India should not be based on the assumption that law and order would break down. It thus failed to appreciate the ground realities of a serious communal conflict, just round the corner, in India. In general the committee desired an atmosphere in which a friendly transfer of power from British government to Indian authorities could take place. They were of the opinion that the Plan would result in the division of India into two or more parts and this would lead straight in the direction of Pakistan. Therefore, the committee decided that the viceroy's plan should be held in reserve for use in case of an emergency.

At the same time, the viceroy should be asked to transfer to other provinces some members of the secretary of state services at present serving in the southern provinces. Some movement of troops from south to north should also be made so as to concentrate them in the north.[161] These changes should be carried out in such a way as not to imply a complete withdrawal of British authority from these provinces.

Attlee conveyed the Cabinet's decision to Wavell on 8 January 1947.[162] He invited Wavell to London as soon as possible for a review of the situation. But Wavell had returned to India and thought it would be useless to plead his Breakdown Plan any more.[163] Later on Wavell was informed by His Majesty's Government that his war time appointment had been terminated.[164]

The Breakdown Plan had a number of shortcomings; therefore, it could not get the desired results. It could have created a conflict between the central government and the provinces due to ambiguity in the central and provincial subjects. The suggestion given by Wavell to overcome this weakness was also unsatisfactory. Wavell had suggested that withdrawal should be made only from four provinces instead of six Hindu-majority ones, so that Congress and Hindus would not get the impression that government was supporting the creation of Pakistan.

Most of the British ministers disliked any scheme that suggested evacuating the largest and most important colony, India. They wished to prolong their authority for at least another two or three decades and were not convinced that the British control had diminished so much that it would be difficult to carry on after March 1948. It was also considered desirable to leave India in the hands of those leaders who could make economic and political treaties with the British government but, they also felt, that the Plan did not guarantee such peaceful transfer of power to a legitimate authority or authorities.

It was feared that the liberation of such a big empire could also create problems for British authorities in other colonies as well. Representatives of the British Commonwealth states had expressed their concerns over this plan as it could also provoke other colonies to demand their liberation as well.[165] Ernest Bevin, the foreign secretary, felt that 'the defeatist attitude adopted by the Cabinet and by Field Marshal Wavell is just completely letting us down.'[166] He was against the fixing of a specific date for withdrawal as it could cause problems for them in the Middle East and suggested Attlee to replace Wavell due to his defeatist approach.[167]

Peter Hennessy writes, 'Attlee did have developed views on some crucial areas of policy, Indian independence particularly, and here he would take the lead in Cabinet and Cabinet Committee, even slapping down (albeit privately) his closest and most important colleague, Bevin, who recoiled from the rush to independence.'[168] The British government was also apprehensive of the communist involvement in the region. It was desired that in the 'Cold War' era the British colonies ought to be united and powerful. They did not wish to leave their possession in an unfriendly atmosphere which would force the colonies to reach out to the USSR.

Wavell's Breakdown Plan needed legislation from the British parliament to put it into force. Labour Party feared that new legislation would not get approval in the parliament on the lines proposed by Wavell.

Attlee felt that the Wavell Plan 'savours too much of a military defeat and does not realize that it is a political problem and not a military one.' Besides, the Labour Party considered the plan and its author, Wavell, a defeatist and an advocate of scuttle. He himself never had a positive opinion of Wavell's political insight and doubted whether he had the finesse to negotiate the next step. The aim of the plan was to avoid the blackmailing by the Congress ministries from the four provinces, as the viceroy was obliged to act upon the advice of the ministers.

Although, the Labour Party rejected Wavell's Breakdown Plan, they agreed in principle to leave India lest the Indians forced them to vacate the country. They announced the date of their final withdrawal as March 1948, a date which Wavell himself had suggested.[169]

All this delay in settling the communal problem and winding up the British rule had the most adverse effect in India. The loyalties of the police and the army to British authority became doubtful. According to Noor-ul-Haq,

> it seems that, by January 1947, the communal feelings in the Armed Forces had grown very strong. The communal composition in the Services was closely monitored by the two communities and the figures appeared in the

press violating the secrecy rules of classified information. Because of the growing communalism in the Armed Forces, Prime Minister Attlee, who stood for the unity of India, got worried that Indian unity could not be achieved if the Indian Armed Forces were spilt on communal lines. He did, however, desire that if the Raj was to come to an end, the loyalty of the Indian soldiers might be transferred to an all India government. He feared that if the British failed to get that, the Indian Armed Forces would undoubtedly split owing to persistent communalism.[170]

The country had been heading towards a civil war which could have been avoided by implementing the Breakdown Plan. Victoria Schofield has recorded:

> Since partition formed part of the eventual solution, it may be conjectured that the Breakdown Plan—taking place over more than a year under Wavell's schedule—would have provided more time for tempers to subside; under Mountbatten, there were less than three months between the announcement of partition in June 1947 and independence celebrations in August. Mountbatten argued that once the plan had been announced time was of the essence, but within Wavell's longer time frame it is possible the violence that accompanied partition could have been considerably lessened, if not averted.[171]

Thus the civil war that broke out during last days of the Raj in India, in which numerous innocent people were slaughtered might have lost a major part of its fury if Wavell's Breakdown Plan had been implemented, the division of India and also the partition of the provinces of Punjab and Bengal would most likely, have taken place peacefully.

According to the instructions of His Majesty's Government, Mountbatten acted as a constitutional head of the government and, therefore, could do nothing to stop bloodshed; rather, he left everything in the hands of the Interior Minister Sardar Patel who made scant efforts to control it. Wavell, on his part, had been impartial and conscious of the rights of all communities and was determined, as an executive head, to suppress all such threats. After his dismissal, extremists became uncontrollable and shed the blood of innocent people in India in the presence of the new governor-general and British forces, the police and the army.

During Wavell's viceroyalty, the devolutionary process of British authority in India was accelerated. He was trying to bring a settlement between the two major political parties to maintain the unity of India.[172] Whitehall rejected his Breakdown Plan because they believed that it was a weak plan of a defeatist soldier and would result in a clash with the Congress. Attlee thought, 'Partition would bring us into immediate conflict with the Congress and permanently embitter our relations with the larger part of India.'[173] This kind of approach emboldened the Congress which promoted violence and bloodshed against the Muslims. Wavell reported to Pethick–Lawrence on 8 January 1947,

> Nehru, in his usual irresponsible vein, addressed the All-India Students Congress Delhi on the curious Congress position in which they were both associated with the Government of India and even running Provincial Governments, but at the same time in opposition; and the Provincial Government Committees have been advised by the Congress Head Office that they should prepare sub-committees in every village against the day of a future struggle.[174]

It proved a great error on the part of Whitehall to ignore the Breakdown Plan as Ian Stephens has recorded,

> he put forward a "Wavell (Breakdown) Plan", politically and militarily clear-cut, whereby British authority would have been withdrawn from the subcontinent much more gradually; that this was turned down; and that had it not been, much of the appalling slaughter at Partition-time, and resulting ill-will between the two successor-States, might have been avoided.[175]

It is obvious that Wavell's personal relations with Attlee were strained and uneasy. Wavell's insistence on carrying out his Breakdown Plan put the Labour government in an awkward position. Wavell was allowed to return to Delhi. The fact was that Attlee had already decided to replace Wavell during his stay in London but did not dare tell him personally.[176] The Congress leadership was annoyed with him too and had been continuously asking the Labour government to replace him. In the last days of the transfer of power, he had become unacceptable both to the Congress and the ruling Labour Party in England. H.M. Close has already challenged the myth that Wavell had become a spent force. But he has concluded wrongly that Wavell was insisting on establishing the 'Lesser Pakistan'. As a matter of fact, Wavell in his Breakdown Plan had developed a strategy to force the Congress and the League to come to terms on the basis of the Cabinet Mission Plan but he was not allowed to carry it through in its entirety. One part of the Breakdown Plan proposed that a phased withdrawal of the British authority from four Hindu provinces of Bombay, Madras, Orissa, and Central Provinces in the first phase be made and then they should withdraw from other provinces. This part of the Breakdown Plan was unacceptable to the Labour government as it could annoy the Congress and give the impression that the British wanted to divide India and to create Pakistan. The Labour government accepted other recommendations which were embodied in the Breakdown Plan but dismissed him from the viceroyalty.

Whitehall had given Wavell a mandate to maintain law and order in India for the duration of the war but, he, as a political thinker, disagreed with them. He advocated granting India freedom to earn the respect and love of the people of India, as had been earned by his hero, Allenby, in Egypt. However, His Majesty's Government did not permit him to carry out his plans. Wavell's failure to achieve his goals was not due to his own indecisions but was really due to the delay and wrong policies of both the Conservative and the Liberal governments regarding India. He also had to face the opposition of the Congress high command due to his insistence on granting Muslims a fair deal under the Cabinet Mission Plan which eventually led to his removal.

Indeed, Wavell worked as an honest broker during the negotiations of the Cabinet Mission, but he failed to check the hostile, biased and negative approach of the Cabinet delegation towards the Muslim League leaders, especially Jinnah. He did go back on his word about the formation of the Interim Government and thus betrayed Jinnah but he did so to avoid embarrassing His Majesty's Government.

He wanted the geographical unity of India at all costs and all his efforts like his initiation of the 'Wavell Plan', supporting the Cabinet Mission Plan and outlining of the Breakdown Plan were directed sincerely towards that end. His opposition to the Cripps Proposals was also based on that principle.

Wavell can also be credited with strongly apprising the British government of the widespread backing by Muslims of the 'Pakistan' scheme so that it could be dealt with effectively before it became unmanageable. He considered the Cabinet Mission Plan as the best antidote to the spreading popularity of the Pakistan scheme and, therefore, wanted the British government and Whitehall to press the Congress strongly in order to gain concessions which would have prevented the emergence of Pakistan; in the end, however, he failed to do so.

Wavell chalked out the Breakdown Plan to reduce the attractiveness of the 'Pakistan Scheme' for the Muslims. In his Breakdown Plan he suggested the division of Punjab, Bengal and Assam on communal basis, something which was not clearly mentioned either in the Cripps Proposals or the Cabinet Mission Plan. His suggestion in the Breakdown Plan that Punjab and Bengal should be divided on a communal basis if Jinnah insisted on the Pakistan demand, was only envisaged as a bargaining point with the Muslim League and never intended for actual implementation because he was dead sure that the League and the Congress would come to terms on a formula for a united India based on the Cabinet Mission Plan. However, since neither of the parties was willing to compromise enough he was proved wrong. In the meantime his Hindu advisers had drawn up an unjust demarcation of the Punjab and the Bengal boundaries on maps, which, when actually implemented during Mountbatten's brief tenure as the viceroy, later on, caused tremendous territorial losses to the newly created state of Pakistan.

NOTES

1. John Barnes and David Nicholson, ed., *The Empire At Bay: The Leo Amery Diaries, 1929–45* (London: Hutchinson and co. Ltd, 1988), p. 896.
2. Ibid.
3. Ronald Lewin, *The Chief*, p. 224.
4. The wartime Coalition Government in UK was headed by Winston Churchill of the Conservative Party and its Cabinet was composed of outstanding political personalities. The India Committee of the British Cabinet, set up in 1942, was the powerhouse for Indian policy- and decision-making. Its members were chosen for their wide knowledge of India. Besides Attlee, the Deputy Prime Minister, who chaired this committee, other well-known ministers included Simon, Anderson, Grigg, Butler, Amery, and Cripps, and Wavell was indirectly answerable to this

committee via the Secretary of State for India, who acted as a middle-man between the Viceroy and the British government. Besides the above, Wavell was also answerable to the War Cabinet and Whitehall with regards to any political initiatives in India.

5. John Barnes, *Amery Diaries*, pp. 904–5.

6. Ibid.

7. Wavell has recorded that 'Amery and Halifax supported my proposals without much enthusiasm while Sir James Grigg, Anderson and Simon all opposed them.' Wavell, *Viceroy's Journal*, p. 17.

8. Mr Turnbull to Sir E. Bridges, 8 October 1943, L/PO/6108a: f 36.

9. Ibid.

10. Ibid. On 8 October, Churchill cancelled the meeting of the Cabinet on India and invited Wavell to see him alone. Winston had a formula for a directive, which, in Wavell's eyes, was mostly meaningless. It entailed instruction to improve the lot of the Indians; to make peace between Muslims and Hindus, and only at the end indicated that political progress during the war was not debarred.

11. Though Wavell always came up to the expectations of Winston and won many laurels in the battlefield, he never received the acknowledgements and recognitions from the Prime Minister Winston Churchill for his services. On June 1941, Churchill wrote to Wavell that he had come to the conclusion that public interest would best be served by the appointment of General Auchinleck to replace you in command of armies of the Middle East. Although he acknowledged and appreciated Wavell's services in the region but was very angry with him, as he had become impatient at Wavell's reluctance to take the offensive against the Germans. He got serious doubts about the intellect and vision of Wavell whom he always saw an unimpressive and boring kind of person. He thought he was more like 'the chairman of the golf club'. Quoted in Ronald Lewin, *The Chief*, p. 26; Churchill transferred him to the position of Commander-in-Chief India in June 1941. Despite Wavell's repeated requests he did not grant him home leave for some days. John Connell, *Wavell: Scholar and Soldier*, pp. 464–507; Wavell was called back to London in April 1943, never to return as Commander-in-Chief for India. The confidence of Churchill on the generalship of Wavell began to waver. Churchill decided to remove Wavell. Their relations became strained and when Wavell returned to England from the United States of America, instead of going back to India, he was told to take some of his overdue home leave.

12. At the farewell party, Wavell once again stressed the need to review the Indian policy and let him carry on his plan. He also used those words which, Amery had warned him not to use. It annoyed Winston and Clement Attlee.

13. Barnes, *Amery's Diaries*, pp. 946–7.

14. Wavell, *Viceroy's Journal*, p. 82.

15. Subsequently, the Cabinet agreed to a revised draft which Wavell described, 'I got back exactly the same in principles, but intransigent and discourteous in tone. It seems to me one of our great mistakes in this country is not to have realized the importance to the Indian mind of good manners and appearance at least of consideration.' Wavell, *Viceroy's Journal*, p. 84.

16. Barnes, *Amery's Diaries*, pp. 907–8.

17. Wavell sent back a revised version of the Cabinet's draft, friendly in tone and clearly showing his desire to keep open the door to negotiations, whereas the Cabinet gave the impression of keeping it closed. Wavell knew his revised draft would infuriate Churchill and it actually did enrage not only him but also the whole of the Cabinet. Wavell, *Viceroy's Journal*, p. 84.

18. Wavell, *Viceroy's Journal*, pp. 86–7.

19. Barnes, *Amery's Diaries*, pp. 907–8.

20. Ibid.

21. Wavell, *Viceroy's Journal*, pp. 86–7; *Transfer of Power*, Vol. IV, pp. 1182–99.

22. Wavell to Amery 15 August 1944, Wavell Collections, L/PO/10/21.

23. Wavell, *Viceroy's Journal*, p. 87.

24. Gandhi–Jinnah talks were expected to be held soon and possibly result in a compromise between the two main parties. Wavell believed that Gandhi had the talent and would manoeuvre successfully as Jinnah would not totally understand his inner feeling and intentions. He wrote that 'I am sure that Gandhi's real object is to get the Working Committee out of detention and that he will go a very long way (with the usual mental reservations) in dealing with Jinnah to secure the co-operation of the Muslim League. Having drafted an agreement of some kind he may tell Jinnah that he is at a disadvantage because the Working Committee, who alone can commit the Congress, are in detention, and may suggest a joint approach to Viceroy to secure their release.' Wavell, *Viceroy's Journal*, p. 87; Wavell to Amery 15 August 1944, Wavell Collections, L/PO/10/21.

25. Sir Jeremy Raisman, the finance member of the Executive Council, informed Wavell on 15 September 1944 that this would have very serious repercussions on India's finances. The War Department also protested at the failure to consult them in advance. The cost would fall, under the Defence Expenditure Agreement between His Majesty's Government and the Government of India, entirely on Indian revenues, and would result in aggravation of inflation in India. Wavell to Amery, 11 September 1944, *Transfer of Power*, Vol. V, p. 25.

26. Wavell to Amery, 15 September 1944. Ibid., p. 34.

27. Churchill to Wavell, 1 October 1944, *Transfer of Power*, Vol. V, pp. 61–2; Wavell, *Viceroy's Journal*, pp. 91–2.

28. Ibid., p. 92.

29. After the Governors' Conference in 1944, he urged the British government to issue the statement that they genuinely meant to give India self-government as soon as difficulties could be overcome. Note By Wavell on 5 September 1944, Wavell Papers, Political Series, April 1944–July 1945, Pt. I, pp. 47–9.

30. Ibid.

31. Ibid.

32. Amery to Wavell, 23 November 1944. Ibid., pp. 128–9.

33. Amery to Wavell, 10 October 1944. Ibid., p. 96.

34. He suggested that addition might be made to it to include the premiers of the non-section 93 provinces, elder statesmen, further representatives of labour and the depressed classes, and the representatives of the fighting services, including those of the states. Amery to Wavell, 10 October 1944. Ibid., p. 99.

35. Other points also came under discussion. For example, it was suggested that a highly skilled technical body which could put forward technically sound proposals, or a politically representative body which could guarantee the support of the parties from which it was drawn for what ever working scheme, might be formed.

36. The meeting was chaired by Attlee and attended by, Sir John Anderson, Leopold Amery, James Grigg, Cripps, Butter, Edward Bridges, Gilbert Laithwaite and Viscount Simon. Meeting of the India committee, 6 December 1944, *Transfer of Power*, Vol. V, pp. 274–79.

37. Wavell, *Viceroy's Journal*, p. 111.

38. Wavell wrote to Amery that 'We missed an opportunity between breakdown of Gandhi–Jinnah negotiations and Sapru's announcement of his Committee. We shall always be late if we only begin consultation when opportunity for action has occurred. I therefore propose that I should come home about January 25th and stay about a fortnight. I cannot come earlier...and can not break the engagement.... Will you please let me know as soon as possible whether my proposals for dates is approved as I have certain engagements to postpone or cancel.' Wavell to Amery, November 1944, Wavell Papers, Political Series, 1944–45, pp. 133–4.

39. Wavell writing to Amery said that 'I definitely do not agree with your remedy. If we held general elections in the present state of feeling there would be a great increase in communal bitterness, with unfortunate results on the war effort; and I do not believe that a constituent assembly on the Cripps model could be formed or would produce any useful result at this stage. I have reason to think that the Muslim League would not agree to a constitution-making body of this kind. Jinnah told Mudie a few days ago that he would not hear of such a proposal, and gave figures to illustrate his objection.; he repeated his opinion in another letter that Jinnah told Mudie during their recent talk that the Muslim League would not accept anything of the kind, as the method of the election to the Constituent Assembly outlined in the Cripps offer would be dissatisfactory to the Muslims.' Wavell to Amery, 5 December 1944, Wavell Papers, Political Series, 1944–45, p. 134.

40. Wavell to Winston Churchill, 10 October 1944, Wavell, *Viceroy's Journal*, pp. 94–99.

41. Ibid.

42. Wavell to Winston Churchill, 10 October 1944, *Transfer of Power*, Vol. V, pp. 126–33.

43. Churchill to Wavell, 26 November 1944, Churchill Papers, Chur 2/43, Churchill Archives Centre, Cambridge.

44. Wavell to Amery, 27 November 1944, Wavell Papers, L/PO/6/108b: f 353.

45. Wavell wrote that 'I have been careful not to commit myself with Jinnah or anyone else. It would be quite impossible for me to shut myself up and refuse to see any of the Indian politicians or to try to find out what they are thinking. I am sure it is right that I should continue to see political personalities as opportunity offers, so as to have a chance to size them up. I think you can trust me not to give away anything.' Wavell to Amery, 27 December 1944, Wavell Papers, Political Series, 1944–45, pp. 134–5.

46. Amery to Wavell, 28 November 1944, Wavell Papers, L/PO/6/108b: f 351.

47. Another development, in Wavell's view, giving urgency to the matter, came with the meeting on 19 November of the moribund Standing Committee of the Non-Party Leaders' Conference under the aged Indian Liberal politician Sir Tej Bahadur Sapru because Wavell thought it would give another excuse to Whitehall to put off his request to implement his plan.

48. The prime minister on 1 January 1945 said that that because of the meeting of the Big Three in Yalta in early February it was impossible for Wavell's visit to take place before the end of that month. Minute by Churchill, 1 January 1945, *Transfer of Power*, Vol. V, p. 173.

49. Wavell to Amery, 12 December 1944, L/PO/10/20.

50. Wavell to Amery, 12 December 1944, Wavell Collections, pp. 137–8.

51. On 11 January 1945 Wavell was informed that His Majesty's Government considered late March the best time for his visit. He continued to press for an earlier date but on 13 March Attlee gave various reasons for postponing the visit till early June. This evoked a very strong protest from Wavell on 15 March and on the next day the government agreed for his immediate visit home. He left for London on 21 March. The War Cabinet, at its meeting on 18 December had invited the India Committee to proceed with 'stocktaking' of the Indian position. On 28 December Attlee invited comments from members of the Committee. Amery contributed on 5 January a long memorandum. On Wavell's arrival at Westminster, India Committee began its proceeding and discussed the Wavell Plan. The correspondence between Amery and Wavell, beginning with the latter's memorandum of 20 September, had been circulated to the War Cabinet by direction of the prime minister on 22 November, but not discussed. On 1 December Wavell suggested that he should fly home unless his proposals were receiving attention. While Amery again restrained him, he simultaneously wrote to Attlee about Wavell's very serious apprehension that we may lose a favourable moment for dealing with the Indian situation. Admitting that representations from me to Winston will have little effect, Amery asked him as 'leader of one half of the coalition' to intervene.

52. Attlee refused to allow Wavell to see a record of discussion on the Indian constitutional problem in the India committee, as 'the making of this request is, I fear, only another example of having a Viceroy with no political experience.' Hugh Tinker remarks that 'Attlee's complaint seems particularly peevish when we recall that the man he chose to succeeded Wavell, Mountbatten, had even less knowledge of British politics.' Hugh Tinker, *Viceroy: Curzon to Mountbatten*, p. 193.

53. Attlee also held that a government responsible neither to parliament nor to a legislature would leave His Majesty's Government powerless to protect the Indian masses, which would be defenceless. He also said that the new members would owe allegiance to an outside body and not to the viceroy, who would be forced more and more into the position of a Dominion Governor-General. Therefore, effective control would pass to an Executive Council 'responsible only to party caucuses.

54. War Cabinet, India Committee I (45), 13th Meeting, 26 March 1945, L/PO/6/108c: ff 268–75.

55. Wavell, *Viceroy's Journal*, p. 126.

56. India Committee Meeting, 27 April 1945, L/PO/6/108d: ff 228–31.

57. Wavell, *Viceroy's Journal*, p. 127.

58. Wavell to Churchill, 24 May 1945, *Transfer of Power*, Vol. V, pp. 1057–58.

59. Churchill to Wavell, 28 May 1945. Ibid., p. 1063.

60. Wavell to Churchill, 24 May 1945. Ibid., pp. 1057–58.

61. Quote in Hugh Tinker, *Viceroy: Curzon to Mountbatten*, p. 197.

62. Wavell went to see Churchill on 31 August 1945 when he had been ousted from the power. He had an hour-long meeting with him. Churchill was in a good mood and 'revealed that the only reason he had agreed to my political move was that India committee had all told him it was bound to fail.' Wavell, *Viceroy's Journal*, p. 168.

63. The Labour victory of 1945, in the eyes of Geoffrey Alderman, 'was a famous one: with the support of nearly 12 million voters as against the Conservative total of just under 10 millions, Labour could rightly claim to have become a, and perhaps the, national party.' Geoffrey Alderman, *Modern Britain, 1700–1983* (London: Croom Helm Ltd., 1986), p. 232.

64. The incoming government included several leaders such as Addison, secretary of state for dominions; Wedgwood Benn, former secretary of state for India; and Pethick–Lawrence, secretary of state for India. Lawrence and his wife had long been supporters of self-government for India. Wavell's observations on his appointment as Secretary of State for India were not unfounded. He said that 'I fear he may have fixed and old fashioned ideas derived mainly from Congress contacts.' His fears soon proved right.

65. Irial Glynn, 'An Untouchable in the presence of 'Brahamans' Lord Wavell's Relationship with Whitehall during His Time as Viceroy of India, 1943–57', *Modern Indian Studies*, Cambridge University Press, (2007), pp. 1–25.

66. Speech of Bevin at Blackpool on 23 May 1945, quoted by Hugh Tinker, *Viceroy: Curzon to Mountbatten*, p. 200.

67. Wavell Collections, MSS Eur D 977/4.

68. The very first telegram which Wavell received from the secretary of state for India on 18 August 1945 indicated that His Majesty's Government intended to take Indian problem in hand at once and seriously. The first instructions, Lawrence issued to Wavell were to hold elections, release political prisoners and to lift ban on the Congress Party. Wavell, *Viceroy's Journal*, p. 163.

69. Wavell went to London on 24 August 1945 and came back on 16 September 1945. He discussed at length the Indian problems and forcefully tried to project his opinion.

70. W. David, McIntyre, *British History in Perspective: British Decolonization, 1946–1947* (London: Macmillan Press Ltd, 1998), pp. 3–4.

71. Casey, the governor of Bengal sought permission from the viceroy to launch an open campaign against the demand for Pakistan to apprise the voters about the practical difficulties it would create, due to its vagueness. He discussed matters with other governors who also shared his views. Though Wavell also agreed with the proposal he was not in favour of going openly against the demand as it could create an impression that the British government in India was partial and a party to it.

72. R.J. Moore, *Churchill, Cripps and India, 1939–1945* (Oxford: Clarendon Press, 1979), p. 147.

73. India and Burma Committee, IB (45), 2nd Meeting, 29 August 1945, L/P&J/10/20: ff 121–8.

74. In the central assembly election, the Congress won 55 seats and 30 Muslims seats were captured by the Muslim League. The Sikh seats went to the Akalis who were uncompromisingly opposed to Pakistan. The Congress lost 4 landlord seats, according to Shiva Rao, because of 'Jawaharlal's strong attacks on the land holds and advocacy of the abolition of permanent revenue settlement.' Shiva Rao to Cripps, 15 December 1945, *Transfer of Power*, Vol. VI, pp. 704–7.

75. Durga Das, *India from Curzon to Nehru and After* (New York: The John Day Company, 1970), pp. 222–3.

76. Apprising Whitehall, on 27 December 1945 Wavell wrote that the Pakistan demand was an inflexible policy of the League, so long as Jinnah controlled it. He, however, argued that many of his supporters realized the difficulties and disadvantages of Pakistan. Wavell to Pethick–Lawrence, 27 December 1945, L/P&J/8/525: ff 229–47.

77. Wavell requested Lawrence to keep it secret so that his negotiations with the Indian leaders for the formation of the Executive Council should not be prejudiced. Wavell to Lawrence, 27 December 1945, L/P&J/8/525: ff 248–51.

78. Moon writes that 'Through no fault of its members the Parliamentary Delegation did not arouse much interest in India and had little effect on the course of events; but probably some of its members did succeed to some extent in bringing home to the Labour Government that Jinnah and the League would not easily be persuaded to drop the demand for Pakistan.' Wavell, *Viceroy's Journal*, p. 208.

79. Besides Wavell, it was a general impression of the people in New Delhi and Whitehall that the only method which could make Jinnah accept less than Pakistan was to offer him a better alternative and to convince him that his Pakistan scheme was unacceptable, for it was flooded with extreme dangers. A number of individuals, officials and secretaries worked hard to investigate the Pakistan scheme. Sir David Taylor Monteath, (permanent under-secretary for India and Burma 1942–1947) and his committee in India Office London prepared 'Proposals For a Provisional Constitution.' It was prepared to give the frustrated protagonists a breathing space if there had been a breakdown. It suggested that a policy should be adopted to ensure there would be minimum loss of face to the image of His Majesty's Government and no ultimate prejudice to conflicting aims of Indians.

80. Draft by India Office, undated, *Transfer of Power*, Vol. VI, pp. 1213–28.

81. Philip Ziegler, *Mountbatten: The Official Biography* (London: Phoenix Press, 2001), p. 352.

82. In his letter to Lawrence on 17 February 1946 Wavell wrote, 'While it is claimed and announced that the Viceroy will be an equal party in the discussions, I have been given no information whatever, since I sent home proposals early in January, of how the mind of the Cabinet is working; and latest telegrams about accommodation seem to give the impression that the Ministers wish to conduct the negotiations at some distance from the Viceroy's House, in order to ensure informal contacts.' Wavell to Lawrence, 13 February 1946, *Transfer of Power*, Vol. VI, p. 1003.

83. Wavell, *Viceroy's Journal*, p. 206.

84. Wavell said that he would not like to be excluded from the discussion as was done at the time of the Cripps Offer. Wavell to Pethick–Lawrence, 13 February 1946,

Transfer of Power, Vol. VI, 1003; Pethick–Lawrence in his reply on 21 February 1946 wrote that the ministers would include him in his discussions and would let him know their policy towards India when they finalize it.

85. Wavell, *Viceroy's Journal*, p. 211.
86. Wavell to Attlee, 1 August 1946, *Transfer of Power*, Vol. VII, p. 100.
87. Wavell to Lascelles, 8 July 1946, Wavell Collection, MSS Eur D977/1, p. 121.
88. Wavell, *Viceroy's Journal*, p. 251.
89. Patrick French, *Liberty or Death*, p. 244.
90. Wavell, *Viceroy's Journal*, p. 305.
91. Sudhir Ghosh, *Gandhi's Emissary*, p. 155.
92. Ibid., p. 171.
93. Wavell, *Viceroy's Journal*, p. 305.
94. Wavell felt sorry about what he had done to the League and Jinnah but the Whitehall, especially Pethick–Lawrence, asked him to adopt such method which could further annoy Jinnah. Wavell wrote to Lawrence on 29 July that 'I do not think that your proposed method is quite fair to Jinnah, since it attempts to pin down the main point on which he will raise objections without disclosing to him the whole proposal. I am certain he will refuse. I feel that I must put the proposal to him as a whole. He is still very sore and I cannot confront him with a demand for what he will call one more concession unless I can let him know what he can hope to get if he makes it. I do not want any further misunderstandings or accusations of bad faith, and this is one of the principle reasons why I prefer a written approach. I cannot see why we are any more committed by an approach in written than oral one, since it is surely not suggested that any proposals put forward orally can be subsequently disowned, any more than ones in writing. Our offer of June 16th was in writing. I therefore still very much prefer to make the approach in the method I have suggested. I will be grateful for an immediate reply as Jinnah's meeting is in a week's time, and Nehru is in Delhi for a few days.' Wavell to Pethick–Lawrence, 19 July 1946, pp. 33–34.
95. Wavell to Lascelles, 8 July 1946, Wavell Collections, MSS Eur D997/1, pp. 121–2.
96. Kevin Jeffreys, *The Churchill Coalition and Wartime politics 1940–1945* (Manchester: Manchester University Press, 1995), p. 209.
97. Richard Symonds writes that 'My introduction to India was considerably influenced by Horace Alexander, a Quaker with extensive experience of India…Horace and the Society of Friends were sometimes were felt by British officials to be unduly sympathetic to Gandhi and to the Indian National Congress.' Richard Symonds, *In the Margins of Independence, A Relief Worker in India and Pakistan, 1942–1949* (Oxford: Oxford University Press, 2001), p. 4; Moon writes that Alexander was a lecturer at Birmingham. Like Agatha, he was member of the Quakers India Conciliation Group. Along with Sudhir Ghosh and a group of young British pacifists of the Friends' Ambulance Unit, he had been engaged on famine relief work in Bengal in 1942–43. He saw himself as intermediary between Gandhi and the world of British officialdom in succession to C.F. Andrews. Wavell, *Viceroy's Journal*, p. 311.
98. Ibid.
99. Sudhir Ghosh, *Gandhi's Emissary* (Calcutta: Rupa & Co., 1967), p. 1.

100. B.R. Nanda, *A Biography of Gandhi*, pp. 244–5.

101. Pethick–Lawrence to Wavell, 26 July 1946, Wavell Collections, pp. 55–6.

102. Wavell was also disturbed as the ministers showed tremendous flexibility towards the Congress. They did not take a strong stand and hence changed with the varying demands of the Congress. Consequently, they altered their plan many times to appease the Congress which ultimately brought failure to the Cabinet Mission plan. Wavell deplored this approach and said that he would not be a party to any unilateral concession to Congress, but he was snubbed. Wavell, *Viceroy's Journal*, p. 287.

103. Pethick–Lawrence, however, apologized for his remarks and behaviour towards Jinnah. Pethick–Lawrence to Jinnah.

104. Gandhi and Nehru had started to interpret the substance and intent of the Cabinet Mission plan according to their own desires and interests. Neither had they thought grouping a compulsory clause nor the powers of the Union Assembly. These statements and resolutions were creating problems for Wavell and His Majesty's Government in implementing the short-term and long-term plan. Wavell knew that if the demand of the Congress regarding the sections and grouping was accepted and if the case was referred to the Federal Court and accepted by it, the Congress would gain nothing. The Muslim League would inevitably refuse to take part, and the process of constitution-making would be held up. Meanwhile, communal stresses in the country would get worse and worse. Therefore, Wavell told Nehru that the question involved was not a legal but a practical one and that if the Federal Court decided on a vital point regarding grouping, that the Congress view was correct, no advantage would be gained by the Congress. The League would undoubtedly walk out of the Constituent Assembly and the whole scheme would break down. Writing to Lawrence on 29 August 1946, Wavell held that compulsory Grouping was the most essential scheme and we must insist on its being observed. He hoped that His Majesty's Government would stand quite firm on the matter of Grouping and the intentions of the Mission must prevail. He hoped that it would help bringing the League into the Interim Government. Therefore he suggested to Whitehall that it would be unwise to call the Constituent Assembly till there was a firmly agreed view on the grouping question. Wavell to Pethick–Lawrence, 29 August 1946, Wavell Collections, pp. 134–5.

105. Wavell said that he could assure that he had no desire or intention to break with Congress. But Nehru's letter was more challenging than anything which was put up while the Mission was out here, and 'we can not go on being perpetually subject to these squeezes'. He suggested that the only way to prevent the Congress was to be firm on the essential points. He informed them that 'Congress are convinced that they have got us on the run and we ought to correct that impression at once'. Wavell to Lawrence, 28 July 1946, Wavell Collections, pp. 33–34.

106. Leonard Mosley, *The Last Days of the British Raj* (London: Weidenfeld & Nicholson, 1961), p. 28

107. Gwyer was Chief Justice of India 1937–1943; Vice-Chancellor of Delhi University 1938–1950.

108. Wavell, *Viceroy's Journal*, p. 324.

109. Attlee said that further delay would only exacerbate the temper of the Congress party leaders and perhaps lead to a definite break between them and the British authorities, as a result of which civil disobedience and anti-British agitation might once more sweep the country. The defeat for the viceroy was considerable. The British government, by overruling him, had demonstrated to the Congress that they no longer had any confidence in him. From this moment, neither side in India, Hindus nor Muslims, needed to consider him as vital figure in their negotiations. By his action of August 1946, Attlee deprived Wavell of most of his strength and left him practically helpless in the face of increasingly intransigent communal leaders with whom he had to deal. Wavell, in this hour of personal humiliation showed remarkable lack of resentment. His instinct was to resign at once, but he was aware of the difficult problem which would confront the British government if he took this action, and of the crisis it might well provoke in India. Leonard Mosley, *The Last Days of the British Raj*, p. 49.

110. Wavell to Lawrence, 28 August 1946, Wavell Collections, Political Series, 28 June to 6 December 1946, Vol. IV, part V, IOR, MSS Eur D977/8, pp. 134–5.

111. Gandhi and Nehru met Wavell on 27 July 1946 and discussed the formation of the Interim Government and the matter of Grouping. Wavell asked them to state clearly their intention about Grouping so that the cooperation of the League could be sought. Nehru was full of hate against the League and Gandhi was quite aggressive about his point of view. Wavell, *Viceroy's Journal*, p. 341.

112. Wavell, *Viceroy's Journal*, pp. 342–3.

113. Nehru to Wavell, 28 August 1946, R/3/1/117: ff 164–5.

114. Wavell to Lawrence, 28 August 1946, R/3/1/117: f 145.

115. Lawrence to Wavell, 28 August 1946, L/PEJ/10/75/: ff 394–5.

116. Ibid.

117. Ayesha Jalal, *Sole Spokesman*, pp. 220–1.

118. Massarat Sohail, *Partition and Anglo-Pakistan Relations*, p. 17.

119. Wavell to Lawrence, 23 November 1946, Wavell Collections, Political Series, 28 June to 6 December 1946, Vol. IV, Part V, IOR, MSS Eur D977/8, pp. 340–1.

120. Wavell to Lawrence, 13 November 1946, Wavell Collections, Political Series, 28 June to 6 December 1946, Vol. IV, Part V, IOR, MSS Eur D977/8, p. 313.

121. Wavell wrote that 'I said that I was quite convinced that without the co-operation of the Muslim League there would be no chance of a united India or of a peaceful transfer of power. Nor would the States be likely to negotiate freely with a one-party Government.' Wavell's interview with Nehru, 23 August 1946, Wavell Collections, Political Series, 28 June to 6 December 1946, Vol. IV, Part V, IOR, MSS Eur D977/8, pp. 127–82.

122. He said that the League had become 'mulish and bloody-minded'. Wavell, *Viceroy's Journal*, 382

123. Wavell stressed that 'His Majesty's Government must now make up its mind whether it will stand by the statement of the Mission or not'. He believed that it would save the Mission's plan by a definite statement on the lines proposed by the League in paragraph 3 of his No. 2459-s, which were in effect the assurances given to the League leaders by the Mission in their interview of 16 May. He assured that 'If His Majesty's Government decides to make such a statement, I should of course

put it first to Jinnah and obtain a definite pledge that the League would come in on this assurance. Otherwise His Majesty's Government must recognize that it has in effect abandoned the plan drawn up by the Mission and has surrendered to Congress.' He however said that he could not guarantee the reaction of Congress to such a statement, but he expected that they would accept it after a great deal of preliminary bluster, and that the majority of Indians, including all sensible and moderate men, would be glad that His Majesty's Government had at last shown some firmness of purpose. He however admitted that the Congress may react with resignation of their Members at the Centre and of all Congress government, followed possibly by widespread violence. He suggested that they could face this only if they had a breakdown plan on the lines which he had proposed. It would help them to get rid of India without serious loss and with some dignity. He warned that If His Majesty's Government decided to adopt the line of surrender to the Congress point of view, he feared that the result would be something approaching civil war leading to the eventual break-up of the Indian Army and chaos throughout India, since the Muslim League was driven to the point of desperation and would use the religious issue to stir up trouble. British troops would be involved in the suppression of civil disturbances and attack on the European community would develop. He professed that the Mission plan would have failed since no constitution that the Assembly would frame without the Muslim League would be acceptable to the Muslims. He said that the States would also not as a whole join either side but many of them were likely to be involved in the general disorder. He emphasized that serious note should be taken of his advice and said that 'I do not think that half-measures or wishful thinking will get us further. His Majesty's Government has a clear-cut issue in front of it, either to stand by the Mission plan or to surrender to Congress, and they must make up their minds at once.' He had done his best to persuade the parties to come together into the government and the Constituent Assembly and make it work, but he admitted that he had failed. Wavell to Lawrence, 24 November 1946, Wavell Collections, Political Series, 28 June to 6 December 1946, Vol. IV, Part V, IOR, MSS Eur D977/8, pp. 127–82, 342–4.

124. Note by Wavell, 2 December 1946, L/P&J/10/111: ff 86–90.
125. Ibid.
126. Narendra Singh Sarila, *The Shadow of the Great Game: The Story of India's Partition* (New Delhi: HarperCollins Publishers in India), 2005, pp. 167–198; H.M. Close, *Attlee, Wavell, Mountbatten and the Transfer of Power* (Islamabad: National Book Foundation), 1997, pp. 80–91.
127. Ian Stephens, *Pakistan*, p. 125.
128. Close, *Attlee, Wavell, Mountbatten*, p. 86.
129. Jenkins to Wavell, 10 November 1945, R/3/1/108: ff 8–11.
130. Minutes by Wavell and Abell, 29–30 November 1945, R/3/1/108: ff 16–17.
131. Ibid.
132. Menon to Abell, 6 December 1945, R/3/1/108: ff 24–29.
133. Wavell to Pethick–Lawrence, 5 December 1945, L/PO/10/22.
134. Wavell to Pethick–Lawrence, 18 December 1945. Ibid.
135. Ibid.
136. Wavell to Pethick–Lawrence, 27 December 1945, L/P&J/8/525: ff 248–51.

137. Ibid.

138. Minute addressed to Gibson, undated, Turnbull Papers, MSS Eur D714/72.

139. Wavell to Lawrence, 27 December 1945, L/P&J/8/525: ff 248–51.

140. Minute addressed to Gibson, undated, Turnbull Papers, MSS Eur D714/72.

141. Ibid.

142. It suggested that a policy should be adopted to ensure that there would be minimum loss of face to the image of His Majesty's Government and no ultimate prejudice to the conflicting aims of Indians. The condition of a provisional constitution for India must be based upon the 1935 Act and such a constitution must continue to provide a unitary framework. It also pointed out that means should be applied to retain India as a single state, without prejudice to the interests of Indian Muslims. Draft by India Office, undated, *Transfer of Power*, Vol. VI, pp. 1213–28.

143. Attlee to Wavell, 6 June 1946. Ibid., pp. 830–32.

144. Wavell to Pethick–Lawrence, 9 August 1946, Wavell Collections, Political Series, 28 June to 6 December 1946, Vol. IV, Part V, IOR, MSS Eur D977/7, pp. 91–94.

145. Wavell told Pethick–Lawrence that the British government should hand over, after a stated plan, the Congress majority provinces to Congress but maintain the existing constitution and British control in North West and North East India. Wavell predicted that under such conditions if the British government was not prepared to change their policy, the British control in India could be maintained for a maximum of one and a half-year or till the spring of 1948. Therefore, a definite plan should be worked out in order to wind up British control from India. He suggested that withdrawal should be completed not later than the spring of 1948 because from the administrative point of view the government could no longer exercise control beyond that date. However, he made it clear that the Breakdown Plan was intended primarily for use in the event of a deadlock before 1 January 1947. He held that the plan should come into operation no later than 1 March 1947.

146. Lawrence to Attlee, 13 September 1946, L/PO/6/117: ff 42, pp. 45–82.

147. Note by Wavell, 2 December 1946, L/P&J/10/111: ff 86–90.

148. Ibid.

149. India Conference in London, 5 December 1946, *Transfer of Power*, Vol. IX, pp. 374–9.

150. India and Burma Committee, IB (46), 8th Meeting, 11 December 1946, *Transfer of Power*, Vol. IX, p. 332–7.

151. Ibid.

152. Ibid.

153. Ibid.

154. Ibid.

155. Ibid.

156. Wavell was sure that it would no longer be possible for Congress to put pressure upon him by threatening to withdraw ministries from the provinces. This threat had in the past been a source of embarrassment because he at that time was in no position to administer the provinces under section 93 of the Government of India Act 1935 because of growing control of the popular governments under the

Congress. India and Burma Committee, IB (46), 11th Meeting, 19 December 1946, *Transfer of Power*, Vol. IX, pp. 383–6.

157. Cabinet CM (46) 108th Conclusions, Confidential Annex, 31 December 1947, R/30/1/9: ff 70–75.

158. Bevin to Attlee, 2 January 1947, R/30/1/8a: ff 72–7.

159. India and Burma Committee. IB (47), 1st Meeting, 3 January 1947, L/P&J/10/46: ff 48–51.

160. India and Burma Committee. IB (47), 2nd Meeting, 6 January 1947, L/P&J/10/46: ff 23–6.

161. Memorandum by the Secretary of State for India, 6 January 1947, India and Burma Committee, Paper IB (47)3. *Transfer of Power*, Vol. IX, pp. 472–4.

162. Attlee said that 'in the event of the Muslim League failing to enter the Constituent Assembly it would be desirable to announce a time limit for the continuance of British rule in India; it was considered that it would not be advisable to fix a day. While it was considered that plans might be made for that event and that troops might be moved, there was strong confirmation for the view expressed by the India Committee that the proposal for the abandonment of all responsibility for four Southern Provinces was unacceptable. The Cabinet did not approve the approach to the problem on the basis of a military evacuation. It was considered that a different approach was required viz. that of close co-operation with the Indian governments at the Centre and in the Provinces in order to work out with them plans for handing over the Government in India, as a going concern. There was a feeling that withdrawal by stages was an encouragement for fragmentation.' Attlee to Wavell, 8 January 1947, L/PO/8/9: ff 66–8.

163. Michael Edwards. *The Last Years of British India* (London: Cassel, 1963), pp. 147–149.

164. Attlee to Wavell, 12 January 1947, Telegram, L/PO/8/9j: ff 42.

165. Sir O. Sargent to Sir D. Monteath, 7 December 1946, L/P&J/10/122: ff 105–6.

166. Bevin to Attlee, 1 January 1947, R/30/1/8a: ff 72–7.

167. Ibid.

168. Peter Hennessy, *The Prime Minister: The Office and its Holders Since 1945* (London: Penguin Books, 2001), p. 160.

169. The new viceroy, Mountbatten, did not like to delay the process of demitting the British authority. Therefore, he claimed the maximum powers from the government to settle issues in India. He learnt from the experiences of the previous Viceroy and acquired plenipotentiary powers.

170. Noor-ul-Haq, *Making of Pakistan: The Military Perspective* (Lahore: Army Education Press, reprinted, 1995–96), pp. 158–9.

171. Victoria Schofield, *Wavell: Soldier and Statesman*, p. 400.

172. The newspaper wrote that 'widespread sympathy with Viscount Wavell, who is regarded as having been given an impossible individual task, and is now made to appear a scapegoat for the failure of the Government to bring the Indian parties together.' *The Daily Telegraph*, 21 March 1947.

173. Attlee to Mr Mackenzie King, 13 February 1947, Telegram, L/P&J/10/77: ff 325–8.

174. Wavell to Lawrence, 8 January 1947, L/PO/10/24.

175. Ian Stephens, *Pakistan* (London: Ernest Benn Ltd, 1963), p. 122.

176. *News Chronicle* indicates that from a present point of view Lord Wavell's departure will be regretted, but there is no need to gloss over the fact that certain errors of judgment have been attributed to his political inexperience in dealing with the astute Indian politicians. *News Chronicle*, 22 March 1947.

6

Wavell's Breakdown Plan, 1945–47

The Breakdown Plan was prepared by Lord Wavell and his closest circle of advisors to deal with the fast-evolving political situation in India. Two main political tendencies had crystallized in post-War India: Keeping India as one geographic entity; the second one was diametrically opposed to it, espoused by the Muslims, who wanted an independent Muslim-majority state. Wavell's Breakdown Plan was formulated with two main goals in mind: Firstly, a safe withdrawal of the British from India; secondly, to avoid a partition of India by attempting to maintain it as one geographic entity. For the first goal, Wavell suggested a 'phased withdrawal' from India, which would be initiated from the Hindu-majority provinces of the south. The second goal was to be achieved by proposing a partition of both the Punjab and Bengal, as a bargaining tool with the Muslim League to deter from pursuing its agenda of a separate Muslim-majority homeland on religious grounds. Although Wavell's overall plan was rejected by His Majesty's Government in London, parts of it were, however, incorporated in the final withdrawal plan laid down by Mountbatten, Wavell's successor, in his June 3 Plan. This included the partitioning of both the Bengal and the Punjab thus dealing a blow to Muslim interests in both those provinces. This chapter tries to detail the overall Breakdown Plan and its implications for the Muslims, particularly, as it ended up shaping the future course of the history of the Punjab. This, in the author's view, has not been attempted before.

INTRODUCTION

Lord Wavell, (the Viceroy of India October 1943–March 1947) conceived of India as a single geographic and administrative unit, and, therefore, was desirous of preserving its political unity. After the failure of the Simla Conference in 1945, in pursuance of precisely such a goal, he came up with a secret scheme which has come to be known in history as Wavell's 'Breakdown Plan'. Although the final shape of this Breakdown Plan took some time to evolve, however, in its earlier forms, it strictly avoided any reference to the idea of Pakistan.

Wavell's proposed Breakdown Plan, so-called in its final shape, required two steps to be taken for a phased withdrawal of British authority from India: Firstly, a withdrawal from the four Hindu-majority provinces of Bombay, Madras, Orissa and the Central Provinces; secondly, a general withdrawal from the rest of the country, before March 1948.

Wavell believed that such a plan of withdrawal would not only avoid a division of India but also the civil war, which to all indications was looming clearly on the horizon. However, before he had a chance to put his plan into operation he was removed from his position as the Viceroy of India because of the Labour government's reservations about some long-term implications of his plan.

A critical, historical understanding of Lord Wavell's Viceroyalty which lasted between October 1943 and March 1947, is important for gaining a true insight into the constantly evolving, dynamic relationship between the three leading political actors of India in that period, the British, the Congress and the Muslim League. While Wavell was stressing to the Attlee administration the need to accept and implement his Breakdown Plan, the British government in London was simultaneously working on a departure plan of its own and it was this policy which was later on adopted by Mountbatten as well.

Voluminous historical literature about the viceroyalties of Lord Linlithgow, 1936–43, and Viscount Mountbatten, March-August 1947, exists about the British government's ideas for the transfer of power into Indian hands during those two viceroyalties, however, Wavell's period is often overlooked by historians; consequently, the historical importance of his Breakdown Plan is not fully appreciated.

Wavell's Breakdown Plan, in this author's view, aimed at preserving the political unity of India by the tactic of denying undivided Bengal and Punjab to the Muslim League if the latter persisted in its demand for a totally independent Pakistan. He expected enough flexibility from both parties so as to reach a compromise for a united India, which was Wavell's desired goal. Although Wavell failed in his efforts for a united India via the implementation of his Breakdown Plan, parts of it, however, were incorporated into Mountbatten's June 3, 1947 partition plan resulting in a serious loss of territory for the newly created Muslim state of Pakistan.

WAVELL'S BREAKDOWN PLAN

Wavell, right from the beginning of his viceroyalty, discerned a variety of complex problems lining the Indian political scene. The main ones were the following: the ever-growing Hindu-Muslim friction on religious lines; the Muslim League's demand for a separate homeland for the Muslims on the basis of its two-nation theory and the expected complications flowing from it; lastly, a state of hibernation induced in the British government following the rejection by both the Congress and the League of the Cripps Proposals in 1942; London was not ready to initiate another attempt at breaking the political impasse in India.

Wavell considered India's geographical and political unity as 'natural' and was, therefore, dead-set against any division.[1] He thought of giving appropriate representation to various communities in the legislature, the new central executive and the services. He wished to see the same kind of treatment being given to the Princely States.[2]

Ian Stephens has written that Wavell had contemplated a date for the final British withdrawal from India and, therefore, 'in fact, at any rate during that crucial December of 1946, his thoughts were evidently more progressive on this point than the Cabinet's.'[3]

H.M. Close has written about Wavell that 'consciously or sub-consciously, was not willing to promote a plan for partition on equality with a plan for unity, and therefore downgraded it with the unattractive name of "Breakdown"'.[4] Based on a rough mental sketch of his 'Breakdown Plan' Wavell directed his advisers Evan Jenkins, V.P. Menon and B.N. Rau to chalk out its details.

Jenkins's 'reserve plan' of 10 November 1945 had suggested the establishment of an Indian union with the right of a province(s) to secede from it and form a separate union. In case the Muslim-majority provinces decided to form a separate union, he suggested partitioning the Punjab, Bengal and Assam to make Pakistan small, weak and unattractive for Jinnah. He believed, 'In the long run I think that the Punjab and probably Bengal might join the original Federal Union on terms- the prospect of partition would be less attractive when it became imminent.'⁵ However, he asked V.P. Menon to chalk out further details.

Abell's input into the Breakdown Plan was that 'Pakistan Provinces would be offered to continue for the time being under the present constitution with the British support they have now. They could watch the formation of Hindustan and they could decide later (by an unspecified procedure) to join the Federation or stay out. It would be made clear that H.M.G. would be ready to grant Dominion Status as under the Cripps Plan to the Pakistan Provinces if they wanted.'⁶

However, B.N. Rau agreed with the 'reserve plan' and suggested that it would be necessary to give large territorial units in the Pakistan Provinces the option of merging themselves into the neighbouring federating provinces of 'Hindustan'. He thought that 'this is the right sort of reserve plan and that it might be acceptable to the Congress.'⁷

V.P. Menon stressed the need for the establishment of a coalition government pledged to assist in the revision of the constitution at the earliest possible moment. He also proposed the adoption of a time-table, so that everybody could see that His Majesty's Government meant business. He disagreed with imposing a constitution suggesting instead convening a convention of important political parties, communities, groups and their representatives which would prepare a constitution. He opined that under the existing plan there was the hope of setting at least one union by the people themselves, as Nehru had suggested. Having got the union, he suggested that they would be in a position to know which units stood out and then to deal with them on that basis.⁸

The general elections (1945-46) had electrified the political atmosphere in India causing the political parties to grow further apart. Pethick Lawrence, Secretary of State for India (1945-1947), inquired of Wavell the actions that would be necessary in the event of their finding it impossible to bring agreement between the parties during the coming summer. Wavell informed him on 5 December 1945 that he and his staff had been considering the 'breakdown plan' for some time but had not finalized it.[9] Wavell's request for a visit to India by David Monteath to chalk out details with his own staff was refused.

In the meantime, Jinnah's expression of a willingness to accept 'frontier adjustments where primarily Hindu and Muslim lands were contiguous to the Hindustan or Pakistan States, as the case may be'[10] was seen as a welcome sign by Wavell as an opening for future negotiations.

According to Wavell's calculations, any contemplated plan for a division of India would affect at least two divisions (Ambala and Jullundur) of the Punjab and almost the whole of Western Bengal, including Calcutta, which could only be joined with the Indian Union. Wavell believed that adoption and enunciation of such a policy by Whitehall would diminish the attractiveness of Pakistan to Jinnah. Wavell, quoting Jinnah, said, 'only the husk' then, would remain.[11] Faced with such a fait accompli and finding his power of negotiation vis-à-vis the Congress reduced drastically Jinnah would try to secure the best possible terms for the Muslims within the Union.[12] Wavell felt, 'No-one believes that Pakistan is in the best interests of India from the practical point of view, and no-one knows where the partition of India, once it starts, will end short of Balkanisation.'[13]

Wavell, on his part, wanted to remove the bargaining power of the Muslim League. He had no doubt that his Breakdown Plan would force the Congress and the League to come to terms, but the best panacea was that 'the Constitution would be made sufficiently attractive to the Muslims to induce them to remain in the Federation from the start.'[14] It appears that Wavell, quite skilfully, had drafted a plan which would be unacceptable to the Muslims and Hindus, and violently opposed by the Sikhs so that each one of them would have to accept the unity of India.

However, the Labour Party had a number of reservations about Wavell's Breakdown Plan primarily because it felt that such a plan would greatly weaken any possibility of compromise on the basis of even a very loose federation. Further, how could it be enforced without an agreement between the two leading parties?[15] They, like Wavell, wanted adoption of measures most helpful in securing a united India. For carrying out the necessary revisions to Wavell's Breakdown Plan, he was provided the services of David Monteath's Committee.[16]

Evan Jenkins had detailed knowledge about the Indian affairs with clear headedness and always showed great commitment for work[17] and as a result Wavell leaned heavily on him.[18] Besides this, Jenkins helped Wavell chalk a comprehensive outline of the Breakdown Plan which he termed as a 'Reserve Plan'. Therefore, Evan Jenkins became Wavell's ultimate choice for Punjab's governorship whose Governor Bertrand Glancy's term of office came to an end in April 1946. Wavell had a feeling that Glancy was a tired man and lacked interest in the provincial affairs of the Punjab.[19] He never discussed the Breakdown plan with Glancy rather relied heavily on his advisers including B.N. Rau, Menon and Evan Jenkins. He was not very happy with Glancy's handling of the general elections in 1945–46 and the food condition in the province.[20]

In the meantime, the protracted negotiations regarding the Cabinet Mission Plan's proposals for both the long and the short-term components further estranged the Hindu-Muslim relations. The delay in forming the Interim Government had caused communal as well as administrative problems. The Calcutta riots following the 'Direct Action Day' turned it even bloodier. The riots once let loose could not be stopped. The Interim Government (September 1946–August 1947) caused more frustration than satisfaction for Wavell.[21] Therefore, he pointed out to Whitehall that they must be ready with a plan which could be put into effect if Congress and League failed to reach an agreement or in case both rejected the Mission's Proposals.[22]

Though Wavell had teamed up with the Cabinet Mission Delegation in presenting the Cabinet Mission Plan, deep inside he was not optimistic about its success, expecting a sudden outbreak of violence owing to unbridgeable differences among the leading parties. Therefore, he suggested to Whitehall an adequate consideration of his 'Breakdown Plan' as well. Details of that plan included handing over the Hindu majority provinces of Bombay, Madras, C.P, UP, Bihar and Orissa, by agreement and as peaceably as possible, to the Congress followed by the withdrawal of troops, officials and European nationals in an orderly manner from these provinces.

Wavell was not unaware of the flaws in his Breakdown Plan and, therefore, suggested means to deal with them. Firstly, he thought that the Muslim League might decline the British offer. Secondly, even if it accepted the Plan, it would result in a division of the Indian army. Thirdly, the actual military operation of withdrawal from Hindustan into Pakistan could be difficult and possibly dangerous. Fourthly, it was an equally grave problem to deal with the large minorities, Hindus and Sikh, in the Muslim provinces. Even at that stage, he still favoured that maximum efforts be exerted to bring about a union of India on . the best terms possible and then affect a total withdrawal.

On 6 June 1946, in a Cabinet meeting presided by Attlee in London, Wavell's Breakdown Plan was discussed at length. The idea of withdrawal from India by a specific date was disapproved. The Cabinet remarked:

> We are anxious to give India her independence and have put forward plans for achieving it. Unfortunately the Leaders of the political Parties of India cannot agree among themselves on a plan for independence. We cannot in these circumstances allow a situation to develop in which there will be a chaos and famine. Accordingly we must maintain our responsibilities until the Indian leaders can find a basis for accepting our offer of independence. Our proposals still remain open.[23]

However, seeing the difficulties facing the Cabinet Mission's proposals and feeling especially pessimistic about Congress's general attitude and supported by a realisation that the continuous attrition faced by the essential services and the army, Lord Wavell again emphasized on his Breakdown Plan.

The Congress-League disagreement over the long-term and short-term parts of the Cabinet Mission Plan, particularly the formation of the Interim Government, caused disharmony, discontent and disappointment and it paved the way for further division among the Muslims on one hand and the Hindus and the Sikhs on the other. With all his good intentions, Wavell was convinced that a coalition government would not only help to bypass the demand for Pakistan but help avoid a civil war as well.

Wavell warned that one party rule would lead to a certain civil war, as was obvious from the carnage on the 'Direct Action Day';[24] Gandhi pounded the table and said, 'If a bloodbath was necessary it would come about in spite of non-violence.' Gandhi in his letter on 28 August told Wavell that Congress would not bend itself and adopt what it considered a wrong course because of 'brutal exhibition recently witnessed in Bengal. Such submissions would itself lead to an encouragement and repetition of such tragedies.'[25]

The Muslim League decided to declare 2 September 1946, the day the Congress-led Interim Government started its tenure, as a day of mourning and Jinnah instructed the Muslims to display black flags which led to communal riots in Bombay, Punjab, Bengal and Bihar. Jinnah's response to Nehru's broadcast was a bitter attack on the Congress and the British Cabinet.[26]

Wavell, aware of the repercussion and the backlash it would bring to induct one party rule in a multi-religious country with hostile feelings, recorded:

> Though the consequences may be serious I think it is as well that things have come to a head. Calcutta with its 4,400 dead, 16,000 injured and over 100,000 homeless showed that a one-party government at the Centre was likely to cause fierce disorders everywhere. Far from having any sobering effects, it had increased communal hatred and intransigence. If Congress intentions are as Gandhi's letter suggests the result of their being in power can only be a state of virtual civil war in many parts of India while you and I are responsible to Parliament. [27]

Penderel Moon has recorded that, 'During the period acute tension that followed the failure of the Cabinet Mission, Khizar's Government remained uneasy in the saddle. Though there were isolated communal incidents, there was no widespread outbreak of violence in the Punjab such as occurred in Bengal and Bihar. But this outward tranquillity deceived no one. All the major communities-Muslims, Hindus and Sikhs-were collecting arms and getting ready for open war.'[28] Evan Jenkins reporting to Wavell informed him that, 'It has suggested to me that in Lahore the Hindus now feel that they are well prepared and wish to provoke a conflict.'[29] He imposed Punjab Public Safety Ordinance on 19 November 1946 to curb communal unrest created by Rashtriya Swayamsevak Sangh (RSS) and the Muslim League volunteers. [30]

But Wavell was quite aware of the growing disorder and hostility between the major communities in northern parts of India. Defending his phased withdrawal from the south to north he argued, 'After all the Congress would be receiving unqualified and immediate power over a very large proportion of India, and it would hardly be to their interest that those provinces should be thrown into chaos. I think that there is prospect that the position might be accepted, and that the Congress would acquiesce in an orderly transfer, whether the Central Government were dismissed or not.'[31]

Therefore, Wavell once again reiterated the implementation of his Breakdown Plan.[32] Called to London in December 1946 along with the Muslim League and Congress leadership to try to sort out their differences over the interpretations regarding the Cabinet Mission Plan, Wavell in his private talks with the leaders of His Majesty's Government and the Whitehall insisted upon implementing his proposals for the 'Breakdown Plan' or else get ready to face serious consequences.[33] He had reached this conclusion because, firstly, Congress had not accepted the Cabinet Mission Plan in full, and secondly, His Majesty's Government by an inadequate expression of its position regarding the 'Grouping Clause' had allowed the political deadlock to continue with the resultant increase in communal tensions; feeling, therefore, that the Cabinet Mission Plan had lost its efficacy, he felt it was time to look for alternate solutions.[34]

Wavell reiterated that his Breakdown Plan was intended for use not merely in case of a widespread administrative deadlock, but also in the event of a political breakdown. He believed that the plan would enable the government to take a firm line with Congress, since it had a reasonable alternative on which to fall back; such a course of action might also enable it to avert a political breakdown.

Since 1945, His Majesty's Government had considered Wavell's ideas about the Breakdown Plan in several meetings of the India and Burma Committee and the Cabinet Committees and Wavell personally pleaded his case on 5 December 1946. Attlee, pointing out the necessity of new legislation, was not optimistic about its outcome. Although granted a personal appearance before the India and Burma Committee, Wavell still felt that his proposed Breakdown Plan did not get the wholehearted approval it deserved.[35]

It was again discussed at 10 Downing Street on 11 December 1946 and it was felt that if either of the two communities refused to cooperate in carrying out the Mission's Plan, then a situation would arise which would justify and necessitate a fresh statement of policy by the government.

Wavell held that if the League refused to participate in the Constituent Assembly, the government would be ready to accept a constitution, drawn up by the present Constituent Assembly, as valid for the Hindu majority provinces only. He pointed out that an announcement by the government favouring the establishment of Pakistan would at once arouse great opposition on the part of Congress. On the other hand, he hoped that 'if they realised that continued intransigence on their part would lead to the establishment of Pakistan, the Congress leaders might become more reasonable.'[36]

Wavell explained that under his 'Breakdown Plan' the Hindu provinces of Bihar and the United Provinces would not be handed over to the Congress in the first stage. Although, politically, they were the most difficult provinces, he had the full concurrence of the Commander-in-Chief on this matter and proposed their retention so as to avoid giving any impression that they were only retaining hold on the Muslim provinces. In the end, Wavell's Breakdown Plan, failed to bypass the Pakistan issue completely though it did succeed in postponing it for a while.[37]

In later discussions of Wavell's Breakdown Plan, issues concerning the religious minorities in either of the two groupings or new territories and agreements with one or more new successor authorities were discussed.

Issues concerning the position of the army were particularly awkward as its control and functioning, in the initial stages, both at the central and the provincial levels, could spark conflicts in its modes of operations. At a later stage, control of the Indian army would have to pass under the command of some specified authority. If no central authority for the whole of India came into being they could not hand all of it over to a government for the Hindu provinces only; therefore, they would be compelled to divide it.[38]

The India and Burma Committee remained unclear about the future of the Princely States. They were unsure about the action with regard to the states adjoining the provinces in which sovereignty was to be handed over and at what stage Paramountcy in respect of those states would have to be surrendered. The rights of minorities would also have to be dealt with and eventually all this would require new legislation in the British Parliament.[39]

Wavell emphasised the importance of announcing at the earliest, in fixed and unequivocal terms, the decision to leave India by a specified date. He believed this would force the leading political parties to come to terms. He said, 'the shock of this announcement might be of value in inducing a sense of responsibility in their minds they still had the sense that in the last resort the British would always be there to maintain law and order.'[40]

Therefore, the British Ministers forwarded their own line of action. They suggested that most of the objections raised were due to the suggestion that there should be a formal transfer of power to the provinces. The 'constitution' of India could be preserved intact until the later stages. The first stage would consist in the removal of the remaining officers of the Secretary of State Services in the four southern provinces and the withdrawal of all British troops from there. The British governors could also be recalled unless the provincial governments specially asked for their retention and Indian governors appointed in their place on the advice of the provincial ministers. There would thus be a complete and absolute 'Indianization' of the services in the provinces while the existing constitution would continue to operate and provinces' relationship with the central government would continue as before. The troops of the Indian army would also remain in the provinces to help avoid the division of India into separate units. Similarly, the termination of Paramountcy of Indian States could also be avoided.

The third sitting of the India and Burma Committee took place on 19 December 1946. Now, Wavell put forward a different version of his Breakdown Plan. He proposed that it should immediately become clear that if the Muslim League were not to be represented in the Constituent Assembly, government would withdraw the governors, Secretary of States Services and British troops from the provinces of Orissa, the Central Provinces, Bombay and Madras within a period of three or four months. The present status of central government and the constitution should be maintained but fresh governors would be appointed on the advice of ministries. In his concluding remarks in favour of the Plan, he said that it would enable him to concentrate his administrative forces and limit his responsibilities. It would cause psychological effect on the two communities and they might go for some form of cooperation.[41]

The India and Burma Committee considered the revised Wavell Plan and held that legislation would be necessary because it completely disregarded the government of India Act 1935. The Secretary of State and the Viceroy could not rid themselves of their responsibilities under that Act without an Act of Parliament. It was, however, desirable to avoid legislation before the final transfer of sovereignty. They thought that such legislation would be difficult to get through the Parliament and, therefore, it might be possible to use the 'convention' that governors would always accept the advice of their ministers. Alternatively, it might be possible to obtain the approval of the parliament to some 'blanket resolution' which would give the government sufficient authority to act. Without such authority they might be charged with abandoning their responsibilities towards the minorities and neighbouring states.

Since the cooperation of the Congress was crucial for any implementation of the Breakdown Plan, it was felt necessary that its introduction be made through a carefully worded statement since an impression, in spite of the retention of Bihar and the United Provinces, of the British withdrawal from southern provinces as implying a tilt in favour of Pakistan could easily be created. The probability was that following the British withdrawal, southern provinces would continue to hand over to the central government the taxes necessary for financing the essential services.

The India and Burma Committee resumed its discussion of Wavell's Breakdown Plan on 20 December.[33] Wavell stressed, feeling the heat from the prime ministers of the four southern provinces, that announcement of a definite date for British departure could lessen their enthusiasm for an immediate, full independence in essential services. The date decided upon was 31 March 1948.

Concerning the transfer of power, it was felt that it could be easily carried out to a central authority representing the Congress-led provinces while concerning the other provinces the power could be handed over individually or to a separate central government for them; it would also result in splitting the Indian army.

The India and Burma Committee in its meeting of 3 January 1947 rejected Wavell's Breakdown plan. The Ministers held that 'it was wrong to press too far the analogy of a military withdrawal. The operation now to be begun was not so much a military as a political operation of great delicacy. It must be regarded not as a withdrawal under pressure, but as a voluntary transfer of power to a democratic government. To an increasing degree the Viceroy would assume the position of a constitutional ruler and he and the British officials would act in conformity with the policy of that Government.'42 All this was, however, not conveyed to Wavell before his departure for India.

The next meeting of the India and Burma Committee took place on 6 January 1947.43 Although the Committee showed appreciation of the fact that the area under the control of the Viceroy would be lessened, thereby reducing his risks, they however, disagreed with Wavell's argument that he would remain unaffected. They felt that his argument was not conclusive enough.

The second argument that the Breakdown Plan would deserve implementation in case a law and order situation arose was also rejected on the grounds that the Committee's plan for vacating India should not be based on the assumption that law and order would be broken. It thus failed to appreciate the ground realities of a serious communal conflict, just around the corner, in India. In general, the Committee desired a friendly atmosphere for transfer of power to Indian authorities. They were of the opinion that the Plan would result in the division of India into two or more parts and this would lead straight in the direction of Pakistan. Therefore, the Committee decided that the Viceroy's plan should be held in reserve for use only in case of an emergency.

Some recommendations concerning the transfer of some members of the Secretary of State Services at present serving in the southern provinces to other provinces and movement of some troops from south to north so as to concentrate them in the north were made.44 These changes were to be carried out in such a way as not to imply a complete withdrawal of British authority from these provinces.

Attlee conveyed the Cabinet's decision to Wavell on 8 January 1947.45 He invited Wavell to London as soon as possible for a review of the situation. But Wavell had returned to India and thought it would be useless to plead his Breakdown Plan any more.[46] His termination, a short while later, ended all hopes of its implementation.[47]

IMPLICATIONS OF THE BREAKDOWN PLAN

The Breakdown Plan fell short of the desirable level of acceptability in the British political circles because it could have created a conflict between the central government and the provinces due to ambiguity in the central and provincial subjects; Wavell's suggestion to overcome this weakness that withdrawal should be made only from four provinces instead of six Hindu-majority ones, to obviate a 'pro-Pakistan' bias was also deemed unsatisfactory.

The main reason for the failure of acceptance concerning Wavell's Breakdown Plan, however, lay with a majority of the British ministers who disliked any scheme that included evacuating the largest and most important colony, India. It was also considered desirable to leave India in the hands of those leaders who could make economic and political treaties with the British government but, they also felt, that the Plan did not guarantee such peaceful transfer of power to a legitimate authority or authorities. Additionally, a chain reaction of other colonies demanding their freedom as well was very worrisome to many leading members of the British political leadership.[48] Ernest Bevin, the Foreign Secretary, felt that 'the defeatist attitude adopted by the Cabinet and by Field-Marshal Wavell is just completely letting us down.'[49] He was against the fixing of a specific date for withdrawal as it could cause problems for them in the Middle East and suggested Attlee to replace Wavell due to his defeatist approach.[50]

The British government was also apprehensive of the communist involvement in the region. They did not wish to leave their former possessions in an unfriendly atmosphere which would force the colonies to reach out to the USSR.

Wavell's Breakdown Plan needed legislation from the British parliament to put it into force. The Labour Party feared that new legislation would not get approval in the Parliament on the lines proposed by Wavell as he was considered a 'defeatist' by the Labour party and an advocate of scuttle.[44] Attlee himself never had a positive opinion of Wavell's political insight and doubted whether he had the finesse to negotiate the next step. Since one of the main aims of the Breakdown Plan was to avoid the blackmailing by the Congress ministries from the four provinces, as a Viceroy was obliged to act upon the advice of the ministers.[43] Although the Labour Party rejected Wavell's Breakdown Plan, they agreed in principle to leave India lest the Indians forced them to vacate the country. They announced the date of their final withdrawal as March 1948, a date which Wavell had suggested.[51]

All this delay in settling the communal problem and winding up the British rule had the most adverse effect in India particularly in the province of the Punjab. The loyalties of the police and the army towards British authority became doubtful. According to Noor-ul-Haq, 'it seems that, by January 1947, the communal feelings in the Armed Forces had grown very strong.....Because of the growing communalism in the Armed Forces, Prime Minister Attlee, who stood for the unity of India, got worried that Indian unity, could not be achieved if the Indian Armed Forces were spilt on communal lines.'[52]

The country had been heading towards a civil war which could have been avoided by implementing the Breakdown Plan. Victoria Schofield has recorded:

> Since partition formed part of the eventual solution, it may be conjectured that the Breakdown Plan-taking place over more than a year under Wavell's schedule-would have provided more time for tempers to subside; under Mountbatten, their were less than three months between the announcement of partition in June 1947 and independence celebrations in August. Mountbatten argued that once the plan had been announced time was of the essence, but within Wavell's longer time-frame it is possible the violence that accompanied partition could have been considerably lessened, if not averted.[53]

Thus the civil war that broke out during the last days of the Raj in India, in which numerous innocent people were slaughtered, might have lost a major part of its fury if Wavell's Breakdown Plan had been implemented, the division of India and also the partition of the provinces of Punjab and Bengal would most likely, have taken place peacefully.

According to the instructions of His Majesty's Government, Mountbatten acted as a constitutional head of the government and, therefore, could do nothing to stop bloodshed; rather, he left everything in the hands of the Interior Minister Sardar Patel who made scant efforts to control it. Wavell, on his part, had been impartial and conscious of the rights of all communities and was determined, as an executive head, to suppress all such threats. After his dismissal, extremists became uncontrollable and shed the blood of innocent people in India in the presence of the new Governor-General and British forces, police and army.

During Wavell's Viceroyalty, devolutionary process of British authority in India was accelerated.[54] Whitehall rejected his Breakdown Plan because they believed that it was a weak plan of a defeatist soldier and would result in a clash with the Congress. Attlee thought, 'Partition would bring us into immediate conflict with the Congress and permanently embitter our relations with the larger part of India.'[55] This kind of approach emboldened the Congress which promoted violence and bloodshed against the Muslims.[56]

It proved a great error on the part of Whitehall to ignore the Breakdown Plan as Ian Stephens has recorded, 'he put forward a "Wavell (Breakdown) Plan", politically and militarily clear-cut, whereby British authority would have been withdrawn from the subcontinent much more gradually; that this was turned down; and that had it not been, much of the appalling slaughter at Partition-time, and resulting ill-will between the two successor-States, might have been avoided.'[57]

It is obvious that Wavell's personal relations with Attlee were strained and uneasy. Wavell's insistence on carrying out his Breakdown Plan put the Labour government in an awkward position. Although Wavell was allowed to return to Delhi following the meetings of December 1946, the fact was that Attlee had already decided to replace Wavell during his stay in London but did not dare tell him personally.[58] The Congress leadership was annoyed with him too and had been continuously asking the Labour government to replace him. In the last days of the transfer of power, he had become unacceptable both to the Congress and the ruling Labour Party in England. H. C. Close has already challenged the myth that Wavell had become a spent force. But he has concluded wrongly that Wavell was insisting on establishing a 'Lesser Pakistan'. As a matter of fact, Wavell in his Breakdown Plan had developed a strategy to force the Congress and the League to come to terms on the basis of the Cabinet Mission Plan but he was not allowed to carry it through in its entirety. The Labour government rejected some of Wavell's main recommendations as put forward in the Breakdown plan but accepted some others which were embodied in it but dismissed him from the viceroyalty.

Wavell can also be credited with strongly apprising the British government of the widespread backing by Muslims of the 'Pakistan' scheme so that it could be dealt with effectively before it became unmanageable. He considered the Cabinet Mission Plan as the best antidote to the spreading popularity of the Pakistan scheme and, therefore, wanted the British government and Whitehall to press the Congress strongly in order to gain concessions which would have prevented the emergence of Pakistan; in the end, however, he failed in his attempt.

CONCLUSION

Wavell was not original in his ideas about the partition of India because Rajagopalachari and Gandhi had earlier suggested the division of the Punjab and Bengal on communal lines as well if Pakistan were to be created. However, Wavell prepared the Breakdown Plan to reduce the attractiveness of the 'Pakistan Scheme' for the Muslims. In his Breakdown Plan, he suggested the division of Punjab, Bengal and Assam on communal basis something which was not clearly mentioned either in the Rajagopalachari Formula (1944), Gandhi-Jinnah talks (1944), Cripps Proposals (1942) or the Cabinet Mission Plan (1946). His suggestion in the Breakdown Plan that Punjab and Bengal should be divided on a communal basis, if Jinnah insisted on the Pakistan demand, was only envisaged as a bargaining point with the Muslim League and never intended for actual implementation because he was dead sure that the League and the Congress would come to terms on a formula for a united India based on the Cabinet Mission Plan. However, since neither of the parties was willing to compromise enough he was proved wrong. In the meantime, his Hindu advisers had drawn up an unjust demarcation of the Punjab and the Bengal boundaries on maps, which, when actually implemented during Mountbatten's brief tenure as the Viceroy, later on, caused tremendous territorial losses to the newly created state of Pakistan.

Notes

1. Qazi Saeed-ud-Din, 'Is India Geographically One', in Rafique Afzal, ed., *The Case for Pakistan* (Islamabad, 1988), pp. 67–76.
2. *Transfer of Power, Constitutional Relations between Britain and India,* Vol. IV, pp. 331–38.
3. Ian Stephens, *Pakistan,* (London: Ernest Benn), p. 125.
4. H.M. Close, *Wavell, Mountbatten and the Transfer of Power,* (Islamabad: National Book Foundation, 1997), p. 86.
5. Jenkins to Wavell, 10 November 1945, R/3/1/108: ff 8–11.
6. Minutes by Wavell and Abell, 29–30 November 1945, R/3/1/108: ff 16–17.
7. Ibid.
8. Menon to Abell, 6 December 1945, R/3/1/108: ff 24–29.
9. Wavell to Lawrence, 5 December 1945, L/PO/10/22.
10. Wavell to Lawrence 18 December 1945, Ibid.
11. Wavell to Lawrence 27 December 1945, L/P&J/ 8 / 525: ff 248–51.
12. Ibid.
13. Minute addressed to Gibson, undated, Turnbull Papers, MSS. EUR/ D. 714/72.
14. Wavell to Lawrence 27 December 1945, L/P&J/ 8 / 525: ff 248–51.
15. Minute addressed to Gibson, undated, Turnbull Papers, MSS. EUR/ D. 714/72.
16. Ibid.
17. Before being selected to be Wavell's private secretary Evan Jenkins was an outstanding member of the Indian Civil services, who had been Chief Commissioner of Delhi, 1937–40, and the Secretary, Department of Supply, 1940-3.
18. Ibid. p. 108.
19. Ibid. p. 178.
20. Ibid. p. 210.
21. Ibid.
22. It suggested that a policy should be adopted to ensure there would be minimum loss of face to the image of His Majesty's Government and no ultimate prejudice to conflicting aims of Indians. The condition of a provisional constitution for India must be based upon the 1935 Act and such a constitution must continue to provide a unitary framework. It also pointed out that means should be applied to retain India as single state, without prejudice to interests of Indian Muslims. Draft by India Office, undated, *Transfer of Power,* Vol., VI, pp. 1213–28.
23. Attlee to Wavell, 6 June 1946, Ibid., pp. 830–32.
24. Wavell Collections, 1946, 134–5.
25. Wavell, *Viceroy's Journal,* 342–3.
26. Tara Chand, History of the Freedom Movement in India, volume 4, p. 486.
27. Wavell to Lawrence, 28 August 1946, R/3/1/117: f 145.
28. Penderel Moon, *Divide and Quit* (London: Chatto & Windus Limited, 1961), 74.
29. Jenkins to Wavell, 31 October 1946, L/PEJ/5/249:ff 34–5.
30. Jenkins to Colville, 30 November 1946, L/P&J/5/249 : 22–3s.
31. Wavell to Lawrence, 23 October 1946, L/PEJ/10/46: ff 490–6.
32. Wavell told Lawrence that the British government should hand over, after a stated plan, the Congress majority provinces to Congress but maintain the present

constitution and British control in the North West and North East India. Wavell predicted that under such conditions if British government was not prepared to change their policy, the British control in India could be maintained for maximum one and a half-year or till the spring of 1948. Therefore, a definite plan should be worked out in order to wind up British control in India. He suggested that withdrawal should be completed not later than the spring of 1948 because, from the administrative point of view, government could no longer exercise control beyond that date. However, he made it clear that the Breakdown Plan was intended primarily for use in the event of a deadlock before 1 January 1947. He held that the plan should come into operation no later than 1 March 1947.

33. Lawrence to Attlee 13 September 1946, L/PO/6/117: ff 42, pp. 45–82.

34. Note by Wavell, 2 December 1946, L/P&J/10/111: ff 86–90.

35. India Conference in London, 5 December 1946, *Transfer of Power*, Vol. IX, pp. 374–9.

36. India and Burma Committee, IB (46) 8th Meeting, 11 December 1946, *Transfer of Power*, Vol. IX, pp. 332–7.

37. Ibid.

38. Ibid.

39. Ibid.

40. Ibid.

41. Wavell was sure that it would no longer be possible for Congress to put pressure upon him by threatening to withdraw ministries from the provinces. This threat had in the past been a source of embarrassment because he, at that time, was in no position to administer the provinces under section 93 of the government of India Act 1935 because of growing control of the popular governments under the Congress party. India and Burma Committee, IB (46) 11th Meeting, 19 December 1946, *Transfer of Power*, Vol. IX, pp. 383–6.

42. India and Burma Committee, IB (47) 1st Meeting, 3 January 1947, L/P&J/10/46: ff 48–51.

43. India and Burma Committee, IB (47) 2nd Meeting, 6 January 1947, L/P&J/10/46: ff 23–6.

44. Memorandum by the Secretary of State for India, 6 January 1947, India and Burma Committee, Paper IB (47)3. *Transfer of Power*, Vol. IX, pp. 472–4.

45. Attlee said that if the Muslim League fails to enter the Constituent Assembly it would be desirable to announce a time limit for the continuance of British rule in India; however, he argued that it would not be advisable to fix a day for the Transfer of power. While it was considered that the plans might be made for that event and that troops might be moved, there was strong confirmation for the view expressed by the India Committee that the proposal for the abandonment of all responsibility for four Southern Provinces was unacceptable. The Cabinet did not approve the approach to the problem on the basis of a military evacuation. It was considered that a different approach was required-viz that if close co-operation with the Indian Governments at the Centre and in the Provinces in order to work out with them plans for handing over the Government in India, as a going concern. There was a feeling that withdrawal by stages was an encouragement for fragmentation.' Attlee to Wavell, 8 January 1947, L/PO/8/9: ff 66–8.

46. Michael Edwards, *The Last Years of the British India* (London: Cassel, 1963), pp. 147–149.
47. Attlee to Wavell, 12 January 1947, Telegram, L/PO/8/9j: ff 42.
48. Sir O. Sargent to Sir D. Monteath, 7 December 1946, L/P&J/10/122: ff 105–6.
49. Bevin to Attlee, 1 January 1947, *R/30/1/8a*: ff 72–7.
50. Ibid.
51. The new Viceroy Mountbatten did not like to delay the process of demitting the British authority. Therefore, he claimed the maximum powers from the government to settle issues in India. He learnt from the experiences of the previous Viceroy and acquired plenipotentiary powers.
52. Noor-ul-Haq, *Making of Pakistan: The Military Perspective* (Lahore: Army Education Press, reprinted, 1995–96), pp. 158–9.
53. Victoria Schofield, *Wavell, Soldier and Statesman* (London: John Murray, 2006), p. 400.
54. The newspaper wrote that, 'widespread sympathy with Viscount Wavell, who is regarded as having been given an impossible individual task, and is now made to appear a scapegoat for the failure of the Government to bring the Indian parties together.' *The Daily Telegraph,* 21 March 1947.
55. Attlee to Mr Mackenzie King, 13 February 1947, Telegram, L/P&J/10/77: ff 325–8.
56. Wavell to Lawrence, 8 January 1947, L/PO/10/24.
57. Ian Stephens, *Pakistan* (London: Ernest Benn Ltd, 1963), p. 122.
58. *News Chronicle* indicates that from a present point of view Lord Wavell's departure will be regretted, but there is no need to gloss over the fact that certain errors of judgment have been attributed to his political inexperience in dealing with the astute Indian politicians. *News Chronicle,* 22 March 1947.

Conclusion

This research is based upon the theory that Wavell was against the partition of India and tried until the last moment of his viceroyalty to maintain the unity of India.

The first real challenge faced by Wavell at the start of his viceroyalty was the political deadlock in India. He wanted to take steps to end it whereas Whitehall had no intention of doing so. He felt that the smooth running of administration during the war required co-operation from major political parties. Therefore, he wanted to constitute an Executive Council consisting of their representatives, however, the authorities in London did not concur with his planning. They advised Wavell to wait until an appropriate moment for that move; he had to wait until the defeat of Germany for such a green signal.

At the beginning of the Simla Conference (1945), there were signs that it would succeed as Indian National Congress had accepted the parity principle between the Caste-Hindus and Muslims and agreed not to nominate any Muslims either. Wavell's insistence on accommodating Khizar Hayat Tiwana's (Premier of Punjab) right to nominate a Muslim to the Executive Council, however, led to his differences with the Muslim League, which in turn led to the failure of the Simla Conference. This break with the Muslim League produced a situation which in its turn also dealt a strong blow to his dream of cooperative team work between the Muslim League and the Congress in the Executive Council. The complex situation which resulted was too much for even a man of Wavell's capabilities and perforce he had to declare the Simla Conference a failure.

However, the Simla Conference is of immense political importance from the Muslim League's point of view. It helped to establish two main points: firstly, it established Jinnah as the sole and undisputed leader of the Indian Muslims; secondly, it also proved that the Muslim League was the most powerful and unmatched political representative of the Muslims. For the Muslims, the acceptance of the principle that they would get representation equal to the Caste-Hindus was in essence recognition of the Two-Nation Theory. Flush with confidence on both counts Jinnah asked the Viceroy to announce the holding of the general elections to verify the respective claims of the League and the Congress. In spite of this, in retrospect, Jinnah once described the Simla Conference as a snare for the goals of Muslims of India, in the failure of which lay the seeds of the future making of Pakistan.

In England, the Labour Party, which had promised to grant India independence, had won the elections and come into power. Also, with the end of the Second World War, they wanted to hand over power to the elected representatives, something which was close to the heart of neither the Congress nor the Viceroy, each for their own reason. Congress leadership was not in favour of calling a quick election because they felt that having been incarcerated for the duration of the war they had lost touch with the masses. Wavell, on his side, felt that the elections would only help to create further divisions between the two main communities in India and wanted to initiate another effort at reconciliation between them in the form of their joint participation and effort at working together in the Executive Council.

Following the elections to the central and the provincial assemblies in 1945–46 both the Muslim League and the Congress gained decisive victories in their respective constituencies. This substantiated Wavell's fears that elections would only help to widen the gulf between them the two leading communities instead of bridging it.

The Muslim League had proved its case as the sole authoritative representative of the Muslims of India whose main demand was for a separate homeland, but neither His Majesty's Government nor Wavell wanted such a solution to India's independence. Therefore, they decided to send a mission comprising of three cabinet ministers of the British Parliament to India. The mission's aim was to try to bridge the political gulf between the two main parties with the aim of transferring the power in India to the elected representatives of the people. It was also supposed to seek an agreement with Indian leaders on the principles and procedures to be followed in framing a constitution for an independent but united India. This mission was known as the Cabinet Mission.

The cabinet delegation and Wavell worked hard to achieve their goal but bereft of any executive powers they failed in their attempt to bring about a negotiated settlement between the two major parties. To break the political impasse they presented their own constitutional scheme for India known to history as the Cabinet Mission Plan (1946).

The Cabinet Mission Plan as presented consisted of two parts, a long-term part and a short-term one. Although initially hesitant, Jinnah was able to convince the League leadership that accepting the plan in full would be in the interest of Muslims at large. The Congress on the other hand, accepted the long-term part of the plan only upon the persuasion of Lords Stafford Cripps and Pethick-Lawrence. However, their acceptance seemed to lack sincerity as they started nitpicking and raising objections in spite of the fact that the Cabinet Mission had stated clearly upon its presentation that their plan had to be accepted or rejected 'as is' without any modifications.

As far as Wavell was concerned the scheme though containing a 'grouping' clause did not defer to the demand for 'Pakistan' as stated by the Muslim League in its Lahore Resolution of 1940. This was exactly what Congress had in mind when it had stated that it was totally opposed to any scheme for the division of India. However, in the end, both His Majesty's Government and the Congress united to defeat Wavell's attempt to keep India united via the Cabinet Mission Plan.

Jinnah and the League had accepted the plan in full because they felt that it contained the seed and substance of 'Pakistan' as envisioned in the Lahore Resolution. In addition Jinnah was afraid that the increasing Hindu–Muslim bitterness might lead to a full-scale civil war which he wanted to avoid at all cost.

Congress remained complacent on the Pakistan issue and preferred to focus on the freedom of India to grab power without caring whatsoever about the cost involved to attain such a goal. Congress considered not only the unity of India vital but also wanted the unitary form of government in the long run which could guarantee economic and industrial development. If these objects were missing, it was ready to allow the League to have Pakistan but of its, i.e. Congress's, choice. Congress demanded that the provinces should be given the choice to opt out from the groups which would help her getting Assam and NWFP provinces in Hindustan. This demand was fantastic claptrap.

Likewise, its attitude towards the demand for Pakistan, which was based on the 'two-nation' theory, remained one of self-deception and negation of principles of nationalism which led them into making wrong calculations and judgments at an extremely crucial period of Indian history. At a time when their thoughts, words, and actions could lead to some serious repercussions, Congress leaders like Gandhi, Patel and Nehru used them extravagantly and, more importantly, without a sense of timing.

Wavell tried, by all means, to achieve his objective of sidetracking the demand for Pakistan and maintaining the unity of India without prejudice to the interests of Muslims in a united India. He believed that, if established, a coalition government consisting of the Congress and the League would be able to solve the communal and constitutional problems facing India. However, because of the wide gulf separating the political parties, Wavell's vision of a coalition government soon began to fade.

Wavell, himself could not be fully absolved of the responsibility for the failure of the Cabinet Mission Plan. The complex political situation put his sense of impartiality and fair play to the test and he was found wanting. He broke the pledge given to the League of allowing it to form the government without the participation of the Congress but then allowed the Congress to form an Interim Government on the same lines, but without the League's participation.

After the formation of the Interim Government by the Congress Wavell felt that it was imperative to bring the League into the government to prevent a wider catastrophe from engulfing India especially following the Direct Action Day killings in Calcutta. (August 1946) He also felt that rule by Congress alone would definitely lead to the division of India. He, therefore, in spite of opposition from His Majesty's Government and the Congress worked to bring the League into the Interim Government.

However, the formation of an Interim Government which Wavell was able to achieve at the centre eventually caused more harm than good to his dream of a united India. He had felt that the Congress would refrain from repeating the blunder it had committed in 1937 by not forming coalition governments in the provinces. That step had caused great damage to the communal harmony in the country and had forced the

Muslim League to adopt the Lahore Resolution in 1940; he was proved wrong once again. Muslim League knew the true intentions of the Congress High Command, that the main leaders of its Working Committee aimed at establishing a unitary form of government under the slogan of a strong centre in a united India.

The coalition Interim Government instead of lessening the political tensions in India helped to increase them as both the League and the Congress declined to work as a team thus exposing their communal agendas. Congress, although a bigger party than the Muslim League, felt frustrated because they were not allowed to act unilaterally, especially because Liaquat Ali Khan, who was the finance member in the Interim Government, created severe problems for the Congress leadership. This forced even Patel to think openly on the lines of partition as the best political solution for India, something which Congress had tacitly accepted since the Rajagopalachari formula of 1942.

The Muslim League, which had withdrawn its acceptance of the Cabinet Mission Plan, joined the Interim Government with the promise that they would accept it. Wavell failed to force the Muslim League either to attend the Constituent Assembly or to resign from the Interim Government. He, as an honest, impartial and keen observer was convinced that unless the Muslim League got a clear-cut statement from the Congress and His Majesty's Government regarding Grouping, it would not accept the long-term part of the Cabinet Mission Plan and would not attend the Constituent Assembly's meetings. The Congress had been demanding Wavell's dismissal since August 1946, the Labour Party also considered him as a spent force. But the fact was that Wavell was neither acceptable to the Congress nor to the British government, for he was too impartial and honest. For the League, he failed to deliver the goods. In fact, he was made ineffective by the command and control of Whitehall.

Wavell thought of India as a single geographic unit and, therefore, wished to maintain its unity. This led him not only to denounce but even attempt to derail the demand for Pakistan. Initially he thought of it simply as a bargaining counter and believed that its creation could be avoided. However, with the passage of time, after he had witnessed the rapidly rising support for the Pakistan demand and increasing popularity of Jinnah as the sole spokesman of the Muslims, he came to the conclusion that it needed to be taken very seriously and dealt with accordingly. This prompted him to suggest to His Majesty's Government to expose the weaknesses of the Pakistan demand as incorporated in the Lahore Resolution. This was the strategy which he suggested should be adopted before the elections in order to lessen the popularity of the League's demand; however, he was not allowed to pursue this course of action.

Following the victory of the Muslim League in the elections Wavell kept Whitehall thoroughly informed of the latest political developments in India so that when the Cabinet Mission proposed its Plan for India it incorporated all those ideas which Wavell thought would help to keep India united in addition to offering the best constitutional arrangement for safeguarding the rights of the minorities, especially the Muslims, in India. What Wavell disliked was the *modus operandi* of the Mission's delegates who tried to sidetrack the Muslim League's point of view by sometimes openly, and at other times, surreptitiously, siding with the Congress delegates. These unfair and sometimes underhanded actions of the Cabinet Mission's delegates aroused fears in Wavell's mind that the Muslim League just might begin to oppose the Cabinet Mission Plan. At the same time his own position *vis-à-vis* the Congress was considerably weakened by such tactics as it came to the conclusion that Wavell could easily be bypassed while taking important decisions concerning India.

While all this activity with regards to the Cabinet Mission Plan was in progress Wavell was also involved in giving finishing touches to his 'Breakdown Plan'. Considerable controversy surrounds the aims and objectives of Wavell's Breakdown Plan. H.M. Close, Narendra Sarila, and Victoria Schofield are of the view that Wavell's Breakdown Plan was designed to give Jinnah a smaller Pakistan. This study shows that Wavell's Breakdown Plan did not aim at the partition of India. He was forced to draft this plan because of the highly depleted strength of the British military and civil forces which would have been unable to properly assert and maintain the government's control over all of India in case the Congress decided to follow up on its threats of civil disobedience as it had during the 'Quit India' movement. The main aims of the Breakdown Plan included the following:

(1) To implement the Cabinet Mission Plan in full which would involve a peaceful transfer of power to the Indians while providing for the safe evacuation of all foreigners and maintenance of a united India after the departure of the British.

(2) In case the two leading parties failed to compromise on the Cabinet Mission Plan, he thought that he would pressurise each of the two parties concerned by trying to make them realise that they would fall far short of their eventual aims if they rejected the Cabinet Mission Plan.

(3) The third and final phase of his Breakdown Plan envisaged the phased withdrawal of British authority from four of the six Hindu-majority provinces but it would retain full control of the Centre and the Muslim-majority provinces from where, he felt, the British still would be in a position to dictate a final and favourable constitutional solution to the political problem.

Whatever the merits of Wavell's Breakdown Plan His Majesty's Government opposed it on the following grounds:

(1) They considered it as indicating a case of 'cut and run' or a 'defeatist' attitude on his part;

(2) In spite of their highly weakened position, something which was obvious to Wavell, His Majesty's Government was unwilling to even entertain the idea of completely cutting its links with India at such short notice.

(3) His Majesty's Government thought that implementation of Wavell's Breakdown Plan would send a wrong signal to the Congress Party, i.e. this would inevitably lead to the creation of Pakistan and this was something that they were loathe to do under any circumstances.

(4) Finally, such a move would have required legislation in the British Parliament and it was highly unlikely that it would get approval in that body. All these moves led to a deterioration of Wavell's relationship with both His Majesty's Government and the Congress and led to his dismissal soon after.

However, several of the ideas included by Wavell in his Breakdown Plan, unfortunately, outlived his presence in India. Whereas he had included the partition of Bengal and Punjab in his Breakdown Plan just to impress upon the Muslim League, the futility of its request for a Pakistan based upon the Lahore Resolution. With the aim of keeping India united, his successor, Lord Mountbatten and his team of Hindu advisors namely V.P. Menon and others, actually included them in their partition plans for these two provinces in June–August 1947; this led to mass migrations and killings of countless innocent people. So those parts of Wavell's Breakdown Plan which were actually put into practice went squarely against Muslims which was not the way he had intended them to be used in the first place. And finally, his dream of preventing the foundation of Pakistan by offering Muslims sufficient concessions within a united India also failed to materialise.

Selected Bibliography

PRIMARY SOURCES

A. Documents and Records (Unpublished)

i. India Office Library and Records (IOR) London

Official Files and Papers

L/P & J/5	Governor's & Chief Secretary's Fortnightly Reports
L/P & J/7	Political Department Files
L/P & J/8	Political Department Collections
L/I/l	Information Department Files
L/WS/1	War Staff Files
R/3/1	Papers of the Office of the Private Secretary to the Viceroy

Private Papers

- Attlee (Clement Richard) Collection, MSS Eur Photo Eur 212
- Birdwood Collections (William Riddell), MSS Eur D686
- Casey Collection, MSS Eur Photo 048
- Christies Papers (Walter Henry John) MSS Eur D718
- Evan Jenkins Papers, MSS Eur D807
- Fazl-i-Husain Collection, Eur E264
- George Cunningham Papers, Mur Eur D670
- Gregory Collection (Gregory Theodore Emmanuel Guggenheim), MSS Eur D1163
- Hugh Dow Collection, MSS Eur E372; MSS Eur D670/5
- James Griggs Collection, MSS Eur D844
- Jinnah (Quaid-i-Azam) Papers MSS Eur D609
- John Gilbert Laithwaite Collection, MSS Eur F138
- Linlithgow Papers, MSS Eur C152, F125
- Listowel Collection, MSS Eur B357; MSS Eur D714
- Lord Irwin Halifax Collection, MSS Eur E220
- Lord Simon Collection, MSS Eur E238
- Lumely Collection, MSS Eur F253
- Major Short Collections, MSS Eur F189
- Maurice Garnet Hallet Collection, MSS Eur E251
- Mountbatten Collection, MSS Eur Neg. 17444/53
- Olaf Caroe Collection, MSS Eur F203

- Pethick-Lawrence Collection, MSS Eur D540
- Robert Francis Mudie Collection, MSS Eur F164
- Sir Reginald Hugh Collection, MSS Eur E215
- Turnbull Papers, MSS Eur D714/72
- Wavell Collection, MSS Eur D977/1–18
- Zetland Collection, MSS Eur F77

ii. Cambridge University Churchill Centre

Churchill Papers, Chur/20/1–200 (Microfilms)

iii. Bodleian Library Oxford

Attlee Papers, MS/23–48

iv. National Documentation Centre, Islamabad

Wavell Collection, MSS/977/1–18
Linlithgow Collection,
Sorabji Collection

v. National Archives of Pakistan, Islamabad

Fatima Jinnah Papers
Quaid-i-Azam Papers
Syed Shamsul Hassan Collection
Archives of the Freedom Movement (All-India Muslim League Records)

vi. Karachi University Library

Freedom Movement Archives, Muslim League Records, and Private Collections

B. NEWSPAPERS

The Civil and Military Gazette (Lahore)
Daily Dawn (Delhi)
Inqilab (Lahore)
Nawa-i-Waqt (Lahore)
Paisa Akhbar (Lahore)
The Times (London)
Zamindar (Lahore)

Press abstracts of the following newspapers available at IOR (Newspapers Section) have been used:

The Amrita Bazar Patrika, Calcutta
Bande Matrum
Daily Telegraph
The Eastern Times
The Hindu, Madras
The Hindustan Times, New Delhi
Muslim Outlook
Paisa Akhbar
The Statesman of Calcutta
The Statesman
The Times of India, of Bombay
The Times
The Tribune

C. PUBLISHED WORKS

Afzal, Rafique, ed., *Selected Speeches and Statements of the Quaid-i-Azam Mohammad Ali Jinnah, 1911–34, and 1947–48*, Lahore: Research Society of Pakistan, 1976.

Afzal, Rafique, ed., *Speeches and Statements of Quaid-i-Millat Liaquat Ali Khan, 1941–51*, Lahore: Research Society of Pakistan, 1975.

Ahmad, Jamil-ud-din, ed., *Some Recent Speeches and Writings of Mr. Jinnah*, Lahore Shaikh MuhammadAshraf, 1952.

Ahmad, Jamil-ud-din, *Speeches and Writings of Mr. Jinnah*, 2 Vols., Lahore: Shaikh Muhammad Ashraf, 1960, 1964.

Ahmad, Jamil-ud-din, ed., *Glimpses of Quaid-i-Azam*, Karachi: Education Press, 1960.

Allana, G., ed., *Pakistan Movement: Historic Documents*, Lahore: Islamic Book Service, 1977.

Amery, Leo, *The Empire At Bay: The Leo Amery Diaries, 1929–45*, ed., Barnes, John and David Nicholson, London: Hutchinson and Co. Ltd, 1988.

Aziz, K.K., ed., *The All-India Muslim Conference, 1928–1935: A Documentary Record*. Karachi: National Publishing House, 1972.

Aziz, K.K., ed., *The Indian Khilafat Movement, 1915–1933: A Documentary Record*. Karachi: National Publishing House, 1972.

Aziz, K.K., ed., *Muslims Under Congress Rule, 1937–39: A Documentary Record*, Vol. I. Islamabad: National Commission on Historical and Cultural Research, 1978.

Banerjee, A.C., ed., *Indian Constitutional Documents*, Calcutta: A. Mukherjee, 1946.

Char, S.V. Desika, ed., *Readings in the Constitutional History of India, 1757–1947*, Delhi: Oxford University Press, 1983.

Chopra, P.N., ed., *The Collected Works of Sardar Vallabhbhai Patel*, Vol. XI, Delhi: Konark Publishers, 1997.

Dobbin, Christine, ed., *Basic Documents in the Development of Modern India and Pakistan*, London: Van Nostrand Reinhold Co., 1970.

Gandhiji's Correspondence with the Government, 1942–44, Ahmedabad: Navajivan Publishing House, 1945.

Gopal, S., ed., *Selected Works of Nehru*, New Delhi: Orient Longmans, 1972–81.

Gwyer, Maurice and A. Appadorai, eds. *Speeches and Documents on the Indian Constitution, 1921–1947*, 2 Vols., Bombay: Oxford University Press, 1957.

Iqbal, Afzal, ed. *Select Writings and Speeches of Maulana Mohammad Ali*, 2 Vols., Lahore: Sh. Muhammad Ashraf, 1969.

Khaliquzzaman, Choudhry, *Pathway to Pakistan*, Lahore: Longman, 1961.

Khan, Aga, *The Memoirs of Aga Khan: World Enough and Time*, London: Cassell Co., 1954.

Khan, Liaquat Ali, comp., *Resolutions of the All-India Muslim League from December 1938 to March 1940*, Delhi, n.d.

Khan, Liaquat Ali, comp., *Resolutions of the All-India Muslim League from March 1940 to 1941*, Delhi, n.d.

Khan, Sir Syed Ahmad, *The Present State of Indian Politics*, ed., Farman Fatehpuri, Lahore: Sang-e-Meel Publications, 1982.

Letters of Iqbal to Jinnah. Lahore: Sh. Muhammad Ashraf, 1942.

Long, Roger D, ed., *Dear Mr Jinnah: Selected Correspondence and Speeches of Liaquat Ali Khan, 1937–1947*, Karachi: Oxford University Press, 2004.

Mansergh, N., E.W.R. Lumby, and Penderel Moon, eds., *Constitutional Relations between Britain and India: The Transfer of Power*, 11 Vols., London: Her Majesty's Stationery Office, 1970–82.

Mirza, Sarfraz Hussain., ed., *The Punjab Muslim Students Federation: An Annotated Documentary Survey, 1937–47*, Lahore: Research Society of Pakistan, 1978.

Nehru, Jawaharlal, *An Autobiography*, London: Bodley Head, 1958.

Pandey, B.N., ed., *The Indian Nationalist Movement, 1885–1947: Select Documents*, London: Macmillan, 1979.

Philips, C.H. *The Evolution of India & Pakistan, 1858–1947: Select Documents on the History of India and Pakistan*, Vol. IV, London: Oxford University Press, 1964.

Pirzada, Syed Sharifuddin, ed., *The Collected Works of Quaid-i-Azam Mohammad Ali Jinnah*, Karachi: East and West Publishing Co., 1984.

Pirzada, Syed Sharifuddin, ed., *Foundations of Pakistan: All-India Muslim League Documents, 1906–1947*, 2 Vols., Karachi: National Publishing-House, 1969–1970.

Pirzada, Syed Sharifuddin, ed., *Quaid's Correspondence*, Lahore: Service Book Company, 1977.

Rajput, A. B., *The Cabinet Mission Plan 1946*, Lahore: Lion Press, 1946.

Rozina, Parveen, ed., *Jamiat-i-Ulama-i-Hind: Documentary Record of the General Sessions, 1919–1945*, Islamabad: National Institute of Historical and Cultural Research, 1981.

Sherkoti, Muhammad Anwaral Hasan, comp. *Khutbat-i-Usmani*, Lahore: Nazir Sons, 1972.

Sherwani, Latif Ahmad, ed., *Speeches, Writings and Statements of Iqbal*, Lahore: Iqbal Academy, 1977.

Sherwani, Latif Ahmad, ed., *Pakistan Resolution to Pakistan*, Karachi: National Publishing Housing Limited, 1969.

The Indian Annual Register 1939–47, ed., N.N. Mitra, Calcutta: The Annual Register Office.

Yusufi, Khurshid Ahmad Khan, ed., *Speeches, Statements & Messages of the Quaid-e-Azam*, 4 Vols., Lahore: Bazm-i-Iqbal, 1996.

Wavell, Archibald, *Wavell: The Viceroy's Journal*, ed., Penderel Moon, Karachi: Oxford University Press, 1974.

Wavell, Archibald, *Other Men's Flower*, Jonathan Cape, 1944.

Wavell, Archibald, *Speaking Generally*, Macmillan, 1946.

Wavell, Archibald, *The Good Soldier*, Macmillan, 1948.

Wavell, Archibald, 'Archibald Wavell, The Triangle of Forces in Civil Leadership', a lecture delivered before the University of St. Andrews 22 October 1947, *Walker Trust Lectures on Leadership No. IX*, (London: Oxford University Press, 1948), pp. 1–24.

SECONDARY SOURCES

A. BOOKS

Afzal, Rafique, ed., *The Case For Pakistan*, Islamabad: NIPS, 1976.

Afzal, Rafique, *Political Parties in Pakistan, 1947–58*, Islamabad: National Commission on Historical and Cultural Research, 1976.

Ahmad, Aziz, *Islamic Modernism in India and Pakistan*, London: Oxford University Press, 1967.

Ahmad, Aziz, *Studies in Islamic Culture in the Indian Environment*, London: Oxford University Press, 1964.

Ahmad, Choudhry Habib, *Tehrik-e-Pakistan aur Nationalist Ulama* (Urdu), Lahore: al-Biyan, 1966.

Ahmad, Jamil-ud-Din, *The Final Phase of the Pakistan Movement*, Lahore: Publisher United, reprint 1975.

Ahmad, Jamil-ud-Din, *Middle Phase of Muslim Political Movement*, Lahore: Publisher United, 1969.

Ahmad, Jamil-ud-Din, ed., *Quaid-i-Azam As Seen by His Contemporaries*, Lahore: Publishers United, 1966.

Ahmad, Jamil-ud-Din, ed., *Some Recent Speeches and Writings of Mr Jinnah*, Lahore: Shaikh Muhammad Ashraf, 1952.

Ahmad, Jamil-ud-Din, ed., *Speeches and Writings of Mr Jinnah*, 2 vols., Lahore, 1960, 1964.

Ahmad, Jamil-ud-Din, ed., *Glimpses of Quaid-i-Azam*, Karachi: Education Press, 1960.

Ahmad, Riaz, ed., *Madr-i-Millat Miss Fatima Jinnah: A Chronology*, Islamabad, 2003.

Ahmad, Waheed, ed., *Letters of Mian Fazl-i-Husain*, Lahore: Research Society of Pakistan, 1976.

Ahmad, Waheed, ed., *Diary and Notes by Mian Fazl-i-Husain*, Lahore, Research Society of Pakistan, 1977.

Alderman, Geoffrey. *Modern Britain, 1700–1983*, London: Croom Helm Ltd., 1986.

Ali, Rabia Umar, *Empire in Retreat: The Story of India's Partition*, Karachi: Oxford University Press, 2012.

Ambedkar, B.R., *Pakistan or the Partition of India*, Bombay: Thacker & Co., 1946.

Ansari, Sarah, *The Sufis, Saints and State Power: The Pirs of Sindh*, Cambridge University Press, 1992.

Aziz, Qutubuddin, *Quaid-i-Azam Jinnah and the Battle For Pakistan*, Karachi: Islamic Media Corporation, 1997.

Allen, Louis, *Burma: The Longest War 1941–45*, London: Butler & Tanner, 1984.

Ali, Chaudhry Muhammad, *The Emergence of Pakistan*, Lahore: Research Society of Pakistan, 1996.

Ali, Chaudhry Rahmat, *Pakistan: The Fatherland of the Pak Nation*, 3rd ed., Cambridge: The Pak National Liberation Movement, 1947.

Aziz, K.K., *Britain And Muslim India*, London: William, Heinemann, 1963.

Aziz, K.K., ed., *Historical Handbook of Muslim India 1700–1947*, 2 Vols. Lahore: Vanguard, 1995.

Aziz, K.K., *Ameer Ali: His Life and Work*, Lahore: Publishers United, 1968.

Aziz, K.K., *The Making of Pakistan: A Study in Nationalism*, Lahore: Adab, Printers, 1975.

Aziz, K.K., *Muslims Under the Congress Rule*, 1937–39, 2 vols., Islamabad: The National Commission on Historical and Cultural Research, 1978, 1979.

Bandyopadhyay, Sekhar. *From Plessey to Partition*, Hyderabad: Orient Longman, 2004.

Bashir, Agha, *The Khaksar Movement, Past and Present: An Appraisal*, Lahore, n.d

Bazalgette, Jack, *The Captains and the Kings Depart*, Oxford: The Amate Press, 1984.

Beg, Aziz, *Jinnah and His Times*, Islamabad: Babur & Amer Publications, 1986.

Bahadur, Lal. ed., *Struggle for Pakistan: Tragedy of the Triumph of Muslim Communalism in India*, New Delhi: Sterling Publishers, 1988.

Bhagwan, Vishnoo, *Constitutional History of India and National Movement*, Part I, Delhi: Amta Ram and Sons, 1974.

Binder, Leonard, *Religion and Politics in Pakistan*, Berkeley: University of California Press, 1961.

Black, Jeremy, *World War Two: A Military History*, London: Rutledge Taylor & Francis Group, 2003.

Brass, Paul R., *Language, Religion and Politics in North India*, Cambridge: University Press, 1974.

Brown, Norman, *The United States and India, Pakistan, Bangladesh*, Cambridge, Mass.: Harvard University Press, 1972.

Burke, S.M., *Landmarks of the Pakistan Movement*, Lahore: Research Society of Pakistan, 2001.

Burke, S. M. and Salim Al-Din Quraishi, *The British Raj In India: An Historical Review*, Karachi: Oxford University Press, 1999.

Cook, Chris & John Stevenson, *Modern European History, 1763–1985*, London: Longmans, 1989.

Callard, Keith, *Pakistan: A Political Study*, London: George Allen and Unwin, 1968.

Chandra, Bipen, *Nationalism and Colonialism in Modern India*, Hyderabad: Orient Longman, 2004.

Chand, Tara, *History of the Freedom Movement of India*, Vol. 4, Lahore: Book Traders, n.d.

Chawla, Mohammad Iqbal, *Islamic Writings in Pakistan: A Case Study of Allama Ghulam Ahmad Parwez*, Lahore: Al-Noor Printing Press, 1991.

Close, H.M., *Attlee, Wavell, Mountbatten and the Transfer of Power*, Islamabad: National Book Foundation, 1997.

Connell, John, *Wavell: Scholar and Soldier*, London: Collins Clear-Type Press, 1964

Connell, John, *Lord Wavell: A Military Biography*, London: Hodder & Stoughton, 1964.

Connell, John, *Wavell: Supreme Commander*, London: Hodder & Stoughton, 1968.

Collins, Larry and Lapierre Dominique, *Freedom at Midnight*, New York: Simon and Schuster, 1975.

Collins, Larry and Lapierre Dominique, *Mountbatten and the Partition of India*, Vol. 1, Delhi: Vikas, 1982.

Coupland, Reginald, *India: A Re-Statement*, London: Oxford University Press, 1945.

Coupland, Reginald, *Report on the Constitutional Problem in India, Part 7, The Indian Problem, 1833–1935*, London: Oxford University Press, 1968.

Dani, Ahmad Hasan, et al., *Quaid-i-Azam and Pakistan*, Islamabad; Quaid-i-Azam University, 1981.

Dani, Ahmad Hasan, ed., *World Scholars on Quaid-i-Azam Mohammad Ali Jinnah*, Islamabad: Quaid-i-Azam University, 1979.

Das, Durga ed., *Sardar Patel's Correspondence: 1945–50*, 10 vols., Ahmedabad, 1972.

Desai, Mahadeo, *Maulana Abul Kalam Azad*, Agra: Shivalal Agarwala & Co., 1946.

Durrani, F.K. Khan, *The Meaning of Pakistan*, Lahore: Sh. Muhammad Ashraf, 1946.

Edwards, Michael, *The Last Years of British India*, London: Cassel, 1963.

Edwards, Michael, *Nehru: A Political Biography*, Harmondworth: Penguin Books, 1973.

Embree, Ainslie T., *India's Search for National Identity*, New York, 1972.

Enver, Khurshid Ahmed, *Life Story of Quaid-i-Azam*, Lahore: Young People Publishing Bureau, 1950.

Faruqi, Ziya-ul-Hasan, *The Deoband School and the Demand for Pakistan*, Bombay: Asia Publishing House, 1963.

Fergusson, Bernard, *Wavell: Portrait of a Soldier*, London: Collins Clear-Type Press, 1961.

French, Patrick, *Liberty or Death: India's Journey or Independence and Division*, London: Harper Collins Publishers, 1997.

Fisher, Louis, *The Life of Mahatma Gandhi*, London: HarperCollins Publishers, 1951.

Ghosh, Sudhir, *Gandhi's Emissary*, London: the Crescent Press, 1967.

Gopal, Ram, *The Indian Muslims: A Political History*, Lahore: Book Traders, 1976.

Gopal, S., *Jawaharlal Nehru: A Biography*, Vol. I. London, 1975.

Gordon, Leonard A, *Bengal: The Nationalist Movement, 1876–1940*. New York: Columbia University Press, 1974.

Griffiths, P.J., *The British in India*, London: Robert Hale, 1946.

Hali, Altaf. *Hayat-i-Jawid*, (Urdu) Lahore: National Book Foundation, reprint, 1986.

Hamid, Abdul, *Muslim Separatism in India*, Lahore: Oxford University Press, 1967.

Hamid, Abdul, *On Understanding the Quaid-i-Azam*. Islamabad: National Committee for Birth Centenary Celebrations of Quaid-i-Azam Mohammad Ali Jinnah, 1977.

Haq, Noor-ul, *Making of Pakistan: The Military Perspective*, Lahore: Army Education Press, reprinted, 1995–96.

Hardy, P., *The Muslims of British India*, Cambridge University Press, 1972.

Hardy, P., *Partners in Freedom and True Muslims: The Political Thought of Some Muslim Scholars in British India, 1912–1947*, Lund: Student Literature Scandinavian Institute of Asian Studies, 1971.

Hasan, Khalid Shamsul, *Sindh's Fight for Pakistan*, Karachi: Shamsul Hasan Foundation for Historical Studies & Research, 1992.

Hasan, Mushirul, *Nationalism and Communal Politics in India, 1916–28*, Delhi: Manohar, 1979.

Hasan, Mushirul, *Muslim Politics in Modern India, 1857–1947*, Meerut: Meenakshi Prakashan, 1970.

Husain, Azim, *Fazl-i-Husain: A Political Biography*. Bombay, 1946.

Hayat, Sikandar, *Aspects of Pakistan Movement*, Lahore: Progressive Publishers, 1991.

Hayat, Sikandar, *The Charismatic Leader: Quaid-i-Azam Mohammad Ali Jinnah and the Creation of Pakistan*, Karachi: Oxford University Press, 2008.

Hennessy, Peter. *The Prime Minister, the Office and its Holders since 1945*, London: Penguin Books, 2001.

Hodson, H.V., *The Great Divide, India, Pakistan and Bangladesh*, Karachi: Oxford University Press, 1969.

Hunter, W.W., *The Indian Musalmans*, Calcutta: Comrade Publishers, 1945.

Hussain, Salma Tasaduq, *Azadi Ka Safar: Tehrik-i-Pakistan Aur Muslim Khawateen* (Urdu), Lahore: Pakistan Study Centre, 1986.

Ikram, Shaikh Muhammad, *Mauj-i-Kausar*, (Urdu). Lahore: Ferozsons, 1966.

Ikram, Shaikh Muhammad, *Modern Muslim India and the Birth of Pakistan*, Lahore: Shaikh Muhammad Ashraf, 1970.

Ikram, Shaikh Muhammad, *Muslim Civilization of Indo-Pakistan*, Lahore: Research Society of Pakistan, 1966.

Ikramullah, Shaista Suhrawardy, *Huseyn Shaheed Suhrawardy: A Biography*. Karachi: Oxford University Press, 1991.

Ikramullah, Shaista, *From Purdah to Parliament*, Karachi: Oxford University Press, 1998.

Iqbal, Afzal, *Life and Times of Mohamed Ali*, Lahore: Institute of Islamic Culture, 1974.

Jafri, S.Q.H., ed., *Quaid-i-Azam's Correspondence with Punjab Muslim Leaders*, Lahore, 1977.

Jalal, Ayesha, *The Sole Spokesman: Jinnah, the Muslim League and the Demand for Pakistan*, Cambridge: University Press, 1985.

Jallandhari, Rashid, *Dar-ul-Uloom Deoband*, Islamabad: National Book Foundation, 1989.

James, Lawrence, *Raj: The Making of British India*, London; Little, Brown and Company, 2001.

Jeffreys, Kevin, *The Churchill Coalition and Wartime Politics, 1940–1945*, Manchester: Manchester University Press, 1995.

Jinnah, Mohammed Ali, *Nationalism in Conflict*, Bombay: Home Study Circle, 1943.

Kadri, Justice Syed Shameem Hussain, *Creation of Pakistan*, Lahore: Army Book Club, 1982.

Kaura, Uma, *Muslims and Indian Nationalism: The Emergence of the Demand for India's Partition, 1928–40*, Delhi: Manohar Book Service, 1977.

Kausur, Inam ul Haq, *Pakistan Movement and Baluchistan*, Quetta: United Printers, 1999.

Kasturi, Bhashyam, *Walking Alone: Gandhi and India's Partition*, New Delhi: Vision Books Ltd., 2001.

Kazmi, Mohammad Reza. *Liaquat Ali Khan: His Life and Work*, Karachi: Oxford University Press, 2003.

Keirman, *Wavell*, London: George g. Harper & Co., 1945.

Khairi, Saeed R. *Jinnah Reinterpreted*, Karachi: Oxford University Press, 1995.

Khaliquzzaman, Choudhry, *Pathway to Pakistan*, Lahore: Brothers Publishers, 1961.

Khan, Abdul Rashid, *The All India Muslim Educational Conference, Its Contribution to the Cultural Development of Indian Muslims 1886–1947*, Karachi: Oxford University Press, 2001.

Khan, Muhammad Anwar, *The Role of N.W.F.P. in the Freedom Struggle*, Lahore: Research Society of Pakistan, 2000.

Khan, Shafique Ali, *Two Nation Theory*, Hyderabad, 1973.

Khan, H.B., *Bar-i-Sagheer Pak-O-Hind Ki Siyasat Main Ulema Ka Kirdar* (Urdu), Islamabad: National Institute of History and Culture, 1985.

Khan, Muhammad Yamin, *Nama-i-Aamal: Yadayn our Taasurat*, (Urdu) Lahore, 1976.

Khan, Salahuddin, ed., *Speeches, Addresses and Statements of Madr-i-Millat Mohtarama Fatima Jinnah: 1948–1967*, Lahore: Research Society of Pakistan, 1976.

Khursheed, Abdus Salam, *History of the Idea of Pakistan*, Lahore: National Book Foundation, 1977.

Kibria, Ghulam, *Pre-Independence Indian Muslim Mindset*, Karachi: City Press Bookshop, 2001.

Kibriya, Mazhar, *Gandhi and Indian Freedom Struggle*, New Delhi: APH Publishing Corporation, 1999.

Kulke, Hermann, Dietmar Rothermund, *A History of India*, 4th ed. London: Routledge, 2004.

Lelyveld, David, *Aligarh's First Generation: Muslim Solidarity in India*, New Jersey: 1978.

Malik, Hafeez, ed., *Iqbal: Poet-Philosopher of Pakistan*, New York, 1971.

Malik, Hafeez, *Moslem Nationalism in India and Pakistan*, Washington D.C.: Public Affairs Press, 1963.

Malik, Iftikhar Haider, *Sir Sikandar Hayat: A Political Biography*, Islamabad: National Institute of Historical and Cultural Research, 1985.

Majumdar, S.K., *Jinnah and Gandhi: Their Role in India's Quest for Freedom*, Lahore: Peoples Publishing House, 1976.

Malik, Ikram Ali, *A Book of Reading on the History of the Punjab, 1799–1947*, Lahore: Research Society of Pakistan, 1970.

Malik, Ikram Ali, *Tarikh-i-Punjab* (Urdu), Lahore: Salman Publishing Company.

Majumdar, S.K., *Jinnah*, Patna: Khuda Bukhsh Oriental Public Library, 1996.

Mansergh, Diana, ed., *Independence Years: The Selected Papers of Indian and Commonwealth of Nicholas Mansergh*, New Delhi: Oxford University Press, 1999.

Mathur, Y.B., *Growth of Muslim Politics in India*, Lahore: Book Trader, 1980.

McIntyre, W. David, *British History in Perspective: British Decolonization, 1946–1947*, London: Macmillan Press Ltd, 1998.

Mehta, Ashoka, and Patwardhan, *Communal Triangle in India*, Allahabad: Kitabistan, 1942.

Menon, V.P., *The Transfer of Power in India*, Princeton: University Press, 1957.

Mirza, Janbaz, *Caravan-i-Ahrar* (Urdu), 6 Vol., Lahore: Maktaba Tabsrah, 1975.

Mirza, Sarfraz Hussain, *The Punjab Muslim Students Federation: 1937–1947*, Islamabad: NIHCR, 1991.

Mirza, Sarfraz Hussain, *Tehrik-i-Pakistan Nawa-i-Waqt Kai Idariun Ki Rushni Mein, 1944–1947* (Urdu), Lahore: Pakistan Study Centre, 1987.

Mirza, Sarfraz Hussain, ed., *Tehrik-i-Pakistan, Siasiati Beri Saghir and Nawa-i-Waqt 1944–47*, Lahore: Pakistan Study Centre, 2000.

Mirza, Sarfraz Hussain, *Youth and the Pakistan Movement*, Lahore: Nazaria Pakistan Foundation, 2004.

Mirza, Sarfraz Hussain, *Women's Role in the Pakistan Movement*, Lahore: Research Society of Pakistan, 1981.

Moin, Mumtaz, *The Aligarh Movement*, Karachi: Salman Academy, 1976.

Moon, Penderel, *Divide and Quit*, London: Chatto & Windus, 1961.

Moore, R.J., *Churchill, Cripps, and India, 1939–4*, Oxford: Clarendon Press, 1979.

Moore, R.J., *The Crisis of Indian Unity, 1917–1940*, Oxford: Clarendon Press, 1974.

Moore, R.J., *Escape From Empire: Attlee Government and the Indian Problem*, Oxford: Clarendon Press, 1963.

Mosley, Leonard, *The Last Days of the British Raj*, London: Weidenfeld and Nicholson, 1961.

Mujahid, Sharif al, *Quaid-i-Azam Jinnah: Studies in Interpretation*, Karachi: Quaid-i-Azam Academy, 1981.

Masood, Mukhtar ed., *Eye-Witness of History: Letters Addressed to Quaid-i-Azam*, Karachi, 1968.

Munawwar, Muhammad, *Dimensions of Pakistan Movement*, Lahore: Pap-Board, 1987.

Nanda, B.R., *Mahatma Gandhi: A Biography*, London: Unwin Books, 1965.

Nanda, B.R., *Three Statesmen, Gokhale, Gandhi, and Nehru*, New Delhi: Oxford University Press, 2004.

Nasr, Seyyed Vali Reza, *Mawdudi and the Making of Islamic Revivalism*, New York: Oxford University Press, 1996.

Nasr, Seyyed Vali Reza, *The Vanguard of the Islamic Revolution: The Jama'at-i-Islami of Pakistan*, Berkeley: University of California Press, 1994.

Nehru, Jawaharlal, *The Discovery of India*, New York: The John Day Company, 1946.

Noman, Mohammad, *Muslim India*, Allahabad: Kitabistan, 1942.

Noman, Mohammad, *Our Struggle 1857–1947: A Political Record*, Karachi: Pakistan Publications, n.d.

Page, David, *Prelude to Partition: The Indian Muslims and the Imperial System of Control, 1920–1932*, Delhi: Oxford University Press, 1982.

Pandey, B.N., *Nehru*, London, 1976.

Pandey, B.N., *The Indian Nationalist Movement*, London: The Macmillan Press, 1979.

Parkash, Dewan Ram, *Cabinet Mission in India*, Lahore: Tagore Memorial Publications, 1946.

Philips, C.H. and Mary Doreen Wainwright, eds., *The Partition of India: Policies and Perspectives, 1935–1947*, London: George Allen & Unwin, 1970.

Pirzada, S.S., *Evolution of Pakistan*, Lahore: All-Pakistan Legal Decisions, 1963.

Prasad, Beni, *The Hindu-Muslim Questions*, London: George Allen & Unwin, 1946.

Prasad, Rajendra, *India Divided*, Bombay: Hind Kitab, 1977.

Pyarelal, *Mahatma Gandhi: The Last Phase*, Vol. 1, Ahmadabad: Navajivan Publishing House, 1956.

Qalb-i-Abid, S., *The Muslim Politics in Punjab 1923–1947*, Lahore: Vanguard, 1992.

Qalb-i-Abid, S., *Jinnah, Second World War and the Pakistan Movement*, Multan: Beacon Books, 1999.

Qalb-i-Abid, S., *Muslim Struggle for Independence: From Sir Syed to Quaid-i-Azam Muhammad Ali Jinnah, 1857–1947*, Lahore: Sang-e-Meel Publications, 1997.

Qureshi, Ishtiaq Husain, *The Muslim Community of the Indo-Pak Sub-continent, 610–1947*, Mouton: The Hague, 1962.

Qureshi, Ishtiaq Husain, *The Struggle for Pakistan*, Karachi: University, 1965.

Qureshi, Ishtiaq Husain, *Ulema in Politics*, Karachi: Ma'aref, 1974.

Qureshi, M.M. Saleem, *Jinnah and the Making of a Nation*, Karachi: Council for Pakistan Studies, 1960.

Qureshi, M.M. Saleem, *The Politics of Jinnah*, Karachi: Royal Book Company, 1988.

Qureshi, Waheed, *Ideological Foundation of Pakistan*, Lahore: Islamic Book Foundation, 1987.

Rahman, Matiur, *From Consultation to Confrontation: A Study of the Muslim League in British Indian Politics, 1906–1912*, London, 1970.

Rai, Lala Lajpat, *Unhappy India*, Calcutta: Banna Publishing Co., 1928.

Rao, V. Pala Prasad, et al., *India-Pakistan, Partition Perspective in Indo-English Novels*, New Delhi: Discovery Publishing House, 2004.

Rajput, A.B., *Maulana Abul Kalam Azad*, Lahore: Lion Press, 1946.

Ravoof, A.A, *Meet Mr. Jinnah*, Lahore: Shaikh Muhammad Ashraf, 1955.

Robinson, Francis, *Separatism Among Indian Muslims, The Politics of the United Provinces Muslims: 1860–1923*, Cambridge: University Press, 1974.

Rizvi, Gowher, *Linlithgow and India: A Study of British Policy and the Political Impasse in India, 1936–43*, London, 1978.

Robb, Peter, *A History Of India*, London: Palgrave, 2002.

Roberts, Andrew, *Eminent Churchillians*, London: 1994.

Saeed, Ahmad, *Muslim India: A Biographical Dictionary, 1858–1947*, Lahore: Institute of Pakistan Historical Research, 1997.

Sarila, Narendra Singh, *The Shadow of the Great Game: The Story of India's Partition*, New Delhi: Harper Collins Publishers in India, 2005.

Sayeed, Khalid bin, *Pakistan: The Formative Phase, 1858–1947*, London: Oxford University Press, 1968.

Saiyid, M.H., *Mohammad Ali Jinnah: A Political Study*, Lahore: Shaikh Muhammad Ashraf, 2 ed., 1953.

Salimi, Safdar, *Khaksar-i-Azam aur Khaksar Tehreek* (Urdu), Lahore, 1957.

Sarkar, Sumit, *Modern India*, New Delhi: Macmillan, 1983.

Schofield, Victoria, *Wavell: Soldier & Statesman*, London: John Murray, 2006.

Seervai, H.M., *Legend and Reality*, Rawalpindi: Services Book Club, 1991.

Shah, Sayed Wiqar Ali, *Ethnicity, Islam and Nationalism: Muslim Politics in the North-West Frontier Province, 1937–47*, Karachi: Oxford University Press, 1999.

Shahnawaz, Jehanara Begum, *Father & Daughter: A Political Autobiography*, Karachi: Oxford University Press, 2002.

Shan, Mohammad, *The Khaksar Movement*, Meerut, 1972.

Sherwani, Latif Ahmad, *The Partition of India and Mountbatten*, Karachi: Council for Pakistan Studies, 1986.

Singh, Sangat, *The Sikhs In History*, New Delhi: Uncommon Books, 1996.

Sinnah, Sachchidananda, *Jinnah As I Knew Him*, Patna: Khuda Bakhsh Public Library, 1993.

Shaft, Alhaj Mian Ahmad, *Haji Sir Abdoolah Haroon: A Biography*. Karachi: Begum Daulat Anwar Hidayatullah, n.d.

Singh, Khushwant, *Train to Pakistan*, London, 1965.

Singh, Jaswant, *Jinnah: India-Partition-Independence*, New Delhi: Rupa & Co, 2009.

Singh, Kirpal, *The Partition of Punjab*, Patiala: Punjab University, 1972.

Smith, Wilfred Cantwell, *Islam in Modern History*, Princeton: University Press, 1957.

Smith, Wilfred Cantwell, *Modern Islam in India: A Social Analysis*. London: Victor Gollancz, 1946.

Sohail, Massarat, *Partition and Anglo-Pakistan Relations, 1947–1951*, Lahore: Vanguard, 1991.

Spear, Percival, *India: A Modern History*, University of Michigan Press, 1961.

Stephens, Ian, *Pakistan: Old Country, New Nation*. London: Ernest Benn, 1967.

Stephens, Ian, *Pakistan*, London: Ernest Benn, 1963.

Suleri, Z.A., *My Leader*, Lahore: Nawa-i-Waqat Press, 1973.

Symonds, Richard, *The Making of Pakistan*, London: Faber & Faber, 1950.

Symonds, Richard, *In the Margins of Independence: A Relief Worker in India and Pakistan, 1942–1949*, Karachi: Oxford University Press, 2001.

Talbot, Ian, *Freedom's Cry: The Popular Dimension in the Pakistan Movement and the Partition Experience in North-West India*, Karachi: Oxford University Press, 1996.

Talbot, Ian, *Inventing the Nation: India and Pakistan*, London: Oxford University Press, 2000

Talbot, Ian, *Punjab Under the Raj, 1848–1947*, New Delhi: Manohar Publication, 1988.

Talbot, Ian, *Khizar Tiwana, the Punjab Unionist Party and the Partition of India*, Karachi: Oxford University Press, 2000.

Talbot, Ian, *Pakistan: A Modern History*, Lahore: Vanguard Book, 1999.

Talha, Naureen, *Economic Factors in the Making of Pakistan: 1921–1947*, Karachi: Oxford University Press, 2000.

Tatla, Darshan Singh, *The Sikh Diaspora: The Search For Statehood*, London: UCL, 1990.

Tendulkar, G.D., *Abdul Ghaffar Khan: Faith is a Battle*, Bombay: Gandhi Peace Foundation, 1967.

Tendulkar, G.D., *Mahatma: Life of Mohandas Karamchand Gandhi*, Delhi: Ministry of Information and Broadcasting, 1960.

Terraine, John, *The Life and Times of Lord Mountbatten*, London: Arrow Books, 1970.

Tinker, Hugh, *The Foundations of Local Self-Government in India, Pakistan and Burma*, London, 1968.

Tinker, Hugh, *Experiment with Freedom: India and Pakistan 1947*, London: Oxford University Press, 1967.

Tinker, Hugh, *India and Pakistan: A Short Political Guide*, London: The Pall Mall Press, 1962.

Tinker, Hugh, *Men Who Overturned the Empires*, London: The Macmillan Press, 1987

Tinker, Hugh, *Viceroy: Curzon to Mountbatten*, Karachi: Oxford University Press, 1997.

Tinker, Hugh, *South Asia: A Short History*, London: Pall Mall Press, 1965.

Tomlinson, B.R., *The Indian National Congress and the Raj, 1929–1942*, London: Macmillan, 1976.

Toosy, Muhammad Sharif (M.R.T.), *Nationalism in Conflict*, Bombay: Home Study Circle, 1943.

Waseem, Mohammad, *Politics and the State in Pakistan*, Lahore: Progressive Publishers, 1989.

Wasti, Razi, *Lord Minto and the Indian Nationalist Movement, 1905–1910*, London: Oxford University Press, 1965.

Wasti, Razi, *Political Triangle in India, 1858–1924*, Lahore: People's Publishing House, 1976.

Wilcox, Wayne, *Pakistan: The Consolidation of a Nation*, New York: Columbia University Press, 1963.

Wolpert, Stanley, *India*, New Jersey: Prentice-Hall, 1965.

Wolpert, Stanley, *Jinnah of Pakistan*, New York: Oxford University Press, 1984.

Wolpert, Stanley, *Morley and India, 1906–10*, Berkeley and Los Angeles: University of California Press, 1967.

Wolpert, Stanley, *Gandhi's Passion, The Life and Legacy of Mahatma Gandhi*, Karachi: Oxford University Press, 2001.

Wolpert, Stanley, *Zulfi Bhutto of Pakistan His Life and Times*, Karachi: Oxford University Press, 1993.

Woodruff, P., *The Men Who Ruled India*, London, 1954.

Woollcombe, Robert, *The Campaign of Wavell: 1939–43*, London: Cassell N Company, 1959.

Zaidi, A.M., ed., *Evolution of Muslim Political Thought*, Delhi: S. Chand & Co., 1975–79.

Zafrullah, Khan, *The Forgotten Years: Memories of Sir Muhmmad Zafrullah Khan*, Batalvi, A.H. ed., Lahore: Vanguard Book Ltd., 1991.

Zaman, Mukhtar, *Student's Role in the Pakistan Movement*, Karachi: Quaid-i-Azam Academy, 1979.

Zaman, Waheed-Uz, *Quaid-i-Azam Mohammad Ali Jinnah: Myth and Reality*, Islamabad: National Institute of Historical and Cultural Research, 1985.

Zaman, Waheed-Uz, *Towards Pakistan*, Lahore: United Publishers, 1978.

Ziring, Lawrence, et al., *Pakistan: The Long View*, Durham; Duke University Press, 1977.

B. Articles in Journals

Afzal, Rafiq, 'Origin of the Idea for a Separate Muslim State', *Journal of the Research Society of Pakistan* (April 1966), pp. 178–82.

Ali, Imran, 'Relations between the Muslim League and the Punjab Unionist Party, 1935–47', *South Asia*, 6 (1976), pp. 51–65.

Barrier, N.G., 'The Arya Samaj and Congress Politics in the Punjab', *Journal of Asian Studies* Vol. 3 (May 1967), pp. 363–79.

Barrier, N.G., 'Muslim Politics in the Punjab, 1870–90,' *The Punjab Past and Present*, Vol. Vl (April 1971), pp. 84–125.

Barrier, N.G., 'The Punjab Government and Communal Politics, 1870–1908,' *Journal of Asian Studies*, No. 3 (May 1968), pp. 523–39.

Baxter, Craig, 'The 1937 Election and the Sikandar–Jinnah Pact,' *The Punjab Past and Present* (October 1976), pp. 356–85.

Chawla, Iqbal, 'Quaid-i-Azam and Rajagopalachari Formula', (Lahore) *South Asian Studies*, vol. 17, No. 19 (January 2002), pp. 1–16.

Chothu Ram, 'Serving the Weak and Raising the Fallen,' *The Punjab Past and Present*, Vol. VI (April 1971), pp. 160–67.

Coalman, J., 'The Round Table Conference,' *The Nineteenth Century and After* (January–June 1932), pp. 24–34.

Garrett, G.T., 'Prospects of the Round Table Conference,' *The Nineteenth Century and After*, (July–December 1931), pp. 417–28.

Gilmartin, D., 'Religious Leadership and the Pakistan Movement in the Punjab,' *Modern Asian Studies*, 13.3 (1979), pp. 485–517.

Glyn, Irial, 'An Untouchable in the presence of "Brahamans", Lord Wavell's Relationship with Whitehall during His Time as Viceroy of India, 1943–57,' *Modern Indian*, (2007), pp. 1–25.

Gordon, R., 'The Hindu Mahasabha and the Indian National Congress, 1915–26,' *Modern Asian Studies*, 9.2 (1975), pp. 145–203.

Jalal, Ayesha, 'Interacting the Raj: Jinnah and Governor-General Issue,' *Modern Asian Studies*, Vol. 19, No. 1 (1985), pp. 29–53.

Jones, K., 'Communalism in the Punjab: the Arya Samaj Contribution,' *Journal of Asian Studies* (November 1968), pp. 39–54.

Jones, K., 'The Khaksars,' *The Indian Review* (August 1940), pp. 477–78.

Moore, R.J., 'Jinnah and the Pakistan Demand,' *Modern Asian Studies*, 17, 4 (1983), pp. 529–61.

Nath, N., 'Sir Stafford Cripps' Mission and Akhand Hindustan', *The Modern Review* (November 1942), pp. 380–86.

Oren, S., 'The Sikhs, Congress and the Unionists in British Punjab, 1937–45,' *Modern Asian Studies*, 8.3 (1974), pp. 397–418.

Owen, H., Negotiating the Lucknow Pact,' *Journal of Asian Studies*, XXXI, 3 (May 1972), pp. 561–87.

Prasad, Bimal, 'The Emergence of the demand for India's Partition,' *International Studies*, 9.3 (1968), pp. 241–78.

Prasad, Bimal, 'The Cripps Mission,' *International Studies*, 15 (1976), pp. 137–60.

Gulshan, Rai, 'The Communal Problem in the Punjab', *The Indian Review* (March 1932), pp. 185–87.

Stuart, Louis, 'An Alternative Scheme,' *The Indian Empire Review'* (November 1939), pp. 425–32.

Talbot, Ian, 'The 1946 Punjab Elections,' *Modern Asian Studies*, 14.1 (1980), pp. 65–91.

Tinker, H., 'Pressure, Preservation, Decision: Factors in the Partition of the Punjab, August 1947,' *Journal of Asian Studies*, 4 (1977), pp. 695–704.

Wallace, P., 'Factionalism and National Integration in the Pre-Independence Congress Party,' *Essays*, pp. 390–402.

Wasti, S. Razi, 'Anjuman Himayat-i-Islam Lahore—A Brief History', *Journal of the Research Society of Pakistan* (April 1966).

C. CHAPTERS IN BOOKS

Ahmad, Jamil-ud-Din, 'The Congress in Office (1937–39)', in *A History of the Freedom Movement*, Vol. IV, part I & II, Karachi University Press.

Ahmed, Rafiuddin, 'Redefining Muslim Identity in South Asia: The Transformation of the Jama'at-i-Islami,' in Martin E. Marty and R. Scott Appleby, eds., *Accounting for Fundamentalism: the Dynamic Character of Movement*, Chicago: University of Chicago Press, 1994.

Amin, Syed Mohammad Rooh-ul, 'Quaid-i-Azam Aur Sooba-i-Sarhad Ke Musha'ikh' (Urdu), in Dr Riaz Ahmad, ed., *Pakistani Scholars on Quaid-i-Azam Mohammad Ali Jinnah*, Islamabad: National Institute of Pakistan Studies, Quaid-i-Azam University, 1999.

Ali, Mehmud, 'My Contact with Quaid-i-Azam 1945–1948,' in Riaz Ahmad, ed., *Pakistani Scholars on Quaid-i-Azam Mohammad Ali Jinnah*, Islamabad: National Institute of Pakistan Studies, Quaid-i-Azam University, 1999.

Haq, Mushirul, 'The Ulema and the Indian Politics', in Rashid Jallandhri and Muhammad Afzal Qarshi, eds., *Islam in South Asia*, Lahore: Institute of Islamic Culture, 1986.

Ispahani, M.A.H. 'Factors Leading to the Partition of British India', in C.H. Philips and Mary Wainwright, eds., *The Partition of India: Policies and Perspectives, 1935–1947*, London: George Allen & Unwin, 1970.

Jalal, Ayesha and Anil Seal, 'Alternative to Partition: Muslim Politics between the Wars,' in Christopher Baker, Gordon Johnson, and Anil Seal, eds., *Power, Profit and Politics*, Cambridge: Cambridge University Press, 1981.

Malik, Iftikhar H., 'Regionalism or Personality Cult? Allama Mashriqi and the Tehreek-i- Khaksar in pre-1947 Punjab,' in Ian Talbot and Gurharpal Singh, eds., *Region & Partition, Bengal, Punjab and the Partition of the Subcontinent*, Karachi: Oxford University Press, 1999.

Moore, R.J., 'The Problems of Freedom with Unity: London's India Policy, 1917–1947', in D.A. Low, ed., *Congress and the Raj: Facets of the Indian Struggle, 1917–1947*, London: Heinemann, 1977.

Mujahid, Sharif al, 'Communal Riots', in *A History of Freedom Movement*, Vol. IV, Part II, Karachi: Pakistan Historical Society, 1970.

Mujahid, Sharif al, 'Jinnah's Rise to Muslim Leadership', in A.H. Dani, ed., *World Scholars on Quaid-i-Azam Mohammad Ali Jinnah*, Islamabad: Quaid-i-Azam University, 1979.

Nandi, Proshanta, 'Visions of Nationhood and Religiosity among Early Freedom Fighters in India', in S.L. Sharma, T.K. Oommen, eds., *Nation and National Identity in South Asia*, New Delhi: Orient Longman, 2000, pp. 145–46.

Roy, Asim, 'The High Politics of India' Partition: The Revisionist Perspective', in, Mushirul Hasan, ed., *Themes in Indian History: India's Partition Process, Strategy and Mobilization*, New Delhi: Oxford University Press, 1993.

Rizvi, S. Muhammad Asif, 'Quaid-i-Azam and the Punjab: 1936–46', in Riaz Ahmad, ed., *Pakistan Scholars on Quaid-i-Azam Mohammad Ali Jinnah*, Islamabad: National Institute of Pakistan Studies, Quaid-i-Azam University, 1999.

Saeed-ud-Din, Qazi, 'Is India Geographically One', in Rafique Afzal, ed., *The Case for Pakistan*, Islamabad, 1988.

Sayeed, Khalid bin, 'The Personality of Jinnah and his Political Strategy', in C.H. Philips and Mary Doreen Wainwright, eds. *The Partition of India: Policies and Perspectives*, London: George Allen & Unwin, 1970.

Sayeed, Khalid bin, 'Political Leadership and Institution Building under Jinnah, Ayub and Bhutto', in Lawrence Ziring, et al., *Pakistan: The Long View*, Durham: Duke University Press, 1977.

Thapar, Romila, 'Religion as History in the Making of South Asian Identities', in S.M. Naseem and Khalid Nadvi, eds., *The Post-Colonial State and Social Transformation in India and Pakistan*, Karachi: Oxford University Press, 2002.

Wilcox, Wayne, 'Wellsprings of Pakistan', in Lawrence Ziring, et al., *Pakistan: The Long View*, Durham: Duke University Press, 1977.

Zaidi, Z.H., 'Aspects of the Development of Muslim League Policy, 1937–47', in C.H. Philips and Mary Doreen Wainwright, eds., *The Partition of India: Policies and Perspectives, 1935–1947*, London: George Allen & Unwin, 1970.

Zaman, Mukhtar, Quaid-i-Azam Mohammad Ali Jinnah As A Parliamentarian', in Riaz Ahmad, ed., *Pakistani Scholars on Quaid-i-Azam Mohammad Ali Jinnah*, Islamabad: National Institute of Pakistan Studies, Quaid-i-Azam University, 1999.

Ziring, Lawrence, 'Jinnah: The Burden of Leadership', in A.H. Dani, ed., *World Scholars on Quaid-i-Azam Mohammad Ali Jinnah*, Islamabad: Quaid-i-Azam University, 1979.

Index

A

ABDA (American, British, Dutch and Australian forces in West Pacific), 16
Abell, 229
Abid, S. Qalb-i-, 9, 36
Abyssinia, 6
Africa, 6
Agricultural Produce Markets Act, XIV of 1939, 40
Ahrar movement, 38
Ajmal, 36
Akali Sikhs, 113
Akbar (Mughal Emperor), 27
Akhand Bharat (Sacred and Great India), 43
Alexander, A.V., 116, 222
Alexander, Horace, 172, 223
Ali, Asif (Congress leader), 176
Ali, Chaudhri Muhammad, 186
Ali, Chaudhry Rahmat, 27
Ali, Syed Ameer, 24
Aligarh, 141
Alipore Suadan, 33
Al-Islah, 41
Al-jamayat (Delhi), 36
Allahabad, 26–7
Allenby, 5, 210, 243
All-India Students Congress Delhi, 242
All-India Women's Organization, 33
All-Parties Convention (1928), 26
Ambala, 12, 230
Ambedkar, Dr, 65, 74, 79, 138
America, 4
American, 13
Amery, Leopold, 17, 20, 63, 67, 72, 78, 80, 89, 94, 209, 210–5
Amritsari, Maulana Sanaullah, 33
Anderson, John, 216
Andrews, C.F., 222–3
Anglo-Sikh union, 44

Anjuman-i-Islahul-Afghania (the Association for the Reformation of the Afghan), 38
Ansari, Sarah, 9, 113
Arakan Peninsula, 17
Arthur, Sir George, 6
Aryans, 23
Asia, 13
Assam Provincial Congress, 138
Assam, 19, 28, 32, 71, 83, 113, 118, 124, 129, 136–8, 142, 229, 244, 260
Attlee, Clement, 5, 7, 17, 20, 63–4, 118–9, 135, 141, 143, 181, 190, 209, 216–9, 220, 222–3, 227, 232–3, 239, 240–2; his statement of 15 March 1946, 116; his 6 December 1946 statement, 136–7
Auchinleck, 18; as Commander-in-Chief in India (1940–41), 18
August Offer of 1940, 19
Aurangzeb, Sardar, 19
Azad Muslim Conference, 37
Azad, Maulana Abul Kalam, 15, 35, 37, 42, 80, 89, 91–2, 117, 119, 127–9, 131, 139, 166, 173, 188, 221; as President of the Congress (1940–46), 34, 80–1, 83, 86, 88, 93
Azhar, Maulana Mazhar Ali, 37

B

Bajpai, 212
Bakhsh, Khuda, 39
Bakhsh, Pir, 39
Balkanization, 226, 231
Balochistan, 71, 118, 124, 137, 139
Bande Mataram (song), 30
Banerjea, Dr Pramatha, 83
Bengal famine (1942–43), 2, 6, 66–7, 211
Bengal Ministry, Dissolution of, 67
Bengal, 22, 28, 32, 35, 71, 78, 113–4, 118–9, 124, 140, 141, 178–9, 182, 187, 212, 225, 229, 230, 241, 244, 265; 1911